Index.

THE
GLASGOW
COOKERY
BOOK

DEDICATION

To six women who shaped domestic science education:
Grace Chalmers Paterson (1843–1925)
Margaret Black (née MacKirdy) (1830–1903)
Isabella (Ella) Scott Scouler Glaister (1880–1954)
Dorothy Humphreys Melvin (1881–1963)
Isobel Scott Gibson (1897–1993)
Juliann McKinnon Calder (1914–2008)

To all the Alumni of the Glasgow and West of Scotland College of Domestic Science, later The Queen's College, Glasgow, who went on to make a difference in the teaching of domestic science and home economics.

All profits received by Glasgow Caledonian University for this publication will be invested to preserve the archives of the University's founding institutions and to facilitate, through a series of scholarships, the evolution of the learning and teaching that began there. Funding of this kind enables Glasgow Caledonian University to develop in ways not possible through core funding alone and so is extremely valuable to the University, its students, and the communities it serves in Scotland and internationally. If you are interested in supporting similar activity at the University, please contact the Development and Alumni Relations Office on 0141 331 8190 to find out more.

Inside cover photos, College students, 1957. Inside front cover, left to right: Catherine Bryson, Penny Broadfoot and Margaret Goodwin. Inside back cover, left to right: Myra Hunter, Penny Broadfoot, Breda Foley, Sine Loudon, Margaret Goodwin, Catherine Bryson, Sheena Ferguson, Myra Sugrue, Sheila Fergusson Also pictured, pages from the notebooks of Ella Cowan, 1909, courtesy of Alex Gray

*Students of The Glasgow and West of Scotland College of Domestic Science,
later The Queen's College, 1946, with Miss Dorothy Melvin, centre*

THE GLASGOW COOKERY BOOK

PUBLISHED BY
WAVERLEY BOOKS
IN ASSOCIATION WITH
**GLASGOW CALEDONIAN
UNIVERSITY**

The Editor's sincere thanks go to:
Sheonagh Beaton • Helen Daye • Mary Farquhar • Morag Fortune • Wendy I'Anson
Elaine Moffett • Betty Orr • Linda Pryde • Fiona Robertson • Gilda Smith • Diane Spiers
Sheena McArthur • Carole McCallum • Penny Grearson • Melanie Armstrong
whose contribution to the new edition of this book has been invaluable

Thanks also to those who edited and retested recipes to create the first metric edition of *The Glasgow Cookery Book* in 1975: the staff of the then Food Studies Department of The Queen's College, who included: Jen Stewart • Mairie MacDonald • Anne Tavern • Pat Bewes • Diane Spiers
Sheena McArthur • Elizabeth Iversen • Morag Cochrane

All at Waverley Books thank Alex Gray for allowing us to publish pages from Ella Cowan's notebooks, the timely discovery of which was the inspiration for us contacting Glasgow Caledonian University and talking about *The Glasgow Cookery Book*

The University Archivist would like to thank the individuals and families who have donated archives and memories which bring the Dough School's history to life. Collections have been preserved in the following names: Christina Bell • Jessie Dick • Jessie Paterson
Janet Levack • Mollie Gofton • Robina Purdon • Kathleen Sangster • Anne Wallace
Moira Bisset • Myra Hunter • Morag Boyd • Jean Lancaster • Elizabeth Smellie
Thank you also to Roy and Rena Kennedy who gifted the Christina W Bell collection

This edition published 2009 by Waverley Books, 144 Port Dundas Road, Glasgow, G4 0HZ

Designed, typeset and edited by Waverley Books

Edited by Eleanor Abraham and Penny Grearson. Index by Margaret Christie

Historical Introduction by Carole McCallum. For a fuller account of the cookery schools, the Glasgow and West of Scotland College of Domestic Science and The Queen's College, Glasgow see Willie Thompson and Carole McCallum, *Glasgow Caledonian University: Its Origins and Evolution* (East Linton: Tuckwell Press, 1998)

Picture Credits:
Archive material on pages ii–xiviii appears courtesy of Glasgow Caledonian University Institutional Archive. With thanks to John Powles, Carole McCallum and Phillip Wallace
Cover by Mark Mechan based on the design by A. Jan Pattison (née Hall) who created the illustrations and cover for the 1975 metric edition. Illustrations by Mark Mechan pages 144, 369; redrawn with reference to illustrations by A. Jan Pattison pages 83, 85, 87, 175, 310, 311, 385
Inside-front and inside-back cover photos by Catherine Webster (née Innes), 1957, courtesy of Myra Hunter. Clippings from *The Bulletin*, pages xix and xxvii, appear courtesy of *The Herald* and *Times* Group. Photographs of Ella Cowan and pages from her notebooks are copyright © Alex Gray. Thanks to Jane Rose of the National Library of Scotland, Bernadette Gallacher of the Mitchell Library and *The Herald* Picture Desk

Every effort has been taken to trace and credit the owners of copyright material in this book, however, the publisher would be glad to hear from any who believe they may have been omitted

ISBN 978-1-84934-003-8

Typeset in Bitstream Humanist and ITC Caslon

Printed and bound in the EU

A catalogue entry for this book is available from the British Library

3 4 5 6 7 8 9 10

CONTENTS

THE GLASGOW COOKERY BOOK

College students, 1926

PREFACE

This new edition of *The Glasgow Cookery Book* comes to print as we near the hundredth anniversary of the book's first publication.

The Glasgow Cookery Book started life as a textbook that was based on actual coursework taught in the classrooms of the Glasgow School of Cookery and the West End School of Cookery. Before its publication, recipes were painstakingly copied down by students, by hand, into their own notebooks – examples of which can be seen in this introduction.

In 1910, two years after the amalgamation of Glasgow's two cookery schools into the Glasgow and West of Scotland College of Domestic Science, the first edition of *The Glasgow Cookery Book* was published, masterminded by the school's then Principal, Miss Ella Glaister. It must have been a great aid to teaching and, in addition, a fantastic opportunity to preserve forever the collected culinary wisdom of the teachers at this new institution.

Anyone you meet who studied at the College, known to most Glaswegians as "the Dough School", will tell you that its regime was exacting. It has left the alumni with an enviable eye for organisation and an expectation of high standards in themselves and others. *The Glasgow Cookery Book*, in all its editions, has always been a book that has prioritised practical and economical cooking methods, and no matter what cookery fashions come and go, there is always a place for such a no-nonsense approach to cooking good food.

The book made a name for itself outside the confines of the College. The general public gradually learned of the reliability of its recipes. Its fame spread not as the result of any marketing campaign but by reputation alone. Mothers bought it for daughters and daughters-in-law, and its common-sense approach made an easy transition from the classroom to the home. There must be few textbooks in existence that have become as well-loved.

Over the years, the book has been revised many times. The edition on which this book is based is that of 1975 – which was the centenary year of the founding of the Glasgow School of Cookery. Published by John Smith & Son Limited (another Glasgow institution), the 1975 print was also noteworthy in that it was the first metric edition and the first edition of the book to be published with the imprint of "The Queen's College".

According to Juliann Calder's foreword, her hope had been that in revising the book they would be able to "link that which is traditional, familiar and reliable with that which is up to date and forward looking."

I echo Miss Calder's hope that in this new edition we have preserved the much-loved content of this book – with around 1000 tried-and-tested recipes – while updating it for today's cook.

E. B. A., Waverley Books

ACKNOWLEDGEMENTS

The Queen's College Special Collection and the Glasgow Caledonian University Institutional Archive, stretching back to the founding of the Glasgow School of Cookery in 1875, are curated at our University as part of Research Collections. As Research Collections Manager, and as someone who has been involved over several years in the crusade to publish a new edition of *The Glasgow Cookery Book*, I am delighted to acknowledge the endeavours and support of those who have helped bring our project to fruition.

We are very grateful for the undertaking by Waverley Books to produce and publish the new edition. So to Ron Grosset and his team, especially Eleanor Abraham for her understanding and sympathetic editing, a huge thank you for having faith in *The Glasgow Cookery Book*, and for inspiring us to renew our efforts when things were looking bleak.

Our original project to publish a new edition started in 2000, initiated and driven forward by Anne Ward who at that time was Chief Cataloguer in Collection Management. Anne's determination over some three years encouraged others to join in, including Sheena MacArthur, Pauline Bell, Fiona Keddie, Catherine McAlinden, and Margie Shields, all members of Queen's College staff. Anne faced multifarious obstacles, and when she moved on from the University, the project, for one reason and another, ground to a halt.

Then along came Ron and his colleagues following a serendipitous approach from Eleanor seeking information about Ella Cowan, a former College of Domestic Science student. A new team was formed to advance the project, and many thanks are due to a number of GCU colleagues, above all Jo Dowling, Head of Development and Alumni Relations, who has been energetic, diplomatic and enthusiastic in driving things forward.

Others deserving thanks are Mansoor Ali, Alumni Relations Officer, who so efficiently organised the editorial team; Fiona Stewart-Knight, Davena Rankin, Alison Arnot, Lynn McGarry, Liz Small and Ailie Ferrari for marketing and administrative support; and Melanie Armstrong for proof-reading.

The sterling and invaluable work of our editorial team, all Queen's College Alumni – Sheonagh Beaton, Helen Daye, Mary Farquhar, Morag Fortune, Wendy I'Anson, Elaine Moffett, Betty Orr, Linda Pryde, Fiona Robertson, Gilda Smith and Diane Spiers – is very gratefully acknowledged.

Many thanks are also due to Carole McCallum, our University Archivist based in Research Collections, for providing the introduction to this new edition, and for being the keeper of our corporate memory.

John Powles
Research Collections Manager
Glasgow Caledonian University

FOREWORD: A COOKERY DETECTIVE STORY

BY ALEX GRAY

It was all Maw Broon's doing, though she wasn't aware of it at the time.

Waverley Books was enjoying the rip-roaring success of the first *Maw Broon's Cookbook* and I was a huge fan. (Have you tried Daphne's chocolate cake?) So I decided to show Ron Grosset of Waverley Books, two very old cookery books that had come into my possession and now resided amongst my extensive collection.

"These," I told him proudly, "are Aunt Ella's cookbooks."

Unlike Maw's gravy-stained and well-used book, Ella Cowan's soft, battered recipe books, dated 1909, were in pristine condition. Handwritten in perfect copperplate, page-numbered and meticulously indexed, Ella's books looked as though they had been a labour of love.

Despite the lack of smudges from ingredients (and cheeky, scribbled comments) these books were uncannily like Maw's own cookbook. In fact, I had used a few recipes from them myself, I told Ron. Looking at his face, Maw might have remarked that Mr Grosset "wis fair gob-smacked". Just what had I shown him? Were these recipe books the life's work of a dedicated cook? Did Ron now have the real-life version of Maw Broon's cookbooks in his hand?

Preparation for the publication of the *But an' Ben Cookbook* was at the time under way. Excitedly, Ron dreamt up a fictional scenario where Ella and Maw meet at an SWRI cake competition and Maw swaps her beetroot chutney recipe for one of Ella's famed cake recipes. (See the *But an' Ben Cookbook* page 122 for details of their "correspondence".) A recipe was chosen from Ella's books for inclusion. At the back of the notebooks was a more hastily handwritten recipe for Semolina Cake, a suitably old-fashioned sounding recipe worthy of inclusion in Maw's new book of homely fare.

You might ask, how had these notebooks come to me, and who was Ella Cowan? In truth, I didn't know very much about her.

All I seemed to recall was that Ella Forbes Cowan had been a Principal Teacher of cookery and that she had attended the "Dough School" in Glasgow.

There are few Glasgow citizens of a certain age who will not have heard of the "Dough School", Glasgow's affectionate nickname for the Glasgow and West of Scotland College of Domestic Science.

Established in 1908, the school was an amalgamation of the Glasgow School of Cookery (established 1875) and the West End School of

Cookery (established 1878). The establishment of the Glasgow School of Cookery was one of the measures taken to try to help alleviate the problems of running a home in a city suffering through overpopulation and the problems associated with the Industrial Revolution.

And so began what one might describe as a cookery detective story.

A visit to the Archivist, Carole McCallum, at Glasgow Caledonian University revealed more about Ella's cookery books. A clue as to their origin lay in the sections entitled "Artisan and Invalid Recipes" and "Household Recipes"; two sections also found within the 1910 edition of the now-famous *Glasgow Cookery Book*.

This was the publication and textbook of the College of Domestic Science (later The Queen's College, now incorporated into Glasgow Caledonian University). It was concluded that Ella's recipe books were most likely her College workbooks containing the information and recipes that went to make up *The Glasgow Cookery Book*'s first edition in 1910 under the direction of the Principal of the College at that time, Miss Ella Glaister.

Carefully set out with hand-drawn diagrams, one could easily imagine the young Ella Cowan neatly copying down details of recipes and housewifery from the blackboard. Little wonder that the books were free from grubby flour stains!

What might have been disappointment that Ella Cowan hadn't invented these recipes herself, or that, even worse, she had just copied them from *The Glasgow Cookery Book*, was soon overtaken by the realisation that these College notebooks were from 1909, a year *before* the famous cookery book was even published.

Carole revealed that these very notebooks were the earliest she had seen and the first definitive proof that *The Glasgow Cookery Book* was based on the notes the women were taught in class.

Carole had been the first to discover the previously unrecorded publication date of the cookery book when she was searching in the minutes of the College's Cookery Committee, dated 16 June, 1910.

> "Miss Glaister states that she was preparing a new book of recipes, which are used in training, and which she hoped to have in the hands of the printers soon. She stated that the first edition of the book would require to be paid for as soon as printed, and the price would be recovered, as the copies sold, and that she thought the book would sell at 1s 6d a copy."

Now I had discovered that Ella's books were indeed the forerunner to the cookery book that would become a household name, I felt impelled to find out more about Aunt Ella and what her life had been like.

Ella Forbes Cowan was the maiden aunt of Hume Rennie, my dear friend and honorary aunt to my two children. It was after Hume's death in 1992 that I was given Ella's cookery books. Childless herself after a late marriage to Dr Tom Rennie – father of our best friend, Tony – Hume became a very close part of our family. When I first met Hume in 1976, Aunt Ella was living in the annexe to Hume's lovely cottage in St Andrews. She died in 1977, her estate passing to Hume and with it her precious cookery books.

Like Ella before her, Hume was an excellent cook, eventually achieving Cordon Bleu status. Her meals may have looked simple, using vegetables and herbs straight from the garden but each mouthful was a delight. And as for her baking! Well, anything she offered up was a very special treat; the oatmeal biscuit recipe she passed to me many years ago simply became known as "Hume Biscuits" within our family lore.

Hume had shared Aunt Ella's passion for cookery although her choice of career had been primary teaching, not domestic science. I discovered that it had been Ella's wish that young Hume follow in her footsteps and attend the College of Domestic Science but after a few months Hume decided it was not for her and she left to study at Jordanhill College instead.

With no children to tell her story and Aunty Hume now gone too, I turned to our friend, Tony Rennie for help. The house in St Andrews yielded up several family photographs including ones of Ella and her companion of many years, Dorothy Herbert, helping Tony to delve into his own memory bank for reminiscences of Ella.

Ella Cowan was born at a time when the daughters of gentlemen were expected to prepare themselves for the task of running their own homes – marriage being a hopeful expectation. The College of Domestic Science ran classes to encourage such diligence and it was to these that Ella made her way in 1909.

Her aim, though, was to become a teacher of domestic science and she fulfilled that aim after graduation, working in the city of Glasgow. After leaving Glasgow she set up home in Cothall, a lovely house on the outskirts of Coupar Angus with Dorothy. (I am amused by the proximity to Dundee and the Broons family; the fictional story Ron had produced seemed almost believable.)

Tony recalls Aunt Dorothy as a fearsome, outspoken person and although Ella was quieter, one was never in any doubt of her firm sense of what was right and what was wrong. But it was the memory of Ella's baking that remains strongest in my friend's memory; any visit to Coupar Angus was a huge thrill with its promise of goodies for a young boy. Eventually the house in Cothall became too big for Ella and so she and Dorothy moved to Lundin Links. When Dorothy died in the early 1970s Ella did not wish to live alone

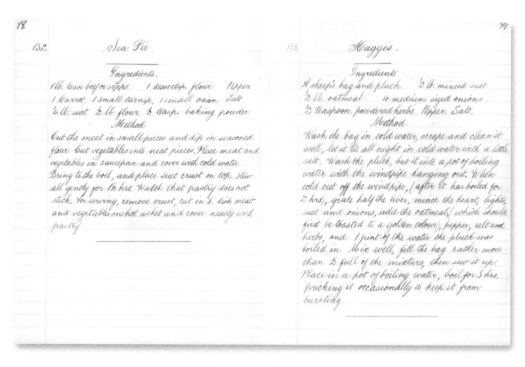

Left: The cover of one of Ella's notebooks.
Above: Pages from inside Ella's notebook. The recipes for Sea Pie and Haggis, above, can still be found in The Glasgow Cookery Book

Below: Ella Cowan (right) and her friend Dorothy Herbert

Pages from Ella's notebooks, including, right, traced diagrams of cuts of meat, that were neatly pinned inside one of the books with brass paper-fasteners

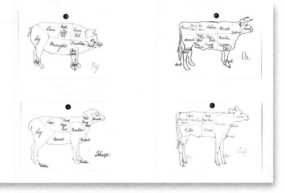

and so she arranged for the annexe to be built onto her niece's home in St Andrews which she had purchased in 1972. By this time Hume was a widow and she welcomed her elderly aunt into St Leonard's cottage, respecting her wish to have her own private apartments.

Hume's elderly school friend, Janey Clark, very kindly gave me more insight into the family and her own memories of Ella. "She was nobody's fool," Janey told me. "She was very direct and spoke her mind, but in a quiet way. She was very exact and particular, like a wee sparrow. And her soups were magnificent. These were the days when one judged a cook by their soups. Brilliant! And the desserts!"

Now that I have found out more about Aunt Ella and the times in which she lived, these two cookery books handed down over the generations are even more precious to me. They are, in fact, part of Glasgow's social history, taking their place in telling the story of *The Glasgow Cookery Book*.

It is with a sense of pride that I think back to the lady who attended the Dough School and gave so much of her life to the teaching of others, passing on much more than a collection of old-fashioned recipes. It is my hope that this new edition, like Maw Broon's books, will encourage many readers to go back to the old ways of cookery and domestic methods and, just as Aunt Ella's books were passed on to me, we might pass such knowledge on for future generations.

Alex Gray, 2009
Alex Gray is an award-winning writer of crime fiction

Alex Gray, (wearing a Queen's College scarf!) with Archivist
Carole McCallum looking at other notebooks donated to
Caledonian University's Institutional Archive

THE GLASGOW COOKERY BOOK: A HISTORY

ONE HUNDRED YEARS

This edition of *The Glasgow Cookery Book* is a new book for one of Scotland's newest Universities. One hundred years on from its original publication, this well-loved icon of the cookery world, to those in the know, remains true to its origins in format and content. A no-nonsense manual that captures the expertise of generations of The Glasgow and West of Scotland College of Domestic Science cookery staff, this centenary edition celebrates the work of the women who shaped domestic science education for the benefit of all.

A NEW BOOK FOR A NEW COLLEGE

As The Glasgow and West of Scotland College of Domestic Science said goodbye to its first Principal in 1910, it also said hello to a cookery publication that would stand the test of time.

In 1908, Miss Ella Glaister was given the onerous task of managing the merger of The Glasgow School of Cookery and The West End School of Cookery. Both schools were established in the second half of the 1870s and were to merge to create Glasgow's new domestic science college. Ella only held the position of College Principal for around two years before taking up the austere-sounding role of Inspectress in Domestic Subjects. However, before leaving, she left a legacy. She arranged for the publication of the first edition of the now famous *Glasgow Cookery Book*.

As part of her role in establishing the new College, Ella seized the opportunity to provide a printed book for cookery instruction rather than have the students copy the recipes down in their own hand as had been the practice in the earlier cookery schools. Her preface to the first edition noted that the recipes included were ones which had been perfected over the years by the College's parent institutions:

> "This book has been compiled specially for the use of Students in training as Teachers of Cookery at this College. The Recipes are those which have been successfully used for many years, and have been proved therefore to be essentially practical. It is hoped that the long-felt want, so often expressed by many, will also be met by this collection of thoroughly reliable Recipes."

Ella Glaister

Isabella (or Ella) Scott Scouler Glaister (1880–1954) took over the running of the Glasgow School of Cookery when Grace Paterson retired in March 1908. When her school amalgamated with The West End School she was appointed Principal. Ella was a pioneering career girl, who eventually married in her late thirties – the only female Principal to marry albeit some years after she left College.

She met Professor Harold Addison Woodruff (veterinary pathologist and bacteriologist) of Melbourne University, a widower with two small sons, during his war service. They married in Australia on June 24, 1919. The College presented her with the perfect gift – a College-made wedding cake.

Ella was the daughter of John Glaister, Glasgow University's Regius Professor of Forensic Medicine and Public Health, and Mary Scott Clarke. She was the eldest of six children, four girls and two boys. Her mother and father both died in the Glasgow influenza epidemic on December 18, 1932, within four hours of each other.

In 1916, Ella's future sister-in-law prepared for her marriage to Ella's brother John by attending the short "Bride's Course" at the College and in 1941 Ella's niece completed a housewifery course and went on to study cordon-bleu cookery eventually becoming a College Governor; it is not uncommon to find generations of the same family benefiting from the College's syllabus. Ella died in March 1954 but during her time in Australia she continued her pioneering work in the field of domestic science education, working with the Invergowrie Homecraft Hostel and the Emily McPherson College of Domestic Economy.

The "long-felt want" she speaks of could be twofold; the want of the students to have the recipes in printed format and the want of those outside the College to get their hands on them! She could never have known the impact this publication would have in time nor the dedicated following it would build world-wide over the next 100 years.

The "Dough School" is still remembered today in Glasgow and beyond, as is its purple-covered book, but what of its origins?

Goodbye Sheep's Head Broth

Above is an example of the handwritten notes that were taken down in class in the early days of the Dough School. These notes were the basis of the first edition of The Glasgow Cookery Book. The pages above are from the College notebooks of Ella Forbes Cowan, (see Foreword by Alex Gray) and were written in 1909. The recipes here are for Suet Pudding and Sheep's Head Broth. While the Suet Pudding recipe survives in this new edition in a similar form to the text above, Sheep's Head Broth has fallen victim to recent government food-safety guidelines and is missing from the book for the first time. Despite this, as was the case in 1909, cookery "from nose to tail", from exponents such as Fergus Henderson, is gaining interest from those who think it is important to waste as little as possible of the meat from the animals that we butcher.

NEW ATTITUDES

The Glasgow School of Cookery came into being at a time when Glasgow was in its heyday as an industrial and imperial centre. However, though there was plenty of work during the Industrial Revolution, this was also a time of great suffering for many. Factory conditions could be bad, working hours long, towns were overcrowded and living conditions unbearable.

The cookery schools were viewed by their founders as one of the answers to the social problems which were the counterpart of Britain's prosperity. Cookery schools opened in various British cities in the last quarter of the 19th century. They went on to play a vital role in the education of girls and in the development of domestic economy as an essential and respected subject.

The National Training School of Cookery was established in London in 1873, the first of its kind in the country. There was a thirst for knowledge in the fields of cookery and hygiene in Victorian Britain and it was felt by groups of a certain class that proper teaching about food and its preparation could improve the life of the working classes in a time of rapid urban growth. How this was to be achieved, however, was not as straightforward as the early pioneers expected. In all of their planning, fundraising and goodwill it would appear that they failed to understand one crucial thing: the daily life, attitudes and priorities of the working classes and, more importantly, its women.

An article in *The Times* of the July 7, 1875 captures the ethos of the schools of cookery as they developed in Britain at this time,

> "…not so much to teach good cooks how to cook better, as to show the great mass of the working people how to make the most of the food material which is nowhere so good, so abundant, and so vilely cooked as in England."

And *The Edinburgh Courant* recorded on April 22, 1875,

> "…Cookery is amongst the middle classes practically a lost art… As far as women in still more humble circumstances, the question is one of really vital importance…The gain physically, morally, and pecuniary, from an improvement of dinners of hardworking people is simply incalculable…The greatest care, then, should be taken to avoid any appearance of exclusiveness in the course of instruction offered."

As the new cookery schools opened their doors they found a number of young ladies at their enrolment classes. Unfortunately, very few of these were "needy" working-class women. Fortunately, the early pioneers were not to be put off easily, for this marked the beginning of a movement to raise domestic work from the lowly status of drudgery – rewarded with social inferiority – to its true position as one of the chief means of securing the health and comfort of the whole community.

THE GLASGOW SCHOOL OF COOKERY

Following on from the example set by developments in London and then by the establishment of the Edinburgh School of Cookery in 1875, James Bain, the Lord Provost of Glasgow, invited Mr J C Buckmaster to address a Glasgow conference. Buckmaster was central to the creation of the National School in London and this conference was with a view to organising a scheme for an "institution of cookery" in the City of Glasgow.

The Bulletin article headline and body:

2   November 6th 1943.   *The Bulletin*

School's Nickname May Be Changed

THE Glasgow and West of Scotland College of Domestic Science may lose its time-honoured nickname, "the dough school," as a result of an appeal made yesterday by Mr Osbourne Hatrick, chairman of the board of governors.

A wave of giggles ran round the listening girls as he remonstrated on the lack of dignity in the title, which is the only one by which the College is known in Glasgow, among students, ex-students, their families and friends, and, he suspected, also among the staff.

Mr Hatrick suggested that the outgoing students might take the opportunity when it arose of referring to the College as "Park Drive," after the street in which it is situated.

The Edinburgh College of Domestic Science is invariably referred to as "Atholl Crescent."

"A good name is a good name, and it shouldn't be submerged," he said.

Councillor Jean Roberts, who handed over diplomas and prizes, criticised large-scale preparation of food.

There was a limit, she said, to the extension of the principle that everything carried out on a large scale was more economical and efficient.

Must Be Appetising

It was more important, she declared, that food should be attractive to look at and appetising to taste than that certain economies should be effected by means of preparing it in the mass. A stage was reached when meals ceased to be savoury when cooked on too large a scale.

Miss D. H. Melvin, Principal of the College, giving the report on session 1942-43, disclosed that 81 diplomas had been gained, 114 housewifery certificates, and 447 short-course certificates.

The following is the list of prize-winners:—

"Margaret Black" memorial prize for best Group I. diploma student, Isobel Melville, Newton-Stewart; prize for best Group II. diploma student, Elizabeth Hogg, Falkirk. "Osbourne Hatrick" prize for best advanced cook's certificate and best Cordon Bleu student, Josephine Cochran, Brookfield; and Myra Whyte, Newton-Stewart. "May J. F. Telnie" prize for best household management certificate student, Mary Cartner,

Carlisle; for best housewife's certificate student, Mary Colville, Kilkenzie. "Margaret Beattie" prize for best institutional (catering) certificate student, Ella Bell, Newry; Myra Whyte, Newton-Stewart, and Josephine Cochran, Brookfield. "Margaret Gettins" prize for best cookery diploma student, Group III., Joan Muirs, Kilmacolm. "Isabella Gray" memorial prize for best housewifery diploma student, Dorothy Scobbie, Bearsden. "Miss M. A. Mavor" prize for best embroidery student, Elizabeth Brown, Glasgow.

"G. W. Service" prize for the best dietitian, Mrs Louisa Harper, Milngavie, and Moira M'Millan, Jordanhill. "Mrs Peter MacLellan" prize for the best laundrywork diploma student, Isobel Melville, Newton-Stewart. For best dressmaking diploma student, Dorothy Scobbie, Bearsden. E.I.S prize for teaching children, Marion Steele, Larkhall, and Jane Ewing, Jamestown. "Isabella Cunningham" memorial prize for best institutional management student, Annie Boag, East Kilbride; Margaret Martin, Mount Vernon; and Lorna Winks, Glasgow. Mrs Cairns prize for work in housewifery subjects, Dorothy Scobbie, Bearsden.

DOMESTIC SCIENCE PRIZEWINNER.—Councillor Mrs Jean Roberts presents Miss Isobel Melville with the Margaret Black Memorial Prize as the best Group I. diploma student at Glasgow and West of Scotland College of Domestic Science prize day yesterday. Corbett.

Article in The Bulletin, November 6, 1943

Dough School versus Do. School

An establishment with such a long and unwieldy name as The Glasgow and West of Scotland College of Domestic Science (Incorporated) was always going to get a nickname, but trust Glaswegians to make it a pun as well.

The "Dough School", born out of local wit and insight, is suggestive of the very act of cooking. In 1943 Mr Osbourne Hattrick, the then Chairman of the Board of Governors, made a plea to change the "time-honoured" nickname but it certainly fell on deaf ears as the moniker has survived to the present day. Even when the College name changed to The Queen's College, the nickname remained despite attempts to encourage the use of the new title.

Some of the College's more recent graduates favour "Do. School" as the preferred nickname but this was originally an administrative shortening of Domestic rather than an affectionate pun given to the institution and its girls.

Both nicknames, however, have a place in the history of the College and the use of both has survived to the present day.

In the Religious Institution Rooms, Bath Street on Saturday November 13, 1875 a motion was passed to initiate the establishment of a Glasgow School of Cookery. The Reverend Frederick Lockhart Robertson was a key instigator in the establishment of this school and, as such, held the position of Chairman of its impressive Board of Directors. Lockhart Robertson was a Presbyterian minister who moved to Glasgow from Greenock where his efforts on behalf of the working classes had gained him great respect. His Glasgow parish was that of St Andrews in the east end where he experienced first-hand great poverty, inhumane living conditions, poor diets and the negative role of drink in the life of the working man.

Glasgow School of Cookery,

THE ALBERT HALL, 285 BATH STREET.

INSTITUTED 1875.

Patronesses.

HER GRACE THE DUCHESS OF HAMILTON.
THE RIGHT HONOURABLE THE COUNTESS OF GLASGOW.
THE LADY ISABELLA GORDON.

Directors.

THE HONOURABLE THE LORD PROVOST OF GLASGOW.

SIR JAMES WATSON.
A. G. MACDONALD, ESQ., PRECEPTOR OF HUTCHESONS' HOSPITAL.
JAMES KING, ESQ., LORD DEAN OF GUILD.
BAILIE COLLINS.
GEORGE BUCHANAN, M.D., PROFESSOR OF CLINICAL SURGERY, GLASGOW UNIVERSITY. .
MICHAEL CONNAL, ESQ.
ANDREW HOGGAN, ESQ.
ARCHBISHOP EYRE.
JAMES AIRLIE, ESQ., SECRETARY, ABSTAINERS' UNION.
A. S. SCHAW, ESQ.

A. ORR EWING, ESQ., M.P.
A. WHITELAW, ESQ., M.P.
ARCHIBALD GILCHRIST, ESQ., DEACON-CONVENER.
BAILIE MORRISON.
W. T. GAIRDNER, M.D., PROFESSOR OF MEDICINE, GLASGOW UNIVERSITY.
DR. ANDERSON KIRKWOOD.
WILLIAM TAYLOR, ESQ.
WILLIAM FORSYTH, ESQ.
THE REV. R. S. OLDHAM.
THE REV. F. LOCKHART ROBERTSON.
D. ROSS, ESQ., H.M. INSPECTOR OF SCHOOLS.

Chairman of Directors—REV. F. LOCKHART ROBERTSON. 204 BATH STREET.

Hon. Secy.—C. D. DONALD, JUN., ESQ., 172 ST. VINCENT ST.   *Secretary*—MISS DODD, 285 BATH ST.

Ladies' Executive Committee.

MRS. SCOTT, 1 Woodside Place.
MRS. MACKENZIE, 6 Blythswood Square.
MRS. AULD, 4 Park Terrace.
MRS. KING, 12 Claremont Terrace.
MRS. GEORGE BUCHANAN, 193 Bath Street.
MRS. GAIRDNER, 225 St. Vincent Street.
MRS. A. BUCHANAN, 17 Sandyford Place.
MRS. MACDONALD, 8 Park Circus.
MRS. HIGGINBOTHAM, Ashfield House. Sauchiehall Street.

MRS. DONALD, 196 Bath Street.
MRS. COLLINS, 3 Park Terrace, East.
MRS. ROBERTSON, 204 Bath Street.
MISS WATSON, 9 Woodside Terrace.
MISS BAIN, 3 Park Terrace.
MISS DONALD, 200 Bath Street.
MISS PATERSON, 8 Claremont Terrace.
MISS HOGGAN, Camphill.

Teachers.

MRS. PRICE and MRS. BLACK,
Of the National Training School of Cookery, South Kensington.

The impressive list of the patrons, directors and committee members of The Glasgow School of Cookery

Grace Paterson

Grace Chalmers Paterson (1843–1925) has an honourable record of public work in Glasgow and the West of Scotland. As well as her pioneering work with The Glasgow School of Cookery, she was one of the first women elected onto the Glasgow School Board, the other being Margaret Barlas, in 1885. In another sphere of education she was closely associated with Miss Janet Galloway and the founders of Queen Margaret College, who did so much to advance the higher education of women at Glasgow University. It is noted in her obituaries that Grace Paterson believed in women and their capacity both for original work and for organising and directing the work of others. She desired votes for women and posts for women, equal pay and equal moral standards. In public life she was "no ornamental figure".

However, the driving force behind The Glasgow School of Cookery was a woman. Grace Paterson was born in Glasgow in 1843 to upper-middle-class parents and she appears, from what is known about her, to have been a striking and forceful personality with the improvement of Glasgow's health, welfare and women's educational opportunities at the forefront of her concerns. On her death in 1925 the words feminist and suffragist were both used to describe her. A central figure of the school's Ladies Executive Committee she was in effect its first and founding Principal. Her role was organisational and she did not undertake teaching duties or their direct supervision.

After much organisation, The Glasgow School of Cookery opened its doors, those of the Albert Hall in Bath Street, to the public on Monday February 21, 1876. Early prospectuses advertise demonstration lessons and practice lessons. The scope of such lessons were class-related, with superior cookery (becoming high-class cookery), plain cookery (becoming plain household cookery) and cookery for the working classes.

An early "satirical" advert using soup as the example dish captures "soup for the different classes" perfectly with "*potage ecossais*" at 25 shillings for 12 lessons, "Scotch soup" at 21 shillings for the dozen lessons and "broth" being 3 shillings for the same:—

"SCHOOL FOR COOKERY

"SUPERIOR Cookery – Tickets, 25s per doz. – Potage Ecossais
This superior soup is prepared as follows:- Choose a few pounds of beef – thick, juicy, nutritious. Next procure a selection of esculent roots, bulbous and otherwise, together with such herbaceous plants as may be in season. Now boil several pints of condensed vapour, placing the beef in the pot while the water is cold, in order to prevent the formation of an albuminous envelope. About an hour before serving throw in the vegetables, previously reduced to atoms by the operation of a mincing knife. Serve hot, in Wedgewood ware, with a ladle argent. When the temperature is below zero this will be found a most excellent and comfortable dish.

"Plain Cookery – Tickets, 21s per doz. – Scotch Soup
Take some pounds of beef, fat rather than lean. Buy some carrots, turnips and onions, together with some parsley, if you can get it. Now boil the beef, and throw in the vegetables, nicely minced, an hour before serving. For cold weather no better dish could be prepared.

"Cookery for the Working Classes – Tickets, 3s per doz. – Broth
Buy some hochs, also tippence worth o' neeps, sibos, carrots, and ingans. Pit the beef intae the pat wi' cauld watter. Bile for an 'oor, and then in wi' the vegetables. When the guidman comes in at one, serve het. Eh, lassies, there's naething like a drap guid kail on a cauld day."

The Bailie, March 22, 1876

Both the time and cost of the actual lessons related to the intended audience. Superior cookery was on a Wednesday and Friday from 3pm to 5pm, plain cookery on Wednesday and Friday from 11am to 1pm and working-class cookery on a Sunday at 7pm. The daytime classes for better-off women were priced to subsidise the cost of evening classes for working women, although budgeting for cookery lessons would probably not have been a priority for a working-class family.

A Glasgow periodical of the day *The Baillie* reported on March 1, 1876:

"What Folk are Saying.
That the Cookery School has been successfully started.
That 70 young lady pupils are already in attendance.

That their husbands, when they get them, will prefer dining at
home.

That restaurants and clubs will be nowhere.

That the minister of St Andrew's lives luckily in the vicinity of
the Albert Hall.

That he knows the value of the creature comforts.

That he thinks the working man's daily bread should be as
well cooked as his own.

That he gives the institution daily the light of his countenance.

That instruction is to be given at a cheap rate to women of the
working class.

That by and by they will be able to prepare nice meals
economically for their husbands.

That drunkenness and wife-beating will belong to the
barbarous past. ..."

This ambitious strategy, perhaps naive in its approach, changed course in
time when the determined and dedicated pioneers realised that it was girls
of school age that they needed to teach if there was to be a long-term benefit
from any form of culinary and domestic economy education.

Margaret Black

Margaret Black FEIS (1830–1903), née Mackirdy, was born in Rothesay and was brought up in the Free Kirk. She married in the early 1870s, but her husband, John Black, a shawl manufacturer, tragically drowned in the River Kelvin in 1874. After his death she directed her energies towards social improvements in a number of spheres including a crusade against the employment of young children in pantomimes. As well as founder and Principal of The West End School of Cookery, she wrote books on cookery and household management. In September 1885 she was created a Fellow of the Educational Institute of Scotland and in 1891 was elected onto the School Board of Glasgow as a temperance and free educationalist candidate.

THE WEST END SCHOOL OF COOKERY

For almost two years, The Glasgow School of Cookery employed a Mrs Margaret Black, financing her initial training at the National Training School of Cookery in South Kensington where she achieved a first class diploma.

In 1878, however, she broke away and set up her own institution: The West End School of Cookery opened its doors at the end of October 1878 in the west hall of the Corporation Galleries in Dalhousie Street. Margaret was a hands-on Principal and a writer of books on cookery and domestic economy. A native of Rothesay, she was widowed at the age of 44 and, much like Grace Paterson, she showed a determined energy and a tireless dedication

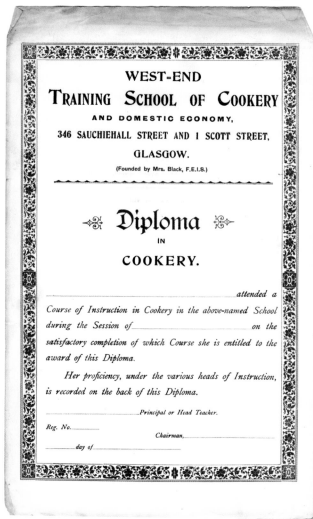

The West End School of Cookery, which opened in 1878, had its own Diploma in Cookery

Glasgow International Exhibition, 1888

The Glasgow School of Cookery won the tender to provide a tearoom close to the Women's Industries Section at the Glasgow International Exhibition from May 2 to November 10, 1888. The tearoom caused

quite a stir and it was reported that at different times a policeman was stationed at the entrance door to regulate the admission of patrons. The profit from this tearoom was £2,825 4s 8d and the money was initially used to lease new premises at 86 Bath Street; premises that remained central to Glasgow's domestic science education over the next 30 years.

Above: The Glasgow School of Cookery tearoom at the Glasgow International Exhibition, 1888. Opposite: The Glasgow School of Cookery students at the Exhibition

in her own beliefs. Central to those beliefs was the temperance movement.

Her school was smaller than the Glasgow School of Cookery, but in 1885 it was also formally recognised as a teacher-training centre, joining her rival institution.

Glasgow in the 1870s had two schools of cookery and, in time, their combined effort resulted in training and instruction being offered in various aspects of cookery, housewifery, laundry work, dressmaking, needlework, millinery, hygiene, sick-nursing and book-keeping.

SURVIVAL AND A NEW STRATEGY

That both schools were able to survive throughout the years following their foundation indicates that they were meeting a significant demand, though neither of them enjoyed a very secure financial position.

Although they both started with the intention of teaching working-class women how to cook better, and thus improve their family life, this approach was not a great success.

Even when the evening classes for working women were offered free they failed to catch on. Lack of interest, lack of available time, a degree of class suspicion and a failed marketing strategy (just how were these working-class women targeted?) may all have contributed to this.

Whatever the reasons, a fresh strategy was needed if the schools were to survive and succeed with their intended objectives. It should be noted that it was also both schools' intention to improve the cooking skills and nutritional standards of middle-class families too.

This fresh strategy targeted girls of school age and heralded the start of a campaign to encourage the recognition of domestic economy as part of the school curriculum. At first, staff went to the board schools to teach the girls. However, in time this effort developed into a teacher-training programme whereby the cookery schools trained domestic science teachers to work in the board schools. No doubt the eventual presence in 1885 of Grace Paterson and later Margaret Black (1891) on the Glasgow School Board accelerated this process.

The cookery schools developed a double function, the training of teachers in domestic science and the provision of instruction for the general public (and domestic servants) both in-house and as visiting lecturers.

If the working classes would not come to the cookery schools, then the cookery classes – and more besides – would reach them in time through the classroom.

THE BIRTH OF THE GLASGOW AND WEST OF SCOTLAND COLLEGE OF DOMESTIC SCIENCE (INCORPORATED)

The 1908 Education (Scotland) Act made provision for the domestic education of schoolgirls, and with this responsibility came the establishment of the new domestic science colleges in Glasgow, Edinburgh and Aberdeen: central institutions under the ultimate control of the Scotch Education Department.

There was no room for two cookery schools in Glasgow, since the new funding could only recognise one. The Glasgow and West of Scotland College of Domestic Science was incorporated on May 20, 1908 – a merger of both of Glasgow's cookery schools.

Whether this merger was popular with the individual institutions or not, it was a necessary action to save both schools and build on their combined work of the past thirty years plus. This work, after all, had gone a long way in establishing and formalising domestic science education.

A NEW BUILDING FOR A NEW COLLEGE

At the time of the merger The Glasgow and West of Scotland College of Domestic Science was spread over five locations – 86 Bath Street, 346 Sauchiehall Street, 504 Sauchiehall Street, 1 Scott Street and 1 Victoria Crescent. This was not an ideal set up for the new College with the students running between sites for different classes.

Plans were set up to raise the money for a purpose-built building in one location; raising this money however was a slow process. Recognition as a central institution meant the College could apply for a building grant but only equivalent to the sum it could raise itself.

Glasgow and its citizens played their part in supporting what was to become a much-loved building.

As part of its fundraising, a public appeal was launched by the Lord Provost and subscription appeals were printed in the *Glasgow Herald*, the *Scotsman*, the *Citizen*, the *Daily Record*, the *Evening Times* and the *Evening Citizen*; the first of these appearing on Saturday April 29, 1911. This raised £6,121 and, along with a Glasgow Corporation grant of £3,000 from the Glasgow Common Good Fund and a variety of other donations, the College raised its half of the estimated £30,000 needed.

Needless to say, the building costs escalated to over £40,000. Mr Walter R Watson was appointed architect for the new building and a site was selected at Park Drive beside the West End Park (now Kelvingrove Park). Building work started in 1913 and continued in the months following the outbreak of the war.

Cooking the Books

The cookery department at the Dough School was dynamic from the start. The first Head of Department, Mary Mackirdy (last Principal of The West End School of Cookery), was published in the subject of domestic science, just like her aunt Margaret Black before her (founder of The West End School).

Mary's *c.*1926 publication *Recipes for You* saw *The Bulletin* herald her as a Scottish Mrs Beaton. The recipes in this book had previously appeared in "Women's Topics" in *The Glasgow Herald*. Margaret Black's publications included *Household Cookery and Laundry Work* (1882), *Hints to Young Housekeepers* (1884), and *Superior Cookery* (1887). She too wrote for the press, including *The Glasgow Weekly Mail*. Margaret's *Hints to Young Housekeepers* records that her reason for initially writing these seasonal papers on cooking and household management was to offer her young sisters the benefit of her experience.

Through further publications, spanning the decades of the 20th century, many were to benefit from the wealth of experience gained and shared by Dough School staff, not only in the revisions and new editions of *The Glasgow Cookery Book*, but in specialised publications that addressed the issues of the day. Examples of this are seen in the collaborative pamphlets created for the Great War on rationing, food economy and war recipes. There was Mary Mackirdy and Mary Andross's (eventual Head of the College's Science Department) 1934 compilation, *Cheap*

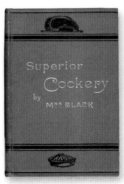

Diets: representing a week's meals, and the early 1940s publications addressing the needs on Scotland's home front. Miss Milligan and her staff wrote *An Economic Budget for the Family with Menus and Recipes* (1940). College cookery staff produced *Some Recipes for War-time Dishes* (1940). Miss Andross and Miss Little shared their expertise in *Food Preservation in War-time* (1940). Misses Orr, Sproat and MacColl expanded choice with their *More Recipes for War-time Dishes* (1941).

Cookery publication covered the whole spectrum and examples include an early College publication entitled *Plain Cookery Recipes*, a 1928 publication from Margery Rhys, a College lecturer, entitled *High Class Cookery* and a 1955 book from the then Head of Cookery, Hilda Ferris, and Margery Rhys covering *Advanced Cookery*.

In "cooking the books" the Dough School shared its expertise and served the community, taking on board the issues of the day in a practical and informed manner. They also took the lid off high-end cooking and allowed household kitchens the chance to experiment and practise in this field, ably guided by their well-written publications.

The Glasgow and West of Scotland College of Domestic Science (Incorporated), 1–6 Park Drive

By the early months of 1915, when the building was nearing completion and equipment was beginning to be installed, the Governors were confronted with a request from the Red Cross. They requested that the new building should be turned over to them for the duration of the war to be used as a hospital.

The College agreed and "Woodside Red Cross Hospital" was formally opened by Lord Provost Dunlop on June 28, 1915, providing 26 wards and 300 beds for the war wounded. The College's Housewifery Committee adopted four wards and their senior diploma students offered to do voluntary service in the hospital. Needlework students also offered their services, sewing and mending as needed.

In years to come, one of the College's Principals, Miss Juliann Calder, wrote of her childhood memories during this period:

"I was just a toddler during the First World War, but my father took me fairly regularly into Kelvingrove Park on a Saturday afternoon. I knew this building [Park Drive] as the 'Soldiers' Hospital' and therefore felt a very intimate connection with it throughout the whole of my life."

It was not until April 29, 1919 that the first college class was held in their new premises and The Glasgow and West of Scotland College of Domestic Science, or "Dough School" as it became affectionately known, settled into the Park Drive building that was to serve it well for many years to come.

COLLEGE WAR WORK

Under the direction of its Principal, Miss Dorothy Melvin, the College carried on its teaching programme throughout the war, but it did even more by contributing its time and expertise to the war effort.

Dorothy Melvin

Dorothy Humphries Melvin, OBE, JP (1881–1963) was College Principal for 36 years, from 1910 to 1946. She originally trained and worked at The Glasgow School of Cookery. Miss Melvin's sisters, Muriel and Greta also taught at the College. She championed the need for a purpose-built College and worked closely with Mr Watson, the architect, to see her vision come to fruition in Park Drive. Guiding the College through two world wars she used its discipline for the benefit of the country while maintaining the educational value of the College. She stretched the main syllabus from six to sixteen subjects during her period in office and embraced the training of international students; students from Turkey and Iceland were at the College in the year of her retirement. Miss Melvin was not only the Principal for an exceptional number of years, she was the Principal during the College's period of birth and establishment. For her work in the College and for her pioneering educational work in both the subject of domestic science and in women's education in general, she was made an Officer of the Order of the British Empire in the Coronation honours list of 1937.

The biggest contribution it made was educating people on the use of food during times of shortage and it worked closely with the newly established Patriotic Food League. Pamphlets on rationing, food economy and wartime recipes were written, there were free courses given to teachers on wartime cookery and experimentation with food substitutes took place with the results being demonstrated to the general public.

Students took up positions in hospitals, canteens and camps, reaching places like Paris, Rouen, Calais, Troyes, Royaumont, Salonica and Corsica. Staff members were released to fill positions in munitions factories and in the kitchens of military hospitals, and full support was given to local and national economy campaigns. The office staff answered questions on food economy and organised the filling of posts, making them a women's employment bureau during this period.

April 1915 saw the College doors opened for male students; soldiers to be precise. This was a teaching initiative that would continue for the duration of the war. Soldier-cook classes offered the men a three-week basic training in cookery before they were sent overseas to put their training to the test.

Students and staff raised money for causes like the Red Cross, the Limbless Hospital, the Scottish Women's Hospital, Bellahouston Hospital and for wheelchairs. The list of their efforts is long and the support they offered was far-reaching, with public lectures and demonstrations taking place throughout Scotland and a variety of organisations – including infant health visitors, nurses, the Voluntary Aid Detachment, Red Cross, and many others – benefiting from the College's know-how and teaching skills.

Soldiers were taught how to cook. The College received reports on the success of these classes, and for soldiers unable to attend The Glasgow Cookery Book *was sent to offer guidance*

COOKERY CLASSES FOR SOLDIERS: SOME NEW CHEFS.

Classes for teaching soldiers cookery are being conducted by the Glasgow and West of Scotland Domestic Science at their branch school in Scott Street. Ladies of the College Committee are interested spectators.—" Bulletin " Photo.

Students of the Glasgow and West of Scotland College of Domestic Science, 1917

Wartime Cookery Classes for the Working Classes

A teaching initiative of 1917 harked back to the early days of the cookery schools when the working classes were again targeted as being in need of help.

".....Cookery demonstrations will be given in the kitchens of working-class housewives in six districts – Calton, Garngad, Hutchestown East and West, Govan and Partick.......[The instructors] will work only with utensils provided in the house where the demonstrations are given, for it is realised that this is the most practical method of teaching economical cookery. It has been left to members of the Infant Health Visitors' Association to select suitable kitchens in each district, the housewives themselves being asked to give invitations to their neighbours so that as many local women as possible may have an opportunity of profiting by the demonstrations. The charge for admission will be a penny per head, and the food cooked will be left with the hostess. It is hoped that similar demonstrations will be arranged in other districts later on."

Glasgow Herald, October 4, 1917

It is not clear just how many women this reached or how much of an impact it made on the attitudes of Glasgow's working-class women. It is also not clear how such demonstrations were accommodated in a Glasgow single end!

PARK DRIVE AND THE BIRTH OF A NEW STUDENT IDENTITY

For 11 years, College students and staff had been dispersed between the various sites, but in 1919 they at last came together under one roof, a unified body with the chance of establishing their own collective identity.

The College was made up of numbers 1 to 6 Park Drive while numbers 7, 8 and 9 were private dwelling houses. The students were not slow to take advantage of their new premises and quickly requested permission to hold dances in the dining hall. A Students' Union was formed in 1920 which grew rapidly with hockey, swimming and golf clubs and choir, dramatic and debating societies. A magazine was produced that received rave reviews in the press and the College entered the wider forum of student activity and competition.

Left: The first edition of the Students Union Magazine, 1921. Cover illustration by Margaret Duncan.
Above: A drawing of millinery students

The College's Golden Jubilee celebrations in 1925 included a civic reception for hundreds of guests at the City Chambers. Around this time the student body came up with the proposition of a welfare scheme aimed at the acquisition of an actual union and playing fields. The figure the students hoped to raise was £10,000 and for two years both students and staff tirelessly fundraised, their activities culminating in a bazaar which took place on November 4 and 5, 1927.

With around £7,200 raised, a playing field was bought at Chesterfield Avenue and in time, through the acquisition and reconstruction of 7, 8 and 9 Park Drive, the long-awaited Students' Union and Recreation and Badminton Hall was complete.

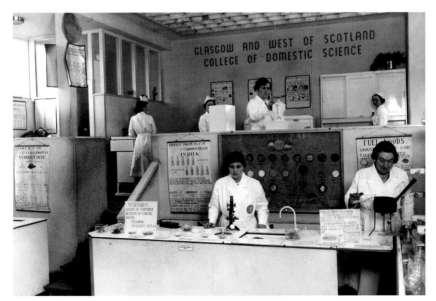

College staff at the Empire Exhibition, 1938. Miss Andross, bottom right

During the 1930s, the College participated in the annual university and public school races in the Gareloch, on the River Clyde. In August 1938 the College yachting crew were the only Scottish representatives to reach the final of the university section of the races. One year later, on August 24, 1939, the team won – not only bringing a victory to Scotland, but introducing an all-female crew to the prestigious list of winners. The girls were Miss Molly G Simpson – Skipper, Miss Edith Mackay, Miss Isobel Crosby and Miss Joan Young. Oxford University had held the Young Challenge Trophy in the university section for the previous four years.

In 1938 the College staff and students made quite an impact at the Empire Exhibition held in Glasgow's southside from May to October. Their contribution would not be out of place in today's society with its eating-related health problems. Housed in the Women of the Empire Pavilion, their stall was a nutrition centre.

Demonstrations centring round dietetics were planned with the expertise of the College staff (Miss Andross and Miss Milligan), and College girls (Misses Hamilton, Main and Lithgow) were employed to work on the stall, although other staff and students were also needed to keep the popular programme on course.

The timetable of demonstrations was split into four sections; diets for the healthy adult, diets for the healthy child, diet in disease and budgeting. Fuel food, vitamins, protective foods, home-grown fruit and vegetables, high- and low-calorie dishes, high- and low-protein diets, low-fat dishes, dishes for the

The College Gets Switched On

The Principal, Miss Melvin, had a strong appreciation of the new domestic power source, electricity. On November 12, 1930 the College formally opened its demonstrative and experimental switchboard to enable students and the public to comprehend modern electricity and its uses. This practice switchboard was the first of its kind to be installed in Scotland and allowed students to blow bulbs, repair fuses and learn the practicalities of electricity as it is applied to the home without danger or disturbance. Large and small purchases in electrical housecraft items began in the 1920s at the College and by 1937 electricity figured prominently.

A five-day Electrical Association for Women (the EAW was formed in 1924) summer school took place at the College in August 1937 and its director, Miss Caroline Haslett CBE, attended the event.

Miss Haslett's own desire to organise this summer school of electrical housecraft in Scotland, she said, started when she heard of the progress being made by the College of Domestic Science, and on a visit last year she had been greatly impressed by its new appliances. The importance, she continued, of the work being done there had convinced her that teachers of Domestic Science were going to be among the most important people in the new world.

She had been greatly impressed by the necessity of teaching children the methods they would have to follow and the tools they would have to use in the new way of living. Of these the most important was the electric motor.

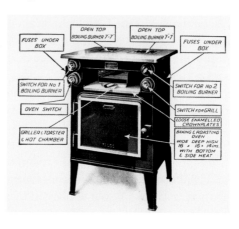

diabetic, common diet errors and wise spending of the food allowance were some of the many topics covered by the demonstration programme over the six-month period.

ANOTHER WAR

The management of very scarce resources, particularly food, was central to the College's teachings in the Second World War. The universal rationing system imposed from January 8, 1940 meant that the work of Britain's domestic science colleges became absolutely invaluable, quite apart from their direct contribution to the war effort in instructing and training military personnel. Rationing was the dominant reality of British civil life through the war years and afterwards.

As with the previous war, and still under the Principalship of Miss Melvin, the College not only passed on its services as an educational institution, in the training of others, but played a vital role allowing its members of staff and students to participate in the war effort of Glasgow, the surrounding area and beyond.

The College taught cookery again in the kitchens of Glasgow's deprived areas

Air Raid Shelter

"A tunnel below their College, discovered 30 years ago during building operations, has been adapted for the girls of the Glasgow and West of Scotland College of Domestic Science. The 100 resident-students of the College have already had an air raid drill from their hostel quarters to the tunnel, ...and each has been supplied with a torch for use in reaching the shelter in time of emergency. Miss D H Melvin, Principal of the College, showing a *Bulletin* woman reporter over the shelter yesterday, pointed out that the main entrance to the tunnel lies alongside the College food store, and that stores could be collected in a few seconds by the girls as they entered. The tunnel, which houses the pipes of the College heating system, has six storeys above it, and is claimed to be capable of accommodating at least 300 of the 800 students and staff, not all of whom attend the College at one time."

The Bulletin, 9 February 1939

St Enoch Canteen

Early in 1941 members of staff, and past and present students, who had been working in other canteens felt that they would like a canteen bearing The Glasgow and West of Scotland College of Domestic Science name. There was no canteen for the forces in St Enoch Station in Glasgow despite there being an urgent demand for one. Sir Andrew H Pettigrew, the then Chairman of the Board of Governors, threw himself into the task of organising this canteen and around £450 was raised. £200 was also gifted from the Central War Relief Fund. Despite cramped conditions the canteen continued until October 1945, when it was handed over to the Women's Voluntary Organisation, eventually closing at the end of 1945. In the four years and five months that the College ran the canteen, it served approximately 1,537,720 people. The Lord Provost opened it on June 2, 1941, the 35th of Glasgow's service canteens. The hexagonal bungalow was decorated in College colours: blue, white and purple.

and held public evening classes on topics like "Catering Without Coupons", "Expanding the Meat Ration", and "Vegetables, Salads and Potatoes in Variety". From 1942, vegetables were grown in the College playing fields at Chesterfield Avenue, including experimental work with herbs and less common vegetables, and cooking with dried eggs was also on the teaching agenda. The College's important cookery and nutrition work especially in the preservation of fruit and vegetables, and the process of bottling and canning, was shared with the general public too, as was its expertise in the area of make-do-and-mend. Mary Andross developed vitamin C sourced from wild rose fruits, and the College advised on fuel-saving techniques. The St Enoch Station canteen and the mobile canteen were tremendous efforts on behalf of the College.

Again, during the war years, the College was an enthusiastic fundraiser raising over £6,000 through initiatives like the "Penny-a-Week Fund", "Salute the Soldier" and "Wings for Victory".

As the war drew to its close, the Ministry of Education focused on the best way to re-integrate women service personnel back into the domestic environment. Courses were started on home-making and post-war domestic efficiency:

GIRLS STEP FROM KHAKI INTO APRONS
Training for Demob Day

After years in the open air, drilling on the parade ground and toughening-up under military discipline, ATS girls of all ranks are finding ordinary domestic work infinitely more trying and a greater strain than any of their wartime duties.

That is the opinion of the majority of girls now undergoing an intensive course in domestic science at the Glasgow and West of Scotland College before returning to their units, where they act as instructors for the thousands of girls who will be demobbed when the peace comes.

Glasgow Evening Citizen, March 9, 1945

London

In October 1944, students from Scotland's three Domestic Science Colleges – Glasgow, Edinburgh and Aberdeen – volunteered to go to London to cook for the builders, joiners, masons and slaters who were repairing the blitzed property. This was all part of Scotland's response to the urgent fly-bomb repair needs of a damaged London when many workers crossed the border to take part in the reconstruction of the city. The Dough School sent 99 girls in all.

THE ROYAL CONNECTION

On September 4, 1944, HRH The Princess Elizabeth agreed to become the Patroness of The Glasgow and West of Scotland College of Domestic Science and in light of her new role, she presented the certificates at Diploma Day on 28 September 1945.

Her patronage automatically ceased on her accession to the throne, but, as Queen she agreed to bestow it again. She came with the Duke of Edinburgh

A Special Day

On September 28, 1945 the College had its first Diploma Day since 1939. If that was not special enough for the students and staff, HRH The Princess Elizabeth was the guest of honour.

"We stood at the door that day awaiting HRH Princess Elizabeth. The sun was shining, the students in white and blue and white uniforms lined the corridors. Their caps were quivering with excitement…. 'Here she comes' – everyone stood up. We all mentally practised our curtsey and forgot our awkwardness when we looked at that sweet face and lovely smile. Down the hall the thrill of Royal patronage seemed to last throughout the proceedings. Miss Melvin read out the diploma list. The Princess presented them and once again we had a most complete demonstration of her charm. She congratulated each student individually and everyone felt she had a personal interview with HRH Princess Elizabeth."

As recorded by Mary Andross,
Head of the College's Science Department.

to open the College's new halls of residence, Gibson Halls, on July 5, 1968 and in the year of their centenary celebration she kindly gave her name to the College on March 19, 1975. The Glasgow and West of Scotland College of Domestic Science became The Queen's College, Glasgow. This change in name however was blithely ignored by Glaswegians who continued calling it the Dough School.

Not having domestic science in the title of the College better reflected its developing syllabus and aspirations for the future, although home economics (as it was now called), dietetics and institutional management remained central to its teaching profile.

The renaming of the College heralded a new era; a new motto "For the Common Weal" was penned and a new coat of arms created.

A NEW FOCUS

Throughout its existence, the College used its expertise for the good of the community, meeting the various needs of the time.

Emigration was a sign of the times in 1949 in Scotland, and evening classes were established to help educate emigrating women to prepare for their new lives in Canada. Talks were given on Canadian life and politics, shopping, budgeting, grooming, travel, a general knowledge of labour-saving equipment, along with practical cookery demonstrations.

A direct result of adapting to a time of plenty, as opposed to the austere times of post-war Britain, was the birth in the 1950s of the full-blown consumer society. This, combined with the virtual disappearance since the war of the domestic servant class, opened up new avenues for the colleges of domestic science in areas of domestic instruction and development, especially as a new range of goods, technologies and facilities appeared on the market. The Colleges' Annual Report for 1961/62 said:

> "… In the last thirty-five years for instance, there have been three distinct phases. There were the days of economic crisis, called The Slump, when the urgency was to help mothers to budget and to prepare reasonably nourishing meals for next to no money, and with no thought of saving time and energy. Then there were, during and after the last war, years of scarcity and 'make do and mend'.
>
> "Now there is a very different picture; women working outside as well as inside the home, time more scarce than money, better housing standards, hire purchase, labour-saving devices and convenience foods, a growing consciousness of the place of art in everyday life, and a different use of leisure."

Teacher training in domestic science developed through the 1950s, 1960s and 1970s under the Principalship of firstly Miss Isobel Gibson and then Miss Juliann Calder.

Changes in the Scottish education system were reflected in course content and entrance requirements, resulting in the development of a Diploma in Home Economics. The establishment of this diploma in 1973 meant that students could be trained to the College's high standard and then decide whether to opt for teacher training or to take their knowledge into the commercial world, industry or to the community at large.

It spread opportunity into other fields of employment and developed to reflect the changes of society. It had always been argued, whether it be domestic economy, domestic science or home economics, that this subject had not only the family unit as its basis but also social, economic and technological developments within its sphere, allowing it to serve many professions and

The Bride's Course

Session 1951–52 marked the end of an era at the College; the final session in which a historically well-attended and much-loved course ceased to run. The College's non-certificated "Three Months' Course of Housewifery" was inherited from The Glasgow School of Cookery and in 1910 its tuition fee was £8 8s. It consisted of the following lessons – 24 cookery practice, 12 needlework, 12 laundry, 12 home nursing, 10 first aid, home book-keeping, continuous housewifery and admission to any demonstrations in progress at time of study. In Session 1920–21 the fee increased to £12 12s, and, over the years, certain changes were made with dietetics and infant management being added to the content.

In 1933, *The Evening News* carried a report on the "Engaged Girls' Course", more popularly known as the "Brides' Course". The text included a mixture of sentimentality, sexism and social reference:

"Love laughs at depression, and bad trade cannot hinder the matrimonially inclined! Crisis or no crisis, this has been a 'bumper' year for weddings in Glasgow, and there is prospect of an even greater spate of brides and bridegrooms in the comparatively near future. One straw which shows the way the wind is blowing is the increase in the number of girls who have enrolled for the 'Engaged Girls' Course' at the College of Domestic Science. 'Three Months' Course' it is called on the prospectus but that is far too unromantic a name for this training in cookery, housewifery and laundry which is specially designed to teach young brides-to-be how to look after their homes and their husbands. No longer can husbands complain of indigestion; no longer do they limp about with 'lumpy' darns in their socks, no longer do they search fruitlessly for a clean collar. The 'Engaged Girls' Course' produces efficient house-keepers who know their job thoroughly and are particularly good at 'feeding the brute'."

The Evening News, October 20, 1933

industries within the community. There was an increasing need for an informed scientific understanding of nutritional problems and of the ways in which modern science and technology were affecting the work of the home and the professional kitchen. Equally important was knowledge of social and economic conditions and community development so that graduates might follow the trends of their time and adapt their skills to contemporary needs. Home economics, dietetics and institutional management were enhanced with the skills of social science and the College also developed social work courses from 1975 onwards. It could be argued, however, that social sciences and social work had always been central to its ethos.

Isobel Gibson

Isobel Scott Gibson, OBE, JP, BSc (1897–1993) was the first Principal to be educated to degree standard, with a BSc in Applied Science from Glasgow University, although she was also a College of Domestic Science graduate. She trained as a teacher, breaking off for two years during the First World War to work in the kitchens of the Erskine Hospital for Limbless Soldiers. Isobel was the daughter of George A Gibson, Glasgow University's Professor of Mathematics.

Migrating from west to east, Miss Gibson was appointed supervisor for domestic subjects under Edinburgh Corporation; then she joined the staff of the Scottish Education Department as HM Inspector. In 1947 she came back to her old College as Principal.

In 1951 Miss Gibson, like Miss Dorothy Melvin before her, was given an OBE (Order of the British Empire) in recognition of her work. During her career she helped the College recover from the Second World War and struggle through the period of scarcity and rationing. She encouraged the academic developments of the College and put much work into the establishment of a proper library at Park Drive. She also played a magnificent role within the International Federation of Home Economics.

At the time of her retirement *The Glasgow Herald* reported the following as part of an interview with her:

"… Homecraft properly taught in schools, she feels can influence for good the whole family structure. She goes so far as to say that schoolboys should learn certain aspects of homecraft, too – 'This is already being done in Scandinavia and America,' she points out, and emphasises that it needn't mean teaching boys what they regard as 'girl's work', but 'simply equipping them to play an equal part in the partnership of marriage'."

The Glasgow Herald, December 21, 1962

ANOTHER MERGER AND A NEW STATUS

From 1976, under its new name, The Queen's College began a process of change; change that gave it a new identity and a new student population. The appointment of the new Principal, Geoffrey Richardson, was in itself something completely new. He was a man, he was English and he was not

Juliann Calder

Juliann McKinnon Calder, BSc (Hons), MEd, FEIS, FAHE, MHCIMA, FSA Scot (1914–2008), know as Sheila by close friends, graduated in 1936 with a Bachelor of Science (Hons) in Chemistry from the University of Glasgow and the following year, 1937, she gained a double qualification in primary and secondary teaching from Jordanhill College of Education. She entered the Dough School as a lecturer in January 1940. The subjects she taught in this position included inorganic chemistry, organic chemistry, physiology and  hygiene and she also developed studies in textiles and plastic materials. Miss Calder qualified with a Masters in Education from Glasgow University in 1948 and became Principal of her College in 1963. It was under her direction that the College changed its name, reflecting its changing academic focus and broadening its student appeal. When the College's new extension was formally opened in September 1975 it was called the Calder Wing in her honour; this new wing primarily catered for the sciences. The ongoing academic development of the College evidenced her strength of leadership through which the talents of all concerned were harnesses to "the common weal". It was fitting that as a mark of her efforts students were enrolled for the first College Degree course in Dietetics, a joint venture with Paisley College of Technology, in September 1976. The 1975 metric edition of *The Glasgow Cookery Book*, in celebration of the College's centenary, was published under Miss Calder's direction. Miss Calder passed away in December 2008; the last of the Glasgow and West of Scotland College of Domestic Science Principals.

trained in the main discipline of the College. In 1991 he was succeeded by John Phillips whose mission for the College placed it as a leading specialist provider of vocational higher education, respected throughout the west of Scotland and nationally and internationally as a centre of excellence in Health and Community Care, and Consumer and Hospitality Management.

Through the 1980s and 1990s the momentum of change accelerated and the College's teaching syllabus expanded. A BA in Home Economics was introduced in 1982 offering a challenging pattern of studies in social sciences, food studies, resource management and textile studies. Other degree courses followed in areas like catering and accommodation management, hospitality management and health-related disciplines. The College had a portfolio of 10 full-time degree courses at the time of its merger with Glasgow Polytechnic. Significantly, in 1989 the Home Economics degree was revised and changed to a BA Consumer and Management Studies. This title catered for a broader subject matter and was aimed at a wider student audience, of both sexes. For those who wished to teach, it was still possible to complete the degree with a Home Economics specialism.

On April 1, 1993 the Queen's College, Glasgow and Glasgow Polytechnic merged to form Glasgow Caledonian University. In the early years of the new millennium, the new University continued developing its mission and tailoring its teaching syllabus and course content to meet its vision. The kitchens are now closed at Glasgow Caledonian University and in 2001 the Park Drive building was sold to Glasgow University.

The early subject legacy of the cookery schools and The Glasgow and West of Scotland College of Domestic Science continues however through the longest running dietetics programme in the UK, through the unique courses offered by the University's Division of Fashion, Marketing and Retailing and through the remaining Queen's College staff and the development of their subject specialisms. Glasgow Caledonian University's mission calls for the promotion of "the common weal"; put simply, that means to use its skills, facilities and knowledge to make a positive contribution to society. This brief introduction offers a historical perspective showing that the University not only adopted The Queen's College's motto, it inherited its proud past of civic social welfare.

Glasgow and West of Scotland College of Domestic Science students in one of the kitchens of the Park Drive building, c. 1930

THE GLASGOW COOKERY BOOK

The Glasgow and West of Scotland College of Domestic Science, becoming The Queens' College, Glasgow, gave Glasgow Caledonian University the Glasgow Cookery Book. Its last female Principal, Miss Juliann Calder, also gave the University its motto "For the Common Weal". There are worse things to inherit than an ethos and a much-loved book.

A good textbook stands the test of time. As Ella Glaister spoke of the "long-felt want" in the first edition of *The Glasgow Cookery Book*, one hundred years later this centenary publication answers the cries to see the book back on the shelf. Historically its content can be traced back to the 19th century and now such content will be taken forward into the 21st century. *The Glasgow Cookery Book* has stood the test of time, and passed with flying colours.

Carole McCallum
University Archivist
Glasgow Caledonian University

Glasgow Caledonian University's Institutional Archive contains many objects and documents pertaining to the College of Domestic Science. The family of Christina Bell, Roy and Rena Kennedy, have gifted many of her notes, books, photographs and examples of her skilled handiwork. Chrissie was a student at the College from 1916 to 1919. This is her College diploma.

GLASGOW CALEDONIAN UNIVERSITY

The originator of the first *Glasgow Cookery Book*, Ella Glaister, could not have begun to imagine the University that would grow from the institution of which she was Principal, the Glasgow and West of Scotland College of Domestic Science.

In the course of a century that has seen *The Glasgow Cookery Book* become a staple on many kitchen shelves around the globe, the "Dough School", as the College was affectionately known, has evolved to become Glasgow Caledonian University, one of the UK's most dynamic and innovative universities. Miss Glaister would, however, approve of the ingredients that have contributed to the recipe for a leading higher education institution.

Today, the University's 17,000 students, drawn from over 100 countries, can choose to study from more than 200 undergraduate, postgraduate and part-time programmes, which encompass subjects as diverse as nursing, optometry, forensics, design, media and the environment through computer game design, business and fashion.

In addition, the University has a thriving campus in Oman, where a further 2000 students are enrolled, and is consistently rated Scotland's best international student experience (International Student Barometer survey), and holds a *Times* Higher Education award for its outstanding support for overseas students.

Far from the kitchens and sedate sewing rooms of the College of Domestic Science, the University's city centre campus today offers world-class, state-of-the-art facilities such as the cutting-edge eMotion Lab, the world's first laboratory created to evaluate how players interact emotionally with computer games; a broadcasting suite; an eye clinic; a fashion factory and a replica hospital ward, complete with "living" mannequins that can breathe, talk and even "suffer" the range of symptoms that the University's nursing students will face in their careers in real-life hospitals.

At the heart of today's campus, the iconic Saltire Centre has – according to *The Guardian* newspaper – rewritten the design book on academic learning spaces to create one of the UK's most advanced study environments. With five floors of futuristic but people-friendly learning spaces, the £23 million centre is the University's library. While it may be devoted to the serious subject of learning, its award-winning dynamic design – from inflatable igloos to talking lifts – raises a smile from its thousands of users and visitors. The hub of the campus, the Saltire blends learning with social spaces and student services. It complements the informal, IT-rich environment of the University's Learning Café, the first in the UK to demonstrate how learning is being revolutionised by technology and to recognise fully that interaction is an essential element of learning.

In addition, Glasgow Caledonian University has established the Caledonian Academy, a revolutionary initiative geared to ensuring the University leads the way in the development and implementation of new and exciting forms of learning and teaching. At its heart is the cutting-edge Second Life project, which uses the virtual world as an innovative learning tool that can be accessed by students, staff and the public. The University's Second Life island – a re-creation of the campus, incorporating other iconic city-centre landmarks – allows visitors to access information and view exhibitions of students' work, for example, as well as enabling students to treat virtual patients or take an exploratory trip inside the human eye.

The university's six academic schools – Built and Natural Environment, Business, Engineering and Computing, Health, Law and Social Sciences, and Life Sciences – offer hundreds of high-quality, career-focused programmes and have forged successful partnerships with both the public and private sectors. The quality of the schools' range of research, which is particularly strong in health, the environment, and biomedical and vision sciences, has been rated world-leading and internationally excellent, and is complemented by more than 40 specialist research centres, including HealthQwest, the Centre for the Social History of Health and Healthcare, The Moffat Centre for Travel and Tourism, Caledonian Creates, Caledonian Environment Centre, Glasgow Centre for the Study of Violence, The Scottish Poverty Information Unit and KIT-OUT the Park.

The colleges of domestic economy, designed to fight the ravages of poor nutrition and alcohol abuse, and to promote new innovations in hygiene, were born out of Victorian philanthropy. The Queen's College's 1975 motto, "For the Common Weal", lives on in today's Glasgow Caledonian University. The University is committed to providing an inclusive learning and teaching environment that applies its knowledge and skills for the social and economic benefit of the communities it serves in Scotland and around the world, from helping train Rwanda's nurses to recruiting students who may have been denied an opportunity to participate in higher education. The University's commitment to "the common weal" is exemplified in projects such as the Caledonian Club, which works with children at nursery, primary and high schools in areas across the city, where, traditionally, few young people have aspired to a university education, showing them everything that the institution has to offer them.

Just like the University, in this new edition celebrating the centenary of the book's first publication, *The Glasgow Cookery Book* has evolved. A classic throughout the twentieth century, this new edition is set to be a key ingredient in kitchens for another century to come.

THE
GLASGOW
COOKERY
BOOK

GLOSSARY OF COOKING TERMS

Al dente	An Italian term, usually used to describe properly cooked pasta, meaning that it is firm to the bite.
Ashet	A flat serving plate.
Aspic	A clarified jelly that is used as a coating for cold foods.
Bain-marie	Also known as a water-bath, a bain-marie can be, e.g. a large roasting tin or saucepan half-filled with water that is just below boiling point. Into or above this another cooking container, such as a bowl, is placed. In this certain foods are cooked at a low temperature. Sauces are cooked in this way to avoid curdling. Roasts may be cooked using a bain-marie to retain moisture and avoid scorching.
Bake blind	To bake pastry on a plate or in a flan ring without the filling.
Bard	To cover the breasts of game or poultry with slices of fat bacon.
Baste	To spoon over with hot oil, gravy or cooking liquid during cooking.
Baton	A cut of vegetable resulting in thin sticks about 5 cm long.
Bind	To add a liquid, such as a beaten egg, to a mixture to make sure it will not fall apart during cooking.
Blanch	To put food into boiling water for a short time and then into cold. This process is used to remove skins from, e.g. tomatoes and peaches, and to prepare vegetables for freezing. Blanching can also be used to remove strong flavours when the food is put into cold water and brought to the boil.
Blend	To mix well till smooth. To mix ingredients together in a blender or food processor.
Blocks	Pieces of vegetables of approximately 8–10 cms long. Square off the sides but try to waste as little of the vegetable as possible.
Bouquet garni	In this book, it is called "bouquet of herbs" (page 27). A small bunch of herbs (e.g. parsley, bay leaf, thyme) used to flavour soups, sauces and stews. Removed at the end of cooking.
Braise	Meat cooked in a closely covered pan; the method is carried out partly, or wholly, on top of the cooker and partly in the oven. The foundation consists of bacon, vegetables and herbs, the flavour from these ingredients being absorbed by the meat.
Brine	A solution of water and salt that is used in preserving food.
Canapé	Small, round slices of bread – plain, fried or toasted – used as a base for savoury mixtures.
Caramelise	To cause sugar to melt and turn brown. To sauté vegetables with butter and sugar until they turn brown.
Chaudfroid	A dish of cooked meat, poultry or fish served cold, coated with a chaudfroid sauce (page 295).
Chiffonade	Shredded leaves, e.g. of lettuce, used as a base for cold savoury dishes.
Clarified butter	Also called drawn butter. Butter that has had the milk solids skimmed from it. Used to seal the top of patés and for frying meat.
Coating consistency	When a liquid is thick enough to coat the back of a spoon.
Cocotte	A small ovenproof dish usually used for baking eggs.

GLOSSARY OF COOKING TERMS

Coddle	A method of cooking eggs that involves a sealed container in hot water.
Collops	Thick pieces of a tender cut of meat.
Concassé	The flesh of a tomato that has been skinned, de-seeded, and then chopped into small dice.
Concasser	To chop roughly.
Consommé	Clear soup, served hot or cold, and garnished.
Cream	To cream butter, or butter and sugar, means to beat air into it to create a light consistency, a bit like whipped cream in appearance.
Croquettes	Minced meat, fish or other savoury mixtures bound together, formed into balls or sausage-shaped rolls, coated with egg and breadcrumbs, and deep-fried in hot oil until golden brown.
Croûte	A slice of fried bread used as a base for savoury dishes, e.g. meat, egg.
Croûtons	Small dice of toasted or fried bread, served with purée soups.
Curd	When milk is soured it turns into a curd.
Curdle	When the solid and liquid parts of a sauce, cake mix, mayonnaise, etc, start to separate.
Cure	A method of preservation of food that can involve any of several substances such as salt, vinegar, smoke, alcohol or sugar.
Deglaze	To add a liquid such as stock, wine or water to a roasting pan or frying pan to loosen flavoursome particles such as fat, browned juices and sediment, in order to make sauce or gravy.
Degorge	To draw the juices from something, e.g. using salt, if such juices would be bitter or if their inclusion would make a dish too moist.
Dice	Small dice are vegetables cut into cubes of 6 mm. Medium dice are cubes of 1 cm. Large dice are cubes of 1.5 cm
Dredge	To coat foods lightly with a fine powder such as flour or icing sugar.
Dropping consistency	When a mixture drops, though with some resistance, from a spoon.
Dumpling	Seasoned dough, shaped into balls, steamed or cooked on top of a stew.
Duxelles	Vegetables, finely chopped and sautéed in butter to be used as an additional ingredient, i.e. in a sauce, as a stuffing or as a garnish.
Emulsion	A liquid where oil and water combine to make a smooth sauce, usually including an emulsifier, such as egg yolk, that makes the sauce stable.
Entré	A main course.
Entrecôte	Another name for sirloin steak.
Escalope	Thin slices of meat; very often veal.
Farce	Stuffing or forcemeat.
Farci	Stuffed.
Fillet	To remove the bones from fish. A boneless cut of meat or fish.
Fleurons	Small shapes of puff pastry used as a garnish.
Flour	To coat a surface in sifted flour.

GLOSSARY OF COOKING TERMS

Fold	To stir a mixture gently with a lifting motion to trap as much air into the mixture as possible.
Forcemeat	A stuffing made from minced meat, vegetables and breadcrumbs.
Fork	To pierce the surface of something with a fork.
Giblets	The heart, liver, gizzard and neck of poultry used for stock and gravy.
Girdle or Griddle	A flat plate of metal on which things are cooked.
Glaze	To make the surface of food look glossy (page 476).
Grate	To rub food through a perforated cutter, known as a grater, in order to reduce it into fine pieces.
Gratin	To serve food au gratin is to cover it in breadcrumbs or cheese and brown it in the oven or under the grill. It is wholly or partly cooked in the dish in which it is served.
Grill	To brown food beneath a source of heat that comes from above.
Grill trivet	The bars of a grill pan, or the wire tray in grill pan.
Hang	To age meat to improve its flavour by hanging it on a metal hook in a cool airy place.
Hors d'oeuvre	A dish served to whet the appetite.
Infuse	To allow something to steep in liquid in order to flavour the liquid.
Julienne	Thin strips of vegetables, a bit like matchsticks, of about 5 cm in length and 3 mm in width.
Lard	The name for pig fat used in cooking. To insert strips of bacon fat into lean meat to improve the flavour; usually done with a larding needle.
Lardons, lardoons	The name given to strips of fat bacon or pork fat.
Liquor	The liquid in which a food is cooked.
Macedoine	A mixture of vegetables or fruits cut in neat pieces. The vegetables are generally used as a garnish.
Maître d'Hôtel, à la	Flavoured with parsley and lemon.
Maître d'Hôtel butter	Small 10p-piece sizes of flavoured butter placed on top of hot cooked meat just before serving which when melted adds flavour and succulence.
Marinade	A sauce made from an acidic liquid (such as vinegar or citrus juice), oil and seasoning, in which meat or fish is soaked before cooking.
Meat extract	Highly concentrated meat stock made from meat (usually beef), salt and (usually) yeast extract. Suitable for diluting in stocks, sauces, soups and as a savoury drink.
Mirepoix	The foundation of vegetables, bacon and herbs used in braising.
Mornay sauce	A white or béchamel sauce containing extra egg yolks and cheese (usually Gruyère), eaten with cooked eggs or fish.
Mousse	A light mixture which is made frothy and bubbly by the addition of whisked egg whites.
Mutton	Lamb more than one year old. Stronger in flavour and takes longer to cook than lamb.
Oxtail	The name for the tail of a beef animal, used in stock, slow-cooked dishes or stew.

GLOSSARY OF COOKING TERMS

Panada	A very thick sauce used as a binding agent for minced meat, fish, etc.
Parboil	To boil food until it starts to soften in order that another cookery process will later finish the cooking.
Paring	The removal of thin peel from fruit and vegetables using a sharp knife.
Pluck	The internal organs of a sheep, i.e. windpipe, liver, lungs (lights) and heart. To remove the feathers from poultry or game.
Poach	Too cook food in gently simmering liquid.
Pound	To mash a foodstuff with an implement like a fork.
Prove	The short period when yeast mixtures are left to rise, after shaping dough and before baking.
Réchauffer	To reheat. A réchauffé is a dish of food reheated.
Reduce	To reduce the amount of a cooking liquid by boiling or simmering in order to intensify the flavour for a sauce or gravy.
Render	To separate animal fat from flesh and bone, through slow roasting in an oven, to produce lard.
Rest	To chill pastry dough for about 30 minutes to relax the gluten, harden the fats and stop shrinkage while cooking.
Rissole	A small patty of meat or vegetables bound together, coated in breadcrumbs and fried.
Roux	Equal quantities of fat and flour cooked together and used as a basis for sauces. The roux may be white, fawn or brown, as desired, depending on the recipe. You make a brown roux by allowing the butter to brown before blending with the flour.
Salmi	A rich stew or casserole of partly roasted game.
Sauté	To cook quickly in hot fat as a preliminary to further cooking. A sauté pan is similar to a stew pan.
Scald	To immerse in boiling water in order to sterilise equipment or kill bacteria, or to loosen the skins of some vegetables.
Season	To use salt, pepper, spices and other flavourings to improve the taste of a dish.
Sieve	To pass ingredients through a sieve.
Strain	To pour through a sieve to remove the solids from the liquid.
Sweat	To soften vegetables by gentle cooking in butter or oil.
Sweetbreads	The name given to the two portions of the thymus gland, commonly of the calf or lamb; sold in pairs.
Stir-fry	To fry food quickly in a wok or large frying pan.
Stock	Liquid flavoured by the lengthy cooking of meat, vegetables or bones in it. Used for soups, sauces and as cooking liquid.
Tart	A filled pie without a pastry top.
Terrine	A paté or a dish of layered meat set in aspic.
Tripe	The lining of the first and second stomachs of the cow. Usually sold pre-prepared and cooked, as cleaning and blanching of fresh tripe takes hours.
Trussing	To tie poultry or stuffed joints of meat with string.
Vol-au-vent	A case of puff pastry used for sweet or savoury fillings.

APPROXIMATE QUANTITIES TO SERVE

Soup:	
Broths, Pulses, Purées	250 ml per person and 250 ml over
Clear and Cream Soups	150 ml per person and 150 ml over
Fish:	
Filleted	100–125 g per person
With bone	150 g per person
Lobster	1 for 2–3 persons
Crab	1 for 2 persons
Meat:	
Without bone	100 g per person
With bone	125–150 g per person
Chops	1 or 2 per person
Croquettes	1 or 2 per person
Sweetbreads	100 g per person
Chicken	1 for 4–6 persons (depending on size of chicken)
Turkey	See roast turkey (page 147)
Duck	1 for 4 persons
Rabbit	1 for 4–6 persons
Ox Tongue	1 for 8 persons
Vegetables, quantities vary according to type:	
Root	100 g, e.g. carrots per person
Potatoes	150 g per person
Green Vegetables	100–150 g per person
Pie or Tart:	
500 g Meat or Fruit 150 g Flour for Pastry	Serves 4–5 persons
Suet Pudding:	
200 g Flour or its equivalent	Serves 6 persons
Cake Mixture Pudding:	
200 g Flour Plain Cake Mixture 2-Egg quantity Rich Cake Mixture	Serves 6 persons
Milk Pudding:	
500 ml Milk	Serves 3 persons

HANDY MEASURES

Ingredients	Millilitre Spoons	Average Household Spoons
Flour, Cornflour, Custard Powder	25 g = 3 level 15 ml spoonfuls	= 3 level tablespoonfuls
Cheese (grated)	25 g = 4 level 15 ml spoonfuls	= 3 level tablespoonfuls
Breadcrumbs	25 g = 6 level 15 ml spoonfuls	= 4 level tablespoonfuls
Sugar	25 g = 2 level 15 ml spoonfuls	= 2 level dessertspoonfuls
Rice (uncooked)	25 g = 2 level 15 ml spoonfuls	= 2 level dessertspoonfuls
Gelatine	10 g = 3 level 5 ml spoonfuls	= 3 level teaspoonfuls
Baking Powder, Spices, etc	1 level 5 ml spoonful	= 1 level teaspoonful

These handy measures are approximate.

UK Liquid Measures Imperial and Metric			
Unit	= (approx.)	UK fluid ounces/ pints	Millilitres
1 teaspoon	1/3 tablespoon	1/5 fl oz	5 ml
1 dessertspoon	2 teaspoons	2/5 fl oz	10 ml
1 tablespoon	3 teaspoons	3/5 fl oz	15 ml
1 cup	16 tablespoons	1/2 pint	285 ml
1 UK fluid ounce	2 tablespoons	1/20 pint	28 ml
1 UK pint	2 cups	20 fl oz	570 ml
1 gill	1/4 pint	5 fl oz	140 ml
1 quart	2 pints	40 fl oz	1136 ml
1/2 UK pint	1 cup	10 fl oz	285 ml
1/4 UK pint	1/2 cup	5 fl oz	115 ml
2 UK pints	1 quart	40 fl oz	1136 ml
1 litre	4 1/2 cups	scant 2 pints	1000 ml
1 UK gallon	4 quarts	8 pints	4560 ml

These measures are approximate. Imperial measures are not used in this book. All of the measures given in the recipes of this book are metric.

TEMPERATURE CHART

Oven Temperatures and Setting Marks			
Heat of Oven	**Thermostat Setting (Gas)**	**Approximate Temperature in °Celsius**	**Approximate Temperature in °Fahrenheit**
Very Cool	¼	110	225
	½	130	250
	1	140	275
Cool	2	150	300
Warm	3	170	325
Moderate	4	180	350
Fairly Hot	5	190	375
	6	200	400
Hot	7	220	425
Very Hot	8	230	450
	9	240	475

Temperatures stated in recipes presume that the oven is preheated.
For fan-oven temperatures please consult your oven manufacturer's instructions.

OILS AND FATS FOR FRYING

Oils and fats for frying.— The term smoking hot fat is seldom used now as the majority of people use oils for frying.

If dripping (rendered fat) or cooking fats are used, faintly smoking fat is at the correct temperature.

To test temperature of oils for frying.— Put a small piece of bread into the fat and allow 40–60 seconds, by which time it should be pale golden brown.

A GUIDE TO FRYING TEMPERATURES

	Approximate Temperature in °Celcius	**Approximate Temperature in °Fahrenheit**	**Time**
Fried Fish	175–182	345–360	3–5 mins
Reheated Food	182–195	360–380	3–5 mins
Fritters and Doughnuts	175–185	345–365	3–5 mins
Potato Chips	182–195	360–380	4–8 mins

AMERICAN MEASUREMENTS

US Liquid Measures
About 30 ml equates to 1 US fluid ounce (a UK fluid ounce is only slightly less, at 28 ml)
A UK Imperial pint is 19 US fluid ounces and approximately 568 ml
The US liquid pint is approximately 473 ml. Our recipes will state a liquid amount that is usually rounded to the nearest 25 ml; just short of 1 US fl oz. In most recipes a US pint measurement will suffice for 500 ml (though it is closer to a US pint plus 2 tablespoons)
British Standards Institute tablespoons are very slightly bigger than the American tablespoon, but only by a small amount, so in most cases can be substituted without a problem
* A UK standard cook's cup is around 285 ml while a US cup is nearer 240 ml, however very few recipes in this book use cupfuls as a measurement. In the ones that do, e.g Seven-cup Pudding (page 238), as long as the UK and US cups are substituted consistently within the recipe you shouldn't encounter a problem

UK/Metric	US Measures		
3.79 litre (round up to 4 litres)	1 gallon	16 cups	4 quarts
0.95 litre (round up to 1 litre)	1 quart	4 cups	2 pints
450 ml (round up to 500 ml)	1 pint	2 cups	16 fl oz
240 ml (round up to 250 ml)	½ pint	1 cup	8 fl oz
120 ml (round up to 125 ml)	¼ pint	½ cup	4 fl oz
25 ml (round up to 30 ml)	1/16 pint	2 tablespoons	1 fl oz
15 ml = 1 UK tablespoon	roughly the same as a US tablespoon		
5 ml = 1 UK teaspoon	roughly the same as a US teaspoon		
1 UK cup = 285 ml	1 US cup plus 2–3 tablespoons approx. See * above		

US Dry Weights			
Metric	US Cups	Metric	US Cups
125 g flour	1 cup	225 g solid fat (such as butter)	1 cup
150 g dried fruit (currants, sultanas, raisins etc)	1 cup	225 g sugar (granulated, castor, superfine)	1 cup
50 g fresh breadcrumbs	1 cup	150 g icing/powdered sugar	1 cup
90 g dried breadcrumbs	1 cup	250 g minced/ground meat	1 cup
125 g suet (shredded)	1 cup	250 g mashed potatoes	1 cup

These measures are approximate.

APPETISERS

STARTERS, HORS D'OEUVRES AND SAVOURIES

STARTERS

HORS D'OEUVRES

SAVOURIES AND CANAPÉS

DIPS

STARTERS

There is a wide variety of foods which are suitable for this course. They should stimulate the appetite and should, therefore, be well flavoured and attractively presented.

I. SUGGESTED FOODS FOR STARTERS

Fish and Seafood	Smoked Salmon – served with buttered brown bread and lemon wedges Prawns – served with Thousand Island Dressing (page 221), and salad Caviare – served plain, in a bowl, on ice, with a lemon wedge, and toast Oysters – served on shell, on ice, with lemon wedges and buttered brown bread Mussels (page 78) Shrimp – potted (page 78), served with Oatcakes (page 376) Scallops – fried (page 77) Fish Croquettes (page 69) – served with Salad (page 209)

Fruits	Grapefruit and Orange – halve and loosen segments with a curved, serrated knife. Or cut off skin and pith and then cut each segment away from its membrane walls. Sprinkle with sugar if liked
	Avocado Pear – halve, stuff or serve with dressing.
	Melon – halve and segment
	    – wedges or balls with ground ginger (optional)
	    – with grapes
	    – with segmented oranges
	    – with thinly sliced Parma Ham
	    – with thin slices of Avocado Pear

Vegetables	Potato Croquettes (page 194) Stuffed Mushrooms, Baked Mushrooms (page 205) Globe Artichoke (page 195)
Soups	See pages 25–47
Meats	Cooked, cured and smoked meats – served with bread (page 363), dip (page 24) and dressings (page 219) Meat Croquettes (page 103) or Chicken Croquettes (page 153) – served with salad (page 219)
Cheeses	Mozzarella cheese – served with with basil, sliced tomato, olive oil and black pepper Cheese and Fruit Salad (page 218) Grilled slice of Goat's Cheese – served with salad leaves (page 212) and Tomato Chutney (page 448)

2. GRILLED GRAPEFRUIT

Ingredients:

½ Grapefruit per person   Sherry *or* Maraschino liquid
Soft brown Sugar   Maraschino Cherries
Small piece Butter

Method:

1. Halve grapefruit and loosen segments. Sprinkle with sugar.
2. Add a few drops of sherry or maraschino, dot with butter.
3. Grill the half grapefruit, in its skin, till lightly browned and heated through.
4. Put cherry in the centre and serve.

3. GRAPEFRUIT AND GINGER

Ingredients:

2 Grapefruit   Sugar to taste
1 teaspoonful preserved Ginger   4 Maraschino Cherries
Sherry

Servings: 4

Method:

1. Skin grapefruit, remove segments (page 13) and divide into four glasses. Add sugar.
2. Sprinkle with a little sherry and top with chopped ginger.
3. Soak cherries in sherry, put one in centre of each serving and chill.

4. GRAPEFRUIT AND MELON COCKTAIL

Ingredients:

1 Grapefruit   25–50g black Grapes
¼ Melon   Little Maraschino liquid

Servings: 4–5

Method:

1. Skin grapefruit and remove segments (page 13).
2. Dice melon, and halve and stone grapes.
3. Mix fruits, add maraschino liquid.
4. Put into glasses and chill.

5. FLORIDA COCKTAIL

Ingredients:

1 Grapefruit   4 Maraschino Cherries
2 Oranges

Servings: 4

Method:

1. Skin grapefruit and remove segments (page 13), place in a bowl. Add sugar.

2. Skin oranges, and remove segments (page 13). Add to bowl. Add a few drops of liquid from cherries.
3. Fill into glasses, put a cherry in the centre and chill.

6. SUMMER COCKTAIL

Ingredients:

Melon ⎫
Cucumber ⎬ Amounts according to number of servings and flavour that predominates
Tomato ⎭
Salad Dressing (1) (page 219)

Method:

1. Dice melon. Skin and dice cucumber. Skin, remove seeds and dice tomato (page 202).
2. Lightly mix with salad dressing.
3. Put into glasses and chill.

7. FRUIT COCKTAIL

Ingredients:

25 ml Pineapple Juice and Water	Juice ½ Lemon
Sugar to taste	
1 Apple	50 g Pineapple
1 Pear	½ Grapefruit
50 g Grapes	1 Orange

Servings: 4–5

Method:

1. Add lemon juice to pineapple juice and water. Add sugar to taste and mix till sugar dissolves.
2. Prepare fruit according to kind and cut up roughly.
3. Add fruit to the liquid and liquidise.
4. Chill. Serve in glasses with maraschino cherry on cocktail stick.

Note: Prepare shortly before use as mixture tends to go brown.

8. TOMATO COCKTAIL

Ingredients:

1 cupful Tomato Juice	1 dash Worcester Sauce
1 teaspoonful Vinegar	1 tablespoonful Lemon Juice
1 teaspoonful Sugar	

Servings: 2

Method:

1. Mix all ingredients and chill.
2. Serve in glasses.

15

9. SHRIMP, PRAWN OR LOBSTER COCKTAIL

Ingredients:

100 g cooked Shrimp, Prawn *or* Lobster
2 tablespoonfuls Mayonnaise (page 220)
1 teaspoonful Tomato Juice *or* Sauce

Dash Worcester Sauce
1 tablespoonful Cream
Lettuce (shredded)

Servings: 3

Method:

1. Clean and shell the shrimp or prawns; divide lobster meat finely.
2. Mix fish, mayonnaise, tomato juice or sauce and Worcester sauce.
3. Stir cream through mixture.
4. Put shredded lettuce in the foot of the glass and add mixture on top.

Note: You could use crème fraîche instead of mayonnaise.

10. CREAM CHEESE AND PINEAPPLE

Ingredients:

Pineapple Rings
Cream Cheese
Mayonnaise (page 220)
Cucumber

Chopped Chives *or* Parsley
Seasoning
Lettuce

Method:

1. Blend cream cheese with a little mayonnaise, add seasoning and chives or parsley.
2. Put a ring of pineapple on a lettuce leaf or shredded lettuce.
3. Fill centre of pineapple ring with cream cheese mixture, decorate with sliced or chopped cucumber and chill.

11. CREAM CHEESE AND PEACHES

Make as above but use half-peaches instead of pineapple.

12. TOMATO JELLY

Ingredients:

250 ml Tomato Juice
Salt and Pepper to taste

10 g Gelatine

Method:

1. Dissolve the gelatine in a very small amount of water.
2. Add to the seasoned tomato juice.
3. Pour into small moulds, cover and allow to set in the fridge.

Note: This quantity will make 4 jellies.

HORS D'OEUVRES

Hors d'oeuvres are hot and cold savoury dishes served to whet the appetite before a main meal, or served with drinks before a group sits down to dinner. These dishes should be served separately, and be neatly prepared and well flavoured.

13. SUGGESTED FOODS FOR HORS D'OEUVRES:

Fish	Sardines, Shrimps, Tuna Fish, Anchovies
Meat	Ham, Tongue, Cocktail Sausages, Salami
Vegetables	Tomato, Cucumber, Sweet Corn, Peppers, Cauliflower, Pickled Onions, Beetroot, Celery, Olives, Potatoes
Fruit	Grapes, Pineapple, Grapefruit
Egg	Hard-boiled
Cheese	Cream Cheese; small dice of, or grated Cheese
Rice and Pasta	Combined with other foods

14. SMOKED FISH PÂTÉ

e.g. Kipper, Findon Haddock

Ingredients:

250 g Smoked Fish	Black Pepper
50 g Butter	Lemon Juice
50 g Cream Cheese	

Servings: 3–4

Method:

1. Poach fish in water to remove some of the salt. Drain.
2. Remove skin and bones.
3. Pound or mash fish with other ingredients till smooth, and put in small bowls.
4. Serve chilled, with fingers of toast or on oatcakes.

15. CHICKEN LIVER PÂTÉ

Ingredients:

250 g Chicken Livers	Salt and Pepper to taste
150 g Butter	1 Shallot (finely chopped)
1 tablespoonful Brandy (optional)	

Servings: 3–4

Method:

1. Wash chicken livers and remove any tubes.
2. Chop shallot and sauté without colouring in 50 g butter.

3. Add livers and continue cooking gently for 10 minutes.
4. Blend or sieve mixture and add the remaining butter, melted, and salt and pepper.
5. Press into small pots and chill.
6. Serve with toast.

SAVOURIES AND CANAPÉS

These are neat, bite-sized and well-flavoured, handed round on trays and eaten with the fingers. They may have as a base a savoury biscuit, a small piece of toast or bread, or various shapes of savoury pastry such as cheese pastry. All croûtes should be of a similar size – i.e., 2-cm square or 2-cm diameter rounds.

16. EXAMPLES OF SAVOURIES AND CANAPÉS

Canapés:

Butter bread or toast, cut into neat shapes, top with any suitable savoury mixture.

Use rounds of savoury pastry, or savoury biscuits, such as oatcakes (page 376), for the same purpose.

Spreads:

Using Cream Cheese.— See cheese biscuits (page 22).

Sardine.—Remove tail, pound, add tomato juice or sauce to flavour.

Anchovy.—Pound, add good pinch mustard.

Lobster or Crabmeat.—Pound, mix with mayonnaise.

17. NORWEGIAN KIDNEYS

Ingredients:

1 Sheep's Kidney	Salt and Pepper
1 teaspoonful Onion (chopped)	Thin slices lean Bacon
Small piece Butter	Flour
1 Mushroom (chopped)	1 Egg (beaten)
Parsley (chopped)	Dried Breadcrumbs (page 477)

Method:

1. Skin, wash and core kidney, chop finely.
2. Sauté onion in melted butter.
3. Add mushroom and kidney, sauté for 3 minutes, add parsley, salt and pepper.
4. Spread a little of the mixture on small strips of bacon.
5. Roll up strips, dip in flour, coat with egg and breadcrumbs, fry in deep oil till golden brown.

18. DEVILS ON HORSEBACK

Ingredients:

6 Prunes	Salt and Pepper
6 Almonds	Pinch Cayenne
6 pieces Streaky Bacon	6 croûtes Bread (fried or toasted)

Method:

1. Soak prunes overnight (or use ready-soaked and pitted prunes).
2. Blanch almonds (or use ready-skinned), toss in salt, pepper and cayenne.
3. Remove stones from prunes and substitute almonds.
4. Wrap prunes in a piece of bacon, place on a skewer.
5. Grill until bacon is cooked.
6. Place on a croûte of fried or toasted bread.

19. SCOTCH WOODCOCK

Ingredients:

Small piece Butter	Pepper
1 Egg	4 croûtes toasted Bread
Tinned Anchovy fillets	Capers

Method:

1. Make scrambled egg.
2. Put scrambled egg on top of buttered croûtes.
3. Put a cross of anchovy fillets over egg with a caper on either side. Add pepper according to taste. Anchovy fillets tend to be salty so salt should not be needed.

20. HADDOCK CROÛTES

Ingredients:

Croûtes fried Bread	Salt and Pepper
1 small Smoked Haddock	1 Tomato (skinned)
125 ml Milk	Pickled Walnut *or* Gherkin
15 g Butter	Chopped Parsley
15 g Flour	

Time: 10 minutes

Method:

1. Skin fish, cook in milk.
2. Melt butter, add flour and milk gradually, bring to the boil.
3. Flake the fish and add to the sauce. Add salt and pepper to taste.
4. Mound on fried croûtes of bread.
5. Skin tomato (page 202), place a slice on top of fish.
6. Slice walnut or gherkin thinly, place on top of tomato.
7. Heat in oven if necessary.

21. CHEESE AND TOMATO TARTLETS

Ingredients:

50 g Cheese Pastry (page 313)	3–4 tablespoonfuls Cream
2 small Tomatoes	Salt and Pepper
50 g Cheese (grated)	Paprika

Time: 7–10 minutes

Oven Temperature: 190°C, No. 5

Position in Oven: Middle shelf

Method:

1. Make pastry. Line patty tins with pastry, prick bases with a fork, bake.
2. Skin and dice tomatoes (page 202), half-fill pastry cases.
3. Mix cheese and cream, season, cover tomatoes.
4. Sprinkle with paprika, brown under grill.

Note: Cream cheese softened with mayonnaise may be piped on top and browned under grill or served cold.

22. CREAMED MUSHROOM TARTLETS

Ingredients:

50 g Short *or* Cheese Pastry (pages 300, 313)	1 level tablespoonful Flour
100 g Mushrooms	Small piece Butter
125 ml Milk	Salt and Pepper
	1 tablespoonful Cream

Time: 8–10 minutes

Oven Temperature: 200°C, No. 6

Position in Oven: Middle shelf

Method:

1. Make pastry. Roll pastry thinly, line small patty tins, fork the bases.
2. Bake.
3. Wash mushrooms, chop finely.
4. Cook mushrooms in milk until tender.
5. Blend flour with a little milk till smoooth. Add to rest of milk. Stir until boiling.
6. Beat butter through mixture, add salt and pepper to taste, add cream.
7. Fill pastry cases, serve hot.

23. DIABLOTINES

Ingredients:

50 g Cheese Pastry (page 313)	40 g Parmesan Cheese
15 g Butter	1 Egg (beaten)
15 g Cornflour	Salt and Pepper
2 tablespoonfuls Milk	Anchovy Paste

Time: 10–15 minutes

Oven Temperature: 180°C, No. 4

Position in Oven: Middle shelf

Method:

1. Make pastry. Line patty tins with thin cheese pastry.
2. Spread on a little anchovy paste.
3. Melt butter, add cornflour, then the milk, mix thoroughly and bring to the boil.
4. Add cheese and beaten egg. Add salt and pepper to taste.
5. Three-quarter fill pastry cases, sprinkle with grated Parmesan cheese.
6. Bake until lightly browned, turn out, serve.

24. PRAWN HORNS

Ingredients:

50 g Cheese Pastry (page 313)	2 tablespoonfuls Mayonnaise
50 g Prawns, *or* 1 tin Prawns	

Time: 10–15 minutes
Oven Temperature: 190°C, No. 5
Position in Oven: Middle shelf

Method:

1. Make pastry. Roll pastry thinly, cut into narrow strips.
2. Wind round horn tins, overlapping each twist, brush with egg.
3. Bake, remove from tins, cool.
4. Wash and chop prawns, mix with mayonnaise.
5. Fill horn cases.

Note: Shrimp, salmon or lobster may be used.

25. SARDINE ROLLS

Ingredients:

50 g Cheese Pastry (page 313)	Chutney
1 tin Sardines	Pepper, chopped Parsley, Paprika

Time: 15 minutes
Oven Temperature: 190°C, No. 5
Position in Oven: Middle shelf

Method:

1. Pound sardines with a fork using enough oil from the tin to give a spreading consistency. Add pepper to taste.
2. Make pastry. Divide pastry in two. Roll each piece into an oblong that is 8 cm wide and 5 mm thick.
3. Spread thin layer of chutney on pastry, cover with sardine mixture.
4. Wet one long edge of pastry and roll over, keeping join underneath. Cut into even-sized rolls.
5. Brush with egg and bake.
6. Serve hot or cold; one end dipped in chopped parsley, the other in paprika.

Note: Larger rolls can be made for picnics.

26. CHEESE STRAWS

Ingredients:

        50 g Cheese Pastry (page 313)   Paprika

Time: 10–15 minutes

Oven Temperature: 190°C, No. 5

Position in Oven: Middle shelf

Method:

1. Roll out pastry into strips 8 cm wide and 5 mm thick.
2. Cut in 5-mm straws, place on baking tin. Bake.
3. When cold, dip one end of straw in paprika.

27. CHEESE BISCUITS

Ingredients:

        50 g Cheese Pastry (page 313)

Time: 10 minutes

Oven Temperature: 190°C, No. 5

Position in Oven: Middle shelf

Method:

1. Roll pastry thinly, cut into 3-cm rounds.
2. Bake, cool.

Cheese and celery topping:

1 tablespoonful Cream Cheese	A little Mayonnaise
A little chopped Celery	Paprika

Mix all ingredients, pile on biscuits and sprinkle with paprika.

Alternative toppings:

Cheese and Walnut	Cheese and Pineapple
Cheese with Chutney	Cheese with chopped Gherkin
Cheese with chopped Shrimp or Prawn	Cheese with chopped Chives

28. CHEESE BUTTERFLIES

Method:

1. As cheese biscuits, above, Step 1.
2. Cut half of the rounds in 2 before baking.
3. Dip rounded edge of halves in paprika.
4. Pile cream cheese mixture on top.
5. Set two halves on either side as wings.

29. CHEESE D'ARTOIS

Ingredients:

100 g Rough Puff Pastry (page 309)   25 g melted Butter
50 g Cheese (grated)   1 Egg (beaten)
Salt and Pepper, pinch Cayenne

Time: 10–15 minutes
Oven Temperature: 200°C, No. 6
Position in Oven: Middle shelf

Method:

1. Roll pastry into two equal-sized squares.
2. Mix cheese, salt, pepper and cayenne, butter and beaten egg.
3. Spread mixture on top of one square of pastry. Wet edges.
4. Put second square on top; brush with egg or milk.
5. Mark into small fingers; bake, cut when hot.

30. CHEESE PUFFS

Ingredients:

25 g Flour and   Pinch Salt, Pepper
    ½ level teaspoonful Baking Powder   Mustard
or
25 g Self-raising Flour   1 Egg (beaten)
50 g grated Cheese   Milk

Method:

1. Mix dry ingredients, add beaten egg and enough milk to make firm dropping consistency.
2. Fry in teaspoonfuls in hot oil until golden brown.
3. Drain, toss in grated cheese.

31. CHEESE AIGRETTES

Ingredients:

15 g Butter   25 g Cheese (grated)
125 ml Water   Pepper and Mustard
40 g Flour   2 Eggs (beaten)

Method:

1. Boil butter and water, add sifted flour.
2. Beat until it forms a ball, add cheese, pepper and mustard.
3. Mix in beaten egg slowly.
4. Fry in spoonfuls in hot oil until golden brown.

DIPS

The consistency of dips should be that of thick cream.

32. SUGGESTED FOODS FOR DIPPING

Cheese Straws	Savoury Biscuits
Potato Crisps	Vegetable Pieces
Cubed Cheeses	Olives
Pickled Onions	Small portions cooked Meat and Sausage

Supply cocktail sticks to your guests to enable them to dip the foods.

33. FOUNDATION FOR MAKING DIPS

1. Mayonnaise
2. Cream, Crème Fraîche
3. Cream Cheese, Blue Cheese
4. Yoghurt (Greek yoghurt is a delicious lower fat alternative to cream),
   Fromage Frais.

When using cream cheese, beat in additional cream or mayonnaise to give the required consistency.

The above foundations are combined with other foods finely chopped, e.g.:
Anchovies, Lobster, Prawns, Shrimps
Cooked Chicken, Smoked Ham, Smoked Sausage
Gherkins, Capers
Crushed Garlic
Red and Green Peppers, roasted or raw
Pineapple
Finely chopped fresh leafy Herbs such as Parsley, Basil, Coriander, Chives and Dill
Chopped roasted Nuts
Sieved fresh Tomatoes

Mustard – Mustard Dip is either English Mustard and Mayonnaise or French Mustard and Cream along with other flavourings, e.g.:
     Mixed herbs in very small quantities
     Chopped cooked mushrooms and onions
     Worcester, Mushroom, Anchovy Sauces

SOUPS

STOCK

MEAT SOUPS

BROTHS

VEGETABLE SOUPS

PURÉE SOUPS

CREAM SOUPS

FISH SOUPS

COLD SOUPS

STOCK

Many soups can be made successfully with water, but where a full mellow flavour is desired it is advisable to use stock. Once made, stock should be chilled immediately (never being allowed to spend any time at room temperature) and thoroughly reheated again before use. Stock will keep for around three days in the refrigerator or three months in the freezer.

Bone stock is suitable for household soups but for consommé it is essential to use meat stock.

When adding vegetables to flavour a stock no one flavour should predominate. For example, too many carrots will produce a very sweet stock. Celery is an indispensible ingredient for soup stocks.

Bouillon cubes may be used instead of stock as a basis for soups and there are many available in different flavours. Follow the instructions on the packet for the correct dilution.

The quantity of stock yielded will vary depending upon the evaporation that has taken place during cooking. Season according to taste.

Boiling will make stock cloudy, so, instead, simmer for several hours to produce a clear stock.

See consommé, steps 4 to 6, page 29, for how to clear a stock.

Note: The use of a pressure cooker reduces the time for stock-making considerably. Bone stock can be made in 1 hour.

1. BOUQUET OF HERBS OR BOUQUET GARNI

A stock must have a balanced flavour, so where a bouquet of herbs is indicated, choose a combination of herbs that will subtly enhance, rather than overpower, the soup. In most soups the following combination will enhance:

Ingredients:

1 Bay Leaf   1 sprig Thyme
3 large sprigs Parsley (including stalks)

You could also include:

1 10-cm piece Celery (including leaves)
2 10-cm pieces Leek
Peppercorns

Method:

1. Tie all together with clean string and drop into stock pot when making stock.
2. Remove and discard when the stock is ready.
3. If including peppercorns, tie the ingredients together in a muslin bag.

Note: A bouquet of herbs is often used in the preparation of sauces.

2. **WHITE BONE STOCK**

Ingredients:

Raw *or* cooked Bones   Small piece Turnip
Water   I Carrot
I Onion   Salt

Method:

1. Wash bones and put into a pan with water to cover.
2. Add salt and bring to boiling point.
3. Boil 4–6 hours, adding vegetables, cut in large pieces, I hour before straining.
Note: Instead of making stock, a bone or piece of meat, e.g. runner or flank, may be added to the water when making soup.

3. **BROWN BONE STOCK**

Make as above, first browning the sliced onion in a little oil.

4. **BROWN MEAT STOCK**

Ingredients:

500 g Hough   I small piece Bone
3 ½ litres Water   (preferably Veal)
25 g Dripping *or* Cooking Fat   2 Onions
I Leek   2 sticks Celery
I medium Carrot   Salt
Bouquet of Herbs (page 27)   A few Black Peppercorns

Method:

1. Cut the meat and skin into small pieces; put into the water along with the bone and salt. Soak 30 minutes.
2. Fry the onion till brown in the fat; pour off surplus fat.
3. Add meat, bones and water, bring very slowly to simmering point and skim. Allow to simmer 4 hours.
4. Add vegetables, herbs, salt to taste and simmer gently for a further hour. Strain and set aside till cold.
5. Remove fat. Stock should be clear if cooking has been slow enough.

5. **CHICKEN STOCK**

Ingredients:

Chicken Bones   I medium Carrot
Salt   I stick Celery
Water   Bouquet of Herbs (page 27)
I Onion

Method:

1. Cut up vegetables roughly.
2. Put all the ingredients in a large pan and cover with water.

3. Bring to the boil and simmer gently for 1–1½ hours.

4. Strain, and skim off the fat when cold.

6. FISH STOCK

Ingredients:

Fish Trimmings	1 stick Celery
Salt	1 Onion
Water	Few Peppercorns

Method:

1. Wash trimmings thoroughly and put into a pan with water to cover.

2. Bring to boiling point and skim.

3. Add celery, onion, peppercorns and salt.

4. Simmer for 30 minutes and strain.

5. Use immediately for fish soups and sauces.

MEAT SOUPS

Clear Soups:

A variety of clear brown soups are made from brown meat stock as follows:

1. One litre brown meat stock (page 28) garnished with 2 tablespoonfuls of cooked diced carrot and turnip.

2. One litre brown meat stock garnished with 2 tablespoonfuls of cooked rice or small pasta shapes.

3. One litre brown meat stock thickened with 25 g cornflour.

7. CONSOMMÉ

Ingredients:

1 litre Brown Meat Stock (page 28)	Whites and shells of 2 Eggs
100 g Lean Beef	Peppercorns
2 tablespoonfuls Tomato Pulp	Salt
1 tablespoonful Sherry (optional)	

Method:

1. Remove all fat from stock (easily done by allowing to chill in refrigerator and then skimming off the hard fat).

2. Mince beef, or shred or cut up finely, and soak with stock in pan for 1 hour.

3. Add tomato pulp, peppercorns and salt to taste.

4. Add egg whites, unbeaten, and crushed shells to stock.

5. Whisk till nearly boiling; remove whisk and allow to boil up and settle three times. Infuse for 10–15 minutes.

6. Decant through clean, scalded cloth. No seasoning should be added after clearing.

7. Sherry may be added before serving.

8. GARNISHES FOR CONSOMMÉ

The garnishes used give the name to the soup. All garnishes are previously cooked, put into a tureen or soup bowl and soup poured over. Allow 2 tablespoonfuls of garnish to 1 litre of soup.

Julienne Garnish.—Thin strips of carrot and turnip about 3 cm long.
Brunoise Garnish.—Very small dice of carrot and turnip.
Parpane Garnish.—Triangles of carrot and turnip and the green of leek.
Pasta Garnish.—Cooked pasta in various shapes.
Tomato Consommé.—250 ml tomato purée is added before clearing the consommé. A garnish of diced tomato (page 202) is added after clearing.

9. HOUGH SOUP

Ingredients:

200 g Hough *or* Shin of Beef (without bone)	Cooking Oil
1 litre cold Water	Bay Leaf
Salt	Peppercorns
1 Onion	40 g Flour *or* Cornflour

Method:

1. Cut the meat in small pieces and put in the water with salt. Soak for 30 minutes.
2. Slice and fry the onion in oil till a good brown colour.
3. Add the meat, water, seasoning and flavouring and bring to simmering point. Simmer 2–3 hours and strain. Reserve the meat.
4. Blend flour or cornflour with a little cold water until smooth. Pour into rinsed pan and pour strained soup over.
5. Cut up about half of the meat very finely and add to the soup.
6. Stir until boiling. Simmer for 5 minutes.
7. Check for seasoning and serve.

10. KIDNEY SOUP

Ingredients:

200–250 g Ox Kidney	Salt and Pepper
1 Onion	1 Carrot
25 g Cooking Fat *or* Oil	Small piece Turnip
Pinch Sugar	2 Cloves
3 litres Brown Bone Stock *or* Water	Bouquet of Herbs (page 27)
40 g Cornflour to each litre	

Method:

1. Split and core the kidney, cut up, wash and dry.
2. Fry the onion till a good brown colour in the fat or oil.
3. Add the kidney with a pinch of sugar and fry well.
4. Add stock or water and seasoning and bring to the boil. Simmer 1 hour.

5. Add vegetables (roughly cut), cloves and herbs and simmer for a further hour. Strain.
6. Cut the kidney into neat dice, add to the soup.
7. Measure and thicken with cornflour that has been blended until smooth with a little stock. Bring to the boil, stirring all the time and simmer for 5 minutes.
8. Check for seasoning and serve.

II. **LIVER OR MOCK KIDNEY SOUP**

Make as kidney soup, using 200–250 g ox liver instead of kidney.

I2. **OXTAIL SOUP**

Ingredients:

I Ox Tail (jointed)	Bouquet of Herbs (page 27)
50 g Cooking Fat *or* Oil	2 Cloves
2 Onions	A few Black Peppercorns
I Bacon rasher	Salt
3 litres Water	A little Mushroom Ketchup
Piece of Turnip	Glass of Sherry (optional)
2 sticks Celery	40 g Cornflour to each litre of Soup
I Carrot	

Method:

1. Cut the tail into joints and wash.
2. Fry the onion in the fat or oil.
3. Add bacon, joints and water. Simmer for 3 hours.
4. Add vegetables, herbs and seasoning and simmer for a further hour.
5. Strain, skim well and measure to determine the amount of cornflour required.
6. Remove meat from joints and cut up finely. Add to soup.
7. Thicken with cornflour that has been blended until smooth with a little stock.
8. Check for seasoning and add sherry if liked.

Note: If liked, soup may be made on previous day without thickening. This allows fat to solidify on top which is then easily removed. On following day, skim soup well, add the cornflour (blended with stock) to thicken, and boil for a few minutes.

I3. **HARE SOUP**

Ingredients:

I Hare	I stick Celery
I teaspoonful Vinegar	I Carrot
2 Onions	100g-piece of Turnip
25 g Cooking Fat *or* Oil	Bouquet of Herbs (page 27)
25 g Bacon	40 g Flour to each litre of Soup
3–3½ litres Water	I tablespoonful Redcurrant Jelly
Salt, Pepper and Cayenne	Port Wine

Method: (See pages 166 and 167 for paunching and jointing of hares and rabbits.)
1. Paunch the hare. Mix the vinegar with the blood and leave aside.
2. Fry onion in oil till a good brown colour.
3. Chop the bacon and joint the hare and add to pot. Add the water and seasoning. Simmer 2 hours.
4. Add vegetables and herbs and simmer 1 hour longer. Strain and keep stock.
5. Remove best parts of hare and shred. Return to the soup.
6. Blend flour with water or stock till smooth and add to soup. Stir until boiling.
7. Add jelly and blood and cook thoroughly without boiling.
8. Check for seasoning and add port wine.

Note: If liked, the best parts of the hare may be used for jugged hare (page 166) and the remainder for soup. A pressure cooker may be used allowing 30–45 minutes, depending on age of hare.

14. MULLIGATAWNY SOUP

Ingredients:

2 Onions (roughly chopped)	Bouquet of Herbs (page 27)
1 Carrot (sliced)	1 level dessertspoonful Salt
25 g Cooking Fat *or* Oil	2 Tomatoes (chopped)
25 g Flour	2 Apples (chopped)
1 level teaspoonful Curry Powder	1 teaspoonful Chutney
1 level teaspoonful Curry Paste	25 g Bacon
1 litre Water	50 g Rice (boiled, page 475)
200 g Chicken Breast	

Method:

1. Fry onion and carrot in fat or oil till brown.
2. Add flour, curry powder and paste and fry lightly with the vegetables.
3. Add water and chicken breast and stir till boiling.
4. Add herbs, salt, tomatoes, apples, chutney and bacon.
5. Simmer 1 hour or till chicken is tender.
6. Strain, dice the chicken, add to the soup and reheat. Check for seasoning.
7. Serve boiled rice separately.

15. TRIPE SOUP

Ingredients:

1 Onion	500 g prepared cooked Tripe
50 g Flour	1 litre Water *or* Chicken Stock
500 ml Milk	Salt and Pepper to taste
1 tablespoonful chopped Parsley	

Method:

1. Prepare and chop onion.
2. Cut tripe into small pieces.
3. Add onions and tripe to the stock or water.

4. Bring to the boil and simmer for 30–40 minutes.
5. Blend flour with a little milk until smooth. Mix with rest of milk. Add some hot soup to this and blend well, return all to pan and stir till boiling.
6. Simmer for 5 minutes, check for seasoning, add chopped parsley and serve.

BROTHS

16. SCOTCH BROTH

Ingredients:

or 250 g Mutton (Flank *or* Shank)   100 g Turnip
250 g Beef (Runner, Flank *or* Hough)   1 small Parsnip
50 g Barley   Small piece of Cabbage
25 g Dried Peas (soaked overnight)   1 Onion *or* Leek
2 litres Water   Salt and Pepper
2 Carrots   Chopped Parsley

Method:

1. Scald barley and put in pan with meat, peas and water.
2. Bring to the boil and simmer 1–1½ hours.
3. Add diced vegetables except cabbage, green of leek and parsley.
4. Season and cook slowly for 30 minutes or until vegetables are tender.
5. Add cabbage and green of leek, shredded. Boil for 10 minutes, check for seasoning, add parsley and serve.

Note: If liked, after cooking, any meat may be removed from the bone, cut finely and returned to the broth.

17. HOTCH POTCH

Ingredients:

500 g Shank *or* Flank of Lamb *or* Mutton   1 small Cauliflower
3 litres Water   500 g Garden Peas
4 Carrots (new)   500 g Broad Beans
4 Turnips (new)   Salt and Pepper
½ small Cabbage   2 teaspoonfuls Sugar
1 small Lettuce   2 tablespoonfuls chopped Parsley
10 Spring Onions

Method:

1. Cut the meat into pieces, add to water, season, bring to boil and simmer for 1 hour 30 minutes.
2. Prepare vegetables, cutting turnip and two carrots into dice.
3. Shred the cabbage and lettuce, chop onion finely. Break the cauliflower into sprigs. Shell peas, shell and skin beans. Grate remaining carrots.
4. Add all the prepared vegetables except grated carrots.

5. Boil for ¾ hour, add grated carrot, sugar and check seasoning.

6. Cook for 10 minutes, check for seasoning, add chopped parsley and serve.

Note: If liked, any meat may be removed from the bone, cut finely and returned to the soup. Any vegetables in season may be added. They should be young and as fresh as possible.

18. CHICKEN BROTH

Ingredients:

1 litre Chicken Stock	1 tablespoonful chopped Parsley
40 g Rice	Salt and Pepper
1 Onion (chopped)	150 ml Milk (optional)
1 Leek (chopped)	

Method:

1. Bring stock to the boil and sprinkle in the washed rice.

2. Add the onion, white of leek and seasoning to stock. Simmer for 30 minutes.

3. Add green of leek cut finely and simmer for 15 minutes.

4. Add a little milk if liked.

5. Add parsley, check for seasoning and serve.

Note: Spaghetti (broken into small pieces) or vermicelli may be substituted for rice.

19. LENTIL BROTH

Ingredients:

200 g Lentils	1 large Potato (diced)
150 g Carrots (2 carrots)	2 litres Water
100 g Turnip (diced)	Ham bone*
2 Onions (diced)	Salt and Pepper

Method:

1. Wash lentils and drain.

2. Put lentils in pan with water and ham bone, bring to boiling point, skim and simmer for 2 hours.

3. Add diced vegetables and seasoning, cook for 30 minutes or till tender.

4. Remove ham bone, check for seasoning and serve.

Note: Ham stock cubes may be used instead of a ham bone, in which case less water will be required. Follow the dilution instructions on the stock cube packet and simmer the soup till the vegetables and lentils are very tender.

20. PEA OR HARICOT BEAN SOUP

Make as lentil broth (above), using peas (green or yellow) or haricot beans instead of lentils but soak them overnight in preparation, then discard the water in which they were soaked.

Note: This soup may be sieved or liquidised.

21. COCK-A-LEEKIE

Ingredients:

1 Chicken *or* boiling Fowl (including giblets if possible)	150 g Carrot (grated)
	2 litres Water
Salt and Pepper	25 g Rice, washed
1 tablespoonful chopped Parsley	250 g Leeks (shredded)

Method:

1. Wash the chicken and remove the giblets.
2. Put in large saucepan with the cold water, salt (and washed giblets if you have them).
3. Bring to boil and simmer gently for 2 hours.
4. Prepare leeks and shred finely. Add to the soup with the washed rice and continue cooking for a further 30 minutes.
5. Remove fowl and giblets and skim any fat from the soup.
6. Ten minutes before serving, add grated carrot and season to taste.
7. Check for seasoning and serve soup with chopped parsley.
8. The chicken can be served as a separate course (page 145).

VEGETABLE SOUPS

22. WHITE VEGETABLE SOUP

Ingredients:

1 kg Vegetables (Potato, Onion, Carrot and Turnip)	1½ litres Water
1 tablespoonful Sago (optional)	Salt and Pepper
1 tablespoonful chopped Parsley	250 ml Milk

Method:

1. Prepare vegetables and cut into fine dice.
2. Add vegetables and seasoning to water, bring to boiling point. Simmer until vegetables are tender, about 1 hour.
3. Sprinkle in sago and simmer until clear (about 15 minutes).
4. Add milk, reheat, check for seasoning and add chopped parsley.

Note: Vegetables may be cut roughly and soup sieved or liquidised.

23. POTATO AND LEEK SOUP

Ingredients:

25 g Butter *or* a little Oil	Salt and Pepper
1 large Onion (finely chopped)	1 Leek (finely shredded)
500 g Potatoes	250 ml Milk
1 litre Chicken Stock	1 tablespoonful chopped Parsley

Method:

1. Fry onion slowly in oil or butter, being careful not to discolour.
2. Add the thinly sliced potatoes, stock and seasoning. Simmer gently for 1¼ hours.
3. Add the shredded leek, simmer for 10 minutes.
4. Break down any large pieces of potato.
5. Just before serving add milk and reheat. Lastly, check for seasoning and add chopped parsley.

24. **CARROT SOUP**

Ingredients:

250 g Carrots	Salt and Pepper
1 small Onion	25 g Flour
1 Bacon rasher	250 ml Milk
1 litre Water	1 tablespoonful chopped Parsley

Method:

1. Grate the carrots, chop the onion.
2. Put in a pan with water and bacon and simmer gently for 1¾ hours. Remove bacon rasher.
3. Blend flour and a little milk till smooth. Add the rest of the milk. Pour a little hot soup over. Return to pan and bring to the boil. Simmer for a few minutes and season. Check for seasoning and add chopped parsley.

Note: Vegetables may be cut roughly and soup sieved or liquidised. Fresh coriander enhances the flavour of carrot soup.

25. **MINESTRONE SOUP**

Ingredients:

1 Ham Bone	100 g Turnip
75 g Haricot Beans	1 small tin Tomatoes
1 litre Water	1 stick Celery
1 Onion	1 small piece Cabbage
A little Butter	25 g Garden Peas
25 g Spaghetti	Parmesan Cheese
Salt and Pepper	

Method:

1. Put the bone, beans and water into a pan and simmer gently for 2 hours.
2. Chop the onion and fry in a little oil or butter till golden brown.
3. Prepare the vegetables and cut into dice. Chop the cabbage.
4. Remove bone. Add all vegetables except peas and cabbage to the soup and simmer for 30 minutes.
5. Break spaghetti into pieces and add to the soup with the peas and cabbage. Cook for 10 minutes.
6. Check for seasoning, serve with grated Parmesan cheese on top.

26. ONION SOUP (1)

Ingredients:

500 g Onions	Salt and Pepper
25 g Butter *or* Oil	1 litre White Bone Stock (page 28)
1 stick Celery	50 g Flour
1 Bay Leaf	250 ml Milk
Small blade Mace	Chopped Parsley (optional)

Method:

1. Melt fat and add finely chopped onion and celery. Cook without discolouring for a few minutes.
2. Add stock, seasoning, mace and bay leaf, and simmer till all is tender, about 45 minutes. Remove herbs.
3. Blend flour and a little milk till smooth. Add the rest of the milk. Pour a little hot soup over. Return to pan and bring to the boil. Simmer for 5 minutes. Check for seasoning and add chopped parsley if liked.

27. FRENCH ONION SOUP

Ingredients:

500 g Onions (thinly sliced)	25 g Butter
1 litre Beef Stock	Salt and Pepper

Method:

1. Cook the onion slowly in the butter until soft and brown (about 20 minutes).
2. Add stock. Cover and cook for 20 minutes.
3. Check for seasoning and serve with toasted French bread on top.

Note: Thin slices of French bread can be lightly buttered and sprinkled with grated cheese on one side. Serve soup in ovenproof bowls. Put bread on top of bowls. Crisp in a moderate oven.

28. CREAM OF MUSHROOM SOUP

Ingredients:

100 g Mushrooms	Bouquet of Herbs (page 27)
20 g Butter	Salt and Pepper
750 ml White Bone Stock (page 28)	40 g Flour
1 small piece Onion	250 ml Milk
Carrot and Turnip	

Method:

1. Wash and dice mushrooms, cook slowly in butter for 5 minutes.
2. Add stock and bring to the boil. Leave the vegetables in large pieces. Add vegetables, bouquet of herbs and seasoning and simmer for 1 hour.
3. Remove pieces of vegetable and bouquet of herbs.
4. Blend flour with milk till smooth, pour a little hot soup over, return to the pan and bring to the boil, simmer for 5 minutes.
5. Check for seasoning and serve.

PURÉE SOUPS

Average proportions for Vegetable Purée Soups: 500 g vegetables to 1 litre liquid.
Exceptions: Strong-flavoured vegetables, e.g. Brussels sprouts, 250 g vegetables to 1 litre.

Purée soups are sieved after cooking and bound together with a starchy substance. The amount of starchy substance varies according to the vegetable used, but is usually 25–50 g to a litre. This substance could be flour, made into a roux (page 291), or cornflour. A grated potato is also a good thickening agent. If a liquidiser is used, less thickening may be required.

Purée soups may be made by either of the following methods:

      (a) 1. Cook vegetables in the liquid.
          2. Sieve or liquidise.
          3. Make a roux of butter and flour (page 291) and add some sieved soup.
          4. Add to soup, bring to boil and cook for 5 minutes.

      (b) 1. Slowly cook vegetables in oil or butter.
          2. Add stock and seasoning and simmer till tender.
          3. Sieve and add a blended thickening agent such as cornflour.
          4. Boil for 5 minutes.

29. ARTICHOKE SOUP

Ingredients:

500 g Jerusalem Artichokes	1 litre Stock
1 Onion	Salt and Pepper
2 sticks Celery	25 g Flour
25 g Butter (and extra for frying)	150 ml Milk

Method:

1. Peel and slice artichokes.
2. Cut up celery and onion and cook slowly in a little butter for 5–10 minutes.
3. Add artichokes and stock, and season and simmer for 1 hour.
4. In another pot, melt 25 g butter, add flour to make a roux (page 291), add milk gradually. Then add some sieved soup and return to soup pot.
5. Stir till boiling. Simmer for 5 minutes.

30. BORSCHT

Ingredients:

200 g Beetroot	25 g Flour
1 large Onion	150 ml Milk
1 litre Stock	150 ml Sour Cream
Salt and Pepper	*or* { 50 ml Cream
½ Lemon	{ 1 tablespoonful Lemon Juice

Method:

1. Scrub, peel and slice beetroot; slice onion.
2. Put into pan, add seasoning and stock.
3. Simmer slowly for approximately 1 hour until beetroot is soft. Sieve.
4. In another pot, melt butter, add flour, add milk gradually. Then add some sieved soup and return to soup pot.
5. Stir till boiling. Simmer for 5 minutes.
6. Add the juice of ½ lemon, return to pan, reheat.
7. Serve topped with a spoonful of sour cream, or cream soured with lemon.

31. BROWN VEGETABLE SOUP

Ingredients:

4 Potatoes	1 ½ litres Stock
3 Onions	Salt and Pepper
2 Carrots	25 g Flour
100 g Turnip	Chopped Parsley
25 g Butter	

Method:

1. Prepare the vegetables and cut up roughly.
2. Melt fat, add vegetables and fry till lightly browned.
3. Add stock and seasoning and bring to boiling point.
4. Simmer till vegetables are tender, about 1 hour. Sieve or liquidise.
5. In another pot, melt butter, add flour to make a roux (page 291), add milk gradually. Then add some sieved soup and return to soup pot.
6. Stir till boiling. Simmer for 5 minutes.
7. Add chopped parsley and serve.

32. BRUSSELS SPROUTS SOUP

Ingredients:

250 g Brussels Sprouts	25 g Butter
1 Bacon rasher (chopped)	25 g Flour
1 Onion (chopped)	150 ml Milk
Salt and Pepper	2 tablespoonfuls Cream (optional)
1 litre Stock	

Method:

1. Remove outer leaves, trim and blanch Brussels sprouts.
2. Put sprouts, onion, bacon and seasoning in a pan with stock.
3. Bring to the boil, simmer till tender, about 30 minutes, sieve.
4. In another pot, melt butter, add flour to make a roux (page 291), add milk gradually. Then add some sieved soup and return to soup pot.
5. Stir till boiling. Simmer for 5 minutes.
6. Add cream just before serving.

33. CAULIFLOWER SOUP

Ingredients:

1 medium Cauliflower	25 g Butter
2 small Onions	25 g Flour
1 Bacon rasher (chopped)	250 ml Milk
Bouquet of Herbs (page 27)	Salt and Pepper
1 litre Stock	

Method:

1. Wash and sprig cauliflower, slice onion, add to stock with seasoning and bacon.
2. Cook 20–30 minutes and force through a sieve or liquidise.
3. In another pot, melt butter, add flour, add milk gradually. Then add some sieved soup and return to soup pot.
4. Stir till boiling. Simmer for 5 minutes and serve.

Note: Broccoli soup can be made the same way. Stilton, blue cheese and smoked cheese are delicious additions to both broccoli and cauliflower soups.

34. CELERY SOUP

Ingredients:

1 head Celery	25 g Butter
1 Potato	25 g Flour
Salt and Pepper	150 ml Milk
1 litre Stock	2 tablespoonfuls Cream (optional)

Method:

1. Wash and cut up celery, reserving the leaves for garnish. Cook slowly in butter for 10–15 minutes.
2. Add stock, potato and seasoning, and simmer till celery is tender, about 1 hour. Sieve (if liquidising, sieve afterwards to remove any stringy celery fibres).
3. In another pot, melt butter, add flour, add milk gradually. Then add some sieved soup and return to soup pot.
4. Stir till boiling. Simmer for 5 minutes.
5. Add cream, check for seasoning, and serve garnished with celery leaves.

35. CHESTNUT SOUP

Ingredients:

750 g Chestnuts	2 tablespoonfuls Cream
1 litre Stock	250 ml Milk
Salt and Pepper	

Method:

1. Blanch and skin chestnuts (page 139).
2. Place in a pan with the stock and seasoning, and simmer till tender, about 1 hour 30 minutes.
3. Sieve or liquidise, add milk and reheat. Add cream before serving.

36. CRÉCY SOUP

Ingredients:

250 g Carrots (chopped)
50 g Turnip (chopped)
1 Onion (chopped)
1 stick Celery (chopped)
1 medium Potato (chopped)
1 litre Stock

Bacon Lardons
Bouquet of Herbs (page 27)
Salt and Pepper
2 level teaspoonfuls Cornflour
2 tablespoonfuls Cream

Method:

1. Fry a few bacon lardons in a pan. Add vegetables.
2. Sweat the vegetables, then add stock, herbs and seasoning and simmer till tender, about 1 hour.
3. Pass the soup through a sieve or liquidise.
4. Blend cornflour to a paste with a little milk. Gradually add a little sieved soup to the blended cornflour. Pour back into pot. Bring to boiling point and simmer for 5 minutes, stirring all the time.
5. Check for seasoning. Add cream just before serving.

37. GREEN PEA SOUP

Ingredients:

1 small Onion (chopped)
500 g fresh *or* frozen Green Peas
    (weigh fresh peas after shelling)
1 Lettuce

1 litre Stock
40 g Flour
Salt and Pepper
2 tablespoonfuls Milk *or* Cream

Method:

1. If fresh peas are used, shell peas and retain half the pods. Wash pods and lettuce.
2. Add lettuce, onion, pods and seasoning to stock. Simmer 30 minutes.
3. Remove lettuce. Liquidise. Pass through sieve. Discard solids.
4. Add peas to stock. Simmer till tender. Liquidise or pass through a sieve.
5. Blend flour with a little sieved soup till smooth, then add to pan.
6. Stir till boiling then simmer for 5 minutes.
7. Check for seasoning. Add milk or cream and serve.

Note: Mint is a nice addition to pea soup. Add a few sprigs when adding the peas.

38. ONION SOUP (2)

Ingredients:

500 g Onions (chopped)
50 g Butter
250 ml Milk
Chopped Parsley

25–40 g Flour
1 litre Stock
Salt and Pepper

Method:

1. In a large pot, melt 25g of butter, add onions, and cook gently without colouring for 5–10 minutes.

2. Add stock and seasoning and simmer for 1 hour. Sieve or liquidise.
3. In another pot, melt the remaining butter, add flour, add milk gradually, then add some sieved soup and return to soup pot.
4. Stir till boiling. Simmer for 5 minutes, stirring continuously.

Note: Grated cheese may be served on top.

39. POTATO SOUP

Ingredients:

750 g Potatoes	1 litre Stock
Small Onion	250 ml Milk
Stick Celery	Parsley (chopped)
Salt and Pepper	Nutmeg (freshly grated)

Method:

1. Peel and chop the potatoes, onions and celery and put into a large pot.
2. Add stock and salt and pepper.
3. Simmer about 1 hour.
4. Sieve or liquidise, add milk and reheat.
5. Check for seasoning. Add a grating of nutmeg, if liked, or chopped parsley.

40. TOMATO SOUP

Ingredients:

or	500 ml tinned Tomatoes	*or*	50 g Flour
	500 g fresh Tomatoes		40 g Cornflour
	1 Onion		150 ml Milk
	1 Bacon rasher (chopped)		1 teaspoonful Sugar
	Salt and Pepper		2 tablespoonfuls Cream (optional)
	1 litre Stock or Water		

Method:

1. Put tomatoes, onion, bacon, stock and seasoning in pan (roughly cutting tomatoes if fresh).
2. Simmer till tender; about 1 hour. Sieve.
3. Blend flour or cornflour with milk, add to sieved soup, bring to the boil and simmer for 5 minutes, stirring all the time.
4. Add sugar. Check for seasoning. If liked, add cream before serving.

41. WHITE LENTIL SOUP

Ingredients:

100 g Lentils	25 g Butter
1 litre Water	25 g Flour
1 Onion	150 ml Milk
Bouquet of Herbs (page 27)	Salt and Pepper
1 stick Celery	2 tablespoonfuls Cream (optional)
	Chopped Parsley (optional)

Method:

1. Wash lentils and put on to boil in the water. Skim when soup comes to the boil.
2. Add celery, onion and herbs. Simmer 1 hour 30 minutes.
3. Sieve or liquidise.
4. In another pot, melt butter, add flour to make a roux (page 291), add milk gradually. Then add some sieved soup and return to soup pot.
5. Stir until boiling. Simmer 5 minutes, stirring all the time. Season.
6. If liked, add cream before serving.

CREAM SOUPS

Average proportions:

40 g Flour
2 Egg Yolks   } to 1 litre Stock
2 tablespoonfuls Cream

Note: To convert a purée soup into a cream soup, add 2 egg yolks and 2 tablespoonfuls of cream to 1 litre of soup.
Yolks may be reduced if flour increased.

42. BONNE FEMME SOUP

Ingredients:

1 litre White Stock (page 28)	2 level teaspoonfuls Sugar
1 tablespoonful Lettuce (shredded)	Salt and Pepper
1 tablespoonful Spinach (shredded)	25 g Flour
1 tablespoonful Cucumber (shredded)	2 Egg Yolks
1 tablespoonful Green Peas	2 tablespoonfuls Cream

Method:

1. Add prepared vegetables, sugar and seasoning to stock. Bring to the boil and simmer for 15 minutes.
2. In a bowl, add a little hot soup to flour and blend. Return to pan and stir till boiling. Simmer for 5 minutes.
3. Mix egg yolk and cream in a bowl. Pour some hot (not boiling) soup into this, stirring well. Then return to pot. Cook through without boiling.

43. CREAM OF CHICKEN SOUP

Ingredients:

1 litre Chicken Stock	1–2 Egg Yolks
25 g Butter	2 tablespoonfuls Cream
25 g Flour	1 tablespoonful chopped Parsley
Salt and Pepper	

Method:

1. Make a roux with butter and flour, gradually add stock, stir till boiling, season, simmer for 5 minutes.
2. Mix egg yolks and cream in a warm bowl. Pour hot (not boiling) soup over the eggs, stirring well. Return to the pot. If the soup has not thickened reheat without boiling.

44. HOLLANDAISE SOUP

Ingredients:

40 g Butter	2 tablespoonfuls Peas
40 g Flour	Salt and Pepper
1 litre Veal *or* Chicken Stock	2 Egg Yolks
2 tablespoonfuls Carrot (diced)	2 tablespoonfuls Cream
2 tablespoonfuls Cucumber (diced)	Chopped Parsley

Method:

1. Cook vegetables in boiling salted water.
2. Melt butter, add flour and cook for a few minutes.
3. Add stock and bring to the boil. Season and simmer for 5 minutes. Add vegetables.
2. Mix egg yolk and cream in a bowl. Pour some hot (not boiling) soup into this, stirring well. Then return to pot. Cook through without boiling.
3. Serve with parsley sprinkled on top.

45. PALERMO SOUP

Ingredients:

1 litre White Stock	40 g Flour
25 g Vermicelli	2 Egg Yolks
250 ml Tomato Pulp	2 tablespoonfuls Cream
Salt and Pepper	

Method:

1. Add the vermicelli and tomato pulp to the stock and simmer for 15 minutes, season.
2. Blend flour till smooth with a little stock. Add to stock and bring to the boil.
3. Mix egg yolk and cream in a bowl. Pour some hot (not boiling) soup into this, stirring well. Then return to pot. Cook through without boiling.

46. ASPARAGUS SOUP

Ingredients:

1 bunch Asparagus (approx. 250 g)	500 ml Chicken Stock
35 g fresh *or* frozen Green Peas	15 g piece Ham
25 g Flour	125 ml Milk
25 g Butter	Salt and Pepper
2 tablespoonfuls Cream	1 Egg yolk

Method:

1. Cut off the asparagus tips and cook until just tender. Set aside.
2. Cut up the rest of the asparagus and cook with peas and ham for 30 minutes in stock.
3. Remove ham and force the soup through a sieve.
4. In another pot make a roux with butter and flour and milk. Add the sieved soup and bring to the boil. Simmer, stirring all the time.
5. Check the seasoning. Add the cooked tips to the soup and reheat.
6. Mix egg yolk and cream in a bowl. Pour some hot (not boiling) soup into this, stirring well. Then return to pot. Cook through without boiling.

47. CREAM OF CORN SOUP

Ingredients:

200 g Sweetcorn	25 g Flour ⎫
1 stick Celery	25 g Butter ⎬ White Sauce
Small piece Turnip	250 ml Milk ⎭
1 small Onion	2 tablespoonfuls Cream
Bay Leaf	2 Egg yolks
1 litre Stock	Salt and Pepper

Method:

1. Put all vegetables and stock in a pan and bring to the boil. Simmer 30–45 minutes until vegetables are tender.
2. Make the white sauce (page 291) and add to the soup.
3. Sieve or liquidise the soup. Return to the pan, check seasoning, bring to boiling point.
4. Mix egg yolk and cream in a bowl. Pour some hot (not boiling) soup into this, stirring well. Then return to pot. Cook through without boiling.

FISH SOUPS

48. FISH SOUP

Ingredients:

50 g Flour	Salt and Pepper
250 ml Milk	1 teaspoonful Lemon Juice
1 litre Fish Stock (page 29)	1 tablespoonful Chopped Parsley
100 g Haddock (cooked)	

Method:

1. Blend flour with a little milk. Gradually add rest of milk. Add stock and bring to boil.
2. Add flaked fish and simmer for 5 minutes.
3. Add lemon juice and parsley.

Note: Smoked haddock is very suitable for this soup.

49. LOBSTER BISQUE

Ingredients:

or 1 Lobster (cooked, page 74)
1 large tin of Lobster
1 teaspoonful Lemon Juice
150 ml Cream
2 litres Fish Stock

2 teaspoonfuls Anchovy Essence
Salt, Pepper and Cayenne
100 g Flour
50 g Coral Butter (see below)

Coral Butter:

50 g Butter

Coral from lobster

Cream butter, add sufficient coral to colour pink.

Method:

1. Take flesh of lobster from shell, lay aside the best parts for garnish.
2. Wash and break up the shell. Add to the stock with the remainder of the lobster meat and seasoning, and simmer for 1 hour. Strain.
3. Add blended flour and diced lobster garnish. Stir till boiling, simmer for 5 minutes.
4. Add anchovy essence, lemon juice and cream, reheat without boiling.
5. Whisk in coral butter gradually.

Note: If lobster meat is required for another dish, this soup may be made from shell only with a little meat added for garnish.

COLD SOUPS

50. ICED CUCUMBER SOUP

Ingredients:

1 large Cucumber (2 small)
1 Shallot *or* Onion
1 litre Water *or* Chicken Stock

1 level tablespoonful Arrowroot
2 tablespoonfuls Single Cream
Salt and Pepper

Method:

1. Peel and remove seeds from cucumber.
2. Garnish – dice some cucumber or use a small ball cutter.
3. Chop onion and put into pan with stock or water. Simmer for 10–15 minutes.
4. Add cucumber, cut up roughly and simmer for 10 minutes.
5. Sieve or liquidise soup. Return to the pan and thicken with the blended arrowroot.
6. Sir in the cream. Garnish with prepared cucumber.

51. **VICHYSSOISE SOUP**

Ingredients:

3 Leeks   Salt and Pepper
2 small Onions   Pinch Nutmeg
500 g Potatoes   250 ml Single Cream
40 g Butter   Chives to garnish
1 litre Chicken Stock

Method:

1. Use only the white part of the leeks (but keep greens for making other stocks), wash carefully and finely shred.
2. Chop the onions. Peel and slice the potatoes.
3. Sauté the leeks and onions until tender.
4. Add stock, sliced potatoes, seasoning and nutmeg.
5. Bring to the boil, simmer gently for 30 minutes.
6. Sieve or liquidise and put in the refrigerator to chill.
7. Add cream and sprinkle with chopped chives before serving.

FISH AND SHELLFISH

FISH

SHELLFISH

FISH

The choice of fish: Fish must be fresh and free from a strong smell.
Whole fish: Flesh should be firm and tail stiff.
Eyes should be bright and gills red.
Fillets of fish: Flesh firm and good colour.

I. FISH IN SEASON

Fish

Cod	October to January
Haddock	September to February
Halibut	March to October
Herring	June to December
Mackerel	April to June
Plaice	May to December
Salmon	January to August
Sea Trout	March to August
Sole	All year
Trout	March to August
Turbot	March to August
Whitebait	March to August
Whiting	November to March

Shellfish

Crab	May to August
Crayfish	All year
Lobster	April to September
Mussels	All year but best in winter
Oysters	September to April
Prawns	February to October
Scallops	October to March
Scampi	February to October
Shrimps	All year

2. FRIED HERRING OR MACKEREL

Ingredients:

Herrings *or* Mackerel	Oatmeal
Salt and Pepper	Fat or Oil for frying

Time: 3–5 minutes each side

Method (I):

1. Clean whole fish, remove head, fins and scales.
2. Score fish across once or twice.
3. Dip in oatmeal seasoned with salt and pepper.
4. Fry in very little hot fat or oil on both sides until flesh leaves the bone.

Method (2):

1. Dip boned herring or mackerel in oatmeal.
2. Fry in a little hot fat or oil flesh side down until oatmeal is crisp.
3. Turn, fry lightly on skin side.

3. GRILLED HERRING OR MACKEREL

Method:

1. Prepare as for fried herring or mackerel (page 51), method (1).
2. Heat grill at medium.
3. Place fish in grilling pan without grid.
4. Cook on both sides until flesh leaves the bone.

Note: Herring may also be boned and grilled, skin side down and should not require turning.

4. POTTED HERRING OR MACKEREL

Ingredients:

Required number of Fish	2 Bay Leaves
Equal proportions Water and Vinegar	10 Black Peppercorns

Servings: Number of Herring or Mackerel
Time: 45–60 minutes
Oven Temperature: 180°C, No. 4
Position in Oven: Middle shelf

Method:

1. Bone herring or mackerel, season, roll up, skin side out.
2. Place in ovenproof dish.
3. Add water and vinegar to come halfway up fish. Add bay leaves and peppercorns.
4. Cover and bake.

Note: Can be served hot or cold with salad.

5. STUFFED HERRING OR MACKEREL

Ingredients:

2 Herring *or* Mackerel (boned)	Butter

Stuffing:

2 level tablespoonfuls Oatmeal	1 tablespoonful Vegetable Oil
1 teaspoonful chopped Parsley	Salt and Pepper

Servings: 2
Time: 20 minutes
Oven Temperature: 180°C, No. 4
Position in Oven: Middle shelf

Method:

1. Place one herring skin side down on a greased baking dish.
2. Mix ingredients for stuffing and spread on fish.

3. Place second herring on top, skin side up.
4. Place small pats of butter on top; bake.

6. FRIED KIPPERS

Ingredients:

Kippers   Fat or Oil for frying

Time: 8 minutes

Method:

1. Remove head and fins.
2. Place in bowl, pour boiling water over.
3. Remove and dry.
4. Fry in a little hot fat or oil, flesh side down.
5. Cook 5 minutes, turn and cook for 3 minutes.

Note: Kippers may be fried as a pair placing flesh sides together (5 minutes on each side).

7. GRILLED KIPPERS

Method (1):

1. Wipe kippers with kitchen towel.
2. Heat grill, put kippers in grilling pan without grid.
3. Grill 3 minutes, turn.
4. Grill flesh side 3 minutes, or until bone leaves flesh.

Method (2):

Kippers may be grilled as a pair placing flesh sides together (5 minutes each side).

8. BAKED KIPPERS

Time: 10–15 minutes
Oven Temperature: 180°C, No. 4
Position in Oven: Middle shelf

Method:

1. Wipe kippers with kitchen towel.
2. Place on top of each other, flesh sides together.
3. Wrap in foil or put in covered baking dish.
4. Bake.

9. STEAMED FISH FILLETS OR STEAKS

Ingredients:

Fish fillets *or* steaks   Lemon Juice
Salt and Pepper   Butter

Time: 20–30 minutes

Method:

1. Rinse in cold water, dry with kitchen towel, season and fold fillets.
2. Place on plate.
3. Add a little lemon juice and pats of butter.
4. Cover with a bowl or aluminium foil.
5. Place over a pan of boiling water for 20–30 minutes.
6. Serve with liquor (juices that come from the fish) or sauce made using liquor.

10. POACHED WHOLE FISH AND CUTS

The term boiling as applied to fish is incorrect. Fish should be cooked under boiling point – this is called poaching.

Method:

1. Wash and clean fish using salt to remove any dark skin or blood.
2. Place fish in simmering salted water, sufficient to cover.
3. I tablespoonful vinegar may be added to each litre of water to flavour and firm the flesh.
4. Allow the fish to poach until cooked.
   Time: 7 minutes to each 500 g and 7 minutes over.
   Thick Fish: 10–15 minutes to each 500 g and 10 minutes over.
5. Drain thoroughly. Serve garnished with parsley and lemon and with a suitable sauce.

Test for readiness:

Whole fish.—This may be tested by inserting a knife in the middle of the back when flesh should leave the bone.

Cut of fish.—The flesh becomes opaque and a white curd will be seen between the flakes. The flesh should leave the bone easily.

II. POACHED FISH

Ingredients:

2 steaks *or* 4 fillets of Fish	Salt and Pepper
150 ml Milk	I tablespoonful chopped Parsley
15 g Butter	Squeeze Lemon Juice (optional)
15 g Flour	

Servings: 2
Time: 10 minutes

Method:

1. Rinse fish in cold water, dry with kitchen towel, season, roll if fillets.
2. Heat milk and butter, add fish, poach gently.
3. Remove to a serving dish, keep hot.
4. Blend flour with a little cooking liquid to a paste. Gradually add rest of liquid, return to pan and stir till boiling.
5. Add lemon and parsley to sauce and pour over fish.

12. STEWED SMOKED FISH

Cook as poached fish recipe, page 54, omitting salt.

13. FILLETS OF FISH WITH CREAM SAUCE

Ingredients:

4 fillets of Fish
Salt and Pepper
Squeeze Lemon Juice
Bouquet of herbs (page 27)

250 ml White Sauce (page 291)
1 tablespoonful Cream

Servings: 2
Time: 15 minutes

Method:

1. Rinse fillets in cold water, dry with kitchen towel.
2. Season, add lemon juice, roll tightly, skin side inside.
3. Put in pan with milk, bouquet of herbs and salt and pepper.
4. Simmer gently.
5. Remove fish to serving dish.
6. Make sauce using strained milk.
7. Add cream to sauce, coat fish.

14. BAKED WHITE FISH

Ingredients:

4 fillets of Fish
150 ml Milk
15 g Butter

Salt and Pepper
1 tablespoonful chopped Parsley

Servings: 2
Time: 15 minutes

Method:

1. Rinse fish in cold water, dry with kitchen towel, season, roll or fold in half.
2. Put in ovenproof dish, add milk, salt and pepper and butter in small pieces.
3. Bake.
4. Sprinkle with parsley and serve.
5. If thickened liquid is preferred, blend 1 teaspoonful of cornflour, add liquid from fish, bring to the boil, stirring all the time, and pour over fish.

15. BAKED SMOKED FISH

Cook as baked white fish recipe, above, omitting salt.

16. BAKED HALIBUT OR TURBOT

Ingredients:

2 small slices Halibut *or* Turbot
½ teacupful Milk *or* White Wine

Salt and Pepper
Butter

Servings: 4
Time: 15–20 minutes
Oven Temperature: 180°C, No. 4
Position in Oven: Middle shelf

Method:

1. Place halibut in a greased ovenproof dish with a cover. Season.
2. Pour milk or wine round.
3. Place small pats of butter on top, cover and bake.
Note: Mushrooms may be baked along with fish.

17. STUFFED COD STEAKS

Ingredients:

2 Cod steaks, tail-cut
25 g Butter

Salt and Pepper
Chopped Parsley

Stuffing:

25 g Breadcrumbs
½ teaspoonful chopped Parsley
Squeeze Lemon Juice

Pinch Mixed Herbs
Egg to bind

Servings: 2
Time: 15–20 minutes
Oven Temperature: 180°C, No. 4
Position in Oven: Middle shelf

Method:

1. Rinse steaks in cold water, dry with kitchen towel, cut out bone, season.
2. Mix stuffing, bind with egg.
3. Spread stuffing over fish.
4. Melt butter in a greased ovenproof dish, and place steaks in it. Bake.
5. Serve sprinkled with chopped parsley.

18. DRESSED STUFFED COD

Ingredients:

1 kg middle *or* tail-cut Cod
   (skinned and filleted)
50 g Butter
25 g Dried Breadcrumbs (page 476)

Pinch Mixed Herbs
Salt and Pepper
Lemon Juice

Stuffing:

50 g Breadcrumbs
Pinch Mixed Herbs

Lemon Rind
Egg to bind

Servings: 4–5
Time: 30 minutes
Oven Temperature: 190°C, No. 5
Position in Oven: Middle shelf

Method:

1. Rinse fish in cold water, dry with kitchen towel, season.
2. Mix stuffing, bind with egg.
3. Melt butter in a greased ovenproof dish, put in one fillet of fish.
4. Spread stuffing on top, cover with other fillet.
5. Mix breadcrumbs and herbs.
6. Baste fish with melted butter, cover with crumb mixture.
7. Bake, basting once or twice with melted butter.
8. Add lemon juice to butter in dish, before serving.

19. BAKED STUFFED SOLE

Ingredients:

4 fillets of Sole	2 tablespoonfuls Browned Crumbs (page 476)
25 g Butter	Chopped Parsley for garnish

Stuffing

25 g Breadcrumbs	1 teaspoonful chopped Parsley
1 Shallot *or* Spring Onion	Egg (beaten) *or* Milk to bind
25 g Shrimps	Salt and Pepper

Servings: 3–4
Time: 20 minutes
Oven Temperature: 180°C, No. 4
Position in Oven: Middle shelf

Method:

1. Chop onion finely. Chop shrimps roughly.
2. Mix ingredients for stuffing and bind with egg.
3. Rinse fillets in cold water, dry with kitchen towel.
4. Melt butter in a greased ovenproof dish.
5. Put in two fillets, spread stuffing on top.
6. Cover with other 2 fillets and sprinkle browned crumbs on top. Bake.
7. Before serving sprinkle with chopped parsley.

20. GRILLED FISH STEAKS

e.g. Cod, Halibut, Tuna or Turbot

Ingredients:

Required number of Fish steaks	Salt and Pepper
Butter for moistening	

Servings: According to size of steaks
Time: Cod and Halibut: 4–5 minutes each side
Turbot: 6–8 minutes

Method:

1. Heat grill.
2. Rinse steaks in cold water, dry with kitchen towel and season.
3. Put steaks in a greased grill pan without grid, dot with butter.
4. Cook until fish changes colour.
5. Turn over, repeat on other side.
6. Add a squeeze of lemon juice to liquid in pan and pour over steaks.

Note: Grilled mushrooms or tomato may accompany this dish.

21. GRILLED WHOLE SOLE OR PLAICE

Ingredients:

1 Sole *or* Plaice (skinned)	Salt and Pepper
25 g Butter	

Servings: 2

Time: 7 minutes each side

Temperature: Moderate

Method:

1. Rinse fish in cold water, dry with kitchen towel and season.
2. Put in a greased grill pan, dot with butter.
3. When cooked, turn and dot other side of fish with butter.
4. Add a little lemon juice to liquid in pan and pour over fish.

Note: Grilled mushrooms or tomato may be served as an accompaniment.

22. GRILLED FILLETS OF FISH

Ingredients:

Fillets of Sole, Plaice, Cod or Haddock	1 teaspoonful Lemon Juice
Salt and Pepper	Chopped Parsley
25 g Butter	

Time: 7–10 minutes

Temperature: Moderate

Method (1): Thin fillets of fish, e.g. Sole or Plaice

1. Rinse fillets in cold water, dry with kitchen towel and season.
2. Put in a greased grill pan without grid, skin side down.
3. Dot with butter.
4. Cook until lightly browned, remove.
5. Add a little lemon juice and parsley to liquid in the pan and pour over fish.

Method (2): Thick fillets of fish, e.g. Cod or Haddock

Make as above. It may be necessary to turn fillets once while cooking.

Note: Can be served with grilled tomatoes, mushrooms or rolls of bacon (page 476).

23. FRIED COD STEAK

Ingredients:

Cod steaks   Oil for frying
Seasoned Flour   Milk

Servings: I steak per person
Time: 3 minutes each side

Method:

1. Rinse fish in cold water, dry with kitchen towel.
2. Mix flour and seasoning, coat steaks.
3. Dip steaks in milk and again in flour.
4. Fry in hot oil on both sides until cooked.
5. Serve with lemon wedges or a suitable sauce.

24. FISH IN BATTER

Ingredients:

Fillets of Fish   Oil for frying
Coating Batter (page 474)

Servings: I fillet per person

Method:

1. Rinse fish in cold water, dry with kitchen towel.
2. Dip each piece in batter, fry in hot fat.
3. Drain, season. Serve with a suitable sauce.

25. FRIED FILLETS OF FISH

Ingredients:

Required number of fillets of Fish   Salt and Pepper
Egg (beaten)   Dried Breadcrumbs (page 477)
Lemon   Oil for frying

Method:

1. Rinse fillets in cold water, dry with kitchen towel.
2. Cut into a convenient size.
3. Dip each fillet into seasoned beaten egg, covering completely.
4. Coat fillets with dried breadcrumbs, pressing crumbs firmly into fish.
5. Fry on both sides in hot oil in frying pan, or deep-fry in hot oil until a light golden brown.
6. Drain well and serve with wedges of lemon and a suitable sauce.

26. RIBBON FILLETS, OR GOUJONS, OF SOLE

Cut fillets into long strips, tie in a loose knot and cook as for previous recipe.

27. FILLETS OF FISH MEUNIÈRE

Ingredients:

4 fillet of Fish
50 g Butter
Seasoned Flour

I teaspoonful chopped Parsley
I dessertspoonful Lemon Juice

Servings: 4

Method:

1. Rinse fillets in cold water and coat with flour.
2. Melt butter in frying pan without browning.
3. Fry fillets for 3 minutes on each side.
4. Add chopped parsley and lemon juice to butter in pan. Pour over fillets.

28. SOLE CHESTERFIELD

Ingredients:

4 fillets of Sole
10 g Butter
10 g Flour   } Panada
2 tablespoonfuls Milk
I Potato (which will later be discarded)

Salt and Pepper
I tablespoonful chopped Shrimps
Oil for frying
I Egg (beaten, for coating)
Seasoned Flour and Breadcrumbs

Servings: 2
Time: 10 minutes
Oven Temperature: 180°C, No. 4
Position in Oven: Middle shelf

Method:

1. Cut a cork-shaped piece of potato for each fillet.
2. Rinse fillets in cold water, dry with kitchen towel and roll round potato.
3. Put on greased baking tin, cover and cook, or poach in a little milk, for a few minutes until fish starts to firm. Allow to cool.
4. Make panada (page 292), add shrimps and seasoning. Cool.
5. Remove potato from fish and fill centre with shrimp mixture.
6. Roll in seasoned flour, egg and crumb, twice.
7. Deep-fry in hot oil till golden brown.

29. SOLE ORLY

Ingredients:

4 fillets of Sole
Oil for frying

Yeast Coating Batter (page 474)

Marinade:

½ tablespoonful Salad Oil
I teaspoonful mixed Vinegars
½ teaspoonful chopped Parsley

½ teaspoonful chopped Shallot
Cayenne Pepper and Salt

Method:

1. Rinse fillets in water, dry with kitchen towel. Soak for 10 minutes in marinade.
2. Dip fillets in batter and deep-fry in hot oil till golden brown.

30. BAKED FILLETS OF FISH (WITH SAUCE)

Ingredients:

4 fillets of Fish	Lemon Juice
Salt and Pepper	250 ml suitable Sauce

Servings: 2
Time: 10–15 minutes
Oven Temperature: 180°C, No. 4
Position in Oven: Middle shelf

Method:

1. Rinse fillets in cold water, dry, season and sprinkle with lemon juice.
2. Fold or roll, skin side inside.
3. Put on greased ovenproof dish. Cover with lid or greased paper. Bake.
4. Serve with suitable sauce such as parsley or egg sauce (page 291).

31. SOLE MAÎTRE D'HÔTEL

Follow previous recipe and coat with maître d'hôtel sauce (page 293).

32. FISH MORNAY

Ingredients:

4 fillets of White Fish	30–50 g Cheese (grated)
Salt and Pepper	250 ml White Sauce (page 291)
250 g Potato Purée	

Servings: 2–3
Time: 8–10 minutes
Oven Temperature: 180°C, No. 4
Position in Oven: Middle shelf

Method:

1. Rinse fillets in cold water, dry with kitchen towel and season.
2. Fold, put in greased ovenproof dish, cover and bake.
3. Pipe border of potato down each side of dish.
4. Add cheese to hot white sauce, coat fish.
5. Sprinkle a little cheese on top – brown under grill.

33. SOLE WITH SHRIMPS

Ingredients:

4 fillets of Sole	1 teaspoonful chopped Parsley
Salt and Pepper	250 ml Shrimp Sauce (page 293)
50 g Shrimps	

Servings: 2
Time: 15 minutes
Oven Temperature: 180°C, No. 4
Position in Oven: Middle shelf

Method:

1. Rinse fillets in cold water, dry with kitchen towel and season.
2. Chop shrimps, add parsley.
3. Spread mixture on fillets, fold over.
4. Place on greased ovenproof dish, cover, bake.
5. Coat or serve with shrimp sauce.

34. SOLE WITH ASPARAGUS

Asparagus can be used in place of shrimps. Serve with Dutch sauce (page 292) and garnish with cooked asparagus spears.

35. BAKED FISH WITH MUSHROOM STUFFING

Ingredients:

4 fillets of White Fish	Lemon Juice
50 g Mushrooms	250 ml White Sauce (page 291)
15 g Butter	2 tablespoonfuls Cream
Salt and Pepper	Chopped Parsley and Paprika

Servings: 2
Time: 15 minutes
Oven Temperature: 180°C, No. 4
Position in Oven: Middle shelf

Method:

1. Rinse fillets in cold water, dry with kitchen towel and season.
2. Wash mushrooms, chop, fry in butter, season.
3. Put mushrooms on top of fillets, fold over.
4. Place on greased ovenproof dish.
5. Squeeze lemon on top, cover, bake.
6. Add cream to hot white sauce, coat fillets.
7. Serve with chopped parsley and paprika.

36. SOLE VÉRONIQUE

Ingredients:

4 fillets of Sole	1 tablespoonful White Wine
50 g green Grapes	Salt and Pepper
250 ml Dutch Sauce (page 292)	

Servings: 2
Time: 15 minutes
Oven Temperature: 180°C, No. 4
Position in Oven: Middle shelf

Method:

1. Skin and stone grapes. Lay aside a few for garnish, slice remainder.
2. Rinse fillets in cold water, dry with kitchen towel and season.

3. Put grapes on top of fillets, fold over and put on a greased ovenproof dish.

4. Cover with greased paper and bake for 10 minutes.

5. Drain, add wine to hot Dutch sauce.

6. Coat fish and garnish with grapes, or add grapes to the sauce.

37. SOLE AMÉRICAINE

Ingredients:

4 fillets of Sole	Salt and Pepper
250 ml Tomato Sauce (page 297)	2 tablespoonfuls Sherry

Servings: 2

Time: 10 minutes

Oven Temperature: 180°C, No. 4

Position in Oven: Middle shelf

Method:

1. Rinse fillets in cold water, dry with kitchen towel, season and fold in half.

2. Place on a greased ovenproof dish.

3. Sprinkle with sherry and cover with greased paper and bake for 10 minutes.

4. Drain and coat with tomato sauce (page 297).

38. SOLE AFRICAINE

Ingredients:

4 fillets of Sole	50 g Rice (boiled, page 475)
1 Banana	Gherkins
250 ml Poivrade Sauce (page 294)	Chillies
1 Egg (beaten)	Dried Breadcrumbs (page 477)

Servings: 2

Time: 10 minutes

Method:

1. Make poivrade sauce.

2. Halve banana widthwise. Cut one half in slices and toss rounds in melted butter.

3. Cut the other half in 4 by the length. Cover in egg and breadcrumbs and fry.

4. Rinse fillets in cold water, dry with kitchen towel, brush with oil and grill, put slices of banana on fillets and heat through.

5. Put on a serving dish. Coat with sauce and serve with boiled rice.

7. Garnish with fried banana, gherkins and chillies.

39. SOLE NORMANDE

Ingredients:

4 fillets of Sole	3 tablespoonfuls Cream
Salt and Pepper	1 dessertspoonful chopped Parsley
2 tablespoonfuls Cider	

Servings: 2–4
Time: 15 minutes
Oven Temperature: 180°C, No. 4
Position in Oven: Middle shelf

Method:

1. Fold fillets, place on a greased ovenproof dish, season.
2. Pour cider over fish, cover, cook for 10 minutes.
3. Remove cover, pour on cream, bake for 5 minutes.
4. Sprinkle with chopped parsley.

40. SOLE CAPRICE

Ingredients:

4 fillets of Sole	Salt and Pepper
25 g Butter	1 dessertspoonful Lemon Juice
A little Chutney	Chopped Parsley
1 Banana	

Servings: 2–4
Time: 10–15 minutes

Method:

1. Rinse fillets in cold water, dry with kitchen towel and season.
2. Put in grill pan, dot with butter, grill.
3. Halve banana by length, grill until soft.
4. Put fillets on serving dish, spread with chutney.
5. Put banana on each fillet.
6. Add butter to grill pan, heat, add lemon juice, pour over, sprinkle with parsley.

41. FISH PORTUGAISE

Ingredients:

4 fillets of White Fish	1 tablespoonful Browned Crumbs
2 Tomatoes	(page 476)

Stuffing:

25 g Breadcrumbs	1 teaspoonful finely chopped Onion
1 tablespoonful Cheese (grated)	Salt and Pepper
1 teaspoonful melted Butter	

Servings: 2–4
Time: 20–30 minutes
Oven Temperature: 180°C, No. 4
Position in Oven: Middle shelf

Method:

1. Rinse fillets in cold water, dry with kitchen towel.
2. Chop onion and blanch it.
3. Place 2 fillets in a greased ovenproof dish.

3. Mix all stuffing ingredients, cover fillets.
4. Place remaining 2 fillets on top, season, cover with sliced tomato.
5. Sprinkle with browned crumbs. Bake.

42. STEAMED FISH SOUFFLÉ

Ingredients:

40 g Butter	1 teaspoonful Vinegar
40 g Flour	Salt and Pepper
250 ml Milk	200 g Haddock *or* Whiting (cooked)
3 Egg Yolks, plus 1 White (beaten)	1 teaspoonful Anchovy Essence
250 ml Anchovy Sauce (page 291)	*or* 1 teaspoonful Fish Sauce (Asian)

Servings: 4
Time: 40 minutes

Method:

1. Flake fish finely.
2. Melt butter, add flour, gradually add milk and bring to boil, stirring all the time.
3. Add seasoning, flavourings and fish.
4. Add egg yolks, one at a time, beating well.
5. Fold in stiffly beaten whites.
6. Put into prepared soufflé dish or greased bowl.
7. Place in large pan, with enough water to come one-third way up dish or bowl.
8. Steam steadily.
9. Turn out, serve with anchovy sauce.

Note: Prepare dish by placing a round of greased paper to fit base of dish and grease. Tie a double band of greaseproof paper round outside of dish to come about 4 cm above top of dish and grease inside top edge.

43. BAKED FISH SOUFFLÉ (1)

Ingredients:

150 g Haddock (cooked)	Salt and Pepper
25 g Butter	1 teaspoonful Anchovy Essence
25 g Flour	*or* 1 teaspoonful Fish Sauce (Asian)
250 ml Milk	1 teaspoonful Vinegar
3 Eggs (separated)	

Servings: 3
Time: 20–30 minutes
Oven Temperature: 220°C, No. 7
Position in Oven: Middle shelf
Size of Dish: 1 litre

Method:

1. Flake fish finely using a fork.
2. Melt butter, add flour, gradually add milk and bring to boil, stirring all the time.
3. Add fish, seasoning and flavourings.

4. Beat in egg yolks, one at a time.
5. Fold in stiffly beaten egg whites.
6. Put into a greased soufflé dish or a deep, greased, ovenproof dish.
7. Bake until brown and well risen.

44. BAKED FISH SOUFFLÉ (2)

Ingredients:

200 g Smoked *or* White Fish (cooked)	25 g Butter
Salt and Pepper	250 ml Milk
2 Eggs (separated)	25 g Semolina

Servings: 3
Time: 20–30 minutes
Oven Temperature: 220°C, No. 7
Position in Oven: Middle shelf
Size of Dish: 1 litre

Method:

1. Heat milk, sprinkle in semolina, stir till boiling, simmer 5 minutes.
2. Add butter, finely flaked fish, seasoning and egg yolks.
3. Beat whites stiffly, fold lightly into mixture.
4. Put into a deep, greased ovenproof dish, bake till well risen and browned.
Note: If white fish is used add 1 teaspoonful each of vinegar and Worcester sauce before folding in egg whites.

45. STEAMED FISH PUDDING

Ingredients:

250 g filleted White Fish	Salt and Pepper
75 g Breadcrumbs	2 Eggs (separated)
1 teaspoonful chopped Parsley	

Servings: 3
Time: 1 hour

Method:

1. Cut fish into small pieces and add breadcrumbs, parsley and seasoning.
2. Bind with the egg yolks.
3. Fold stiffly-beaten whites into the mixture.
4. Put into a greased bowl, steam.
5. Serve with parsley sauce (page 291) or anchovy sauce (page 291).

46. FISH CUSTARD

Ingredients:

250 g filleted White Fish	2–3 Eggs (lightly beaten)
1 tablespoonful seasoned Flour	Salt and Pepper
500 ml Milk	

Servings: 3
Time: I hour
Oven Temperature: 180°C, No. 4
Position in Oven: Middle shelf

Method:

1. Cut fish in pieces
2. Dip in seasoned flour.
3. Place in a greased ovenproof dish.
4. Heat milk slightly, pour over lightly beaten eggs.
5. Season and strain over fish.
6. Place dish in a baking tin with a little water in the base.
7. Bake till set and brown.

47. FISH PIE

Ingredients:

250 g cooked White Fish   250 ml Parsley Sauce (page 291)
300 g Creamed Potatoes (page 194)   Salt and Pepper

Servings: 3–4
Time: 20 minutes
Oven Temperature: 180°C, No. 4
Position in Oven: Middle shelf

Method:

1. Flake fish using a fork, add to parsley sauce, place in a deep, greased, oven-proof dish.
2. Cover with creamed potatoes, smooth and mark with a fork.
3. Brush with milk. Heat thoroughly till browned on top.

48. SCALLOPED FISH

Ingredients:

200 g cooked Fish   25 g Dried Breadcrumbs (page 477)
250 ml White Sauce (page 291)   *or* 25g Crushed Potato Crisps

Servings: 3
Time: 10–15 minutes
Oven Temperature: 180°C, No. 4
Position in Oven: Middle shelf

Method:

1. Flake fish roughly, season.
2. Put in a greased ovenproof dish or scallop shells. Coat with sauce.
3. Sprinkle dried breadcrumbs or crushed potato crisps on top.
4. Bake for 15 minutes.

Note: Parsley, cheese or egg sauce can be used.

49. **KEDGEREE**

Ingredients:

250 g cooked White *or* Smoked Fish   25 g Butter
100 g Rice (boiled, page 475)   Salt and Pepper
1 Egg (hard-boiled)   Chopped Parsley

Servings: 4

Method:

1. Flake fish using a fork.
2. Melt butter, add all ingredients.
3. Stir until well heated through.
4. Mound on a hot dish, sprinkle with parsley.

50. **FISH CAKES**

Ingredients:

250 g cooked White *or* Smoked Fish   Salt and Pepper
250 g cooked Potatoes   1 Egg (beaten)
25 g melted Butter   Dried Breadcrumbs (page 477)
Oil for frying   *or* Fish Dressing

Servings: 3–4

Method:

1. Remove skin and bone from fish.
2. Mash potato, mix with fish, seasoning and butter.
3. Form mixture into four even-sized cakes on a floured chopping board.
4. Brush with egg and coat in dried breadcrumbs.
5. Fry in hot oil in a frying pan for 3–5 minutes on each side till golden brown.
6. Drain and serve.

51. **FISH AND RICE CAKES**

Ingredients:

50 g Rice (boiled, page 475)   1 tablespoonful Tomato Sauce (page
150 g cooked White Fish   297)
1 Egg (beaten)   Salt and Pepper
Dried Breadcrumbs (page 477)   Oil for frying
or Fish Dressing

Servings: 3–4

Method:

1. Flake fish, mix with rice, season, add tomato sauce (page 297) and
   sufficient egg to make a firm mixture.
2. Form mixture into four even-sized cakes on a floured chopping board.
3. Brush with egg and coat in dried breadcrumbs.
4. Fry in hot oil in a frying pan for 3–5 minutes on each side till golden brown.
5. Drain and serve.

52. FISH CROQUETTES

Ingredients:

250 g cooked White *or* Smoked Fish

Salt and Pepper

or ½ teaspoonful Anchovy Essence

½ teaspoonful Fish Sauce (Asian)

Egg (beaten for coating)

25 g Butter ⎫
25 g Flour ⎬ Panada
100 ml Milk ⎭

Dried Breadcrumbs (page 477)

or Fish Dressing

Servings: 4

Method:

1. Make panada (page 292).
2. Add finely flaked fish, seasoning and anchovy essence.
3. Spread on plate, allow to cool.
4. Form mixture into four even-sized croquettes on a floured chopping board.
5. Brush with egg and coat in dried breadcrumbs.
6. Fry in hot oil in a frying pan for 5 minutes till golden brown.
7. Drain and serve.

53. RUSSIAN FISH PIE

Ingredients:

100 g Flaky *or* Rough Puff
  Pastry (page 309)

200 g White *or* Smoked Fish (cooked)

125 ml Anchovy Sauce (page 291)

Salt and Pepper

1 Gherkin (chopped)

1 teaspoonful Capers (chopped)

1 hard boiled Egg (chopped)

Servings: 4–6

Time: 40 minutes

Oven Temperature: 230°C, No. 8, for 10 minutes

180°C, No. 4, for 30 minutes

Position in Oven: Middle shelf

Method:

1. Flake fish, add sauce and mix together with other ingredients.
2. Roll pastry into a 25 cm square.
3. Put fish mixture on centre, wet edges of pastry and fold as an envelope.
4. Brush with egg, decorate with pastry leaves and bake in hot oven.

54. SALMON PATTIES (OR VOL-AU-VENTS)

Ingredients:

200 g Puff Pastry (page 310)

100–150 g Salmon (cooked)

250 ml Béchamel Sauce (page 293)

Salt and Pepper

Servings: 8 Patties

Time: 20–25 minutes

Oven Temperature: 180°C, No. 4

Position in Oven: Middle shelf

Method:

    1. Make patty (vol-au-vent) cases (page 311).

    2. Make the sauce, add flaked salmon and season: fill patty cases and put on the tops. Heat thoroughly before serving.

    Note: Shellfish may be used in the same way.

55. POACHED SALMON, TROUT OR SEA TROUT

Ingredients:

    Water to cover

    I level tablespoonful Salt

    I tablespoonful Vinegar – whole fish only   } to each litre water

Method (1) To serve hot:

    1. Wash fish, dry with kitchen towel and put in boiling salted water to cover.

    2. Lower heat and poach (page 54).

    3. Drain thoroughly.

    4. Serve with sliced cucumber, and Dutch sauce (page 293) or Hollandaise sauce (page 295).

Method (2) To serve cold:

    1. Wash fish, put in boiling salted water to cover.

    2. Bring back to boiling point, boil for 2 minutes and turn off heat.

    3. Leave in water till cold.

    4. Serve with salad and mayonnaise (page 220).

Method (3) Frozen Salmon, Trout or Sea Trout:

    1. Put frozen fish into boiling salted water.

    2. Bring back to the boil, and complete cooking by either method 1 or 2 from point 2 onwards.

56. FRIED SALMON STEAK

Ingredients:

Salmon steaks, 2–3 cm thick   250 ml Cucumber Sauce

Seasoned Flour   (page 291)

Butter *or* Oil for frying

Time: 4–5 minutes each side

Method:

    1. Dip steaks in seasoned flour.

    2. Melt butter until hot without allowing to brown.

    3. Fry steaks gently.

    4. Serve with cucumber sauce (page 291).

57. GRILLED SALMON STEAK

Ingredients:

2 Salmon steaks (2 cm thick)   Sliced Cucumber

Salt and Pepper   25 g Butter

Servings: 2

Time: 10–12 minutes

Temperature: Moderate

Method:

1. Place steaks in grill pan, season, dot with butter.
2. Cook 4 minutes, turn, season, add butter.
3. Cook 6 minutes. Remove fish. Add a little lemon juice to liquid in pan and pour over.
4. Serve with sliced cucumber.

Note: Bone should leave flesh easily when cooked.

58. SALMON MAYONNAISE

Ingredients:

500 g cooked Salmon	Fine Cress
250 ml Mayonnaise (page 220)	Radish (sliced)
1 tablespoonful Water	Crisp Lettuce Leaves
2 level teaspoonfuls Gelatine	Tomato
Cucumber (sliced)	

Servings: 4–6

Method:

1. Remove skin and bone from salmon.
2. Dissolve gelatine in water and add to mayonnaise.
3. Coat salmon with mayonnaise.
4. Decorate with cucumber, radish and cress.
5. Serve on a bed of shredded lettuce.
6. Surround with tomato, radish and cucumber.

59. FRIED TROUT

This recipe is suitable for small fish

Ingredients:

Trout	Seasoned Flour
Butter *or* Oil for frying	

Method (1):

1. Clean trout. Dip in seasoned flour.
2. Fry 4–6 minutes on each side – time will vary according to size of fish.

Method (2):

1. Split fish down back, remove bone.
2. Dip in seasoned flour, fry for 3 minutes on flesh side.
3. Turn, fry for 4–6 minutes on skin side.
4. Serve with a suitable sauce.

60. **TROUT MEUNIÈRE**

Ingredients:

I Trout   Butter *or* Oil for frying
Seasoned Flour

Beurre Noir:

25 g Butter   I dessertspoonful White Wine Vinegar
I dessertspoonful Parsley (chopped)   *or*   Lemon Juice

Method:

1. Clean trout. If large, score sides, or split and bone.
2. Dip in seasoned flour, fry in hot oil for 6 minutes on each side till golden brown.
3. Put on serving dish, keep hot.
4. Melt 25g butter, allow to brown, add vinegar or lemon juice gradually.
5. Add parsley and pour over trout.

61. **BAKED TROUT**

Ingredients:

Trout   Bay Leaf (optional)
Lemon Juice

Servings: Depending on size
Time: 20–30 minutes
Oven Temperature: 180°C, No. 4
Position in Oven: Middle shelf

Method:

1. Clean trout.
2. Put bay leaf and a squeeze of lemon juice in body.
3. Wrap in foil.
4. Bake.
5. Serve with maître d'hôtel butter (page 110).

62. **WHITEBAIT**

Ingredients:

Required weight Whitebait   Flour
Oil for deep-frying   Brown Bread and Butter
Lemon   Salt

Method:

1. Wash in cold water, iced if possible.
2. Drain.
3. Dry.
5. Sprinkle generously with flour.
6. Place in frying basket, shake to get rid of surplus flour.
7. Fry for 3 minutes in deep, hot oil. Remove.
8. Reheat fat, replace fish for I minute to crisp.

9. Drain. Sprinkle with salt.

10. Serve with lemon wedges and bread.

Note: If a large quantity is being fried, do first frying in batches, all together in second frying. Use a thermostatically controlled deep-fat frier.

63. BOILED COD ROE

Ingredients:

1 Cod Roe   250 ml Parsley Sauce (page 291)

Time: 20–30 minutes

Method:

1. Wash roe.
2. Tie in cloth or wrap in aluminium foil.
3. Put into boiling salted water, simmer 20–30 minutes.
4. Skin and slice.
5. Coat with parsley sauce, if liked.

64. FRIED COD ROE

Ingredients:

500 g boiled Cod Roe   Oil for frying
Seasoned Flour

Servings: 3–4 according to size

Method:

1. Slice roe and toss in seasoned flour.
2. Fry in hot oil in a frying pan until browned.

Note: May be served with bacon, in which case roe is fried after bacon in bacon fat.

65. SALT FISH (LING OR COD)

Ingredients:

500 g Ling *or* Cod   250 ml Parsley Sauce (page 291)

Method:

1. Cut fish into squares and soak overnight.
2. Remove from soaking water and wash. Dry with kitchen towel.
3. Put in fresh cold water and boil 1½–2 hours.
4. Drain well and remove bones and skin.
5. Flake lightly and put in hot serving dish.
6. Coat with parsley sauce.

66. CURRIED FISH

Ingredients:

500 g fillet Fish   250 ml Curry Sauce (page 297)
200 g Rice (boiled, page 475)

Servings: 4
Time: 7–10 minutes

Method:

1. Cut fish into medium-sized pieces.
2. Put into hot curry sauce.
3. Simmer gently.
4. Put into serving dish, serve rice separately.

SHELLFISH

67. BOILED LOBSTER OR CRAB

These should be chosen live and be heavy for their size

Method:

1. Leave crab or lobster in very cold water for 20 minutes.
   Or put in freezer for 5–10 minutes.
2. Plunge into boiling salted water (2 tablespoonfuls of salt for each litre water).
3. Boil according to size. 10 minutes for first 400 g and 3 minutes for each further 400 g. Overcooked lobster will be tough. When cooked, shell is red and the antennae come off easily when pulled.
4. Allow to cool in the water.

68. DRESSED CRAB

Ingredients:

1 cooked Crab	1–2 tablespoonfuls Breadcrumbs
Salt and Pepper	Chopped Parsley
Mayonnaise	Egg Yolk (hard-boiled)

Method:

1. Remove small claws and lay aside. Remove large claws, take out flesh.
2. Take off the apron, break up and remove white flesh. Discard grey gills.
3. Take out all soft flesh from shell.
4. Mix soft flesh and white flesh, add salt, pepper and mayonnaise to taste.
5. Add 1–2 tablespoonfuls breadcrumbs depending on size of crab.
6. Polish shell with a little oil, replace mixture in shell.
7. Garnish with white flesh, chopped parsley and hard-boiled egg yolk, chopped.

69. DRESSED LOBSTER

Ingredients:

1 cooked Lobster	Chopped Parsley
Mayonnaise *or* Salad Dressing	

Servings: 2

Method (1):

    1. Remove small claws, lay aside for garnish.

    2. Remove large claws, crack open and take out the flesh.

    3. Halve lobster down back of shell; remove stomach bag, grey gills and intestine; discard.

    4. Take white flesh from tail and grey creamy matter from body.

    5. Mix all flesh in a bowl with a little seasoning and mayonnaise.

    6. Put into washed shells.

    7. Serve as you would dressed crab (page 74).

Method (2):

    1. Remove meat from shell. Cut up and serve with salad and dressing.

70. GRILLED LOBSTER

Ingredients:

1 part-cooked Lobster (page 74)	Salt and Pepper
25 g Butter (melted)	Chopped Parsley
Lemon	

Servings: 2

Time: 8–10 minutes

Method:

    1. Follow method for boiled lobster (page 74). Remove lobster from cooking water a few minutes before full cooking time is up.

    2. Remove claws. Crack large claws and remove flesh.

    3. Split lobster down back. Discard stomach bag, grey gills and intestine.

    4. Place on grill pan, brush with butter, lay claw flesh on top, brush with butter.

    5. Season, put under hot grill.

    6. Serve with a squeeze of lemon, melted butter and chopped parsley.

71. LOBSTER NEWBURG

Ingredients:

1 Lobster (cooked, page 74)	150 ml Double Cream
25–50 g Butter	2 Egg Yolks
2 tablespoonfuls Sherry	75 g Rice (boiled, page 475)

Servings: 4

Method:

    1. Follow method for boiled lobster. Remove claws, split lobster down back.

    2. Remove flesh from claws and tail, discard intestine, grey gills and stomach bag.

    3. Melt butter, add sliced flesh and heat through.

    4. Season, add sherry and creamy matter from body.

    5. Cook for 3 minutes. Remove and keep hot.

    6. Add cream and egg yolks to butter in pan, whisk until creamy, without boiling.

    7. Strain sauce over lobster.

    8. Serve with a border of hot, boiled rice.

72. LOBSTER THERMIDOR

Ingredients:

1 medium Lobster (cooked, page 74)	1 large Tomato
25 g Butter	150 ml White Sauce (page 291)
½ teaspoonful Onion (finely chopped)	2 tablespoonfuls Cream
½ glass White Wine	Parmesan Cheese (grated)
50 g Mushrooms	

Servings: 2

Method:

1. Follow method for boiled lobster. Split lobster by length.
2. Remove flesh from shell and claws. Discard intestine, grey gills and stomach bag.
3. Dice tail flesh roughly.
4. Heat butter, add onion, cook 3–4 minutes.
5. Add lobster and white wine, simmer 5 minutes.
6. Skin tomato, remove seeds and chop. Add finely chopped mushrooms.
7. Cook all slowly for 5 minutes.
8. Season, add sauce and cream.
9. Put into half shells, sprinkle with cheese and grill until crisp.

73. SCALLOPS

Choice.—Choose those heavy for their size.

To Open.—Place 2–3 minutes in a warm oven, when shell will open.

To Prepare.—Remove black part, also grey gills. Cut meat from shell, wash in several waters to remove sand.

Cooking.—Scallops should be cooked till they are firm on the outside but still tender on the inside and springy to the touch.

74. BAKED SCALLOPS

Ingredients:

4 Scallops	250 ml Béchamel Sauce (page 292)
½ teacup White Wine	25 g Cheese (grated)
1 small Shallot *or* piece Onion	

Servings: 2

Time: Approx. 10 minutes

Oven Temperature: 190°C, No. 5

Position in Oven: Middle shelf

Method:

1. Open, remove from shells, and clean scallops and shells in several waters.
2. Bake in a covered pot in white wine and chopped shallot till cooked (about 8–10 minutes, scallops cook quickly).
3. Remove cooked scallops and slice.
4. Add wine and shallot liquor to béchamel sauce, mix in cooked scallop slices.
5. Season, divide the mixture into shells.
6. Sprinkle with cheese, grill until brown.

75. **FRIED SCALLOPS**

Ingredients:

Required number, allowing 2 per person Salt and Pepper
Beaten Egg   Tomato Sauce (page 297)
Dried Breadcrumbs (page 477)   Butter, for frying

Time: 1–2 minutes each side depending on size

Method:

1. Prepare scallops by removing black part and grey gills.
2. Wash well, remove red part.
3. Cut in two across height of scallop, if large.
4. Dip scallops and red part in egg, and coat in seasoned dried breadcrumbs.
5. Fry scallop pieces and red pieces quickly in melted butter.
6. Serve with tomato sauce.

76. **SCALLOPS AU GRATIN**

Ingredients:

4 Scallops   25 g Butter
250 ml Milk   25 g Flour
1 Bay Leaf   50 g Cheese (grated)
Salt and Pepper   3 tablespoonfuls Breadcrumbs

Servings: 2

Method:

1. Wash scallops.
2. Cut in two across height of scallop, if large.
3. Place milk, bay leaf and seasoning in pan, simmer for 10 minutes, add scallops and simmer till they are firm outside and tender inside (about 5 minutes).
4. Strain the milk from the scallops and reserve.
5. Melt butter, add flour and then gradually add strained milk from scallops.
6. Stir until boiling. Remove from heat and add cheese. Stir till cheese is melted. Add scallops.
7. Put mixture in scallop shells or a flat, greased ovenproof dish.
8. Sprinkle with breadcrumbs, grill until brown.

77. **FRIED SCAMPI OR DUBLIN BAY PRAWNS**

Ingredients:

Fresh *or* frozen Scampi   Dried Breadcrumbs (page 477)
1 Egg (beaten)   Oil for frying
Seasoned Flour   Tartare Sauce (page 298)

Method:

1. Shell. Wash, dry, toss in seasoned flour.
2. Coat in egg and dried breadcrumbs.
3. Deep-fry in hot oil until lightly browned. Drain thoroughly.
4. Serve with tartare sauce.

Note: If frozen scampi are used, thaw completely before coating.

78. POTTED SHRIMPS

Ingredients:

250 g Shrimps (cooked *or* frozen)   Pinch Nutmeg
50 g Butter (clarified page 477)   Salt and Pepper
Pinch Powdered Mace

Method:

1. Shell shrimps.
2. Melt butter in pan.
3. Add all ingredients, heat in butter for 2–3 minutes.
4. Rub through sieve or strainer, or pound.
5. Put into jars and cover closely with clarified butter.
Note: If frozen shrimps are used, thaw completely before using.

79. MUSSELS

Mussels are in season all year but are best in the winter months.

To prepare:

Mussels must be fresh. If shell is open tap it, and if it does not close discard.
Scrub and scrape shells, wash thoroughly in several waters until water is clear.
All traces of sand must be removed.

80. MUSSELS MARINIÈRE

Ingredients:

2 litres Mussels   Salt and Pepper
1 Onion   6 tablespoonfuls White Wine *or* Stock
Bouquet of Herbs (page 27)   25 g Butter
Chopped Parsley   2 level teaspoonfuls Flour

Servings: 4

Method:

1. Prepare mussels.
2. Put mussels, chopped onion, wine and seasonings into a pan, cover.
3. Bring to the boil shaking pan occasionally. Simmer 3 minutes. Check carefully and discard any mussels that do not open.
4. Pour liquid into a small pan.
5. Cream butter and flour and stir into liquid over a low heat. Bring to boil and add chopped parsley.
6. Remove one shell and the beard from each mussel.
7. Put mussels on serving dish and pour sauce over.

MEAT AND OFFAL

MEAT

A GUIDE TO CUTS AND COOKING METHODS

BEEF

Ref.	Cuts	Methods of Cooking
A	Neck or Sticking Piece	Manufacturing purposes
B	Fore-knap Bone	Stock
C	Fore-hough	Stock, soup and stew
D	Gullet	Stew
E	Brisket Braising Steak	Rolled – boil fresh or pickled Stew, braise
F G	Thick Runner Thin Runner	Boil, soup
H	Shoulder	Stew, pies
I J	Flank (Nineholes) Flank (Top Rib)	Boil, soup
K	Flank (Face of)	Manufacturing purposes
L	Rib Roast Rib Eye Steak	Roast on bone or rolled Grill, fry
M	Sirloin Roast Sirloin Steaks	Roast on bone or rolled Grill
N	Pope's Eye	Grill, fry, braise or roast
O	Rump – Silverside Topside Side of Rump	Slow-roast, boil fresh or pickled Stew, pot roast or braise Stew, pot roast or braise
P	Hind Hough	Stock, soup, stew
Q	Hind-knap Bone Tail	Stock Soup, stew

From the inside of the animal	
Fillet	Grill, fry, braise or roast
Skirt of Beef	Soup, stew
Kidney	Soup, stew
Liver	Soup, stew
Tripe	Soup, stew

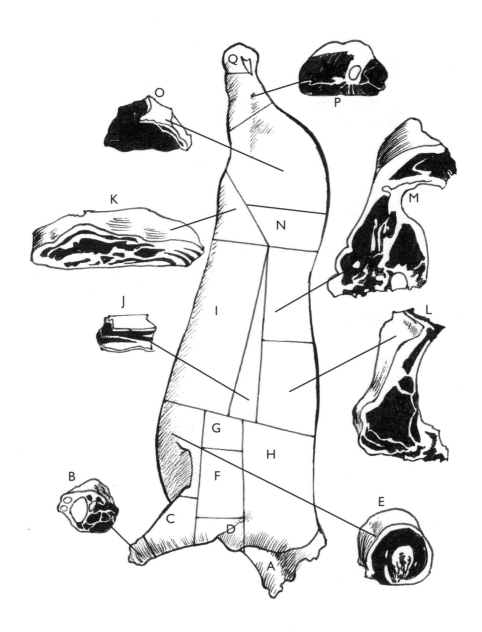

LAMB OR MUTTON

Ref.	Cuts	Methods of Cooking
A	Neck	Boil, stew, use for broths
B	Shank	Soup
C	Breast	Stew, stuff and roast
D	Shoulder (Runner Cut)	Boil, stew, braise, roast
E	Shoulder (Back Rib Cut)	Boil, stew, braise, roast
F	Loin – Cutlet End, Best End of Neck or Single Loin Chop	Grill, fry, bake, roast in a piece
G	Loin – Double Loin Chop	Grill, fry, bake, roast in a piece
H	Flank	Stew, soup
I	Gigot (Leg) Chump End	Roast, braise, boil. Chops: grill, fry or bake
J	Gigot (Leg) Shank End	Roast, braise, boil. Chops: grill, fry or bake

From the inside of the animal	
Kidney	Grill, fry, stew
Liver	Grill, fry, stew

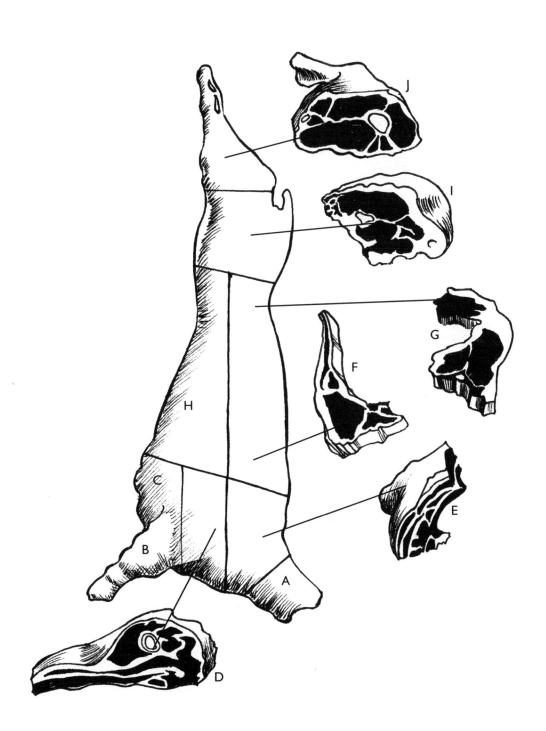

PORK

Ref.	Cuts	Methods of Cooking
A	Head	Can be boiled or roasted, used for potting
B	Trotter	Use for Potted Hough (page 104)
C	Fore Hough	Stock, soup, boiling
D	Flank	Salted and boiled or sliced thinly and use for pies
E	Gigot (Leg)	Roast. Cut into chops, fry, grill, bake
F	Trotter	Use for Potted Hough (page 104)
G	Loin (Double Loin) Chop	Fry, grill, bake, roast in a piece
H	Loin (Single Loin) Chop	Fry, grill, bake, roast in a piece
I	Shoulder	Roast, stew, boned and rolled roast. Salted and boiled

From the inside of the animal	
Kidney	Grill, fry, stew
Fillet	Roast, fry, stew

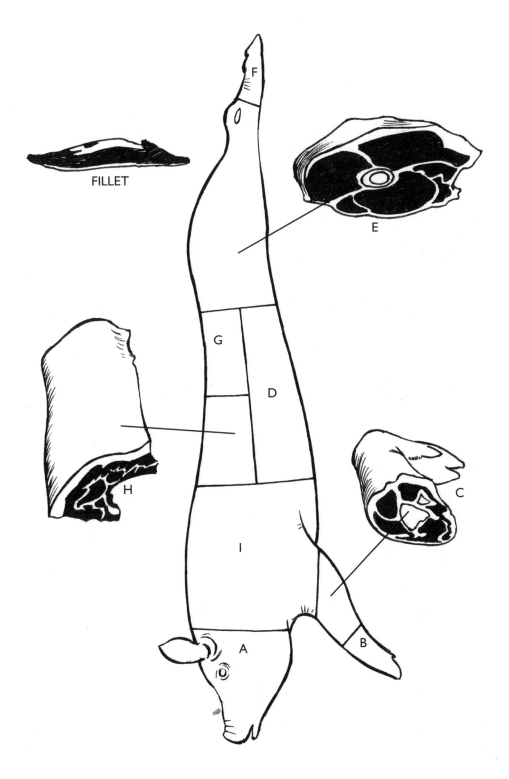

FILLET

F

E

G

D

H

C

I

B

A

BOILING

I. BOILING CHART

This is a method suitable for coarser cuts of meat, i.e. meat that contains a lot of connective tissue. The term boiling is a bit of a misnomer because although the cooking water is brought to the boil, the meat should be simmered slowly rather than boiled or it will harden. The pan should be big enough to cover the meat completely with water.

The shape of the meat will affect cooking time. A thick piece will take longer to cook than a thin piece of equal weight.

Meat	Cuts	Guide to Cooking Time	Accompaniments
Beef Fresh cuts, 2 kg or under	*Thin:* Nineholes, Runner, Flank	1¼ hrs for 1st kg plus 40 mins for each added kg	Carrot and Turnip
	Thick or Rolled: Silverside, Brisket	1½ hrs for 1st kg plus 1¼ hrs for each added kg	
Cuts over 2 kg	As above	50 mins per kg and 50 mins over	As above
Salt cuts, 2 kg or under	Brisket, Silverside, Topside	1½ hrs for each kg	Carrot and Turnip, Kale or Cabbage, Savoury Balls
Salt cuts over 2 kg	As above	1 hr 10 mins per kg plus 1 hr	As above
Mutton/Lamb Cuts 2 kg or under	Neck, Flank, Shoulder, Leg	1½ hrs for 1st kg plus 40 mins for each added kg	Carrot and Turnip, Caper or Onion Sauce
Cuts over 2 kg	As above	40 mins per kg plus 40 mins	As above
Pork, Salt Cuts, 2 kg or under	Flank, Shoulder, Leg	1½ hrs for each kg	Carrot and Turnip, Parsley Sauce, Pease Pudding
Cuts over 2 kg	As above	1 hr 10 mins per kg plus 1 hr	As above
Ham 2 kg or under	Gammon (Middle, Corner, Prime collar Fore-hough) *Boned and Rolled*	1½ hrs for each kg	Mustard or Parsley Sauce, Butterbeans or Peas
Cuts over 2 kg	As above	1 hr per kg plus 1 hr	As above

2. BOILED BEEF

Ingredients:

Meat for boiling (e.g. Brisket)	Carrot
Salt	Turnip

Method:

1. Weigh meat and calculate cooking time (page 88).
2. Wipe meat and tie in shape if necessary.
3. Put in a pan with boiling water to cover, bring back to boiling point and simmer gently for the required time.
4. Add blocks of carrot and turnip ¾ hour before serving.
5. Serve meat with blocks of carrot and turnip and some of the liquor in which the meat has been boiled.

Note: Broth (page 33) can be made in conjunction with the boiling meat.
Boiled ham can be cooked as above and served with parsley sauce (page 291).

3. BOILED SALT BEEF

Ingredients:

Salt Beef	Savoury Balls (page 307)
Carrot and Turnip	

Method:

1. Weigh meat and calculate cooking time (page 88).
2. Put in cold water to cover and bring slowly to boiling point. If very salty change the water.
3. Simmer gently for the required time.
4. Add blocks of carrot and turnip ¾ hour before serving.
5. Add savoury balls (also known as dumplings) 30 minutes before serving.
6. Serve the meat with carrot, turnip and savoury balls.

Dumplings:

1. Make up the savoury balls and divide into 4–6 portions, roll in flour.
2. Add to the pan with the meat and keep simmering briskly for 30 minutes.

Note: Alternatively a layer of tin foil can be placed over the pan and the dumplings placed on this.

Traditionally kale or cabbage was added to the meat 20 minutes before serving.

4. BOILED MUTTON

Ingredients:

Mutton (Shoulder *or* Flank)	250 ml Parsley, Onion *or*
Salt	Caper Sauce (page 291)
Carrot and Turnip	

Method:

1. Cut off surplus fat, wipe meat and tie in shape if necessary.
2. Weigh meat and calculate cooking time (page 88).

3. Put in a pan with boiling salted water to cover, bring back to boiling point and simmer gently for the required time.
4. Add blocks of carrot and turnip according to taste I hour before serving.
5. Serve meat with blocks of carrot and turnip and suitable sauce.

5. BOILED SALT PORK

Ingredients:

Flank of Pork   Pease Pudding (page 200)
Blocks of Carrot and Turnip
250 ml Parsley Sauce (page 291)

Method:

1. Weigh meat and calculate cooking time (page 88).
2. Put in cold water to cover and bring slowly to boiling point. If very salty, change the water.
3. Simmer gently for the required time.
4. Add blocks of carrot and turnip according to taste I hour before serving.

Note: Serve with carrot and turnip, parsley sauce and pease pudding (page 200).

6. STEAMED STEAK

Ingredients:

or 500 g Shoulder Steak   I medium Carrot
500g Skirt of Beef   Piece of Turnip
25 g seasoned Flour   2 tablespoonfuls of Water or Stock
2 small Onions   Chopped Parsley

Servings: 4–5
Time: 2–3 hours

Method:

1. Cut the meat into neat even-sized pieces.
2. Dip in seasoned flour and put in a bowl with layers of sliced vegetables.
3. Pour on water or stock.
4. Place bowl in a pan with boiling water coming halfway up the bowl.
5. Steam steadily. Serve with chopped parsley sprinkled on top.

STEWING

This method of cooking is very suitable for the cheaper cuts of meat as the slow cooking makes them tender.

Finer cuts of meat can also be cooked by this method allowing a shorter cooking time. The meat can be stewed on top of the cooker, in a casserole in the oven or in a slow cooker.

7. **STEWING CHART**

Meat	Cuts	Cooking Time on Top of Cooker	Additions to Stews
Beef	Rump	2 hours	Onion, Carrot, Turnip, Swede, Parsnip, Celery, Suet Pastry, Savoury Balls or Dumplings, Haricot Beans, Potatoes
	Shoulder	2 hours	
	Hough	3 hours	
	Skirt of Beef	3 hours	
Veal, Lamb and Mutton	Shoulder	2 hours	
	Gigot Chops	1 hour	
	Chump Chops	1 hour	
	Breast	2 hours	
	Neck	2 hours	
	Flank	2 hours	

8. **IRISH STEW**

Ingredients:

or 500 g Neck of Mutton (sliced)
500 g Lamb Shoulder Chops
2 large Onions
1 kg Potatoes

Salt and Pepper
1 teacupful Water
Chopped Parsley

Servings: 4
Time: 1½–2 hours

Method:

1. Cut the meat into neat pieces.
2. Slice onion thinly and cut potatoes into thick slices.
3. Put meat, onions, potatoes and seasoning in layers into the pan.
4. Add the water and stew gently till tender, about 2 hours.
5. Shake pan occasionally and, if necessary, add a little more water.
6. Pile up on serving dish and sprinkle liberally with chopped parsley.

Note: If some of the potatoes are preferred whole, add half of the potatoes sliced at the beginning and the remainder whole (or if large, halved) 40 minutes before serving the stew.

9. WHITE STEW OF VEAL

Ingredients:

500 g Shoulder of Veal	Salt and Pepper
I Onion	25 g Flour
2 Cloves (stuck into onion)	250 ml Milk
Bouquet of Herbs (page 27)	25 g Butter
250 ml Water	Rolls of Bacon (page 476)

Servings: 4–5

Time: I hour 30 minutes

Method:

1. Cut veal into pieces and put in stewpan with onion, stuck with cloves, and bouquet of herbs.
2. Add the water, bring to the boil, skim and season. Cook very gently for I hour 30 minutes.
3. Blend flour and milk, gradually mix in 125 ml of the hot liquid, return to pan and boil. Add butter in small pieces and beat into sauce.
4. Serve with rolls of bacon.

10. BROWN MEAT STEW (I)

Ingredients:

500 g Steak (Rump *or* Shoulder)	Oil for frying
25 g Flour	500 ml Water
Salt and Pepper	100 g Carrot
1–2 Onions	100 g Turnip

Servings: 4–5

Time: 2 hours

Method:

1. Cut meat into pieces of suitable size and dip in seasoned flour.
2. Slice onions and fry them a golden brown in the oil.
3. Brown the meat, add remainder of flour.
4. Add water and seasoning, bring to the boil and simmer gently.
5. Add carrot and turnip to stew, cut into blocks, I hour before serving.
6. Serve with gravy poured over meat and vegetables.

11. BROWN MEAT STEW (2)

Ingredients:

500 g Beef (Rump, Shoulder, Hough *or* Skirt)	Salt and Pepper
Oil for frying	100 g Carrot
1–2 Onions	100 g Turnip
25 g Flour	500 ml Water

Servings: 4–5

Time: 2–3 hours (according to cut)

Method:

1. Heat oil in a pan. Slice onions and fry them till a golden brown colour.
2. Cut the meat in even-sized pieces and brown on both sides.
3. Add water and seasoning, bring to boil and simmer gently.
4. Add carrot and turnip to stew, cut in blocks, 1 hour before serving.
5. Blend flour with a little cold water, add some of the hot gravy to it, return to pan and boil up, stirring all the time.
6. Serve with gravy poured round meat and vegetables.

Note: If meat is very coarse, 1 dessertspoonful of vinegar added along with the water, helps to soften the fibres.

12. BROWN MEAT STEW (3)

Ingredients:

500 g Rump Steak	500 ml Water
(2½ cm thick, in one piece)	1–2 Onions
Salt and Pepper	Oil for frying
100 g Carrot	25 g Flour
100 g Turnip	

Servings: 4–5
Time: 1½–2 hours

Method:

1. Slice onions and fry lightly in a little oil; draw to the side of the pan. Brown the meat.
2. Place onions on top of meat, put lid on pan and cook slowly for 30–40 minutes.
3. Blend the flour with a little water. Gradually add rest of water and add to the pan with seasoning. Boil up, stirring all the time.
4. Add carrot and turnip to stew, cut in blocks, and continue cooking for 1 hour or until meat is tender.
5. Serve with gravy strained over meat and vegetables.

Note: The meat may be cut up if preferred. The vegetables may be cooked separately and served with the stew.

13. EXETER STEW

Ingredients:

As for Brown Meat Stew, plus extra cupful water.
Savoury Balls (page 307)

Servings: 4–5
Time: 2–3 hours

Method:

1. Steps 1 and 2 of the method for brown meat stew, above, may be used, adding savoury balls 30 minutes before serving.

2. An extra teacupful of water should be added to the stew as savoury balls absorb some of the liquid.
3. Serve savoury balls round stew.
4. This stew may be cooked in a casserole.

14. SEA PIE

Ingredients:

As for Brown Meat Stew (1) (page 92)   150 g Suet Pastry (page 307)
Servings: 4–5
Time: 2–3 hours

Method:

1. Steps 1 and 2 of the method for brown meat stew, page 93, may be used, adding a round of suet pastry, 20–30 minutes before serving.
2. Roll pastry into a round a size smaller than stew-pan. Place on top of meat.
3. Cook stew steadily for another 20 minutes.
4. Divide pastry into 4 or 6 pieces. Place meat and vegetables on serving dish with pastry on top; pour gravy round.

Note: An extra cupful of water should be added to the stew as the suet pastry absorbs some of the liquid. This pie can also be cooked in the oven.

15. BEEF OLIVES

Ingredients:

500 g Rump Steak	1 Onion
(cut thinly in one piece)	*50 g Forcemeat (page 137)
500 ml Water	Oil for frying
Salt and Pepper	25 g Flour

Servings: 5
Time: 1 hour 30 minutes

Method:

1. Make up forcemeat.
2. Cut the steak into strips 6–8 cm wide.
3. Place 1 teaspoonful forcemeat on each piece; roll up and tie with string or secure with toothpicks.
4. Heat a little oil and fry sliced onion till golden brown; lightly brown the olives.
5. Add water and seasoning and bring to boiling point. Simmer gently 1–2 hours or till tender.
6. Blend the flour, add hot gravy and return to pan; boil up, stirring all the time.
7. To serve; remove string from beef olives, place on hot serving dish and strain gravy over.

Note: Sausagemeat may be used instead of forcemeat.

16. **VICTORIA STEAK**

Victoria Steak can be made in a similar way to beef olives (page 94) using ham forcemeat (page 137).

Keep the steak in *one* piece; place the forcemeat on the steak, roll up and tie with string. Continue from beef olives, step 4.

17. **STEWED OX-TAIL**

Ingredients:

1 Ox-Tail jointed (cut into rounds)	Salt and Pepper
Oil for frying	1 small Carrot
1 Onion (chopped)	Small piece Turnip
1 litre Water	25 g Flour
Bouquet of Herbs (page 27)	1 tablespoonful Tomato Ketchup

Servings: 4–6
Time: 5 hours

Method:

1. Fry onion in a little hot oil.
2. Wash tail and separate into joints. Cut off excess fat.
3. Place tail in pan with onion, water, bouquet of herbs and seasoning; bring to the boil and cook steadily for 4 hours.
4. Add carrot and turnip in blocks and cook for 1 hour longer.
5. Skim. Blend flour, add stock from stew, making up to 500 ml if necessary; boil.
6. Add ketchup; season and serve.

Note: A pressure cooker is most suitable for cooking ox-tail.

18. **HARICOT MUTTON**

Ingredients:

500 g Mutton *or* Lamb Shoulder Chops	100 g Carrot
25 g Fat *or* 25 ml Vegetable Oil	100 g Turnip
1 small Onion	25 g Flour
250 ml Water	50 g Haricot Beans (cooked)
Salt and Pepper	Parsley (chopped)

Servings: 4
Time: 2 hours

Method:

1. Heat a little oil and fry sliced onion till a golden brown colour. Draw to the side of pan, then fry meat lightly.
2. Add water, seasoning and vegetables cut in neat blocks. Simmer 2 hours.
3. Thicken gravy with blended flour, boil up, add cooked beans.
4. Serve sprinkled with chopped parsley.

19. STEWED LAMB

In one piece

Ingredients:

500 g Lamb Shoulder *or* Gigot (cut thick)	6 Small Carrots
1 Onion	2 White Turnips
Oil for frying	200 g Green Peas
500 ml Water	25 g Flour
Salt and Pepper	

Servings: 4

Time: 2 hours

Method:

1. Cut onion into rings and fry lightly in a little oil.
2. Fry meat lightly on both sides.
3. Add water and seasoning.
4. Simmer about 1 hour, add vegetables and cook for 1 hour longer.
5. Blend flour with cold water. Pour hot gravy from pan over blended flour and mix till smooth. Return to heat and boil up.
6. Serve with vegetables around the meat.

20. BROWN STEW OF VEAL

Ingredients:

500 g Shoulder of Veal	Bouquet of Herbs (page 27)
2 level tablespoonfuls seasoned Flour	Salt and Pepper
1 Onion	500 ml Water
Oil for frying	50 g grilled Bacon (if liked)

Servings: 4–5

Time: 1½–2 hours

Method:

1. Cut the veal into neat pieces and dip in seasoned flour.
2. Slice the onion and fry till a golden brown colour in a little oil in a frying pan.
3. Brown the veal in the pan with the onion.
4. Add water to the pan. Add bouquet of herbs and seasoning. Stew very gently for 1½–2 hours or till veal is tender.
5. Serve with grilled bacon.

21. VEAL OLIVES

Ingredients:

500 g Shoulder of Veal	Salt and Pepper
1 Onion	25 g Flour
Oilf for frying	50 g Bacon and Mushroom Stuffing
500 ml Stock	(page 138)

Servings: 5

Time: 1 hour 30 minutes

Method:

1. Make up bacon and mushroom stuffing.
2. Cut veal into strips 6–8 cm wide.
3. Place 1 teaspoonful stuffing on each piece; roll up and tie with string.
4. Make fat hot and fry sliced onion till golden brown; lightly brown the olives.
5. Add water and seasoning and bring to boiling point. Simmer gently for 1 hour 30 minutes or till tender.
6. Blend flour, add hot gravy and return to pan; boil up, stirring all the time.
7. To serve: remove string from olives, place on a hot serving dish and strain gravy over.

22. STEWED SAUSAGES

Ingredients:

500 g Sausages	1 dessertspoonful Flour
250 ml Water	Gravy Browning *or* Granules
Salt and Pepper	

Servings: 4–5
Time: 1 hour

Method:

1. Fork the sausages and put into a cold stew pan.
2. Cook slowly till fat flows then more quickly to brown and crisp skins.
3. Pour off any fat and add water and seasoning. Stew gently for 45 minutes.
4. Thicken with blended flour and gravy browning, or with gravy granules.
5. If liked, serve with apple sauce (page 296).

23. SWEET AND SOUR PORK

Ingredients:

500 g lean Pork Gigot	Oil for frying
200 g Rice (boiled, page 475)	

Sauce:

1 tin (approx. 300 g) Pineapple Chunks	4 tablespoonfuls Vinegar
75 g Soft Brown Sugar	Salt
1 tablespoonful Soy Sauce	1 small Green Pepper (thinly sliced)
2 level tablespoonfuls Cornflour	1 small Onion (thinly sliced)
1 small Carrot (thinly sliced)	

Servings: 4
Time: 1 hour

Method:

1. Remove excess fat from pork and cut meat into cubes.
2. Fry in hot oil until golden brown on all sides.
3. Drain pineapple juice from the tin and make up to 250 ml with water.
4. Add vinegar, brown sugar, soy sauce, and salt.

5. Blend cornflour with a little of this liquid. Add to remaining liquid, pour over the meat and bring to the boil.
6. Cover and simmer for 1 hour until meat is tender.
7. Prepare and slice onion and carrot; remove seeds from pepper and slice.
8. Add sliced pepper, carrot, onions and pineapple 20 minutes before serving.
9. Serve with 200 g of boiled rice.

24. MEAT IN A CASSEROLE OR SLOW COOKER

Ingredients:

500 g Meat	250 ml Water
Salt and Pepper	50–100 g Carrot
1 large Onion	50–100 g Turnip

Servings: 4–5
Oven Temperature: 180°C, No. 4
Position in Oven: Middle shelf

Method:

1. Trim off excess fat and cut meat into even-sized pieces.
2. Prepare vegetables and cut in slices.
3. Put meat and vegetables in layers in a casserole, add water.
4. Cover and cook.
5. Serve sprinkled with chopped parsley.

Meat in a casserole, variations:

Name of Stew	Meat Suitable	Time to Cook	Variation of Recipe	Variation of Method
Casserole of Steak	Shoulder Steak	2–2½ hrs	15 g Flour	Dip steak in seasoned flour before cooking
	Rump Steak	2 hrs	As above	As above
Steak and Kidney Casserole	Shoulder or Rump Steak	2–2½ hrs	25 g Flour 2 Sheep Kidneys or 100 g Ox Kidney 100 g Mushrooms 3 Tomatoes	Dip meat and kidney in seasoned flour. Add mushrooms 20 mins before serving and halved tomatoes 10 mins before serving
Hot Pot	Neck or Shoulder Mutton	2–3 hrs	1 extra Onion 1 kg Potatoes Omit Carrot and Turnip	

Haricot Mutton	Neck or Shoulder	2 hrs	15 g Flour 50 g Haricot Beans (cooked)	Dip chops in seasoned flour before cooking. Add beans before serving
Rice and Mutton Casserole	Shoulder Chops	2 hrs	25 g Rice	Wash rice and sprinkle in bottom of casserole
Lamb Casserole	Shoulder or Gigot	2 hrs	15 g Flour 200 g Green Peas Spring Carrot and Turnip	Dip lamb in seasoned flour before cooking. Add peas ½ hr before serving
Veal Casserole	Forequarter or Knuckle	2 hrs	15 g Flour Pinch of Thyme 100 g lean Bacon 2 Tomatoes	Dip veal in seasoned flour. Layer in casserole with vegetables, bacon, thyme. Add halved tomatoes, 10 mins before serving

25. MINCE

Ingredients:

500 g Mince
25 g Flour
Salt and Pepper

500 ml Water *or* Stock
1 Onion (chopped)

Servings: 4–5
Time: 30– 45 minutes

Method:

1. Brown mince in its own fat (drain some away if necessary). Add chopped onion, flour and seasoning in a pan and cook till onion softens.
2. Add water or stock, simmer slowly for 30–45 minutes.
3. Serve with boiled potatoes, savoury balls (page 307), boiled rice, macaroni, or fingers of toast.

26. STEAMED MEAT ROLL

Ingredients:

500 g Mince
100 g lean Smoked Bacon (minced)
100 g Breadcrumbs
1 tablespoonful chopped Parsley
½ teaspoonful Mixed Herbs

1 teaspoonful Worcester Sauce
Salt and Pepper
1 Egg
Dried Breadcrumbs (page 477)

Servings: 6–8
Time: 1 hour 30 minutes

Method:

1. Mix meat and all dry ingredients.
2. Bind with egg.
3. Press into a well-greased, steaming-jar or -bowl and cover with greased paper.
4. Steam steadily for 1 hour 30 minutes. Serve or leave in jar or bowl till cold with a weight on top.
5. Turn out and toss in dried breadcrumbs.
6. Serve with a salad.

Note: This may be boiled in a cloth and served hot or cold.

27. DUTCH ROAST

Ingredients:

500 g Mince	Salt and Pepper
100 g Ham *or* 2 Sausages	2 Eggs (beaten)
100 g Breadcrumbs	Breadcrumbs to coat
1 tablespoonful chopped Parsley	25 g Butter *or* 25 ml Vegetable Oil
½ teaspoonful Mixed Herbs	250 ml Tomato Sauce (page 297)

Servings: 6–8   **Time:** 1 hour
Oven Temperature: 190°C, No. 5
Position in Oven: Middle shelf

Method:

1. Mix meats, breadcrumbs, parsley, herbs and seasoning; bind with half of egg and add water if necessary.
2. Shape into a roll, coat using rest of beaten egg and with breadcrumbs.
3. Heat butter or oil in ovenproof dish, put in roll and baste. Cook for approximately 1 hour, basting and turning frequently.
4. Drain roll and serve on hot dish accompanied by tomato sauce.

28. STEWED DUTCH ROLL

Ingredients:

Dutch Roast (above)	1 Onion (sliced)
25 g Butter *or* 25 ml Oil	

Method:

1. Make as Dutch roast, step 1 of method.
2. Shape into a roll.
3. Heat oil or butter in stew pan and fry sliced onion golden brown.
4. Add meat roll and carefully brown in hot fat.
5. Add enough water to come halfway up roll and simmer gently for 1 hour.

Note: Vegetables can be added 30 minutes before end of cooking time and served around meat.

29. HAMBURG STEAKS (HAMBURGERS)

Ingredients:

500 g Mince
100 g Bacon (minced)
50 g Breadcrumbs
1 tablespoonful chopped Parsley
1 Egg

or

1 small teaspoonful Mixed Herbs
  (optional)
Salt and Pepper
250 ml Tomato Sauce (page 297)
250 ml Brown Sauce (page 293)

Servings: 6–8
Time: 30 minutes
Oven Temperature: 180°C, No. 4
Position in Oven: Middle shelf

Method:

1. Mix mince, bacon, breadcrumbs, parsley, herbs and seasoning, and bind with egg.
2. Shape into 6 or 8 flat cakes.
3. Grease a roasting tin, place in steaks and cover with thickly greased paper.
4. Bake for 30 minutes.
5. Arrange on hot serving dish and serve with sauce.
Note: Hamburg steaks can also be fried. May be served in rolls.

30. STEWED MINCE PATTIES

Ingredients:

250 g Mince
50 g Breadcrumbs
Salt and Pepper

1 large Onion (sliced)
125 ml Water
Vegetable Oil

Servings: 4 medium-sized patties
Time: 1 hour

Method:

1. Mix mince and breadcrumbs. Add a little water if necessary.
2. Form into 4 portions.
3. Work with floured hands into patties about 2–3 cm thick.
4. Heat sufficient oil to cover bottom of pan. When hot, fry sliced onion and patties.
5. Add water and seasoning, bring to boil and simmer for 1 hour.

31. SHEPHERD'S PIE

Ingredients:

200 g Cooked Meat
1 medium Onion
125 ml Beef Stock

500 g Creamed Potatoes (page 194)
Salt and Pepper
Butter *or* Oil

Servings: 4
Time: 30 minutes
Oven Temperature: 200°C, No. 6
Position in Oven: One-third from top

Method:

1. Chop onion. Heat oil or butter in a frying pan and in it fry onions till soft.
2. Remove excess fat and all gristle from meat. Mince the meat. Add the fried onion and some seasoning.
2. Mix thoroughly and place in the bottom of an ovenproof dish.
3. Add stock.
4. Place creamed potatoes on top. Smooth and mark with a fork.
5. Bake until thoroughly heated, about 30 minutes. The top should be well browned.

32. SAVOURY MEAT PIE

Ingredients:

500 g Potatoes (mashed)	1 tablespoonful Tomato Sauce
200 g Corned Beef	(page 297)
1 Small Onion	5 ml spoon Mixed Herbs
Seasoning	40 g Butter
Oil for frying	

Servings: 4
Time: 20 minutes
Oven Temperature: 190°C, No. 5
Position in Oven: Middle shelf

Method:

1. Boil potatoes. Chop onion and fry in a little oil.
2. Chop beef roughly.
3. Mix beef, onion, seasoning, tomato sauce and herbs.
4. Mash potatoes, season, beat in butter.
5. Put half of the mashed potatoes into bottom of a deep ovenproof dish.
6. Place beef mixture on top, cover with remaining potatoes.
7. Place dots of butter on top, bake.

33. MEAT CAKES

Ingredients:

100 g Cooked Meat		A little Milk and Seasoned Flour
100 g Potatoes (cooked)	or	1 Egg (beaten) and Breadcrumbs
Salt and Pepper		Small piece Butter
Oil for deep-frying		

Servings: 6 medium cakes

Method:

1. Mince meat finely, mash potatoes. Mix together with butter and seasoning. Form into flat cakes.
2. Coat with milk and seasoned flour, or beaten egg and breadcrumbs.
3. Deep-fry in hot oil. Drain well and serve.

34. MEAT CROQUETTES

Ingredients:

100 g cooked Meat	Salt and Pepper
1 small Onion (parboiled)	1 teaspoonful chopped Parsley
25 g Butter	A little Worcester Sauce
25 g Flour	1 Egg (beaten) and Breadcrumbs
125 ml Stock	Oil for frying

Servings: 4 medium croquettes

Method:

1. Mince meat and onion finely.
2. Melt butter in pan, add flour then stock and cook thoroughly. Add meat, onion, parsley, seasoning and a little Worcester sauce; mix well; turn onto a plate to cool.
3. Divide into portions and shape into croquettes.
4. Coat with beaten egg and breadcrumbs and deep-fry in oil. Drain well, serve.

35. CURRIED MEAT

Ingredients:

300 g lean Meat	3 level teaspoonfuls Curry Powder
1 level tablespoonful dried Coconut	1 tablespoonful Chutney
500 ml Stock	25 g Sultanas
1 small Apple	1 teaspoonful Lemon Juice
1 small Onion	1 tablespoonful Milk *or* Cream
25 g Butter	Salt and Pepper
1 level teaspoonful Curry Paste	200 g Rice (boiled, page 475)

Servings: 4

Time: 1 hour 30 minutes

Method:

1. Soak coconut in stock.
2. Chop apple and onion and fry in butter till golden brown.
3. Add curry powder and paste and fry gently for 10 minutes.
4. Add flour and, gradually, the strained stock. Bring to the boil, stirring all the time. Season.
5. Cut meat in small pieces, discarding most of fat; add to the sauce and simmer till tender, about 1 hour.
6. Add chutney and sultanas. Simmer a further 20 minutes.
7. Serve with boiled rice.

Accompaniments that could be served with Curries:

Banana	Thin Onion Rings
Mango Chutney	Raisins
Lime Chutney	Coconut (finely grated)
Naan Bread	Poppadoms
Chapatis	Tomato

36. CURRY OF COLD MEAT OR CHICKEN

Ingredients:

500 ml Curry Sauce (page 297)   100 g Rice (boiled, page 475)
200 g Cooked Meat *or* Chicken

Servings: 3

Method:

1. Make curry sauce.
2. Cut the cooked meat into neat pieces. Add to sauce and heat slowly. Heat through thoroughly.
3. Serve with boiled rice.

37. POTTED HOUGH

Ingredients:

2 Pig's Feet *or* 1 Knap Bone   4 litres cold Water
1 kg Hough *or* Shin   Salt

Method:

1. Clean the feet. Put in a pot with enough cold water to cover. Bring to boiling point, pour away the water and wash the feet again.
2. Remove fat from hough and cut up roughly.
3. Put hough and feet, or knap bone, in a pot with 4 litres of water and a little salt and simmer gently for 4 hours.
4. Remove meat from bones and cut up very finely.
5. Put bones back in the pan with the liquor and seasoning; boil until the liquid starts to jelly when cold. Test a little on a chilled plate. Strain.
6. Add meat, allow to cool, then stir to distribute meat. Put into a mould and leave till set.
7. Turn out and serve with salad.

Note: A pressure cooker may also be used – use 2 litres of water for the above quantity of meat and bones. Cook for approximately 1 hour.

38. POTTED MEAT

Ingredients:

1 kg Rump Steak   100 g Butter
2 Cloves   Salt and Pepper
250 ml Water   Anchovy Essence (optional)

Method:

1. Remove any fat from meat. Cut into small pieces.
2. Stew with cloves and water till tender, for 1 hour 30 minutes to 2 hours.
3. When cold, put through a mincer.
4. Add melted butter, a little gravy (in which meat was cooked), seasoning and anchovy essence. Pound well.
5. Put into jars, pressing down well.
6. Clarify a little butter (page 477) and pour on top of the meat.

39. VEAL CAKE

Ingredients:

500 g Veal (minced)

or 200 g Ham (minced)
200 g Sausagemeat
100 g Breadcrumbs
1–2 Eggs (hard-boiled, sliced)

1 tablespoonful Onion (chopped)
1 tablespoonful Parsley (chopped)
Salt and Pepper
1 Egg (beaten)
A little Stock

Servings: 8–10
Time: 1½–2 hours
Oven Temperature: 180°C, No. 4
Position in Oven: Middle shelf
Size of Tin: 13–15 cm

Method:

1. Grease the bottom of a cake tin and line with slices of hard-boiled egg.
2. Mix the rest of the ingredients together, seasoning and binding with beaten egg. Adding a little stock, if necessary.
3. Put mixture into cake tin, pressing it down well.
4. Steam for 2 hours or place in a tin of water and bake in oven for 2 hours.
5. Turn out and serve with brown sauce (page 293).

To serve cold:

When cooked, place weight on top and leave till cold. Turn out and serve sliced with salad.

40. VEAL AND HAM MOULD

Ingredients:

250 g Fillet of Veal (sliced)
100 g Bacon
1 Egg (hard-boiled)
Salt and Pepper

Pinch Ground Mace
A little grated Lemon Rind
2–3 level teaspoonfuls Gelatine

Servings: 5–6
Time: 1–1½ hours
Size of Tin: 13–15 cm in diameter

Method:

1. Grease tin and line bottom with a piece of greased paper.
2. Arrange sliced hard-boiled egg on the bottom of the tin.
3. Fill up with veal and bacon in layers. Sprinkle each layer with seasoning, mace and lemon rind.
4. Dissolve gelatine in stock and pour over meat. Cover with greased paper and steam. When cooked allow to cool.
5. Turn out and serve on a bed of lettuce.

Note: Alternatively, the mould may be baked in a moderate oven 190°C, No. 5, for 1–1½ hours.

FRYING

This method of cooking is only suitable for pieces of fine-grained meat about 2–3 cm thick.

41. SUITABLE CUTS

Beef.—Fillet Steak, Pope's Eye Steak, Sirloin Steak, Rib Eye Steak.
Lamb.—Single and Double Loin Chops, Chump or Gigot Chops.
Pork.—Loin and Gigot Chops, Fillet.
Veal.—Fillet, Loin.
Gammon.—Steaks.
Kidneys.—Sheep's, Calf's, Pig's.
Liver.—Sheep's, Calf's, Pig's. (Ox Liver and Kidney are not suitable for frying as they are too coarse).
Poultry.—Joints.
Sausages and Bacon.

42. FRIED STEAK AND ONIONS

Ingredients:

250 g Steak (Fillet, Pope's Eye, Rib Eye *or* Sirloin, 3 cm thick)	Oil for frying
	Salt
2 Onions	125 ml cold Water

Servings: 2
Time: 12–15 minutes

Method:

1. Beat the steak.
2. Cut the onions into thin rings.
3. Heat a little oil and fry the onions until cooked and a light brown colour.
4. Drain and place on a hot serving dish, cover.
5. Add a little more oil if necessary.
6. Fry the steak quickly on one side and then on the other.
7. Reduce heat, then keep turning the steak every 2 minutes, until cooked to personal taste.
8. Serve steak with onions on top.

Gravy:

1. Add a pinch of salt to the sediment in the pan.
2. Stir well, then add cold water.
3. Remove excess fat from surface.
4. Boil up, stirring to dissolve the sediment in the pan.
5. Pour round the steak.

43. **FRIED SAUSAGES AND APPLES**

Ingredients:

500 g Pork Sausages   4 Eating Apples

Servings: 4–5

Time: 10–15 minutes

Method:

1. Fork the sausages.
2. Put in a cold frying pan and cook slowly until fat begins to flow.
3. Turn the sausages till brown all over, allowing about 15 minutes.
4. Wash, core and slice apples into 1-cm rings. Fry for 2–3 minutes on each side and serve with sausages.

44. **FRIED LAMB OR MUTTON CHOPS**

Ingredients:

4 Loin *or* Gigot Chops   Oil for frying
Salt and Pepper   4 Tomatoes

Time: 10–12 minutes

Method:

1. Trim off excess fat. Season.
2. In a frying pan, heat enough oil to cover the bottom. Put in the chops and brown quickly, first on one side then on the other. Cook more slowly, turning the chops every 2 minutes, allowing altogether 10–12 minutes according to thickness.
3. Wash tomatoes, cut in halves and season.
4. Fry cut side down first, then turn, allowing 2–3 minutes altogether.
5. Serve chops with the tomatoes round them.

45. **LAMB CUTLETS OR LOIN CHOPS**

Ingredients:

6 Cutlets *or* Loin Chops   1 Egg (beaten)
Oil for frying   Breadcrumbs
Salt and Pepper   250–500 ml Tomato, Espagnole
                                       or Brown Sauce (pages 297, 294, 293)

Servings: 3–6

Time: 8–10 minutes

Method:

1. Prepare cutlets, season and coat with beaten egg and then breadcrumbs.
2. Fry in shallow oil for 8–10 minutes according to thickness, turning the cutlets after 4–5 minutes.
3. Drain and serve with a suitable.

46. FRIED PORK CHOPS WITH APPLE RINGS

Ingredients:

4 Pork Chops (2 cm thick)	Oil for frying
Salt and Pepper	2 Cooking Apples
A little Flour	I tablespoonful Brown Sugar

Servings: 4
Time: 20 minutes

Method:

1. Wash and dry chops and sprinkle with salt, pepper and flour.
2. Heat a little oil in a frying pan and cook chops about 20 minutes, turning every 2 minutes, allowing them to brown well.
3. Peel and core apples and cut into rings about I cm thick. Fry along with chops till soft, sprinkling them with brown sugar a few minutes before they are ready; serve with the chops.

47. FRIED PORK CHOPS DULCE

Ingredients:

4 Pork Chops (2 cm thick)	4 slices Eating Apple (I cm thick)
4 Peach halves (fresh *or* tinned)	4 tablespoonfuls Orange Juice
I tablespoonful Chutney	125 ml Red Wine, Stock *or* Water

Servings: 4
Time: 15–20 minutes

Method:

1. Remove fat from chops.
2. Heat a little oil in a strong frying pan.
3. Fry chops in oil slowly for 15–20 minutes turning frequently.
4. Drain and dry peaches, fill centres with chutney.
5. Add to frying pan along with apple slices and cook for 7 minutes.
6. Before serving chops, put I tablespoonful orange juice over each, season.
7. Place apple ring on chop, top with peach.
8. Add wine to pan, boil up, pour over chops in serving dish.

48. SAVOURY PORK CHOPS

Ingredients:

4 Pork Chops (2 cm thick)	I tablespoonful White Wine
25 g Butter	I teaspoonful Mustard
Small piece Shallot (chopped)	A little Meat Extract
3–4 Gherkins (chopped)	200 ml Stock

Servings: 4
Time: 20 minutes

Method:

1. Fry chops in butter for about 7 minutes on each side.
2. Remove chops from pan but keep warm.
2. Fry shallot in remaining fat and add gherkins, wine, mustard, extract and stock. Cook for about 5 minutes.
4. Pour over chops.

49. WIENER SCHNITZEL

Ingredients:

3 Fillets of Veal	50 g Breadcrumbs
25 g Flour	Butter *or* Oil for frying
Seasoning	Lemon Wedges
1 Egg	

Garnish:

1 Egg (hard-boiled, yolk sieved, white chopped)	Capers

Servings: 3

Time: 6–8 minutes

Method:

1. Trim and flatten fillets.
2. Season, coat with flour.
3. Dip in beaten egg and coat with breadcrumbs.
4. Fry in hot oil or butter, 3 minutes on each side.
5. Serve with lemon wedges and garnish.

Note: Veal should be cut from the leg and be very thin.

GRILLING

This method of cooking is only suitable for pieces of fine-grained meat about 2–3 cm thick.

50. SUITABLE CUTS

Beef.—Fillet Steak, Pope's Eye Steak, Sirloin Steak, Rib Eye Steak.
Lamb.—Single and Double Loin Chops.
Pork.—Loin Chops.
Veal.—Loin Cutlets.
Gammon.—Steaks.
Kidneys.—Sheep's, Calf's, Pig's.
Liver.—Sheep's, Calf's, Pig's (Ox Liver and Kidneys are not suitable for grilling as they are too coarse).
Poultry.—Breast.
Bacon and Sausage.

51. GRILLED STEAK AND ACCOMPANIMENTS

Ingredients:

A thick Steak (Fillet, Pope's Eye,   Butter *or* Oil
   Rib Eye *or* Sirloin)   Potato Chips (page 193)
Seasoning

Time: Maximum of 12–15 minutes

Maître d'Hôtel Butter:

25 g Butter   Lemon Juice
Salt, Pepper, Cayenne   1 teaspoonful chopped Parsley

Cream the butter, add seasoning, squeeze of lemon juice and chopped parsley.

Method:

1. Trim and season the steak. Brush over with oil or place pats of butter on top. Heat grill.
2. Brown the meat quickly on both sides, then reduce heat and keep turning every 2 minutes till cooked to personal taste.
3. Spread with maître d'hôtel butter and serve with potato chips.

52. GRILLED CHOPS

Ingredients:

Single *or* double Loin Chops   Seasoning
Butter   Lemon Juice

Time: 12–15 minutes

Method:

1. Trim off excess fat, beat and season with salt, pepper and lemon juice.
2. Heat the grill and trivet and rub over with fat.
3. Place on the chops and put pats of butter on each.
4. Brown quickly on both sides, lower the heat and continue cooking, turning the chops every 2 minutes; allow 12–15 minutes according to thickness.

53. MIXED GRILL

Ingredients:

Loin Chops   Tomatoes
Sheep's, Calf's *or* Pig's Kidney   Seasoning
Sheep's, Calf's *or* Pig's Liver   Butter *or* Oil
Sausages   Potato Chips (page 193)
Bacon   Maître d'Hôtel Butter
Mushrooms   (see recipe 51, above)

Time: 15 minutes

Preparation:

1. Chops: Wipe, remove surplus fat. Beat and season. Brush with oil or place pats of butter on top.
2. Kidneys: Skin, split, core and wash. Brush with oil or place pats of butter on top.

3. Sausages: Pierce with a fork.
4. Liver: Remove skin and tubes, wash. Brush with oil or dot with butter.
5. Bacon: Remove surplus fat.
6. Mushrooms: Remove stalks and skin, if necessary. Season and put a small piece of butter on each.
7. Tomatoes: Wash and halve tomato. Season and put a piece of butter on top.

Method:

1. Heat the grill and brush trivet (wire tray) with oil.
2. Put on chops and sausages.
3. Brown quickly on both sides, cooking for 4 minutes.
4. Add liver, kidney and mushrooms and cook for a further 2–3 minutes on each side.
5. Add bacon and tomatoes and cook a further 2 minutes on each side. Cook approximately 15 minutes altogether.
6. Put a piece of maître d'hôtel butter (see recipe 51) on meat and vegetables (optional) and serve with potato chips.

54. **MIXED BAKE**

Ingredients:

2 Steaks	4 Mushrooms
2 Sheep's Kidneys	2 Tomatoes
2 Sausages	Salt and Pepper
2 Bacon rashers	25 g Butter *or* 25 ml Oil

Servings: 2
Time: 20 minutes
Oven Temperature: 220°C, No. 7
Position in Oven: Middle shelf

Method:

1. Prepare steaks as for grilled steak (page 110) and other ingredients as for mixed grill (page 110).
2. Heat butter or oil in a baking tin; put in steaks and sausages and baste. Cover with greased paper.
3. After 7 minutes, put in kidneys and mushrooms.
4. Five minutes before serving, put in bacon and tomato.

55. **ZINGARA CUTLETS**

Ingredients:

6 Cutlets *or* Lamb Chops	300 g Green Pea Purée (page 200)
Vegetable Oil	500 ml Tomato Sauce (page 297)
Salt, Pepper, Cayenne	

Servings: 3–6
Time: 20 minutes
Oven Temperature: 180°C, No. 4
Position in Oven: Middle shelf

Method:

1. Prepare cutlets, place in a greased tin and pour a little vegetable oil over.
2. Cover with greased paper and bake in a moderate oven 20 minutes.
3. Heat green pea purée and tomato sauce.
4. Drain the cutlets and arrange them on a serving dish; coat with thick tomato sauce and serve with piped green pea purée and thin tomato sauce poured round.

56. PORK FILLETS, STUFFED AND BAKED

Ingredients:

2 Pork Fillets	250 ml Water
Sage and Onion Stuffing (page 137)	Salt and Pepper
25 ml Vegetable Oil	Meat Extract (if necessary)
Fat Bacon	Apple Sauce (page 296)
1 level tablespoonful Flour	

Servings: 6
Time: 1 hour
Oven Temperature: 220°C, No. 7
Position in Oven: Middle shelf

Method:

1. Split fillets lengthwise without cutting through.
2. Spread stuffing on one fillet and lay the other on top. Fix with skewers.
3. Heat the oil in roasting tin along with a little salt. Put fillets in and baste well. Cover with strips of bacon fat.
4. Cook for 20 minutes at 220°C, No. 7, reduce to 190°C, No. 5, for remaining time.
5. Lift meat onto a hot, flat serving plate. Pour fat from tin, add water and boil up.
6. Blend flour with some cold water. Add liquor from tin. Return to tin and stir till boiling.
7. Add seasoning and meat extract (or gravy granules) if colour of gravy is pale. Serve gravy in a sauce boat.
8. Apple sauce may also be served.

ROASTING

This method of cooking is suitable for finer cuts of beef, mutton, lamb, pork and veal.

The shape and proportion of bone affects the cooking time, i.e. thick pieces require longer than thin pieces of the same weight.

Rolled meat and stuffed meat take longer to cook than meat on the bone.

Beef and lamb can be served rare. Mutton, veal and pork must be thoroughly cooked.

57. ROASTING CHART

Meat	Cuts	Guide to Cooking Times	Accompaniments
Beef Cuts 2 kg or under	Sirloin, Rib or Pope's Eye, Point of Rump *Boned and Rolled* Ribs, Silverside	{ 1 hour 15 mins for 1st kg plus 40 mins for each added kg { 2 hrs for 1st kg plus 1 hr for each added kg	Unthickened Gravy Roast Potatoes (page 192, 193) Yorkshire Pudding (page 475) Horseradish Sauce (page 298)
Cuts over 2 kg	As above	45 mins per kg plus 45 mins	As above
Lamb and Mutton Cuts, 2 kg or under	Gigot (leg), Chump End, Middle Gigot Loin *Rolled or Stuffed Lamb or Mutton* Flank rib, Shoulder	{ 1 hr 30 mins for 1st kg plus 50 mins for each added kg 1hr 30 mins–2 hrs { 2 hrs for 1st kg plus 1 hr for each added kg	Thickened Gravy (page 477) Mint Sauce (page 298) Mint Jelly (page 458) Onion Sauce (page 291) Redcurrant Jelly (page 457)
Cuts over 2 kg	Gigot (leg) *Rolled, Stuffed Meat*	1 hr per kg and 1 hr over	As above
Veal Cuts, 2 kg or under	Leg Loin, Fillet *Rolled and Stuffed* Shoulder	{ 1 hr 30 mins for 1st kg plus 1 hr 15 mins for each added kg 1 hr 30 mins–2 hrs { 2 hrs for 1st kg plus 1 hr for each added kg	Thickened Gravy (page 477) Lemon Wedges Rolls of Bacon (page 476)
Cuts over 2 kg	As above	1 hr per kg plus 1 hr	As above
Pork Cuts, 2 kg or under	Shoulder, Gigot (leg) Loin, Fillet *Rolled and Stuffed* Shoulder, Gigot (leg), Loin	{ 1 hr 30 mins for 1st kg plus 1hr 15 mins for each added kg 1 hour 30 mins–2 hrs { 2 hrs for 1st kg plus 1 hr for each added kg	Thickened Gravy Apple Sauce (page 296) Sage and Onion Stuffing (page 137)
Cuts over 2 kg	Shoulder, Gigot (leg)	1 hr per kg plus 1 hr	As above

58. **ROAST BEEF**

Ingredients:

Sirloin, Rib *or* Pope's Eye   Vegetable Oil

Accompaniments:

Gravy (unthickened)   Yorkshire Pudding (page 475)
Roast Potatoes (page 102, 193)   Horseradish Sauce (page 298)
Time: See page 113   **Oven Temperature:** 220°C, No. 7
Position in Oven: Middle shelf

Method:

1. Tie up the meat if necessary. Weigh it and calculate cooking time (page 107).
2. Heat the oil in a roasting tin, sprinkle in a little salt, place meat in tin and baste the cut sides well.
3. Cook in the middle of a hot oven, 220°C, No. 7, for 15–20 minutes; reduce heat to 180°C, No. 4, and continue cooking till the meat is ready. Beef may be served underdone.
4. One hour before the meat is cooked add potatoes and baste.
5. Bake Yorkshire Pudding, placing on the top shelf in the oven, 30 minutes before meat is cooked and raise oven heat to 200°C, No. 6.

Gravy:

1. Pour the fat from the roasting tin into a bowl, leaving the sediment in tin. Separate any meat drippings from fat and return to tin.
2. Add 250 ml cold water to the tin and skim off any fat which solidifies. Stir well to dissolve all sediment; place tin over the heat and boil up gravy. Season and serve in a sauce boat. If thickened gravy is preferred, allow 2 level teaspoonfuls flour for each 250 ml liquid; blend, pour hot gravy over, return to pan and boil.

59. **ROAST LAMB OR MUTTON**

Ingredients:

Gigot (leg), Loin *or* Best End Neck (jointed)   Vegetable Oil
2 level teaspoonfuls Flour for each 250 ml Gravy

Accompaniments:

Lamb: Thickened Gravy (page 477)   New Potatoes
             Mint Sauce (page 298)   Green Peas
Mutton: Thickened Gravy, Redcurrant Jelly (page 457), Onion Sauce (page 291)
Oven Temperature: 220°C, No. 7
Position in Oven: Middle shelf

Method:

1. Weigh the meat. Calculate the cooking time (page 113). Cooking time will vary according to the shape of the meat. A piece of gigot will take longer than an equal weight of loin which is a much thinner joint.
2. Heat oil in a roasting tin, sprinkle in a little salt, place the meat in and baste the cut sides well.
3. Cook in the middle of a hot oven, 220°C, No. 7, for 15–20 minutes, then

reduce the heat to 180°C, No. 4, and continue cooking till the meat is ready.

4. Place the meat on serving dish.

5. Make the gravy. Pour the fat from the roasting tin into a bowl, leaving the sediment in tin. Separate any meat drippings from fat and return to tin. Add 250 ml cold water to the tin, and skim off any fat solidified, stir well to dissolve the sediment. Place tin over the heat and boil up gravy.

6. Blend 2 level teaspoonfuls flour; pour some of the hot gravy over, return to the tin; boil up, stirring all the time. Season and serve in a sauce boat.

60. ROAST STUFFED LAMB OR MUTTON

Ingredients:

1 kg Shoulder *or* Flank Lamb *or* Mutton (boned)	50 g Forcemeat (page 137) 2 level teaspoonfuls Flour for each
25g Fat *or* 25ml Cooking Oil	250 ml Gravy

Time: 2 hours   **Oven Temperature:** 220°C, No. 7
Position in Oven: Middle shelf

Method:

1. Weigh the meat and calculate cooking time (page 113).

2. Prepare the forcemeat and place in cavity left after shoulder is boned or spread on flank mutton after boning; roll up the latter and fasten securely with string.

3. Heat oil in a roasting tin, sprinkle in a little salt, place meat in and baste cut sides.

4. Cook in the middle of a hot oven, 220°C, No. 7, for 15–20 minutes then reduce the heat to 180°C, No. 4, and continue cooking till the meat is ready.

5. Remove some of the string from the meat to make carving easy and place mutton on a hot flat serving dish.

6. Make the gravy. Pour the fat from the roasting tin into a bowl, leaving the sediment in tin. Separate any meat drippings from fat and return to tin. Add 250 ml of cold water to the tin and skim off any fat which solidifies. Stir well to dissolve all sediment, place tin over the heat and boil up the gravy.

7. Blend 2 level teaspoonfuls flour, pour some of the hot gravy over, return to the tin, boil up, stirring all the time. Season and serve in a sauce boat.

61. ROAST VEAL

Ingredients:

Leg of Veal	2 level teaspoonfuls Flour
Vegetable Oil	250 ml Water
Salt and Pepper	

Accompaniments:

Thickened Gravy (page 477), Lemon Wedges, Rolls of Bacon (page 476)
Oven Temperature: 220°C, No. 7
Position in Oven: Middle shelf

Method:

1. Weigh the meat and calculate the cooking time (page 113).
2. Heat the oil in a roasting tin and sprinkle in a little salt; place the meat in the tin and baste the cut sides.
3. Cook in the middle of a hot oven, 220°C, No. 7, for 15–20 minutes, then reduce the heat to 180°C, No. 4, and continue cooking till the meat is ready.
4. Make the gravy. Pour the fat from the roasting tin into a bowl, leaving the sediment in tin. Separate any meat drippings from fat and return to tin. Add water and skim off any fat which solidifies, place tin over the heat and boil up.
5. Blend the flour with cold water, pour some of the hot gravy over, return to the tin and boil up, stirring all the time. Season and serve in a sauce boat.
6. Serve accompanied by rolls of bacon and wedges of lemon.

62. ROAST STUFFED VEAL

Ingredients:

Fillet of Veal (boned)	2 level teaspoonfuls Flour
50 g Forcemeat (page 137)	250 ml Water
Vegetable Oil	Rolls of Bacon (page 476)
Salt and Pepper	Lemon Wedges

Oven Temperature: 220°C, No. 7
Position in Oven: Middle shelf

Method:

1. Make the forcemeat and spread on the veal; roll up and tie securely with string.
2. Follow directions for roast veal (page 115).

Note: When cooked, remove some of the string from the meat to make carving easier.

63. ROAST PORK

Ingredients:

Loin (jointed and scored), Gigot (leg)	Vegetable Oil
or Shoulder (boned and rolled)	2 level teaspoonfuls Flour
Salt	for each 250 ml Gravy

Accompaniments:

Thickened Gravy (page 477)	Sage and Onion Stuffing (page 137)
Apple Sauce (page 296)	

Oven Temperature: 220°C, No. 7
Position in Oven: Middle shelf

Method:

1. Weigh the pork and calculate the cooking time (page 113). Pork must be thoroughly cooked.
2. Make the sage and onion stuffing; separate the lean and the fat of the pork and into this pocket put the stuffing.

3. Heat the oil in a roasting tin and sprinkle in a little salt. Place the meat in the tin and baste the cut sides.

4. Cook in the middle of a hot oven, 220°C, No. 7, for 15–20 minutes, then reduce the heat to 190°C, No. 5, and continue cooking till the meat is ready.

5. Place the meat on the serving dish.

6. Make the gravy. Pour the fat from the roasting tin into a bowl, leaving the sediment in tin. Separate any meat drippings from fat and return to tin. Add 250 ml cold water to the tin and skim off any fat which solidifies, stir well to dissolve the sediment, place tin over the heat and boil up.

7. Blend 2 level teaspoonfuls flour, pour some of the hot gravy over, return to the tin; boil up, stirring all the time. Season and serve in a sauce boat.

64. POT ROASTING

This method may be carried out in a pan, covered roaster or casserole. It is particularly suitable for coarser cuts of meat.

Suitable cuts:

Beef.—Rump, Topside, Silverside, Brisket.

Mutton, Lamb.—Shoulder, Breast (rolled).

Veal.—Fillet, Breast (stuffed and rolled).

Method:

1. Weigh the meat. Calculate cooking time allowing an extra 30 minutes.

2. Heat oil in pan or casserole. Sprinkle in a little salt, baste cut sides of meat, cover. Cook at a moderate temperature on top of the cooker or in the oven.

3. Place the meat in a serving dish.

4. Make the gravy. Pour the fat from the pan or casserole into a bowl, leaving the sediment in tin. Separate any meat drippings from fat and return to pan. Add 250 ml cold water and skim off any fat which solidifies. Stir well to dissolve the sediment, place pan over the heat and boil up.

5. Blend two level teaspoonfuls flour; pour some of the hot gravy over, return to the pan, boil up, stirring all the time. Season and serve.

Note: If the cut of meat is very coarse, add a little water to the pan or casserole.

BRAISING

This is a method of cooking which traditionally requires both top and bottom heat and is a combination of stewing and roasting. It is very suitable for cuts of meat too small for roasting.

65. SUITABLE MEATS FOR BRAISING

Beef.—Topside, Rump, Fillet, Pope's Eye.

Mutton.—Gigot or Chump, Shoulder (boned and rolled).

Veal.—Fillet or Gigot.

Ham.—Middle Gammon, Corner Gammon.

Offal.—Sweetbreads, Heart, Tongue.

Game.—Older Game Birds and Poultry, small Chickens and Pigeons.

If the meat is lean, lard or bard it.

To Lard – Insert strips of bacon fat across the grain of the meat with a larding needle. Cut the strips of fat (lardoons) 5 mm thick by 5 mm wide by 6 cm long.

To Bard – Lay pieces of fat bacon over the food to be braised, e.g. small chickens and game birds.

Method:

For details, see the following recipes for braised meats.

Time – This is calculated as for roasting (page 113).

66. BASIC BRAISING METHOD

Ingredients:

500 g suitable Meat	Stock
Larding Bacon	

Mirepoix:

1 Carrot	25 g Bacon
Small piece Turnip	Bouquet of Herbs (page 27)
1 Onion	6 Peppercorns
Piece Celery	Mushroom Trimmings
25 g Butter *or* 25 ml Vegetable Oil	

Garnish:

Green Peas *or* French Beans	Mushrooms and Tomatoes
Carrot and Turnip	Celery and Peppers

Servings: 5

Time: 1 hour

Oven Temperature: 180°C, No. 4

Position in Oven: Middle shelf

Method:

1. Cut even-sized pieces of carrot and turnip for the garnish; cut up the remainder roughly for the mirepoix, also onion and celery.
2. Use a stew pan with a tight-fitting lid.
3. Heat the butter or oil in the pan and fry the vegetables and bacon until a good brown colour.
4. Add the herbs, put lid on pan and sauté while preparing meat.
5. Cut strips of larding bacon 5 mm thick and 5 mm wide by 6 cm long. Insert these into the meat with a larding needle (a hollow skewer that can "thread" strips of fat into meat). Or insert fat into slits made in meat with a paring knife.
6. Place meat on mirepoix, cover with greased paper, put lid on pan and fume for one-third of the time, i.e. cook in steam from mirepoix.
7. Add enough stock or water to cover the vegetables and cook one-third of the time.

8. Put the pan with lid on, into a moderate oven and cook for the remaining one-third of the time.
9. Remove the lid for the last 10 minutes to crisp the lardoons.
10. Remove meat, strain stock from vegetables and skim well. If necessary, reduce by boiling. Pour round meat and arrange cooked garnish of choice.

67. BRAISED MEAT IN A CASSEROLE

Ingredients:

500 g suitable Meat (in one piece, page 117–18)
100 g Carrot
1 Bacon rasher (diced)
1 Onion

Small piece Turnip
Bouquet of Herbs (page 27)
Salt and Pepper
250 ml Water

Servings: 4–5
Time: 2 hours
Oven Temperature: 180°C, No. 4
Position in Oven: Middle shelf

Method:

1. Prepare and cut up the vegetables and put in a shallow, covered ovenproof dish or casserole with bacon, seasoning and herbs.
2. Place the meat on top and add water. Cover with greased paper, put on lid.
3. Cook in a moderate oven for 20–30 minutes, reduce to 150°C, No. 2, and continue cooking for 1 hour 30 minutes or until meat is tender.

68. BRAISED MEAT IN PAN

Ingredients:

500 g suitable Meat (page 117–18)
1 Onion
25 g Cooking Fat *or* 25 ml Vegetable Oil
1 Bacon rasher (diced)
100 g Carrot

Small piece Turnip
Bouquet of Herbs (page 27)
Salt and Pepper
250 ml Water

Servings: 4–5
Time: 1 hour 30 minutes

Method:

1. Cut onion in rings and fry in fat or oil along with diced bacon.
2. Cut carrot and turnip into large pieces and put in pan; add herbs and seasoning.
3. Put meat on top of vegetables and put on pan lid. Cook gently for 20 minutes.
4. Add water and continue cooking for 1 hour or until meat is tender.
5. Serve meat and vegetables with liquor poured round. If liked, thicken it with 2–3 level teaspoonfuls flour blended till smooth with water.

HAM

69. BOILED HAM (COLD)

Ingredients:

Gammon (Middle, Corner *or* Hough)   6 Peppercorns
I Bay Leaf   Browned Crumbs (page 476)

Method:

1. Weigh gammon and calculate the cooking time (see page 88).
2. Soak in cold water for several hours.
3. Remove from water and dry. Put in pan and cover with cold water, add the flavouring and bring slowly to the boil, skimming occasionally. Allow water to simmer for the required time.
4. Remove from heat and leave gammon to cool in liquid (about 2 hours).
5. Take gammon out of liquid; remove skin and cover the fat thickly with browned crumbs.
6. Cut in slices and serve.

70. BAKED HAM (I)

This method is particularly suited to strongly flavoured ham

Ingredients:

I kg Gammon (Middle, Corner *or* Hough)   Soft Brown Sugar
Cloves

Time: 2 hours
Oven Temperature: 190°C, No. 5
Position in Oven: Middle shelf

Method:

1. Wash ham and soak for several hours.
2. Boil the ham for I hour.
3. Remove ham from water and cool for 30 minutes.
4. Wrap completely in cooking foil and bake in a moderate oven, for I hour.
5. About 15 minutes before cooking is complete, remove foil and skin the ham.
6. Score the fat in diamonds, stud with cloves and dredge heavily with brown sugar.
7. Return to the oven for 15 minutes.

71. BAKED HAM (2)

Ingredients:

I kg Middle Gammon   Browned Crumbs (page 476)

Time: 2 hours
Oven Temperature: 190°C, No. 5
Position in Oven: Middle shelf

Method:

1. Wash ham and soak for 2–3 hours in cold water.
2. Dry and wrap completely in cooking foil.
3. Put in baking tin and bake in a moderate oven for about 2 hours.
4. Unwrap and skin ham and sprinkle fat with browned crumbs.

Note: A paste of flour and water (200 g flour) may be used instead of foil, but 15 minutes extra cooking time should be allowed to give time for heat to penetrate.

72. BAKED HAM (3)

The method incorporates a glaze to help with the browning

Ingredients:

2 kg middle Gammon	Cloves
50 g Brown Sugar	6 Pineapple rings
125 ml Pineapple Juice	

Time: 3–3½ hours

Method:

1. Cook ham as in recipe 71.
2. Make glaze by dissolving sugar in pineapple juice and boiling to reduce.
3. Score the fat of the gammon into diamonds, stud the fat with cloves and brush with glaze.
4. Brown in hot oven, 200°C, No. 6, for 10–15 minutes.
5. Heat pineapple in remaining glaze.
6. Serve ham garnished with pineapple rings.
7. Serve hot or cold.

73. BAKED GAMMON IN CIDER

Ingredients:

1 Gammon Steak (200 g, 2-cm thick)	2 level teaspoonfuls Cornflour
1 level teaspoonful Mustard	1 tablespoonful Milk
1 level teaspoonful Demerara Sugar	Chopped Parsley
250 ml Cider	

Servings: 2

Time: 20–30 minutes

Oven Temperature: 200°C, No. 6

Position in Oven: Middle shelf

Method:

1. Soak gammon in cold water for 30 minutes; dry and cut off the rind.
2. Lay gammon in an ovenproof dish. Mix mustard, sugar and 1 tablespoonful cider. Spread mixture over the gammon and leave for 15 minutes.
3. Pour the rest of the cider over, cover the dish and bake.
4. Blend the cornflour in a small pan. Drain liquor from baking dish. Add to the cornflour and boil.
5. Season with pepper, add milk and parsley. Pour sauce round ham.

74. FRIED GAMMON STEAK

Ingredients:

I Gammon Steak (200 g, I cm thick)   2 Tomatoes
Butter   Breadcrumbs
4 Mushrooms

Servings: 2
Time: Approx. I5 minutes

Method:

1. Soak the gammon in cold water for 30 minutes. Dry and cut off rind and surplus fat.
2. Put fat in frying pan and, when melted, remove rind. Add enough butter to cover the bottom of the pan.
3. Place gammon in hot fat and fry quickly for 2 minutes on each side. Draw to the side of the pan and cook more gently.
4. Wash and slice mushrooms, fry for 5 minutes at side of pan.
5. Turn the gammon. Slice tomatoes thickly and fry all for 3–4 minutes longer.
6. Lift the mushrooms and tomatoes on top of gammon. Add enough breadcrumbs to pan to absorb fat, season if necessary, and serve on top of gammon.

75. GRILLED GAMMON

Ingredients:

I Gammon Steak (200 g, I cm thick)   Seasoning
25 g Butter   Lemon Juice
2 Tomatoes   Chopped Parsley
8 Mushrooms

Servings: 2
Time: Approx. I5 minutes

Method:

1. Soak gammon in cold water for 30 minutes.
2. Dry it and remove the rind.
3. Snip the fat in towards the lean meat with a pair of scissors.
4. If necessary, use a skewer to keep the steak in shape while cooking.
5. Rub butter over one side of steak. Grease bars of grill pan with some of the butter.
6. Lay steak on the bars, buttered side up, and put under a well-heated grill for 2–3 minutes.
7. Turn steak, rub with butter and put it back under grill for a further 3 minutes.
8. Lower heat and cook gammon more gently for 5 minutes longer each side.
9. Prepare tomatoes and mushrooms, season and put a small pat of butter on each.
10. Grill beside gammon allowing I0 minutes for mushrooms and 4–5 minutes for tomatoes.
11. Melt a little butter in grill pan, add pepper and lemon juice.
12. Sprinkle gammon with parsley and pour liquor from pan over it.

76. SPICED GAMMON

Ingredients:

I slice uncooked Gammon
  (200 g, I cm thick)
I level teaspoonful dry Mustard
½–I level teaspoonful
  Ground Cinnamon

Fresh Orange Juice
2 Dessert Apples
I level teaspoonful Cornflour
I–2 level tablespoonfuls Brown Sugar

Servings: 2
Time: 30–40 minutes
Oven Temperature: 190°C, No. 5
Position in Oven: Middle shelf

Method:

1. Wash gammon and soak in cold water for 30 minutes.
2. Mix mustard, cinnamon and brown sugar and spread on gammon.
3. Put in casserole with enough orange juice to almost cover. Cover dish and bake till gammon is tender.
4. Core apples but do not peel. Cut in quarters and cook gently in remainder of juice.
5. Remove apples and arrange on top of gammon; keep hot. Thicken juice with blended cornflour. Serve with gammon.

77. GAMMON STUFFED WITH APRICOTS

Ingredients:

2 slices uncooked Gammon (200 g each,
  I cm thick)
I teaspoonful Lemon Juice
25 g Breadcrumbs
I Egg
I small Onion
A few Almonds

25 g Raisins
I small tin Apricots
Pepper
Nutmeg
250 ml Liquid (water plus syrup
  from tin Apricots)

Servings: 4
Time: 45 minutes
Oven Temperature: 190°C, No. 5
Position in Oven: Middle shelf

Method:

1. Wash gammon and soak for 30 minutes. Remove rind and some of the fat.
2. Prepare and finely chop onion. Blanch and chop almonds. Wash raisins, chop half the apricots.
3. Mix with breadcrumbs, pepper and nutmeg, and bind with egg.
4. Spread mixture between 2 slices of gammon. Lay in an ovenproof dish and pour syrup over.
5. Bake, basting occasionally.
6. Put remaining apricots round gammon, baste with the hot syrup and leave to heat through.

OFFAL

78. FRIED KIDNEYS AND BACON

Ingredients:

3 Sheep's Kidneys   3 Tomatoes
6 Bacon rashers   Salt and Pepper

Servings: 3
Time: 15 minutes

Method:

1. Skin, split, core, wash and dry kidneys.
2. Fry the bacon lightly, place on ovenproof dish, cover.
3. Fry kidneys in fat left from bacon, first on one side, then on the other, taking in all 7–10 minutes.
4. Wash tomatoes and cut in halves; season, place cut side down in the fat and fry for 1 minute, turn and cook for another 2 minutes or till soft.
5. Arrange kidneys on serving dish, place bacon on top and tomatoes around.

Note: Put the tomatoes to cook several minutes before the kidneys are ready so that both will be ready for serving at the same time.

79. GRILLED KIDNEYS, BACON AND MUSHROOMS

Ingredients:

3 Sheep's Kidneys   Salt and Pepper
6 Bacon rashers   A little Vegetable Oil
6 large Mushrooms   40 g Butter

Servings: 3
Time: 15 minutes

Method:

1. Skin, split, core, wash and dry kidneys.
2. Remove rind from bacon, trim and wash mushrooms.
3. Baste the kidneys with oil; season. Grill for 5 minutes, turn.
4. Season the mushrooms, put small piece of butter on top and place beside the kidneys. Grill for 5 minutes, turn.
5. Add rashers of bacon to grill pan and continue cooking for another 5 minutes; turn the rashers during cooking.
6. Serve.

80. STEWED KIDNEYS

Ingredients:

6 Sheep's Kidneys *or* 2 Calf's Kidneys   2 Cloves
    or ½ Ox Kidney   Salt and Pepper
1 small Onion   1 tablespoonful Sherry

Oil for frying
1 tablespoonful seasoned Flour
50 g Mushrooms
250 ml Water

or

500 g Creamed Potatoes (page 194)
75 g cooked Pasta
Parsley

Servings: 3

Time: 30 minutes for Sheep's and Calf's Kidneys,
2 hours for Ox Kidney

Method:

1. Slice the onion and fry it in oil, then draw it to the side of the pan.
2. Remove the skin from the kidneys, split the sheep's kidney in two, and remove the core of fat. Remove the core of fat from the ox kidney and calf's kidney and cut into 8 or 10 pieces; wash the kidneys and roll in seasoned flour.
3. Fry the kidneys lightly in oil.
4. Wash and stalk the mushrooms.
5. Add water, mushroom stalks, cloves and seasoning to the pan. Simmer gently till cooked.
6. Add the mushrooms 15 minutes before serving.
7. Blend any remaining seasoned flour with water; gradually blend with the hot liquid from the pan; return to pan and boil up, with sherry added, if liked.
8. Put kidney and mushroom on serving dish, pour gravy over.
9. Border with creamed potatoes or macaroni tossed in parsley.

81. KIDNEY LORRAINE

Ingredients:

3 Lamb's Kidneys
50 g lean Bacon
250 ml Stock
15 g Butter
2 level teaspoonfuls Cornflour
Seasoning

½ Green Pepper
50 g Mushrooms
1 small Onion
1 teaspoonful Tomato Purée
1 tablespoonful Yoghurt

Servings: 2–3

Time: 20 minutes

Method:

1. Prepare kidneys and cut in quarters. Peel and chop onion. Cut bacon into strips. Wash and quarter mushrooms. Chop green pepper.
2. Melt butter; fry bacon and onion for 2–3 minutes. Add kidney and fry a further 3 minutes.
3. Blend cornflour with a little stock. Add the remaining stock, tomato purée, mushrooms, and green pepper to the pan.
4. Add the blended cornflour. Season and bring to the boil.
5. Cover and cook for 15 minutes or until kidney is tender. Stir in yoghurt and serve.

82. KIDNEY TURBIGO

Ingredients:

3 Lamb's Kidneys
12 Pickling Onions
25 g Butter
50 g Chipolata Sausages
50 g Button Mushrooms

I level dessertspoonful Flour
I teaspoonful Tomato Purée
I tablespoonful Sherry
250 ml Brown Meat Stock (page 28)
Parsley and Seasoning

Servings: 3
Time: 25 minutes

Method:

1. Skin and core kidneys. Prepare onions.
2. Melt butter, fry kidneys and sausages till brown. Remove and set aside.
3. Fry mushrooms and cook quickly with the onions for 2–3 minutes.
4. Stir in flour, tomato purée, sherry and stock and bring to boil. Add seasoning and re-place sausages and kidneys.
5. Cover and simmer gently for 20–25 minutes.
6. Serve sprinkled with parsley.

83. FRIED LIVER AND BACON

Ingredients:

200 g Calf's *or* Sheep's Liver
75 g fat Bacon
I level tablespoonful seasoned Flour

250 ml Water
Salt and Pepper

Servings: 3–4
Time: 10–12 minutes

Method:

1. Wash and dry the liver, remove skin and tubes. Cut into suitably sized pieces and dip in seasoned flour.
2. Cut bacon into pieces of a suitable size. Fry lightly. Place on serving dish, cover and keep hot while liver is fried.
3. Fry the liver in the fat drawn from the bacon. Cook for 3–4 minutes on one side, turn, and cook for 3–4 minutes on second side. Place on serving dish.
4. Add any remaining flour to fat in pan. Mix well, gradually add water. Boil up, stirring all the time, season.
5. Strain gravy over the liver, arrange the bacon on top.

84. LIVER HOT POT

Ingredients:

250 g Sheep's *or* Pig's Liver
I level tablespoonful Flour
Salt and Pepper
500 g Potatoes

I Onion
I pinch Sage
250 ml cold Water
Chopped Parsley

Servings: 3–4
Time: I hour
Oven Temperature: 180°C, No. 4
Position in Oven: Middle shelf

Method:

1. Wash the liver, remove skin and tubes.
2. Cut into pieces of suitable size and dip in seasoned flour.
3. Parboil an onion, chop it finely and mix with sage.
4. Arrange the liver in layers in an ovenproof dish with the onion and sage sprinkled between layers.
5. Pour water over the liver.
6. Cut the potatoes into slices; cover the liver with them.
7. Bake I hour in a moderate oven. Remove lid 15 minutes before cooking time is up.
8. Serve with chopped parsley sprinkled on top.

85. STEWED LIVER AND BACON

Ingredients:

200 g Liver (Sheep's, Calf's *or* Ox)	Oil for frying
I level tablespoonful seasoned Flour	250 ml cold Water
I Onion	75 g Bacon
I teaspoonful Tomato Purée	

Servings: 3
Time: 30 minutes for sheep's and calf's
I hour 30 minutes for ox

Method:

1. Wash the liver, remove skin and tubes.
2. Cut into pieces of suitable size and dip in seasoned flour.
3. Slice the onion and fry till a golden brown colour in the oil.
4. Lightly fry the liver, add tomato purée.
5. Add the water, stir till boiling, then simmer gently until tender.
6. Serve with fried or grilled bacon.

86. LIVER À LA FRANÇAISE

Ingredients:

200 g Calf's *or* Sheep's Liver	125 ml Stock *or* Water
75 g thin Bacon rashers	Few drops Worcester Sauce

Seasoning mixture:

4 level tablespoonfuls Breadcrumbs	Grating of Nutmeg
I dessertspoonful chopped Parsley	I Egg (beaten, to bind)
Salt and Pepper	

Mix all ingredients together and bind with beaten egg to make a spreading consistency.

Servings: 3–4
Oven Temperature: 180°C, No. 4
Position in Oven: Middle shelf

Method:

1. Wash the liver, remove skin and tubes.
2. Lay slices of liver on a well-greased ovenproof dish. Put some of the seasoning mixture on each slice and a strip of bacon on the top.
3. Pour in water or stock; cover with lid or paper.
4. Cook slowly in a moderately hot oven till tender, about 30 minutes.
5. Remove the lid or paper, crisp the bacon, add Worcester sauce to gravy and serve.

87. SWEETBREADS

Calf's and lamb's sweetbreads are used and they should be very fresh, lamb's having the more delicate flavour. (Sweetbreads are the thymus and pancreas glands.)

Allow approximately 75g per person. The time of cooking will vary according to the size of the sweetbreads.

Preparation of Sweetbreads:

1. Wash and soak for 30 minutes in cold, salted water.
2. Put in a pan with cold water to cover, bring to the boil, then place at once into cold water with a little salt and lemon juice in it; wash the sweetbreads again.
3. Trim off any fat, skin or tubes. The sweetbreads are now ready for cooking by different methods.

88. SWEETBREADS WITH CREAM SAUCE

Ingredients:

250 g Sweetbreads	Small piece Mace
Salt	1 teaspoonful Peppercorns
Piece Lemon Rind	25 g Butter
500 ml Stock	25 g Flour
1 small Onion	125 ml Milk *or* Cream
Stick Celery	Salt and Pepper
Piece Carrot	Lemon Juice

Garnish:

Cooked Ham	Grilled Bacon
Fried Bread	

Servings: 3
Time: 1–1½ hours

Method:

1. Prepare the sweetbreads (see recipe 87 above), put in a pan with stock, vegetables, lemon rind and seasonings, and simmer till cooked; the time varies from 1–1½ hours.

2. Put sweetbreads on serving dish, cover and keep hot. Strain stock.
3. Melt the butter, add the flour and cook for a few minutes without discolouring. Remove from the heat.
4. Add 250 ml stock gradually, beating well. Season.
5. Stir till boiling and cook for 3 minutes. Add milk or cream and lemon juice.
6. Coat the sweetbreads and garnish.

89. FRIED SWEETBREADS

Ingredients:

250 g Sweetbreads (page 128)	1 level teaspoonful seasoned Flour
250 ml Water	1 Egg (beaten)
1 Onion	Breadcrumbs (to coat)
2 Cloves	3 Bacon rashers (to serve with)
Bouquet of Herbs (page 27)	Oil for deep-frying
1 Bacon rasher (diced)	

Servings: 2–3
Time: 1 hour 45 minutes

Method:

1. Prepare the sweetbreads (page 128).
2. Put into a pan with 250 ml water, onion, cloves, bouquet of herbs and diced bacon, and stew for 1 hour 30 minutes.
3. Remove from pan and press between plates till cold.
4. Dip in seasoned flour, coat with beaten egg and breadcrumbs and deep-fry in oil till golden brown.
5. Serve with grilled bacon rashers. A white sauce (page 291) may be made from the liquor in which the sweetbreads were stewed.

90. BRAISED SWEETBREADS

Ingredients:

500 g Sweetbreads	Stock
2 rashers Fat Bacon	Meat Glaze (page 476)

Garnish:

Green Peas	Mushrooms

Servings: 4–5
Time: 1 hour approx.
Oven Temperature: 190°C, No. 5
Position in Oven: Middle shelf

Method:

1. Prepare the sweetbreads (page 128).
2. Braise the sweetbreads using the basic braising method (page 118), laying bacon over sweetbreads.
3. When ready, serve the sweetbreads with the braising liquor poured round.
4. Garnish with cooked mushrooms and green peas.

91. **VOL-AU-VENT OF SWEETBREADS**

Ingredients:

200 g Puff Pastry (page 310) *or* Ready-made Vol-au-vent Pastry Cases

Filling:

Sweetbreads with Cream Sauce (page 128)   100 g Bacon
50 g Mushrooms

Servings: 4
Time: Filling, 1 hour; Pastry, 30 minutes
Oven Temperature: 200–230°C, No. 7–8
Position in Oven: Middle shelf

Method:

1. Make and bake vol-au-vent cases (page 311) from the puff pastry or bake ready-made vol-au-vent pastry cases.
2. Make sweetbreads with cream sauce. Sweetbreads should be cut into bite-sized pieces.
3. Cook mushrooms and bacon; chop finely. Add to sweetbreads.
4. Reheat and fill cases with hot sweetbread mixture; replace tops and serve.

92. **CASSEROLE OF OX HEART**

Ingredients:

1 Ox Heart	Bouquet of Herbs (page 27)
100 g Streaky Bacon (cut thickly)	2 level tablespoonfuls Flour
1 glass Red Wine	Stock
½ head Celery	100 g Button Onions

Servings: 4–6
Time: 3 hours
Oven Temperature: 180°C, No. 4

Method:

1. Wash the heart well and cut away veins and arteries.
2. Cut bacon and heart into cubes and fry till brown.
3. Sprinkle with flour, mix thoroughly and brown the flour.
4. Add wine, stock and bouquet of herbs and cook for 2 hours in a covered casserole.
5. Add button onions and celery, sliced. Cook for a further hour.
6. Serve garnished with triangles of fried bread and accompanied by redcurrant jelly.

93. **BRAISED STUFFED HEARTS**

Ingredients:

2 Sheep's *or* Calf's Hearts	50 g Forcemeat (page 137)

Garnish:

75 g Mushrooms	4 Tomatoes

Servings: 4–6
Time: 3 hours
Oven Temperature: 190°C, No. 5
Position in Oven: Middle shelf

Method:

1. Wash the hearts well and cut away veins and arteries. Fill cavities with forcemeat. Skewer, if necessary.
2. Braise the hearts using any braising method (page 118).
3. When ready place in serving dish. The strained braising liquor can be thickened with cornflour or flour. Pour round the hearts.
4. Garnish with cooked mushrooms and tomatoes.

94. BOILED TONGUE

Ingredients:

1 Ox Tongue	Bouquet of Herbs (page 27)
1 Onion	6 Peppercorns
Small piece Carrot	250 ml Parsley Sauce
Small piece of Turnip	

Servings: 6–8, depending on size
Time: 3–4 hours

Method:

1. Wash and soak the tongue for 1–2 hours or, if strongly pickled, for 3–4 hours.
2. Put into a large pan with water to cover; bring slowly to the boil and skim. Add onion, carrot, turnip, peppercorns and herbs.
3. Boil gently, allowing 1 hour 10 minutes per kg plus 1 hour over. A small tongue will take longer in proportion to its size and not less than 3 hours.
4. When cooked, bones and gristle can be removed easily from the root. Skin the tongue taking care not to break the tip.
5. Slice and serve with parsley sauce.

To serve cold:

After skinning, roll tightly with the tip round the root and press into a round cake tin. Fill up with tongue stock. Cover, put a weight on top and leave overnight, then turn out.

95. DRESSED TONGUE

Method:

1. Prepare and cook as for boiled tongue, above.
2. After skinning, shape on a board, placing a rolling pin under tip to arch it. Leave overnight.
3. Trim off some of the root part, brush with melted meat glaze and decorate with coloured savoury butter.
4. Fix a frill round the root.

96. STEWED TRIPE AND ONIONS

Ingredients:

500 g cooked Tripe   Salt and Pepper
250 ml Milk   25 g Flour
2 Onions

Servings: 3
Time: 1 hour

Method:

1. Cut the tripe into even-sized pieces and put into a pan with the milk and blanched, sliced onions.
2. Simmer for 1 hour.
3. Blend the flour with a little cold milk, or water, pour some of the hot milk from the pan over, return to pan and boil up.
4. Season to taste and serve with toast.

97. HAGGIS

Ingredients:

1 Sheep's Stomach Bag and Pluck   1 level teaspoonful powdered Herbs
(this means the sheep's liver,   200 g Pinhead Oatmeal (toasted)
heart and lights [lungs])   2–4 level tablespoonfuls Salt
100 g Suet   1 level teaspoonful Black Pepper
4 medium-sized Onions (blanched)

Method:

1. Wash the bag in cold water, scrape and clean it well. Leave overnight in cold water.
2. Wash the pluck and put it in a pan of boiling water and boil for 2 hours, with the windpipe hanging out. Have a small bowl under the windpipe to catch any drips.
3. Place the cooked pluck in a large bowl, cover with liquor in which it was boiled and leave overnight.
4. Next day, cut off the windpipe, grate the liver, chop the heart, lights, suet and onions.
5. Add the oatmeal, which should first be toasted but not coloured, salt, pepper, herbs and 500 ml of the liquid in which the pluck was boiled.
6. Mix well, fill the bag rather more than half-full of the mixture, then sew it up and prick it.
7. Place in boiling water, simmer for 3 hours, forking occasionally to prevent bursting.
8. If liked, the bag may be cut into several pieces to make smaller haggises; cook 1½–2 hours.

Alternative method of preparing and using the stomach bag:

1. Get the stomach bag cleaned by the butcher.
2. Wash it thoroughly. Put it in a pot of cold water and bring to boiling point; this will cause the bag to contract.
3. Take it out of the pan immediately, wash and scrape it well and lay in salted water till required.
4. Take the stomach bag, keeping the fat or smooth side inside, and fill it, but not quite full. Sew up the opening.
5. Put into boiling water and simmer for 3 hours.

STUFFINGS

STUFFINGS

Herbs indicated are dried herbs, though fresh can also be used. A mixed herbs mixture could contain thyme, marjoram, rosemary, parsley, sage etc. A larger quantity is required of fresh herbs than dried. A tablespoon of fresh is the equivalent to a teaspoon of dried herbs.

1. FORCEMEAT

This is a suitable stuffing for veal, chicken, rabbit etc

Ingredients:

100 g Breadcrumbs
50 g Suet
3 teaspoonfuls chopped Parsley
1 teaspoonful Mixed Herbs

Rind of ½ Lemon (grated)
Seasoning
1 Egg
Milk, if necessary

Method:

Mix all dry ingredients, and bind with egg and milk.

2. SAGE AND ONION STUFFING

Ingredients:

2 large Onions
50 g Breadcrumbs
1 level teaspoonful Sage

Salt and Pepper
Milk *or* Egg (to bind)

Method:

1. Parboil onions, chop, mix all ingredients.
2. Bind with beaten egg or milk.
3. Use for stuffing meat or poultry.

Note: If preferred, stuffing may be cooked on its own in a greased ovenproof dish for 30 minutes until firm, then cut into slices.

3. HAM FORCEMEAT

Ingredients:

50 g Breadcrumbs
½ level teaspoonful dried Mixed Herbs
1 teaspoonful chopped Parsley

25 g chopped Ham *or* lean Bacon
Salt and Pepper
1 Egg (to bind)

Method:

Mix all dry ingredients together and bind with beaten egg.

4. **BACON AND MUSHROOM STUFFING**

Ingredients:

50 g Breadcrumbs	I teaspoonful chopped Parsley
50 g Mushrooms	Salt and Pepper
25 g lean Bacon	I Egg (beaten)

Method:

1. Skin and chop mushrooms, chop bacon, add to breadcrumbs.
2. Season the mixture, add chopped parsley.
3. Add enough beaten egg to bind.

5. **SAUSAGEMEAT STUFFING**

Ingredients:

500 g Sausagemeat	I teaspoonful chopped Parsley
150 g Breadcrumbs	Seasoning
I teaspoonful dried Mixed Herbs	I Egg
I teaspoonful dried Thyme	

Method:

Mix all ingredients together well, using beaten egg to bind.

6. **OATMEAL STUFFING**

Ingredients:

100 g Oatmeal	I small Onion (chopped)
50 g Suet	Salt and Pepper
I tablespoonful chopped Parsley	Milk

Method:

Mix all the dry ingredients and moisten with milk. Use for stuffing the body of a boiling fowl or the neck of a roasting chicken.

7. **RAISIN STUFFING**

Ingredients:

75 g Breadcrumbs	50 g Raisins
25 g Butter (softened)	Salt and Pepper
I tablespoonful chopped Parsley	I Egg (beaten)

Method:

1. Mix butter into breadcrumbs using a knife. Add raisins and parsley.
2. Season and bind with beaten egg.
3. Use to stuff ducks and other birds.

8. CHESTNUT STUFFING

Preparation of chestnuts:

1. Slit chestnuts on rounded side.
2. Put in pan of cold water, bring to the boil, boil for 3–5 minutes.
3. Remove pan from heat.

In order to skin the chestnuts while hot, remove a small quantity from the hot water at a time. The outer and inner brown skins should come away clean.

Ingredients:

300 g Chestnuts	25 g Butter
75 g Breadcrumbs	I Egg
I Onion (chopped)	Seasoning
I tablespoonful chopped Parsley	Stock *or* Water

Method:

1. Prepare the chestnuts.
3. Simmer for 30–45 minutes in a little stock or water to cover till they are tender.
4. Strain. Chop finely in a food processor or, for a smoother stuffing, press through a sieve or purée in a food processor and mix with the other ingredients. Add melted butter, bind with egg.

Note: Tinned chestnut purée could be used instead of fresh chestnuts.

POULTRY

POULTRY

Poultry is a term for birds that are bred to be eaten. This includes chicken, turkey, duck, goose and guinea fowl.

Flavour	Flavour will depend on how the poultry has been fed and kept. Free range birds will have better-tasting flesh than battery birds, though they may be slightly tougher because they have been allowed to have exercise
Preparation	Giblets should be removed as soon as possible from the bird and stored separately in the refrigerator
Trussing	Trussing helps the bird to retain a good shape while cooking. However, large birds should not be trussed
Frozen birds	Frozen birds must be defrosted slowly in the bottom of a refrigerator. A 5-lb bird will take 24 hours to defrost; a 10-lb bird will take at least 36 hours
Storing	Fresh poultry will generally keep for two days in the bottom of the refrigerator, but do not eat poultry that is beyond its sell-by date
Stuffing	Stuffed poultry will take longer to cook than poultry that is not stuffed. Adjust cooking times according to weight Small birds can be stuffed in neck and body cavities Medium-sized birds may be stuffed in the body cavity but not with a meat stuffing Large birds such as turkeys should not be stuffed in the body cavity Stuffing can be placed between the bird's loosened skin and the breast meat to keep the breast moist

1. TO DRAW A CHICKEN OR FOWL

Method:

1. Singe off any fine downy feathers by turning the bird over a gas flame or with a lighted taper, taking care not to blacken the skin.
2. Cut the skin round the leg, between foot and joint. Break the bone at that point and draw the sinews.
3. Slit the neck skin up the back; cut off close to the head; remove the crop and windpipe.
4. Cut off the neck close to the body, leaving a long neck skin.
5. Push the fingers into the neck opening, loosen the heart and lungs.
6. Raise the tail end of the bird upwards towards the worker. Make an incision between the vent and the tail. Insert forefinger and hook it round the end of the intestine. Slit the remainder of the skin around the vent, taking care not to pierce the intestines.
7. Hook two fingers round the gizzard, which will be felt as a hard lump, and pull out all the internal organs together.
8. Separate the giblets – liver, heart and gizzard. Remove greenish gall sack

from the liver, taking care not to break it. Cut round the thick outer skin of the gizzard and peel off the flesh (discard lining and contents).
9. The giblets and neck are used to make stock for gravy or soup.

2. **TO TRUSS A CHICKEN**

Trussing should not be done to large birds as it prevents the inside of the legs from being cooked as quickly as the breast.

With trussing needle and string:
1. Fold the wing pinions under the bird.
2. Press legs down to plump the breast.
3. Push the threaded trussing needle through the end of the wing joint and at the drumstick joint, through the body cavity and out at the same position on other side.
4. Fold neck skin round to the back. Take a stitch through it to hold it in place and tie off the strings.
5. Re-thread needle. Take a stitch under the breast bone. Cross string ends round legs and tie off under the parson's nose.

With skewers:
1. Insert a skewer in the same way as the trussing needle above.
2. Tie legs down firmly as above.

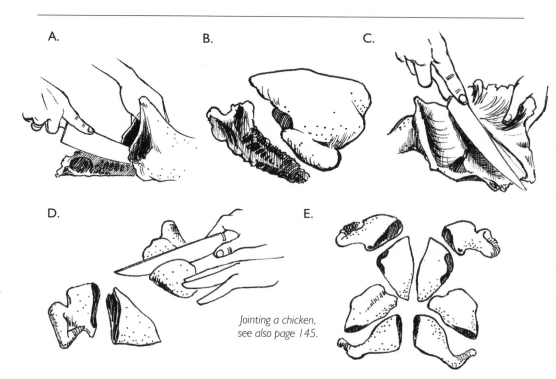

A.

B.

C.

D.

E.

Jointing a chicken, see also page 145.

3. JOINTING A CHICKEN

See artwork on page 144.

1. Cut off each leg at the point where they join the body.
2. With scissors or a knife, cut from the neck down either side of the backbone, cutting through flesh and bones (A). Take out backbone (B) and keep for stock.
3. Put bird breast-downwards (C). Cut along either side of breastbone and discard. Cut down the centre of the bird; this gives two breast portions.
4. To make four portions, cut behind the last rib, from the back to the breast (D).
5. You will have two leg portions (which could be further divided at the joint into drumstick and thigh), two wing–breast portions and two breast portions (E).

4. BOILED FOWL

Ingredients:

1 Fowl (1½–2 kg)	Oatmeal Stuffing (page 138)

Accompaniments:

500 ml White Sauce, Egg Sauce (page 291), *or* Mushroom Sauce (page 292)
Servings: 6
Time: 2–3 hours

Method:

1. Stuff body cavity of prepared fowl, sew up vent; truss (page 143, 144).
2. Put fowl and giblets into boiling salted water to cover and simmer for 2–3 hours or longer according to size and age, until the leg meat is tender and juices run clear when thickest part of leg is tested with a skewer.
3. Remove string and serve with a suitable sauce.

5. ROAST CHICKEN

Ingredients:

1 Chicken	50 g Butter
Forcemeat (page 137)	Salt and Pepper
or Oatmeal Stuffing (page 138)	

Accompaniments:

Thickened Gravy (page 477)	Watercress
Bread Sauce (page 296)	French Salad (page 213)
Rolls of Bacon (page 476)	

Servings: 4–5
Time: 1¼–1½ hours, depending on size of chicken
Approx. 20 minutes per 500 g plus 20 minutes
Oven Temperature: 200°C, No. 6
Position in Oven: Middle shelf

Method:

1. Make stuffing and put it under neck skin, folding skin round back. Truss if appropriate (page 143, 144).

145

2. Rub butter all over, particularly the breast. Season with salt and pepper. Cover breast with greased greaseproof paper. (See note below.)
3. Put chicken in oven and cook for 1¼ –1½ hours, basting regularly with cooking juices.
4. Test by piercing thickest part of leg with a skewer or fork. Juices should run golden and clear. If juices run pink, cook for longer.
5. Rest for 15 minutes in a warm place before carving.

Note: If cooking foil is used, cover the bird loosely with foil and allow 2 hours cooking time. Remove foil, baste breast and allow to brown for last 30 minutes.

Gravy:

Giblets from the bird	Water
Sediment from roasting pan	2 level teasponfuls Cornflour
Salt and pepper	

1. Simmer the giblets in salted water for 1 hour. Strain and reserve the giblet stock.
2. Pour fat from roasting tin into a bowl, leaving the sediment in the tin.
3. Add 250 ml of your giblet stock and boil up. Thicken with blended cornflour, allowing 2 level teaspoonfuls to 250 ml.
4. Season to taste.

6. ROAST FOWL

This recipe is intended for cooking an older, tougher bird.
Most chickens available in supermarkets will be young birds

Ingredients:

1 boiling Fowl	50 g Butter
Forcemeat (page 137)	Salt and Pepper
or Oatmeal Stuffing (page 138)	Thickened Gravy (page 477)

Servings: 4–6

Time: 2 hours 30 minutes (but this will depend on size and age of bird)
Approx. 20 minutes per 500 g plus 20 minutes

Oven Temperature: 190°C, No. 5

Position in Oven: Middle shelf

Method:

1. Stuff the body cavity of the prepared fowl. Sew up vent.
2. Truss if appropriate (pages 143, 144).
3. Put into boiling salted water to cover, and boil gently for 1 hour 30 minutes. Remove from the pan and dry the surface.
4. Rub butter all over, particularly the breast. Season with salt and pepper. Cover breast with greased greaseproof paper. (See note below.)
5. Cook in a moderate oven for 1 hour.
4. Test by piercing thickest part of leg with a skewer or fork. Juices should run golden and clear. If juices run pink, cook longer.
5. Rest for 15 minutes in a warm place before carving.

6. Make thickened gravy (page 477) and serve as roast chicken (page 145).
Note: If cooking foil is used, cover the bird loosely with foil and allow longer cooking time. Remove foil, baste breast and allow to brown for last 30 minutes.

7. ROAST TURKEY

Ingredients:

1 Turkey	75 g Butter
100 g Streaky Bacon	Butter Paper *or* Cooking Foil

or Sausage Stuffing (page 138)
Chestnut Stuffing (page 139)

Accompaniments:

Thickened Gravy (page 477)	100 g lean Bacon, for Rolls of Bacon
Bread Sauce (page 296)	(page 476)
Cranberry Sauce (page 297)	500 g Chipolata *or* small Sausages

Method:

1. Prepare as for roast chicken (page 145).
2. Stuff the neck end with chestnut or sausage stuffing (if more stuffings required, roast separately, wrapped in foil in roasting tins).
3. Rub with butter and place slices of streaky bacon on the breast. Cover with greased paper. (See note below.)
4. Melt 75 g butter in roasting tin, put the turkey in and cook for 20 minutes at 220°C, No. 7, then reduce heat and follow timetable below. Baste regularly.

Weight	Number of Servings	Oven Temperature	Cooking Time
4–5 kg	10–14	170°C, No. 4	3–4 hours
5–6 kg	14–16	170°C, No. 4	4–4½ hours
6–8 kg	16–20	150°C, No. 3	4½–5 hours
8–9 kg	20–25	150°C, No. 3	5–6 hours
10 kg	25–30	150°C, No. 3	6½ hours

5. Test by piercing thickest part of leg with a skewer or sharp knife. Juices should run golden and clear. If juices run pink, cook longer.
6. Rest for 15 minutes in a warm place before carving.
Note: If cooking foil is preferred then cover bird loosely with foil and allow 1 hour longer cooking time. Uncover bird, baste breast and allow to brown at higher temperature for last 30 minutes.

8. ROAST DUCK

Ingredients:

1 Duck	Sage and Onion Stuffing (page 137)

Accompaniments:

Thickened Gravy (page 477)	Apple Sauce (page 296)

Servings: 3–4
Time: 1½–2 hours
Oven Temperature: 220°C, No. 7
Position in Oven: Middle shelf

Method:

1. If necessary, singe and draw duck as for chicken.
2. Cut off first bone of wings. Cut off feet.
3. Stuff the body cavity with sage and onion stuffing.

To truss:

1. Turn the "apron" under the tail and skewer.
2. Truss through points of wings and through legs. The finished bird should have a sausage-like shape with none of the joints showing as in a fowl.

To cook:

1. Prick skin all over with a fork and rub with salt. Put the bird in roasting tin, breast-side down and cook for 30 minutes.
2. Turn bird and cook for the remainder of the time.
3. Remove bird. Pour off all the fat and make gravy from the juices, thickening with cornflour, 10 g to 250 ml.

9. ROAST GOOSE

Ingredients:

1 Goose   150 g Sage and Onion Stuffing (page 137)

Accompaniments:

Thickened Gravy (page 477)
Apple Sauce (page 296)

Servings: 8
Time: 2–3 hours depending on size of bird
Approx. 20 minutes per 500 g plus 20 minutes
Oven Temperature: 220°C, No. 7
Position in Oven: Lower half

Method:

1. Draw as for chicken. Cut off wings at first joint.
2. Stuff the body with sage and onion stuffing.
3. Truss as for roast duck (page 147). Rub skin with salt.
4. Put bird in roasting tin and cook in hot oven, 220°C, No. 7, for about 20–30 minutes.
5. Pour off all the fat that has collected and lower heat to 180°C, No. 4. Add a little water to roasting tin and continue cooking for 2–3 hours depending on size of bird.
6. Remove bird to a hot serving dish. Pour off all the fat and make thickened gravy from the juices, thickening with cornflour, 20 g to 500 ml.
7. Serve with apple sauce.

10. **GUINEA FOWL**

Ingredients:

Guinea Fowl | Rashers of Streaky Bacon
75 g Raisin Stuffing (page 138) | 50 g Butter
or Sausagemeat Stuffing (page 138)

Accompaniments:

As for Roast Chicken

Servings: 3–4
Time: 45–60 minutes
Oven Temperature: 220°C, No. 7
Position in Oven: Middle shelf

Method:

1. Draw as for roast chicken (page 145).
2. Stuff the body with raisin stuffing or sausagemeat stuffing; this helps to keep the flesh moist as it is inclined to be dry.
3. Truss and cook as for roast chicken (page 144–45).

11. **CASSEROLE OF CHICKEN**

Ingredients:

1 Chicken *or* 4 Chicken Joints | 500 ml Stock
3–4 level tablespoonfuls seasoned Flour | 100 g Mushrooms
50 g Butter | Chopped Parsley

Servings: 4–6
Time: 1½–2 hours
Oven Temperature: 220°C, No. 7
Position in Oven: Middle shelf

Method:

1. Divide the chicken into pieces suitable for serving.
2. Dip each piece in seasoned flour and fry in butter till brown. Add any remaining flour to pan and brown lightly, add stock, boil up.
3. Arrange joints in casserole and pour liquid over.
4. Cover and put in a hot oven until the liquid boils.
5. Reduce the heat to 180°C, No. 4, and cook gently until tender when tested with a skewer.
6. The time will depend on the age of the chicken, but an average time is 1½–2 hours.
7. Add prepared mushrooms to casserole 30 minutes before serving. Sprinkle with finely chopped parsley and serve.

Note: Casserole of fowl may be cooked in the same way as above but requires 2½–3 hours to cook.

12. CHICKEN IN CIDER

Ingredients:

1 Chicken (jointed)	250 ml Cider
25 g seasoned Flour	100 ml Tomato Pulp *or* Passata
50 g Butter	Bouquet of Herbs (page 27)
1 Onion	

Servings: 4–6
Time: 1–1¼ hours
Oven Temperature: 180°C, No. 4
Position in Oven: Middle shelf

Method:

1. Skin the chicken joints and toss in seasoned flour.
2. Fry joints in half the butter, then fry the onion till brown; put both into a casserole.
3. Heat the remaining butter in a pan and allow to brown. Add flour and make a brown roux (page 291). Add the cider slowly, then the tomato pulp and cook for a few minutes.
4. Pour sauce over the chicken in the casserole and add the bouquet of herbs.
5. Cook in a moderate oven for 1 hour or until the chicken is tender.
6. Remove the bouquet of herbs before serving.

13. FRIED CHICKEN

Ingredients:

1 Chicken	8 Mushrooms
1 level tablespoonful seasoned Flour	4 Tomatoes
50 g Butter *or* Oil for frying	

Servings: 4
Time: 30 minutes

Method:

1. Cut the chicken into neat joints.
2. Coat well with seasoned flour.
3. Shallow-fry in butter or oil for 20 minutes.
4. Add seasoned, prepared mushrooms and cook for 7–10 minutes.
5. Add halved, seasoned tomatoes and fry for 2–3 minutes.
6. Serve chicken with mushrooms and tomatoes.

14. GRILLED CHICKEN JOINTS OR POUSSINS

Ingredients:

Chicken Joints *or* Poussins	Salt and Pepper
(cut in halves)	Cooking Oil *or* melted Butter

Time: 20–30 minutes
Grill: Medium to high

Method:

1. Season chicken joints or poussins.
2. Brush inside of poussin with oil or melted butter.
3. Place on a heated grill pan and put under grill. Cook for 20–30 minutes, turning frequently and brushing liberally with oil or melted butter.
4. Serve with some of the liquor from grill pan.

15. KROMESKIES OF CHICKEN

Ingredients:

75 g cooked Chicken	Pinch ground Mace
25 g Butter	*or* grated Nutmeg
25 g Flour } Panada	Salt, Pepper, Cayenne
125 ml Stock	Thin strips Bacon
1 tablespoonful Cream	Coating Batter (page 474)

Servings: 3

Method:

1. Make a panada (page 292) with the flour, butter and stock; add cream, seasonings, mace. Chop the chicken finely and add to panada.
2. Turn onto a plate and leave to cool.
3. Take 2 teaspoonfuls of the chicken and panada mixture, place on a strip of bacon and roll the bacon round.
4. Dip in the coating batter and fry in very hot oil.
5. Drain well and serve.

16. FRICASSÉE OF CHICKEN

Ingredients:

A cooked Chicken (jointed)	Lemon Juice
Grilled Bacon	Seasoning
1 tablespoonful Cream	

Sauce:

40 g Butter	250 ml Chicken Stock
40 g Flour	125 ml Milk

Servings: 4

Method:

1. Make white sauce (page 291) with butter, flour, stock and milk.
2. Cut chicken into joints and remove skin.
3. Heat joints thoroughly in sauce.
4. Place chicken on serving dish.
5. Add cream, lemon juice and seasoning to sauce. Coat chicken and serve with grilled bacon.

Note: This is a good method for using up left-over chicken.

17. CHICKEN MARENGO

Ingredients:

1 Chicken
2 tablespoonfuls Vegetable Oil
250 ml Tomato Sauce (page 297)
250 ml Espagnole Sauce (page 294)

A little Onion (chopped)
8 Mushrooms
3 tablespoonfuls Sherry
10–25 g Almonds (whole, blanched, skinned and roasted in a hot oven)

Servings: 4–6
Time: 1 hour
Oven Temperature: 180°C, No. 4
Position in Oven: Middle shelf

Method:

1. Joint and skin chicken.
2. Brown joints in oil.
3. Place joints in a casserole, add hot sauces, onion and prepared mushrooms. Cover and put in oven.
4. Stir occasionally, and just before serving add sherry.
5. Scatter with roasted almonds.

18. CHICKEN VICTORIA

Ingredients:

2 Leg joints of Chicken (cooked)
4 Bacon rashers

250 g Green Pea Purée (page 200)
500 ml Tomato Sauce (page 297)

Stuffing:

25 g Oatmeal
1 teaspoonful Onion (finely chopped)
1 tablespoonful Butter (melted)

1 small teaspoonful chopped Parsley
Salt and Pepper

Servings: 4

Method:

1. Divide each leg into two joints.
2. Mix together stuffing ingredients.
3. Remove bone from joints and fill with oatmeal stuffing; wrap a rasher of bacon round each portion. Heat thoroughly in tomato sauce.
4. Arrange joints on a serving dish, coat with tomato sauce.
5. Spoon hot green pea purée between the joints.

19. CHICKEN MARYLAND

Ingredients:

4 Chicken Joints
25 g seasoned Flour
1 Egg
50 g Butter
Seasoning

2 Bananas
Dried Breadcrumbs (page 477)
Tomato Sauce (page 297)
Watercress

Corn Fritters:

I small tin Sweetcorn Kernels	Seasoning
25 g Flour	2 tablespoonfuls Milk
I Egg (beaten)	

Servings: 4 **Time:** 30 minutes
Oven Temperature: 180°C, No. 4
Position in Oven: Middle shelf

Method:

1. Prepare cornfritters. Drain sweetcorn. To a bowl add flour, seasoning, beaten egg and milk and mix well to make firm consistency. Add drained sweetcorn. Beat well.
2. Bone chicken joints and divide in two.
3. Coat pieces in beaten egg, and dip in seasoned flour. Fry in melted butter for 10–15 minutes until golden brown.
4. Put into a baking dish, bake in moderate oven for 20 minutes.
5. While chicken is baking, fry corn fritters by dropping spoonfuls into melted butter. Flatten out. Fry until golden brown, turn, fry second side.
6. Cut bananas in half lengthwise, and once across. Coat in beaten egg and breadcrumbs. Fry bananas until golden brown.
7. Serve chicken joints surrounded by fritters and fried banana. Serve on a bed of watercress with tomato sauce.

20. CHICKEN CROQUETTES

Ingredients:

150 g cooked Chicken (minced)	Seasoning
25 g Butter	I Egg (beaten)
25 g Flour } Panada	Dried Breadcrumbs (page 477)
125 ml Chicken Stock	Oil for deep-frying

Servings: 3

Method:

1. Mince chicken, or chop finely.
2. Make a panada (page 292) with the butter, flour and stock. Boil until thick, season.
3. Add chicken, mix thoroughly.
4. Put onto plate, spread out, allow to cool.
5. Divide into six equal portions.
6. Form into a sausage shape, coat in beaten egg and dip in breadcrumbs.
7. Deep-fry in oil.

Note: These may be fried in a shallow pan when they should be formed into cakes.

GAME

GAME

1. GAME SEASONS

Grouse	12th August to 10th December
Blackcock and Ptarmigan	20th August to 10th December
Partridges	1st September to 1st February
Wild Duck	Various, September to February
Pigeon	Available all year
Pheasants	1st October to 1st February
Woodcock (Scotland)	1st September to 31st January
(England and Wales)	1st October to 31st January
Snipe	August to January
Quails	Available all year
Hares	September to March
Rabbit	Available all year, wild or farmed
Venison	Complicated and varies (though farmed or frozen may be available all year)

2. PREPARATION OF GAME

Hanging of Game	1. Game is hung to develop the flavour and to make it tender; it should never have an unpleasant smell 2. The length of time for hanging game depends on the age of the bird, the kind of bird, the time spent in transit, the weather and personal taste. In warm or humid weather, allow a shorter time 3. Game should be hung in a cool, dry airy place. It should be sprinkled with pepper 4. It may be hung by the neck with the feathers on, till blood drops from the beak and the breast feathers can be plucked easily 5. Pheasants may be hung for 6–14 days Partridges may be hung for 7–8 days Grouse may be hung for 3–4 days 6. Water-birds, such as wild duck, teal and widgeon, should hang for only 2 days, otherwise a rancid flavour develops
Plucking	1. When plucking, put the feathers into a basin or pail lined with damp paper to keep them from flying about 2. Hold the bird in the left hand and begin plucking under one wing, work over the back, then under the other wing 3. Work over the breast and down to the tail 4. Lastly pull out pinion feathers 5. Pull the feathers against the way they are lying and give a sharp jerk, taking care not to break the skin

To tell when birds are young	1. Grouse, partridges, snipe and quails, when young, have short, round leg spurs 2. Old grouse and partridges have yellow legs and dark bills. They are not good for roasting, but may be used for casseroles 3. Woodcock, when old, have pointed leg spurs, and the feet hard and thick; when young, their spurs are blunt 4. When the bills look soft and unsightly, and the throat is muddy, it is always a sign that the birds have been dead for a long time 5. In venison, when young, the fat is clear and bright 6. If hares have sharp claws, ears damp, and the cleft in the lip narrow, it is a sign that they are young
Drawing	Draw as for chicken (page 143). Keep the feet on but cut off the toes. Traditionally, snipe and woodcock are not drawn, for the trail is considered a delicacy by gourmets. If preferred they may be drawn as for other birds
Trussing	1. Cut off the toes and cut the wing at the first joint 2. Make a slit in the skin above the vent-hole and pull the tail through 3. Press the legs firmly against the body 4. Pass a skewer through the wing joint and the joint between the thigh bone and the drumstick, then through the body cavity. Repeat this process, putting the skewer, after it has passed through the body, first through the leg joint, then through the wing 5. Cross the legs, tie them together and tie down onto the tail

3. THE COOKING OF GAME

Young birds should be roasted; older birds should be braised or cooked in a casserole. The length of time of cooking will depend on time of hanging and age of bird. See individual recipes for variations.

Cooking Times for Roast Game	**°C**	**Gas Mark**	**Time**
Pheasant	190°C	Gas 5	45–60 mins
Partridge	190°C	Gas 5	20–30 mins
Grouse	190°C	Gas 5	20–30 mins
Blackcock	190°C	Gas 5	45–60 mins
Wild Duck	200°C	Gas 6	40 mins
Pigeon	200°C	Gas 6	25–35 mins
Quail	180°C	Gas 4	20 mins
Snipe	190°C	Gas 5	15–20 mins

Cooking in foil

The bird should be loosely wrapped in cooking foil and placed in the tin without fat and cooked till tender. If, at the end of cooking, the breast is not brown, open the foil, increase the heat of the oven and leave the bird for 10 minutes.

Accompaniments to roast game:

> Clear Gravy
> Game Chips *or* Potato Crisps (page 193)
> Bread Sauce (page 296)
> French Salad (page 213)
> Browned Crumbs (page 476)
> Watercress

Accompaniments to roast wild duck and all water birds:

> As above, but serve Orange Salad (page 216) instead of French Salad
> Bigarade Sauce (page 294)

4. ROAST PHEASANT

Ingredients:

1 Pheasant	50 g Cooking Fat *or* Oil
25 g Butter	A little Flour (for dredging)
Slices of Streaky Bacon (for barding)	250 ml Water

Accompaniments:

Clear Gravy	Game Chips *or* Potato Crisps
Bread Sauce (page 296)	(page 193)
Browned Crumbs (page 476)	French Salad (page 213)
Watercress	

Servings: 3–4

Time: 45–60 minutes

Oven Temperature: 190°C, No. 5; 220°C, No. 7

Position in Oven: Middle shelf

Method:

1. Pluck and draw the pheasant; put a piece of butter inside the body to keep it moist. Truss.
2. Put slices of streaky bacon on the breast, cover with thickly-greased paper.
3. Heat fat or oil in roasting tin. Place the pheasant in the tin and cook in a moderate oven from 45–60 minutes, according to age of bird.
4. Ten minutes before the pheasant is ready. Remove paper, baste pheasant with hot pan juices. Dredge with flour and baste again.
5. Return to the oven, now set at 220°C, No. 7, and leave till brown, about 10 minutes. Place bird on serving dish.
6. Pour fat from tin, leaving sediment. Add 250 ml cold water, skim off solidified fat; stir well, boil up and season.
7. Serve with whichever accompaniments are preferred.

5. ROAST GROUSE

Ingredients:

Grouse	25 g Butter
Rashers of Streaky Bacon	50 g Cooking Fat *or* Oil

Accompaniments:

As for Roast Pheasant (page 159)

Servings: 2–3
Time: 20–30 minutes
Oven Temperature: 190°C, No. 5
Position in Oven: Middle shelf

Method:

1. Pluck, draw and truss as for pheasant.
2. Cook as roast pheasant (page 159) and serve with accompaniments of choice.

6. ROAST PARTRIDGE

Ingredients:

Partridge	50 g Cooking Fat *or* Oil
25 g Butter	Croûte Fried Bread
Rashers of Fat Bacon	

Accompaniments:

As for Roast Pheasant (page 159)

Servings: 1–2
Time: 20–30 minutes
Oven Temperature: 190°C, No. 5
Position in Oven: Middle shelf

Method:

1. Pluck, draw and truss as for pheasant, putting knob of butter inside the body to keep the bird moist.
2. Cook as roast pheasant (page 159) and serve on fried bread with accompaniments of choice.

7. ROAST PIGEONS (1)

Ingredients:

2 young Pigeons	Strips of Streaky Bacon
50 g Cooking Fat *or* Oil	2 Croûtes Fried Bread

Accompaniments:

Thickened Gravy (page 477)	Bread Sauce (page 296)
Watercress	

Servings: 4
Time: 25–35 minutes
Oven Temperature: 190°C, No. 5
Position in Oven: Middle shelf

Method:

1. Draw, singe and wipe the pigeons.
2. Cut off the toes, scald and scrape the feet.
3. Remove wing at the first joint.
4. Truss like roast chicken (page 144), but cross the pigeon's legs.

5. Heat fat or oil in a roasting tin, sprinkle in a little salt.
6. Place bacon rashers on breasts of pigeons, cover with thickly greased paper and place in tin; or wrap loosely in cooking foil, and place in tin without fat.
7. Cook in a moderate oven for 40 minutes or till tender. Remove trussing thread or skewers and place birds on croûtes of fried bread.

Thickened gravy:

1. Pour fat from roasting tin, leaving sediment in tin. Add 250 ml of water for each pigeon.
2. Thicken with cornflour, allowing 2 level teaspoonfuls per 250 ml gravy. Return to heat and boil up.
3. Serve pigeons garnished with watercress.

8. ROAST PIGEONS (2)

Ingredients:

2 young Pigeons	Rashers Streaky Bacon
50 g Cooking Fat *or* Oil	

Accompaniments:

As for Roast Pheasant (page 159)

Servings: 2
Time: 25–35 minutes
Oven Temperature: 190°C, No. 5
Position in Oven: Middle shelf

Method:

1. Prepare and roast the pigeons as for Roast Pigeons (1).
2. When cooked, if birds are not brown, dredge with flour, baste and brown in the oven for 5 minutes, to froth.
3. Put birds on serving dish.
4. Pour fat from tin, leaving sediment.
5. Add 250 ml cold water and skim off solidified fat. Stir well and boil up. Season.
6. Serve with accompaniments.

9. STEWED PIGEONS

Ingredients:

2 Pigeons	Salt, Pepper, Cayenne
25 g Butter	25 g Ham (optional)
500 ml Stock	1 level tablespoonful Flour
100 g Mushrooms	A squeeze of Lemon Juice

Servings: 4
Time: 1–2 hours

Method:

1. Pluck and clean the pigeons and cut in two. Trim mushrooms.
2. Fry pigeon joints quickly in butter in a stew pan, add stock, mushroom trimmings and seasoning. Add the ham (if liked, it may be fried with the pigeons).

161

3. Stew gently for 1–2 hours till pigeons are tender.

4. Add the mushrooms 30 minutes before serving.

5. Remove the birds and the mushrooms and keep hot.

6. Thicken the gravy with the flour, add lemon juice, strain over the pigeons.

10. WILD DUCK

Ingredients:

Wild Duck	25 g Butter
50 g Cooking Fat *or* Oil	

Accompaniments:

Clear Gravy	Game Chips *or* Potato Crisps
Bread Sauce (page 296)	(page 193)
Browned Crumbs (page 476)	Orange Salad (page 216)
Watercress	Bigarade Sauce (page 294)

Servings: 3–4

Time: 40 minutes

Oven Temperature: 190°C, No. 5

Position in Oven: Middle shelf

Method:

1. Pluck, draw and clean as for pheasants.

2. Put butter inside the body.

3. Truss and cook as for roast pheasant (page 159).

Note: Some wild duck has a fishy flavour. This can be lessened by putting 1 cm boiling water in the roasting tin and basting the bird frequently with this for the first 15 minutes.

Drain. Brush breast with some melted butter and roast.

If it is felt that the gravy is still fish flavoured, then serve the bird with a suitable sauce such as Bigarade (page 294).

11. BRAISED GAME BIRDS

Suitable for older birds not easily made tender by roasting

Ingredients:

1 *or* 2 Game Birds	Rashers of Streaky Bacon
Stock	

Mirepoix:

1 Carrot	Bouquet of Herbs
A small piece of Turnip	6 Peppercorns
1 Onion	25 g Butter
A piece of Celery	Mushroom Trimmings
25 g Fat Bacon	

Oven Temperature: 180°C, No. 4

Position in Oven: Middle shelf

Time: Depends on age and size of bird
Pheasants 1½–2 hours
Partridge 1–1½ hours
Grouse 1–1½ hours
Blackcock 1½–2 hours

Method:

1. Pluck, draw and truss game birds.
2. Bard the breasts with streaky bacon.
3. Prepare mirepoix as for braised meat (page 118) in a pan.
4. Place birds on mirepoix, cover with greased paper, put lid on pan and fume for a third of cooking time.
5. Add stock to cover vegetables, replace paper and lid.
6. Cook a third of the time on top of the cooker and a third in the oven.
7. Remove the bacon from the breasts, put the birds on an ashet.
8. Skim the fat from the pan juices and boil juices to reduce for gravy. Serve with the birds.

12. **CASSEROLE OF GAME**

Suitable for older birds not easily made tender by roasting

Ingredients:

1 *or* 2 Game Birds (depending on size)	1 small Onion
25 g seasoned Flour	50 g Mushrooms
100 g Bacon	500 ml Stock
25 g Butter	150 ml Cider *or* Red Wine

Time: 2 hours
Oven Temperature: 180°C, No. 4
Position in Oven: Middle shelf

Method:

1. Draw and joint the birds; dip in seasoned flour.
2. Cut up bacon and fry lightly in pan or casserole; remove bacon, add the butter and brown the joints; remove from pan and brown chopped onion.
3. Place onion, bacon and game joints in a casserole; add the mushroom stalks and seasoning. Add stock and cider almost to cover contents of casserole.
4. Cook gently in the middle of a moderate oven for about 2 hours or till game is tender; this depends on the age of the birds. Half an hour before the game is cooked add the prepared mushrooms.

13. **SALMI OF GAME**

Ingredients:

1 Pheasant	Crescents of Pastry
500 ml Espagnole Sauce (page 294)	1 tablespoonful Sherry
50 g Mushrooms	1 Glacé Cherry

Servings: 4–5
Time: 45 minutes
Oven Temperature: 180°C, No. 4
Position in Oven: Middle shelf

Method:

1. Roast bird until almost cooked.
2. Divide into pieces and remove the skin. Keep warm.
3. Add pan sediment, chopped mushrooms and sherry to Espagnole sauce.
4. Put prepared meat in a casserole, cover with sauce and continue cooking for 30 minutes. Garnish with pastry crescents.

14. VENISON

Venison seasons vary greatly depending on the species and sex of the deer and the area of the country. Generally speaking, doe venison is in season from February/March till October, buck venison from October till June. It may be available farmed or frozen all year round.

To hang	1. Venison should hang for 7–14 days before cooking 2. Wash and dry carefully 3. Dust with ground ginger or pepper to keep off flies 4. Examine the venison every day, dry it and dust again with ginger or pepper 5. Wash and dry before using
Methods of cooking	Haunch or Saddle – Roast Loin – Roast or braise or cut into chops and grill Shoulder – Roast, braise or stew Neck – Cut into chops and stew The haunch and the loin are the best parts. These prime cuts from a very young animal may be roasted without prior marinading

To marinade	For older animals it is advisable to marinade, as follows
	    2 parts Oil to 1 part Vinegar
	    Bay Leaf
	    A little thinly sliced Onion
	    Peppercorns
	1. Put the marinade into a dish large enough to hold the piece of venison; the marinade should cover the bottom of the dish
	2. Place the meat in the marinade, and leave for 1–3 days turning frequently
	3. Drain the venison, do not wash it

15. ROAST VENISON

Ingredients:

Haunch, Loin or Shoulder of Venison	Pork fat (for barding)
Marinade (see 164, 476)	Dripping *or* Butter

Accompaniments:

Clear Gravy	Redcurrant *or* Rowan Jelly

Oven Temperature: 400°C, No. 6.

Time: Allow 30 minutes per 500 g plus 30 minutes

Method:

1. Marinade joint for 1–3 days. Remove joint from marinade and drain.
2. Bard joint with pork fat or cover with heavily greased paper.
3. Melt dripping in a roasting tin and put joint in. After 20 minutes lower oven temperature to 190°C, No. 5 and continue cooking, basting from time to time. The tin may also be covered loosely with foil, which should be removed for the last 30 minutes of cooking to allow meat to brown.

16. GRILLED VENISON CUTLETS OR STEAKS

Ingredients:

or 4 Venison Cutlets from neck (2.5 cm thick)	Salt and Pepper
4 Venison Steaks from leg	8 Mushrooms
50 g Butter *or* Cooking Oil	4 Tomatoes

Servings: 4

Time: 15 minutes

Method:

1. Trim cutlets. Dot with butter or brush with oil. If liked, cutlets may be marinaded before grilling (page 164, 476).
2. Grill slowly, turning every 2 minutes, allowing, in all, about 15 minutes. Brush with oil or melted butter during cooking.
3. Wash mushrooms, remove stalks, season and dot with butter or brush with oil. Grill, allowing 8–10 minutes.
4. Wash, halve and season tomatoes; dot with butter or brush with oil. Grill, allowing about 3 minutes.
5. Serve cutlets with gravy from grill pan poured over. If liked, a teaspoonful of rowan jelly may be added to gravy in grill pan.
6. Garnish with mushrooms and tomatoes.

17. STEWED VENISON

Ingredients:

500 g Venison (Shoulder, Neck *or* slices from the Haunch, boned)	1 Onion (sliced)
2 level tablespoonfuls seasoned Flour	500 ml Water
25 g Dripping *or* Butter	1 tablespoonful Redcurrant *or* Rowan Jelly

Servings: 5

Time: 2 hours

Method:

1. Beat meat, cut into neat pieces and coat in well-seasoned flour.
2. Fry sliced onion in dripping or butter, then brown pieces of venison.
3. Add water; bring to the boil and simmer very gently for 2 hours or until tender.
4. Add redcurrant or rowan jelly to the gravy and boil up, or serve jelly separately.

18. TO SKIN, PAUNCH AND JOINT A HARE

To skin:

As for rabbit (page 167).

To paunch:

Paunching is most easily carried out at the sink.

1. Remove internal organs without breaking diaphragm.
2. Place hare on its back, pierce throat well into chest with a sharp knife and hold head aside, allowing blood to drip into a bowl. Break diaphragm and remove heart and lungs.
3. Add 1 teaspoonful vinegar or flour to blood to prevent it clotting.

To joint:

As for rabbit (page 167), but as joints are large, divide each hind leg into three portions and the back into 5–6 portions.

19. JUGGED HARE

Ingredients:

1 Hare	50 g Flour
75 g Dripping **or** Butter	1 litre Water
1 Onion (chopped)	Salt and Pepper
1 Clove	1 tablespoonful Redcurrant
1 teaspoonful Peppercorns	Jelly
Bouquet of Herbs (page 27)	150 ml Port **or** Red Wine

Forcemeat:

50 g Breadcrumbs	½ level teaspoonful Salt
25 g Suet (chopped)	Pepper
1 tablespoonful chopped Parsley	A little Anchovy Essence
½ level teaspoonful Thyme	2 Eggs (beaten, 1 to bind and 1 to coat)

Servings: 8

Time: 2½–3 hours

Oven Temperature: 200°C, No. 6

Position in Oven: Middle shelf

Method:

1. Skin, paunch and wash hare.
2. Cut into joints and fry in dripping or butter.
3. Place joints, chopped onion and flavourings in a casserole. Blend flour and stock, season, pour into frying pan, bring to the boil and pour over joints in casserole. Cover and stand in a tin of hot water.
4. Place in a fairly hot oven, 200°C, No. 6. Reduce heat to 180°C, No. 4, when cooking has started and simmer gently for 2–3 hours.
5. Add jelly and blood, and wine if liked, reheat thoroughly.
6. Make forcemeat balls by mixing dry ingredients and suet, and binding with half of beaten egg. Form into balls, coat with rest of beaten egg and breadcrumbs and deep-fry in hot oil.
7. Serve on top of joints in casserole.

20. TO SKIN, CLEAN AND JOINT A RABBIT

Rabbits can be bought fresh or frozen and are usually sold cleaned and skinned ready for cooking. Your butcher can joint it for you.

To skin:

1. Cut off paws.
2. Pull skin away from flaps.
3. Push hind legs upwards through skin.
4. Cut skin at tail and pull skin up to forelegs.
5. Push forelegs through skin and continue to pull skin up to ears.
6. Cut through the ears close to the head and pull the skin off over the head or head may be discarded.

To clean:

1. Cut off head, split it open and remove the eyes. Soak the head in cold water.
2. Remove kidneys, break through the thin skin and pull out heart and liver.
3. Remove gall bladder from liver and discard.
4. Wash liver, heart and kidneys.

To joint:

1. Divide into joints as follows:
   2 hind legs;
   2 forelegs;
   3 pieces of back.
   Open ribs up front and chop into 2 pieces.
2. Wash all thoroughly.

21. BROWN STEW OR CASSEROLE OF RABBIT

Ingredients:

1 Rabbit (jointed, reserve liver and kidneys)	1 small Apple (chopped, optional)
1 Onion (thinly sliced)	2 Cloves
50 g Butter	Salt and Pepper
3 level tablespoonfuls seasoned Flour	50 g Bacon (fried)
500 ml Water *or* Stock	50 g Forcemeat (page 166 or 137)

Servings: 4–6

Time: 1 hour 30 minutes for young rabbits; 2 hours 30 minutes for older rabbits

Oven Temperature: 180°C, No. 4

Position in Oven: Middle shelf. Could also be cooked in a lidded casserole pot on top of the cooker.

Method:

1. Joint rabbit and dip in seasoned flour.
2. Slice onion and fry in butter until golden brown and then set aside.
3. Add joints of rabbit and brown them.
4. Add water or stock, onions, liver and kidneys, apple, cloves, seasoning and remaining flour. Simmer or bake in a moderate oven till tender.
5. Arrange joints on serving dish, pour gravy over. Serve with fried bacon and fried forcemeat balls.

Note: If liked, bacon may be stewed with the rabbit.

22. WHITE STEW OF RABBIT

Ingredients:

1 Rabbit (jointed)	50 g Butter
500 ml Water *or* Stock	250 ml Milk
50 g Flour	1 Onion (thinly sliced)
Seasoning	A little Lemon Rind
Rolls of Bacon (page 476)	Bouquet of Herbs (page 27)

Servings: 4–6

Time: 1½–2 hours

Method:

1. Soak rabbit in cold salted water for 30 minutes.
2. Bring a pot of water or stock to boil, add onion and lemon rind and bouquet of herbs. Add rabbit, salt, boil for 2 minutes and simmer for 1 hour 30 minutes.
3. Lift out joints and let stock settle, then pour off clear part of liquid.
4. Add 250 ml of water or stock to 250 ml milk.
5. Melt butter in pan, add flour, cook for a few minutes, then gradually add liquid and stir till boiling. Simmer for 8 minutes to cook out flour. Sauce should coat the back of a spoon. Add more milk if too thick. Season.
6. Add joints of rabbit to the sauce and heat through.
7. Serve joints coated with the sauce.
8. Garnish with rolls of bacon, fried bacon or fried bread.

Note: If the rabbit is dark in colour it may be blanched before cooking.

MEAT PIES AND PASTRY DISHES

MEAT PIES AND PASTRY DISHES

1. STEAK AND KIDNEY PIE

Ingredients:

150 g Rough Puff *or* Flaky Pastry (page 309)
500 g Shoulder Steak

30 g Ox Kidney *or* a Sheep's Kidney
2 level tablespoonfuls seasoned Flour
A little Water and some Stock

Servings: 5
Time: 2 hours approx.
Oven Temperature: 220–230°C, Nos. 7–8
Position in Oven: One-third from top
Size of Pie dish: 500 ml

Method:

1. Make the pastry, cover and set aside.
2. Cut steak into neat strips approx. 2 cm thick, removing excess fat.
3. Skin, split, core, wash and cut up kidney.
4. Dip the meat in seasoned flour, roll up with a piece of kidney in the centre of each strip and put upright in pie dish; half-fill with water.
5. Roll out the pastry a little larger than size of pie dish; cut off a continuous strip round pastry sufficient to fit the rim of the pie dish. Wet rim of pie dish and apply pastry strip.
6. Wet rim of pastry and cover with the remaining pastry, rolling larger if necessary.
7. Press onto rim and trim edges with a knife and flake round edge with a fork to seal.
8. Make a hole in the centre; brush top with beaten egg or milk.
9. Roll out scraps of pastry, cut leaves, decorate pie, arranging leaves round hole in pie. Brush the leaves with egg.
10. Bake in a hot oven for the first 20 minutes, then reduce the heat to 180°C, No. 4, and bake for another 1 hour 30 minutes till meat is cooked.
11. When ready, fill up the pie with boiling stock through hole in centre of pie.

Note: The meat may be stewed and cooled, then placed in pie dish and covered. The baking time will be reduced to 1 hour.

2. VEAL AND HAM PIE

Ingredients:

150 g Flaky Pastry (page 309)
500 g Shoulder of Veal
100 g Streaky Bacon
Salt and Pepper
Bouquet of Herbs

Grated Lemon Rind
Pinch powdered Mace
1 *or* 2 Eggs (hard-boiled)
Little Water *or* Stock

Servings: 5–6
Time: 2 hours approx.
Oven Temperature: 220–230°C, Nos. 7–8
Position in Oven: One-third from top
Size of Pie dish: 500 ml

Method:

1. Cut the veal in 5 cm pieces and put in pie dish in layers with bacon and seasoning, herbs, lemon rind and mace.
2. Cut eggs in thick slices and lay on top. Half fill pie dish with stock or water.
3. Cover as steak and kidney pie (page 171).
4. Bake in a hot oven for first 20 minutes, then reduce heat to 180°C, No. 4, and continue cooking for a further 1–1½ hours, until meat is tender.
5. Fill up with stock through hole in centre of pie and serve hot or cold.

3. RABBIT PIE

Ingredients:

200 g Rough Puff *or* Short Pastry (pages 309, 307)	2 level tablespoonfuls seasoned Flour
1 Rabbit (cleaned and jointed)	Oil for frying
100 g Bacon	Pinch Mixed Herbs
2 Eggs (hard-boiled)	Stock *or* Water

Servings: 6
Time: 2 hours
Oven Temperature: 220–230°C, Nos. 7–8
Position in Oven: One-third from top
Size of Pie dish: 750 ml

Method:

1. Cut the rabbit and bacon into small pieces and the eggs into quarters.
2. Dip the pieces of rabbit into seasoned flour and fry in oil.
3. Put them in the pie dish with the herbs, bacon and hard-boiled eggs. Add enough stock to half fill the dish.
4. Cover with pastry as steak and kidney pie (page 171).
5. Bake in a hot oven for first 20 minutes, then reduce heat to 180°C, No. 4, and continue cooking for 1 hour 30 minutes or until meat is tender.
6. Fill up with hot seasoned stock through hole in centre of pie.

4. GAME PIE

Pastry
Ingredients:

200 g Flour	Pinch Salt
100–125 g Butter	Water, if necessary
1 Egg	

Method:

1. Mix salt with flour and rub in butter.
2. Make to a stiff paste with egg.

**Filling
Ingredients:**

2 Pigeons *or* 1 Pheasant	100 g cooked Ham *or* Tongue
6 Mushrooms	Salt and Pepper
1 Egg (hard-boiled)	2 tablespoonfuls Water

Servings: 6   **Time:** 2 hours
Oven Temperature: 220°C, No. 7
Position in Oven: Middle shelf
Size of Tin: 10-cm pie tin or cake tin with loose bottom

Method:

1. Cut the meat into small pieces, removing bones and skin. Cut mushrooms, egg, ham or tongue into strips and mix all well together, season.
2. Roll out half the pastry and cut the rounds to fit top and bottom of tin.
3. Roll out remainder to fit round the side of tin.
4. Line sides allowing 1 cm to lie on bottom of tin. Wet edge and drop in base. Press firmly.
5. Place the filling loosely in the prepared mould, piling it high in the centre.
6. Wet round the edges and cover with the remainder of the pastry. Trim and make a hole in the centre. Brush with egg and decorate.
7. Bake in a hot oven, 220°C, No. 7, for 20 minutes, then reduce heat to 180°C, No. 4, and continue cooking, giving, in all, 2 hours' cooking time.

To Serve Hot.—Fill with stock made from game bones.
To Serve Cold.—Dissolve 1 level teaspoonful of gelatine in 125 ml of game stock and when almost cold fill up the pie.

5. RAISED PORK PIE

Ingredients:

250 g Hot Water Pastry (page 312)	½ level teaspoonful Sage
500 g Pork	Little Water *or* Stock
Seasoning	

Servings: 5–6 (make one pie or
a number of small pies)
Time: 2 hours
Oven Temperature: 200°C, No. 6
Position in Oven: Middle shelf

Method:

1. Cut the meat into very small pieces and mix with the seasoning. Use any bone or rind for making stock.
2. Take two-thirds of dough and keep remainder warm.
3. Knead and shape the large piece of dough with the fingers into a hollow pie.
4. Fill with the seasoned meat, well pressed down.

5. Wet edges of pastry. Roll remaining pastry to form a lid, cover meat with this, press edges firmly and make a little hole in the middle.
6. Trim edges and decorate pie with leaves of pastry. Brush top with egg.
7. Fix a band of greased greaseproof paper round pie.
8. Bake according to size. Allow 2–2½ hours for the full quantity and about 1 hour for small pies, reducing temperature when the pie is well browned.
9. Fill up through hole in centre of pie with a little boiling stock.

6. RAISED VEAL AND HAM PIE

Make as raised pork pie (page 173), using the following filling:

500 g shoulder of Veal	Salt and Pepper
1–2 Eggs (hard-boiled)	Pinch Herbs and Mace
100 g Streaky Bacon	Grated Lemon Rind

7. RAISED MUTTON PIE

Make as raised pork pie (page 173), using lean mutton instead of pork. Season with salt and pepper and a pinch of mixed herbs, if liked.

8. ROMAN PIE

Ingredients:

100 g Short Pastry (page 307)	1 Tomato
200 g Veal	Salt, Pepper, Cayenne
50 g Macaroni	250 ml suitable Sauce
Very small piece Shallot *or* Onion	(e.g. Tomato, page 297)
50 g grated Cheddar Cheese *or* Parmesan	

Servings: 4
Time: 1 hour
Oven Temperature: 220°C, No. 7
Position in Oven: Middle shelf
Size of Tin: 15 cm diameter

Method:

1. Cut the veal into small pieces and stew for 1 hour.
2. Boil the macaroni till al dente.
3. Chop the shallot or onion finely and mix all the ingredients together.
4. Thickly grease a cake tin. Roll out two-thirds of the pastry and line the tin.
5. Fill prepared tin with the mixture and cover with remaining third of pastry.
6. Bake, reducing heat after 15–20 minutes to 190°C, No. 5, for remaining time.
7. Turn out and serve with tomato sauce (page 297).

9. PLATE MINCE PIE

Ingredients:

150 g Short Pastry (page 307)
200 g cooked Meat
2 level teaspoonfuls Flour
150 ml Stock *or* Gravy   } *or* 200 g cooked Mince (page 99)
1 teaspoonful Ketchup
Salt and Pepper

Servings: 4–5
Time: 1 hour
Oven Temperature: 220°C, No. 7
Position in Oven: Middle shelf

Method:

1. Mince the meat finely. Mix the flour smoothly with a little stock or gravy. Add seasoning and ketchup and mix all together.
2. Roll out half the pastry very thinly and line a metal enamelled plate or pie tin with it.
3. Spread the meat mixture nearly to the edge of pastry. Wet edge of pastry.
4. Roll out the other piece of pastry to cover the meat, press edges well together. Trim neatly and from the trimmings cut out decoration for the top. Brush with egg.
5. Bake for 20 minutes in a hot oven; reduce the heat to 180°C, No. 4 for the remaining time.

10. SAUSAGE ROLLS

Ingredients:

200 g Rough Puff Pastry (page 309)   500 g Sausages
Little Milk *or* Egg

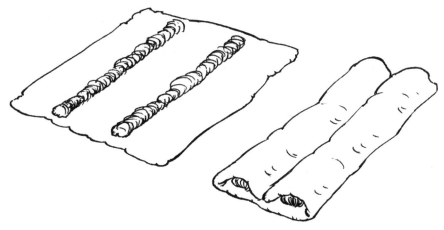

How to roll sausage rolls.

Servings: 8
Time: 30 minutes
Oven Temperature: 220°C, No. 7
Position in Oven: One-third from top

Method:

1. Skin sausages and roll in flour.
2. Roll pastry thinly into an oblong.
3. Put sausages end to end on the pastry in two rows, 2 cm in from sides of strip (see illustration page 175).
4. Dampen side edges of pastry and fold to meet in middle.
5. Cut into two long rolls and flake cut edges.
6. Cut to lengths as required (4–10 cm).
7. Arrange on baking tray and glaze with egg.
8. Bake in a hot oven for 30 minutes. Serve hot or cold.

11. CORNISH PASTIES

Ingredients:

200 g Short Pastry (page 307)	1 raw Potato (small)
or 200 g Rump Steak	Salt and Pepper
200 g Mince	Egg *or* Milk for glazing
½ small Onion	

Servings: 6
Time: 1 hour
Oven Temperature: 220°C, No. 7
Position in Oven: Top shelf

Method:

1. Cut the steak into small pieces or use mince. Chop the onion finely, dice or grate the potato, season.
2. Divide pastry in six, roll each piece into a round the size of a saucer.
3. Put some mixture on each round. Wet edge of pastry halfway round, bring edges together and crimp with a fork to seal. Glaze with egg or milk.
4. Bake at 220°C, No. 7, for 20 minutes, reduce to 180°C, No. 4, for remainder of time.
5. Serve hot or cold.

12. CHICKEN PATTIES OR VOL-AU-VENTS

Ingredients:

100 g Puff *or* Flaky Pastry (pages 309)	50–75 g cooked Chicken
125 ml Béchamel *or* Velouté Sauce (page 292)	2–3 Mushrooms
	Salt and Pepper
25 g cooked Ham *or* Tongue	Little Cream

Servings: 4 patties
Time: 20–25 minutes
Oven Temperature: 230°C, No. 8
Position in Oven: One-third from top

Method:

1. Make pastry, form four patty cases (see page 311) and bake.
2. Make sauce.
3. Add diced chicken, ham, chopped cooked mushrooms, seasoning and cream to the sauce. The mixture should be soft and creamy.
4. Fill the pastry cases with the mixture, put on the tops and serve.

13. RISSOLES IN PASTRY

Ingredients:

50 g Pastry, Short *or* Flaky (pages 307, 309)	10 g Butter
50 g cooked Chicken *or* other cooked Meat	10 g Flour
Small piece Ham	2 tablespoonfuls Stock
2–3 Mushrooms (cooked)	Seasoning
Egg and Breadcrumbs	

Method:

1. Mince chicken, ham and mushrooms.
2. Make a roux with the butter and flour (page 291) and blend with stock.
3. Add all ingredients and seasoning, and mix well.
4. Turn the mixture onto a plate to cool.
5. Roll pastry very thinly and cut in rounds with a cutter.
6. Put a teaspoonful of mixture on each. Dampen edges of pastry. Fold edges together and press firmly.
7. Coat with egg and breadcrumbs and fry to a good brown colour.

14. STEAMED MEAT PUDDING

Ingredients:

150 g Suet Pastry (page 307)	2 level tablespoonfuls seasoned Flour
500 g shoulder Steak *or* skirt of Beef	2 tablespoonfuls cold Water
1 Sheep's Kidney	

Servings: 5–6
Time: 3–4 hours
Equipment: Pudding-shaped basin

Method:

1. Cut the meat into thin slices and dip in seasoned flour.
2. Wash, skin and core the kidney, cut into small pieces; put a piece on each slice of steak and roll up.
3. Set aside one-quarter of the pastry for the top.
4. Grease a pudding basin and line with the pastry.

5. Fill it with meat and kidney, sprinkle on remaining flour.
6. Add water, turn edge of lining onto meat, and wet edge. Cover the pudding with remaining pastry. Press the lid on firmly.
7. Cover with greased paper and steam in a covered pan for 3–4 hours. Check water in pan regularly. Top up with boiling water if necessary.
8. Turn onto a hot serving dish; cut a hole in the top of the pastry and fill up with stock.

15. SAVOURY MINCE ROLL

Ingredients:

100 g Suet Pastry (page 307)   1 small Onion
200 g Mince   Salt and Pepper
Brown *or* Tomato Sauce (page 297)

Servings: 4–5
Time: 2 hours

Method:

1. Mix together mince, finely chopped onion and seasoning.
2. Make the pastry and roll out into an oblong about 15 cm x 30 cm approx.
3. Spread the meat nearly to the edge, moisten edge of pastry.
4. Roll up and press the ends.
5. Place in a greased meat-roll jar and steam for 2 hours.
6. Turn out and serve with brown or tomato sauce (page 297).

Note: Alternatively meat and pastry can be put in layers in a pudding basin.

VEGETABLES

METHODS OF COOKING VEGETABLES

ROOT VEGETABLES

GREEN VEGETABLES

METHODS OF COOKING VEGETABLES

A guide to the classification in this section:

> **Root Vegetables.**—Those grown below the ground (we have included onions in this chart for convenience, onions are bulbs as opposed to roots).
> **Green Vegetables.**—Those grown above the ground.
> **Peas, Beans and Pulses.**—Pod vegetables.
> **Vegetable Fruits and Squash.**—Those which have their seeds on the inside.
> **Mushrooms.**—And other edible fungi.
> Vegetables supply vitamins A, B group and C, and the minerals calcium and iron. These nutrients are easily destroyed if vegetables are too old, or cooked for too long. Fresh is best but frozen vegetables have more nutrients in them than old vegetables. Vegetables are high in fibre and most are low in calories. See pages 435–436 for how to freeze fresh vegetables.

1. ROOT VEGETABLE CHART

Vegetable	Preparation	Method of Cooking	Time
Jerusalem Artichokes	Wash and peel thinly. Slice or leave whole	Boiling Stewing Steaming Roasting	20–30 mins 20 mins 40 mins 30 mins
Beetroot	Rinse off earth and wash carefully, taking care not to break skin	Boiling (Other methods page 190)	1–3 hrs (according to size)
Carrots	Wash, scrape or peel. Leave whole or slice	Boiling Stewing Steaming Roasting Stir-frying	20–40 mins 20–40 mins 40 mins 40 mins 5–10 mins
Celeriac	Wash and peel thinly and cut into slices or dice	Boiling Stewing	20 mins 20 mins
Kohl Rabi	Remove green leaves. Wash and peel fairly thickly and cut into slices or dice	Boiling Stewing	20–40 mins 45 mins
Parsnips	Wash and peel thinly, cut into slices	Boiling Stewing Steaming Roasting	30 mins 40 mins 40 mins 40 mins
Sweet Potatoes	Wash and peel, cut into thick slices	Boiling Roasting	20 mins 25–30 mins

Turnip (old) Swede	Wash and peel thickly. Cut into neat blocks	Boiling Stewing Steaming Roasting	30–40 mins 30–40 mins 30–40 mins 30–40 mins
Turnip (new)	Wash and peel. Cut into slices or keep whole if small	Boiling Stewing Steaming Roasting	20–30 mins 20–30 mins 20–30 mins 20–30 mins
Onions (incl. Shallots)	(Classification – bulbs) Remove outer skin. Slice or chop	Boiling Stewing Roasting Frying (page 191)	45 mins–1 hr 45 mins–1 hr 45 mins–1 hr 5–20 mins
Potatoes Old New	Scrub and peel thinly Scrub and scrape	Boiling (For other methods pages 192–5)	20–30 mins 20 mins

2. BOILING ROOT VEGETABLES

Method:

1. Prepare vegetables and put into sufficient boiling salted water to cover.
2. Put lid on and cook steadily till tender.
3. Drain thoroughly, toss in butter, and sprinkle with chopped parsley, or coat with a white sauce (page 291).

Note: Old turnips may be mashed.

3. STEAMING ROOT VEGETABLES

Method:

1. Put the prepared vegetables into an electric steamer, a steamer over a pan of boiling water or, to save fuel, over a pan already cooking, e.g. steamed pudding.
2. The vegetables may be served tossed in butter and sprinkled with chopped parsley or coated with a white sauce (page 291).

4. STEWING ROOT VEGETABLES

On top of the cooker or in the oven

Method:

1. Prepare vegetables and put into a pan with a little stock or water and 25 g butter.
2. Add seasoning.
3. Cook slowly till tender. Time will vary according to size of vegetables.
4. Serve in the liquor in which they are cooked, reducing it if necessary. (If a sauce is to be served, the liquor should be used and the quantity made up with stock or milk.)

5. ROASTING OR BAKING ROOT VEGETABLES

Method:

1. Prepare vegetables and put into a roasting tin with some olive oil or cooking oil and a little salt or place round a piece of meat while roasting.
2. Bake till tender, turning occasionally.
3. Drain well and serve hot.

6. FRYING ROOT VEGETABLES

Most root vegetables may be fried but they should be cooked previously, except onions and potatoes. Carrots and parsnips may be coated with egg and breadcrumbs or dipped in batter after cooking, then deep-fried in hot oil.

7. POTATO CHART

Potatoes turn green when they have been exposed to the light and this is toxic in quantity. Cut off any green parts before cooking. Store potatoes in a cool, dark, dry place.

Type of cooking	Suitable potatoes	Examples of suitable varieties
Boiling/steaming	Small new (waxy) potatoes, with skins on Large, old (floury) potatoes, peeled	Charlotte Desiree Maris Piper Jersey Royal Nicola Duke of York
Mashing	Dry, old, floury potatoes	Desiree King Edward Kerr's Pink
Baking	Dry, floury potatoes	Desiree Golden Wonder Maris Piper Kerr's Pink
Roasting	Dry, old, floury potatoes	Desiree Golden Wonder Maris Piper Maris Peer King Edward Kerr's Pink

Frying, chipping	Firm, dry, floury potatoes	Desiree Golden Wonder Maris Piper Maris Peer King Edward
Salad	Small, firm, waxy new potatoes in their skins	Charlotte Jersey Royal Nicola
Gratin, dauphinoise	Firm, waxy potatoes	Charlotte Nicola Duke of York

8. GREEN VEGETABLES CHART

Vegetables	Preparation	Method of Cooking	Time
Asparagus	Cut stalks equal in length, scrape white part lightly and tie in bundles	Boiling Steaming Roasting Grilling	5–10 mins 5–10 mins 10–15 mins 5–10 mins
Broccoli	Wash and cut roughly or sprig – may be tied in bundles	Boiling Steaming Stir-frying	10–15 mins 10–15 mins 5–10 mins
Brussels Sprouts	Remove withered leaves, and trim base of stalk	Boiling Steaming	10–20 mins 10–20 mins
Cabbage —Spring	Remove coarse outside leaves. Cut in quarters, remove hard stalk. Wash and shred	Boiling Stir-frying	10 mins 5 mins
—Winter	As above	Boiling	10–12 mins
—Savoy	As above	Boiling Stir-frying	10–15 mins 5 mins
Red Cabbage	As above	Boiling Stewing Casseroling (page 196) Add vinegar during cooking to retain colour	15–20 mins 20–30 mins 20–30 mins

Cauliflower	Remove outside leaves. Wash, trim and cut a cross in base of stalk, or sprig cauliflower	Boiling (whole) Boiling (sprigs) Frying (sprigs) Steaming	15–20 mins 10–15 mins 10–15mins 10–15 mins
Celery	Remove green tops and root. Separate stalks and wash well. Scrub, if necessary, to remove sand. Cut in lengths	Boiling Stewing Stir-frying Raw	20–30 mins 40–50 mins 5 mins
Chicory or Belgian Endive	Remove outer leaves if necessary, trim ends and wash well. Towards end of season blanch – to remove bitter flavour	Boiling Raw, thinly sliced, served with other salad leaves.	10 mins
Fennel	Remove outer layer and wash well. Cut into quarters, slice or chop	Frying Roasting Stewing Braising Raw (thinly sliced)	15–20 mins 30–40 mins 20–25 mins 20–25 mins
Globe Artichoke	Peel off outer leaves and trim green parts of inner bud to leave white heart and remove prickly "choke". Rub with half a lemon. Simmer immediately Or, snap off stalk at base of artichoke. Cut to make base flat. Rub with half a lemon. Simmer immediately	Boiling Add vinegar or lemon juice to cooking water Boiling (To eat, in this case, pull off leaves one at a time and dip in melted butter. Eat fleshy part only. Discard choke)	30–45 mins 30–45 mins
Kale (curly)	Wash well, strip leaves from stalk unless young and tender	Boiling	30 mins
Leeks	Remove the root and coarse outside leaves. Split in two lengthways and wash thoroughly. Cut into lengths	Boiling Stewing Frying	10–20 mins 30 mins 5 mins
Spinach (baby)	Wash well, remove coarse stalks	Boiling (wilting)	5 mins

9. BOILING GREEN VEGETABLES

Method:

1. Prepare vegetables and put into enough boiling salted water just to cover.
2. Cook rapidly with the lid on for the required time.
3. Drain thoroughly, add a piece of butter and toss over heat. Serve.

Note: Cauliflower may be coated with a white sauce (page 291), cheese sauce (page 291) or tomato sauce (page 297).

Leeks may be coated with white or cheese sauce.

10. STEWING GREEN VEGETABLES

Most green vegetables are not suitable for stewing but the
exceptions are celery, chicory and leeks

Method:

1. Prepare vegetables and cook in a small quantity of stock or water with a piece of butter and seasoning.
2. Serve with the liquor in which cooked or use the liquor, along with milk, to make a sauce to coat the vegetables.

Note: These vegetables may be stewed in a casserole in the oven, but allow longer time than when cooking on top of the cooker.

11. FRYING GREEN VEGETABLES

Celery strips and cauliflower sprigs may be coated in egg and breadcrumbs or dipped in batter (page 474) and deep-fried in hot oil. They can be cooked previously but left slightly underdone to prevent break down when put into the batter.

12. STIR-FRYING

Prepare vegetables according to type. Cut into even-sized pieces. Heat cooking oil in a wok or sauté pan and stir-fry vegetables over a medium heat until cooked but still crunchy in texture.

13. PEAS, BEANS, PULSES AND SWEETCORN CHART

Vegetable	Preparation	Cooking Method	Cooking Time
Pea (fresh, garden)	Wash, shell	Boil Steam Stir-fry	10 mins 10 mins 10 mins
Pea (dried, split, green or yellow)	Wash	Boil	1–2 hours

Sugar Snap Pea or **Mange Tout**	Wash, destring	Boil or Steam Stir-fry	10 mins 10 mins
Broad Beans (fresh) **Broad Bean (dried)**	Wash, shell Soak overnight	Boil or Steam Stir-fry Boil	10 mins 10 mins 1–2 hours
Haricot Bean (dried)	Soak overnight	Boil then simmer in water with a pinch of bicarbonate of soda	1–2 hours
French Beans (fresh)	Young – wash, remove tops and tails. Old – Top and tail and remove fibrous thread from down the side. Shred	Boil Boil Stir-fry	10 mins 20 mins 5 mins
Runner Beans (fresh)	String as for older French beans. Wash and slice	Boil Stir-fry	20 mins 5–10 mins
Sweetcorn **Baby Sweetcorn**	Use as soon as possible after buying	Boil Steam Stir-fry	10 mins 10 mins 2–5 mins
Lentils (red, split) **Lentils (brown)**	Wash	Boil then simmer	20 mins 30 mins
Butter or Lima Bean (fresh) **Butter or Lima Bean (dried)**	Wash, shell Soak overnight	Boil Steam Boil then simmer in water with a pinch of bicarbonate of soda. Cook till soft and serve with butter	10–15 mins 10–15 mins 1–2 hours
Chick Peas (dried)	Soak overnight	Boil then simmer in water with a pinch of bicarbonate of soda	5–6 hours
Kidney Beans (dried)	Soak overnight. Discard water. Rinse beans then cover with fresh water and boil vigorously for at least 10 minutes. Failure to do this can cause food poisoning	Boil (in addition to the 10 minutes vigorous boiling done as preparation)	1–2 hours

14. BOILING FRESH PEAS AND BEANS

Method:

1. Put into enough boiling salted water just to cover.
2. Cook rapidly with the lid on for the required time.
3. Drain thoroughly, add a piece of butter and toss over heat. Serve.

15. STIR-FRYING FRESH PEAS AND BEANS

Heat cooking oil in a wok or sauté pan and stir-fry over a medium heat until cooked but still firm in texture.

16. VEGETABLE FRUITS AND SQUASH CHART

Vegetable Fruit	Preparation	Cooking Method	Cooking Time
Tomato	Wash before use. In some dishes, scald, skin and seed before chopping and including in the recipe (concassé, see page 202, recipe 65, Skinning and Seeding Tomatoes)	Grill Fry Stew Process for sauces (stew then blend) Slice raw for salads (page 211)	5 mins 10 mins 10 mins 10 mins
Sweet Pepper	Wash, cover in oil and roast or grill to blister skin in order to loosen and remove skin. Red, orange and yellow peppers are sweeter than green; red being the sweetest. Chop in strips	Stew Process for sauces Roasted in salads Griddle	30 mins 20 mins 30 mins or till soft with crisp edges 10 mins
Chilli Pepper	Destalk, slice in half, remove the seeds and discard (they are the hottest part of the chilli), and run under cold running water. Chop finely into long strips, then dice	Stew Stir-fry Raw in salad	Follow recipe 2–3 mins
Aubergine	Wash, slice crosswise. Salt to encourage juices to be drawn out (dégorger). Stand in salt for 30–60 minutes, then rinse	Stew Stuff and bake Stir-fry Deep-fry in batter Griddle	30 mins 30 mins 5–10 mins 5–10 mins 5–10 mins

Avocado	Halve with a sturdy knife. Chop firmly into the avocado stone with your knife and then twist. If properly ripe, stone will easily come out	Slice and eat raw Purée	
Squash and Pumpkin	Remove peel with a Y-shaped peeler. Halve and de-seed. Chop into large chunks	Roast Bake Steam Boil	30 mins 30 mins 30 mins 30 mins
Cucumber	Wash. Eat with or without peel. Can be deseeded by cutting lengthwise and scooping out seeds. If cucumber is bitter, salt to draw out bitter juices	Raw in salads and dipping sauces Pickled Cooked in soup	Follow recipe
Marrow	Wash, skin and slice or chop	Bake Stuff and bake Stew Stir-fry Steam	15 mins 30 mins 30 mins 5–10 mins 15 mins
	Slice thinly. Coat in batter or seasoned flour (or seasoned cornflour)	Deep-fry	Cook fritters just till golden brown
	Marrow flowers: wash. Coat in light batter	Deep-fry	5 mins or till light brown
Courgette	Wash, skin, slice, ribbon with a Y-shaped peeler, or chop.	Bake Griddle Stuff and bake Stew Stir-fry Boil or steam	15 mins 10 mins 20 mins 20 mins 5–10 mins 10 mins
	Cut into fingers or long strips. Coat in batter or seasoned flour (or seasoned cornflour)	Deep-fry	Cook fritters just till golden brown
	Courgette flowers: wash. Coat in light batter	Deep-fry	5 mins or till light brown

ROOT VEGETABLES

17. **BOILED BEETROOT**

In choosing beetroot, select those which are dark and firm

Method:

1. Wash carefully, taking care not to break the skins.
2. Put into boiling salted water and cook the beetroot till tender, the time varying according to the size and the age of the beetroot, from 1–3 hours.
3. Test for readiness. When pressed with fingers skin should come off quite easily.

Methods of serving:

Hot:

Remove the skin from the beetroot, cut into thick slices or cubes; toss in melted butter and serve sprinkled with chopped parsley. Or, after skinning, cut into slices and coat with white sauce (page 291).

Cold:

When cold, peel and slice. Pour over a little vinegar or equal parts of vinegar and water in which a little sugar has been dissolved.

18. **BOILED BEETROOT (QUICK METHOD)**

Method:

1. Peel and slice beetroot or cut into dice.
2. Put into boiling salted water to just cover the beetroot and cook gently until tender, the time depending on the size of the pieces of beetroot, but approximately 20–30 minutes.
3. Some colour will come out of the beetroot at first, but it will be re-absorbed during cooking. When the beetroot is ready there should be practically no liquid left in the pan.
4. Add a little butter, shake over the heat and serve sprinkled with chopped parsley.

19. **BAKED BEETROOT**

Method:

1. Wash the beetroot.
2. Wrap in greased paper or foil.
3. Place on a baking tray and put into the middle of a moderate oven, 180°C, No. 4. The cooking time will be about the same as for boiling, according to size and age of the beetroot.
4. Baked beetroot may be tested and served as for boiled beetroot.

20. **FRIED ONIONS (1)**

Method:

    1. Prepare the onions and slice thinly.
    2. Melt some butter or cooking oil in a frying pan and add the onions.
    3. Stir while they are frying.
    4. When tender, brown and crisp, drain well.
    Note: Strongly flavoured onions may be blanched before frying.

21. **FRIED ONIONS (2)**

Method:

    1. Prepare the onions and cut into rings. Separate the rings.
    2. Dip the rings in milk then in seasoned flour.
    3. Deep-fry in oil till golden brown and crisp.
    4. Drain thoroughly and sprinkle with salt and pepper.

22. **ROOT VEGETABLE CASSEROLE**

Ingredients:

2 Carrots	Stock *or* Water
2 Parsnips	25 g Butter
2 medium Onions	Seasoning
Large piece Turnip	

Time: 1 hour
Oven Temperature: 180°C, No. 4
Position in Oven: Middle

Method:

    1. Prepare vegetables according to kind, and slice.
    2. Grease a casserole and arrange vegetables in layers.
    3. Season and half fill with stock or water.
    4. Put dots of butter on top and cover.
    5. Cook at 180°C, No. 4, until tender, about 1 hour.
    Note:
    1. Any selection of root vegetables may be cooked in this way. Most green
       vegetables are unsuitable, the exceptions being – chicory, celery and leeks.
    2. This casserole is suitable to serve with roasts, casseroles, pies, etc, that are
       cooked in the oven as it saves fuel.

23. **BOILING POTATOES IN THEIR SKINS**

After scrubbing, make a slit round the middle of the potato just through skin. Cook as for any boiled root vegetable (page 182).

24. STEAMING POTATOES

Method:

1. Scrub and peel potatoes or leave skins on, slitting them round the middle.
2. Put into an electric steamer or steam over a pan of boiling water and cook till tender, time varies according to size and variety of potatoes: average-sized potatoes will require about 30–45 minutes.

25. NEW POTATOES

Method:

1. Scrub and scrape potatoes.
2. Cook in boiling salted water for 20–25 minutes or until tender. A sprig of mint may be added.
3. Drain and toss in butter and chopped parsley or oatmeal.

Note: New potatoes do NOT mash successfully.

26. BUTTERED NEW POTATOES

Method:

1. Choose small potatoes.
2. Scrub and scrape potatoes.
3. Melt sufficient butter to cover the bottom of a pan.
4. Toss potatoes in the butter, put lid on pan and cook till tender, about 30 minutes. Time will depend on the size of the potatoes.
5. Shake pan occasionally to prevent potatoes sticking.
6. Before serving, remove lid and continue cooking for a few minutes to crisp.

27. BAKED POTATOES IN JACKETS

Method:

1. Choose even-sized potatoes.
2. Scrub and pierce them deeply with a fork.
3. Rub with a buttered paper or brush with oil.
4. Place directly on oven shelves or on a baking tray. Bake in a hot oven, 200–220°C, No. 6–7, for approximately 1 hour.
5. Pierce potatoes to test for readiness.

28. ROAST POTATOES (1)

Method:

1. Choose even-sized potatoes and peel.
2. Heat some cooking oil in a roasting tin, add potatoes and baste.
3. Bake in a moderate oven, 180°C, No. 4, until tender: 1 hour for average-sized potatoes. Baste several times in oil during cooking.

Note: When roasting meat, the potatoes are usually cooked round the joint.

29. ROAST POTATOES (2)

Method:

1. Prepare potatoes and parboil for 8–10 minutes.
2. Drain and cook as in recipe 28 but allow less time. Cook at 200°C, No. 6 for about 40 minutes.

30. FRIED POTATOES (1)

Method:

1. Peel potatoes and cut into slices.
2. Heat sufficient cooking oil to cover the bottom of a frying pan.
3. When hot, add potatoes; brown on one side, turn and cook on the second side until potatoes are tender.
4. Drain well, season and serve.

31. FRIED POTATOES (2)

Method:

1. Slice some cooked potatoes and fry as in method (1) having the fat rather hotter and allowing a shorter time.
2. Drain well, season and serve.

32. POTATO CHIPS

Method:

1. Choose large potatoes and peel.
2. Cut into thick slices, cut lengthwise into chips. Soak in cold water for 1 hour, drain and dry thoroughly.
3. Deep-fry in hot oil (page 9) and leave until they rise to the surface.
4. Remove chips, reheat fat.
5. Return chips to fat to finish browning.
6. Drain well, sprinkle with salt and serve.

Note: Instead of removing chips from pan and reheating fat, the chips may be left in the pan until cooked and golden brown.

33. GAME CHIPS OR POTATO CRISPS

Method:

1. Prepare potatoes and slice very thinly.
2. Leave in cold water 1 hour; drain and dry very thoroughly.
3. Deep-fry in hot oil (page 9) until golden brown, stirring with a metal spoon to prevent sticking together.
4. Drain, season and serve with grilled meats and game.

34. **POTATO STRAWS**

Prepare and cook as potato chips (page 193), but cutting much smaller.

35. **STOVED POTATOES**

Ingredients:

500 g Potatoes	125 ml hot Water *or* Milk
1 large Onion	Salt and Pepper
Small piece of Butter	

Method:

1. Prepare and slice potatoes and onion.
2. Melt butter in a pan and fry onion, add potatoes. Season and add water or milk.
3. Put lid on pan and cook slowly for 35 minutes.
4. Stir occasionally to prevent sticking.

36. **CREAMED POTATOES**

Ingredients:

500 g Potatoes	2 tablespoonfuls Milk
Small piece Butter	Salt and Pepper

Method:

1. Prepare as boiled potatoes (page 182).
2. Mash, or put through a potato ricer. Add milk and butter, beat until creamy over a gentle heat.

37. **POTATO CROQUETTES**

Ingredients:

250 g Potatoes (cooked)	Salt and Pepper
25 g Butter	Egg (beaten)
1 Egg Yolk	Dried Breadcrumbs (page 477)

Servings: 6

Method:

1. Sieve potatoes, add butter, egg yolk and seasoning. Mix well.
2. Shape into croquettes, coat with egg and breadcrumbs. Re-coat if necessary.
3. Deep-fry in hot oil until golden brown.
4. Drain well and serve.

38. **DUCHESS POTATOES**

Ingredients:

250 g Potatoes (cooked)	1 Egg Yolk
Small piece Butter	Salt and Pepper

Servings: 6   **Time:** 20–30 minutes
Oven Temperature: 180°C, No. 4
Position in Oven: Middle

Method:

1. Pass potatoes through a sieve, add butter, egg yolk and seasoning. Mix well.
2. Put mixture into a piping bag with large star pipe and pipe onto a greased baking tray.
3. Brush with beaten egg and bake in a moderate oven, 180°C, No. 4, for 20–30 minutes or can be brushed with egg after 10 minutes.

39. **ALMOND POTATOES**

Ingredients:

250 g Potatoes (cooked)	50 g Cheese (grated)
Small piece Butter	Salt and Pepper
1 Egg Yolk	Egg (beaten, for coating)
Almonds (blanched and shredded finely)	Oil for frying

Servings: 6
Time: 20 minutes
Oven Temperature: 200°C, No. 6
Position in Oven: Middle

Method:

1. Pass potatoes through a sieve, add butter, egg yolk, grated cheese and seasoning. Mix well.
2. Form into balls and coat with beaten egg and toss in shredded almonds.
3. Deep-fry in hot oil until golden brown.
4. Drain well and serve.

Note: May be baked in a hot oven, 200°C, No. 6, for 20 minutes.

GREEN VEGETABLES

40. **GLOBE ARTICHOKES**

Globe artichokes consist of three parts:

1. The fleshy leaves of which the base only is eaten;
2. The choke which lies below the leaves and which is inedible;
3. The base or heart.

They are usually served as a separate course, e.g. appetiser.

To serve hot:

1. Trim off the lower leaves and cut the stalk so that the artichokes will remain upright on the serving dish.
2. Wash the heads and put into a pan of boiling, salted water.
3. Cook 30–45 minutes.
4. Test for readiness: pull one of the leaves; it should come away easily.
5. Drain well.
6. Serve with melted butter or Hollandaise sauce (page 295).

To serve cold:
> 1. Prepare as above and allow to become cold.
> 2. Serve with an oil and vinegar dressing.

41. ASPARAGUS

Asparagus requires careful cooking as the tips cook more quickly than the stems

Method:
> 1. Cut or snap the stalks into equal lengths (stems will snap easily above the woody part of the stem).
> 2. Tie in bundles and cook in sufficient boiling water just to cover; put a saucer under the tips to raise them above the surface of the water. Alternatively, steam the asparagus in an electric steamer or over a pan of boiling water.
> 3. Cook until the asparagus is tender, about 5–10 minutes. The cooking time varies with the age of the asparagus.
> 4. Drain well.
> 5. Serve with melted butter poured over the tips or serve with Hollandaise sauce (page 295).

Note: White asparagus needs to be cooked for twice as long as green.

42. RED CABBAGE

May be prepared and cooked exactly like other varieties of cabbage (page 184) or in a casserole in the oven, as below

Method:
> 1. Wash and shred cabbage, sprinkle with vinegar.
> 2. Put into a casserole with a little butter, seasoning and some stock.
> 3. Cook slowly till tender.

43. FRIED PARSLEY

Method:
> 1. Wash the parsley and pick the leaves from the stalks. Dry thoroughly in a cloth.
> 2. Put in a frying basket, lower gently into deep, hot oil.
> 3. When the spluttering noise ceases, the parsley is ready.
> 4. Drain, season, use at once.

44. SEA KALE

Method:
> 1. Wash in several rinsing waters, take off the roots, tie in bundles and put into boiling salted water, to which a good squeeze of lemon juice has been added.
> 2. Cook until tender, about 30 minutes.
> 3. Serve on toast with melted butter, or with a suitable sauce poured over.

45. **BRAISED SEA KALE**

Ingredients:

4 heads Sea Kale	Sprig Thyme
1 Onion	Seasoning
Bay Leaf	2 Bacon rashers
3 sprigs Parsley	Stock

Time: 40 minutes

Oven Temperature: 180°C, No. 4

Position in Oven: Middle

Method:

1. Remove the roots and wash the sea kale. Slice the onion and put in a casserole. Place the sea kale on top.
2. Add the herbs and stock to come halfway up the sea kale. Season.
3. Put rashers of bacon on top.
4. Cook in a moderate oven, 180°C, No. 4, till tender, about 40 minutes.
5. The sea kale can be served separately or with the bacon and onion.

46. **BUTTERED OR CREAMED SPINACH**

Ingredients:

1 kg Spinach	Squeeze Lemon Juice
25 g Butter	125 ml Cream (optional)
Pinch Sugar	Croûtes of Fried Bread *or* Toast
Pinch Nutmeg (optional)	

Method:

1. Prepare and cook spinach (page 185). Sieve or liquidise.
2. Add butter, sugar, nutmeg and lemon juice.
3. Reheat, adding cream if liked.
4. Pile on toast or croûtes of fried bread.

47. **SPINACH BEET**

A variety of beet grown for its leaves and stalks. The green leaves and the white stalks may be cooked separately or the two parts may be cooked together

Method, leaves and stalks together:

1. Wash the spinach beet well.
2. Shred the leaves and slice the stalk portion.
3. Put into a little boiling salted water and cook till tender, about 5 minutes. Drain well.
4. Add a piece of butter, seasoning, and toss over the heat.

Leaves:

1. Wash thoroughly and shred as for cabbage.
2. Cook in a little boiling salted water, about 5 minutes. Drain well.
3. Return to the pan with a piece of butter and shake of pepper. Toss over the heat.

Stalks:

1. Wash the stalks. Cut into 10-cm lengths.
2. Cook in a little boiling salted water for 10 minutes. Drain.
3. Toss in butter and chopped parsley.

48. BRUSSELS SPROUTS AND CHESTNUTS

Preparation of chestnuts:

1. Slit chestnuts on rounded side.
2. Put in pan of cold water, bring to the boil, boil 3–5 minutes.
3. Remove pan from heat.
4. In order to skin the chestnuts while hot, remove a small quantity from the hot water at a time. The outer and inner brown skins should come away clean.

Cooking:

1. Cook chestnuts in a little stock or water till tender. About 30–45 minutes.
2. Prepare the Brussels sprouts.
3. Boil or steam for 10–20 minutes or till tender. Do not overcook or they will be bitter.
4. Combine sprouts and nuts, season lightly, toss in butter.

Note: Good as an accompaniment to roast chicken or roast turkey.

PEAS, BEANS, PULSES AND SWEETCORN

49. BROAD BEANS

Preparation:

Wash well. If beans are very young they may be cooked and eaten in their skins. Older beans may have to have their skins removed before or after cooking.

To Cook:

1. Remove beans from pods. Cook in boiling, salted water. Cook till tender, time will vary according to the age of the beans, but 10 minutes approx.
2. Drain. Add piece of butter and toss over the heat.
3. Serve sprinkled with chopped parsley or with a parsley sauce (page 291).

50. DRIED PEAS AND BEANS

Preparation:

Wash the dried peas or beans, cover well with cold water and soak overnight.

To Cook:

1. Drain the soaking water from the beans. Rinse. Put beans and enough fresh water to cover them in a pan.

2. Put on lid and bring to the boil for 10 minutes.

3. Cook till tender, about 1–2 hours. Add salt about 10 minutes before serving.

4. Drain well. Add a piece of butter and shake well.

5. Serve sprinkled with chopped parsley.

Note: Dried kidney beans (page 187) need soaking overnight, draining, rinsing, rapid boiling for at least 10 minutes before using in any recipe or they will be poisonous. Butter beans require less cooking than haricot beans.

51. SWEETCORN OR CORN-ON-THE-COB

Corn should be used when it is turning yellow; if it is too ripe it is difficult to make tender.

Method:

1. Remove the husks and silky thread from the corn.

2. Place in boiling salted water and cook for about 15 minutes.

3. Drain well and serve with melted butter.

Note: Cooked on the cob in this way, the corn can be served as a side dish.

Alternatively the grain may be cut from the cob using a sharp knife, and cooked separately.—

Method:

1. Put the uncooked grain into a pan with seasoning, a little milk and a piece of butter.

2. Cook for approximately 15 minutes.

3. Serve with any liquor left after cooking.

Note: Baby corn is best stir-fried as it is pleasantly crunchy but has little flavour.

52. FRESH GREEN PEAS

Method:

1. Shell peas and rinse in cold water.

2. Boil gently in salted water with a pinch of sugar and a sprig of mint, for 5–10 minutes or until tender.

3. Drain well and serve with a knob of butter.

53. DRIED PEAS

Method:

1. Wash the dried peas.

2. Cover well with cold water and soak overnight.

3. Put peas and their soaking water in a pan. Add enough cold water to cover as during soaking the peas will have absorbed a lot of the water.

4. Put on lid and bring to the boil.

5. Cook gently for about 1–2 hours, adding salt about 10 minutes before serving.

6. Drain well. Add a piece of butter and shake well. Serve.

54. PEASE PUDDING

Ingredients:

200 g dried Split Peas   Salt and Pepper
50 g Butter   Dried Breadcrumbs

Method:

1. Wash and soak peas in water overnight.
2. Put in a pan, cover with more water and boil for 2 hours.
3. Drain well, sieve or liquidise, add butter and seasoning.
4. Grease a pudding basin, sprinkle thickly with breadcrumbs and pack in mixture.
5. Bake at 190°C, No. 5 for 30 minutes.
6. Allow to shrink, turn out and serve with boiled salt pork (page 90).

55. GREEN PEA PURÉE

Ingredients:

Cooked Potatoes ⎫
Cooked Green Peas ⎬ Equal quantities   Melted Butter
Seasoning ⎭   Milk

Method:

1. Sieve potatoes and peas. Season.
2. Add melted butter and milk to moisten. Heat thoroughly.

VEGETABLE FRUITS

56. AUBERGINE, OR EGG PLANT, PREPARATION

1. Wash and remove stalk, leave the skin on.
2. Split in half lengthways or slice.
3. Sprinkle with salt and leave for about 30 minutes to 1 hour. This is done primarily to remove excess moisture and is advisable if aubergines are being fried. Aubergines are cultivated to be less bitter than they used to be, but salting will also remove any bitter juices.
4. Rinse to remove salt, and dry before cooking as in the following three recipes.
Note: Small aubergines may be served whole.

57. STEWED AUBERGINES

Method:

1. Melt sufficient butter in a pan to cover the bottom.
2. Add the prepared aubergines, shake over the heat and add a little stock.

3. Cover and stew till tender, approximately 20 minutes.
4. Serve with the liquor in which they have been cooked, reducing it if necessary.
5. Serve sprinkled with chopped parsley.

58. FRIED AUBERGINES

Method:

1. Prepare aubergines and cut into slices.
2. Season and coat with either egg and breadcrumbs or seasoned flour or dip into batter (page 474).
3. Fry in hot oil till golden brown.
4. Drain well before serving.

59. BAKED AUBERGINES

Method:

1. Prepare aubergines.
2. Put in a greased casserole, season, dot with butter, add a little stock, cover.
3. Bake at 170°C, No. 3, for 30 minutes or till tender. The time will vary according to the size of the aubergines.

60. BOILED COURGETTES

Method:

1. Wipe courgettes and cut in slices.
2. Add to boiling salted water and cook until tender, about 10–15 minutes.
3. Drain well and toss in butter.
Note: Small courgettes may be served whole.

61. STEWED COURGETTES

Method:

1. Wipe courgettes and cut in slices.
2. Melt sufficient butter or oil to cover the bottom of a pan.
3. Add prepared courgettes, shake over the heat and add tablespoonful of stock or water.
4. Add seasoning and cook slowly for 15–20 minutes or until tender.
5. Serve with the liquid in which they have been cooked reducing it if necessary.
6. Serve sprinkled with chopped parsley or other herbs.

62. SWEET PEPPER PREPARATION

Method:

1. Wash well.
2. Split and remove seeds and stalks.
3. Cut into strips 2–3 cm wide.

63. STEWED PEPPERS

Ingredients:

4 Peppers	Small piece Butter
125 ml Stock *or* Tomato Juice	Seasoning

Method:

1. Prepare peppers.
2. Put into a pan with stock or tomato juice, butter and seasoning.
3. Stew gently till tender, about 20 minutes.
4. Serve with the liquor from the pan, reducing if necessary.

64. DEEP-FRIED PEPPERS

Method:

1. Prepare peppers, slice.
2. Coat with egg and breadcrumbs or dip in batter (page 474).
3. Deep-fry in hot oil until golden brown. Drain thoroughly.

65. SKINNING AND SEEDING TOMATOES

Method:

1. Cut a cross in bottom of tomato.
2. Place in a bowl of boiling water, and leave until skin starts to peel away from the cuts.
3. Put into cold water, and, when cool enough to handle, drain the water away and peel off skin.
4. To remove seeds, cut tomatoes in half crosswise, squeeze each half and shake out the seeds or prise them out with a finger.

Note: When tomatoes are required as an ingredient but the moisture from their seeds is troublesome (e.g. in sandwiches) seeding is recommended. Diced tomatoes are more attractive looking when they are peeled and seeded. Liquid from the seeds need not be wasted; sieve and add liquid to stock or sauces.

66. BAKED TOMATOES (1)

Method:

1. Wash them and place on a greased ovenproof dish, stalk side down and cut a cross on the bottom.

2. Cover with buttered paper.
3. Bake in a moderate oven, 180°C, No. 4, till hot but not broken, about 10 minutes, but this will depend on the size and firmness of the tomatoes.
4. Serve as a vegetable or to garnish meat dishes.

67. BAKED TOMATOES (2)

Method:

1. Wash tomatoes and cut in two across the stalk.
2. Season each half and dot with butter or brush with oil.
3. Place on a greased baking dish, cover with buttered paper or lid.
4. Bake in a moderate oven, 180°C, No. 4, about 10 minutes, but this will depend on the size and firmness of the tomatoes.
5. Sprinkle with chopped parsley and serve.

68. FRIED TOMATOES

Method:

1. Wash, halve or slice tomatoes, and season.
2. Fry in a little butter or cooking oil, placing the cut side down first then turn and fry on second side.

69. GRILLED TOMATOES

Method:

1. Wash tomatoes. Cut in two across the stalk.
2. Season each half, and dot with butter or brush with cooking oil.
3. Grill for 2–3 minutes. The time will depend on the size and firmness of the tomatoes.

70. VEGETABLE MARROW PREPARATION

Method:

1. Wash the marrow and cut into quarters.
2. Remove seeds and peel fairly thickly.
3. Cut into neat pieces.

71. BOILED VEGETABLE MARROW

Method:

1. Prepare marrow.
2. Cook in boiling salted water till tender, time depending on size of pieces.
3. Drain well.
4. Toss in melted butter and chopped parsley or coat with a white, cheese or tomato sauce (pages 291, 297).

72. STEWED VEGETABLE MARROW

Method:

1. Prepare marrow.
2. Melt sufficient butter in a pan to cover the bottom. Add the marrow cut in pieces and toss in the butter.
3. Add a little stock.
4. Put on the lid and cook gently till tender, about 15 minutes.
5. Put into a vegetable dish and keep hot.
6. Use the liquid from the pan along with milk to make a sauce. Season well.
7. Coat marrow with sauce.

Note: Another method is to reduce the liquid and pour it over the marrow.

73. STEAMED VEGETABLE MARROW

A very watery vegetable, it may be steamed instead of boiled

Method:

1. Prepare marrow.
2. Put into a steamer, season and place steamer over a pan of boiling water or cook in an electric steamer.
3. Steam till tender, about 15 minutes.
4. Serve as for boiled marrow (page 203).

74. RATATOUILLE

Ingredients:

3 Tomatoes	1 Pepper
3 Courgettes	2 cloves Garlic (optional)
2 Aubergines	3 tablespoonfuls Olive Oil
2 small Onions	Salt and Pepper

Time: 1 hour
Oven Temperature: 180°C, No. 4
Position in Oven: Middle

Method:

1. Peel and chop tomatoes.
2. Slice courgettes. Slice and salt aubergines.
3. Remove core and seeds from pepper and cut in strips.
4. Slice onions and crush garlic if used.
5. Heat oil and fry onion and garlic for 2–3 minutes.
6. Rinse aubergines to remove salt, dry and add to pan along with courgettes. Fry 2–3 minutes on each side.
7. Season mixture, add shredded peppers and tomatoes, cover pan and cook very gently for one hour either on top of cooker or in oven, 180°C, No. 4.

Note: Ratatouille can be served either hot or cold.

MUSHROOMS

It has become quite fashionable to forage for mushrooms. If you do not know what you are looking for this can be dangerous. Do not pick and eat anything from the wild if you are not sure what it is.

Mushrooms may be washed but they can absorb a lot of water if soaked too long. Peel large mushrooms and wipe smaller ones clean with a damp, clean cloth or kitchen towel, or use a soft brush. Fry in butter before adding to stews, casseroles or sauces.

75. MUSHROOM PREPARATION

Method:
1. Clean mushrooms by peeling, if large, or wiping with a damp, clean cloth.
2. Trim and remove stalks if necessary.
3. Mushroom stalks may be used in making stocks for soup and sauces.

76. BAKED MUSHROOMS

Method:
1. Prepare mushrooms.
2. Place on a greased ovenproof dish or baking tin, dot with butter, season, and cover with greased paper.
3. Bake in a moderate oven, 180°C, No. 4, till tender, for about 20 minutes. If cooked in a baking tin, pour over any liquid from the tin when serving the mushrooms.

77. GRILLED MUSHROOMS

Method:
1. Prepare mushrooms.
2. Heat and brush the grill pan with oil.
3. Brush the mushrooms with melted butter or oil.
4. Place on grill pan with rounded side upwards. Grill 4–5 minutes.
5. Turn the mushrooms so that the hollow side is uppermost.
6. Put a small piece of butter or a little oil and a sprinkling of salt on each one.
7. Return to the grill for another 4–5 minutes. Sprinkle with pepper and serve.

78. FRIED MUSHROOMS

Method:
1. Prepare mushrooms and season.
2. Melt a little butter or oil in a frying pan and add the mushrooms to the pan.
3. Fry gently till tender, about 10–15 minutes.
4. Serve with any liquor from the pan poured over.
5. Sprinkle with chopped parsley.

79. STEWED MUSHROOMS

Ingredients:

250 g Mushrooms	Salt and Pepper
25 g Butter	15 g Flour
125 ml Milk *or* Stock	Toast (buttered, optional)

Method:

1. Prepare mushrooms.
2. Melt the butter in a pan, add the mushrooms and stalks, cook gently for a few minutes.
3. Season, and add stock or milk. Stew gently for 20 minutes.
4. Thicken the liquid wth the flour, boil up and serve as a vegetable or on toast.

80. CREAMED MUSHROOMS

Ingredients:

250 g Mushrooms	4 tablespoonfuls Cream
15 g Butter	Toast
Salt and Pepper	Chopped Parsley
10 g Flour	

Method:

1. Prepare mushrooms.
2. Put into a pan with the butter, salt and flour sprinkled on top.
3. Add milk or cream, put lid on pan and cook very slowly for about 15 minutes.
4. Serve as a vegetable or on toast with a little pepper and chopped parsley sprinkled on top.

81. STUFFED MUSHROOMS

Ingredients:

250 g Mushrooms	Chopped Parsley
1 small Onion	Seasoning
25 g Brazil *or* other Nuts	Squeeze Lemon Juice
Small piece Butter	

Method:

1. Prepare mushrooms.
2. Chop the stalks, onion and nuts, mix well, add seasoning and lemon juice.
3. Put the mushrooms on a greased ovenproof dish, hollow side uppermost.
4. Put a little of the prepared mixture on each mushroom. Dot with butter.
5. Bake in a moderately hot oven, 180°C, No. 4, till tender; about 20 minutes.

MISCELLANEOUS

82. VEGETABLE STEW

Ingredients – any of the following vegetables are suitable for stewing, according to season:

Carrot	Parsnip
Turnip	Onion *or* Leek
Potato	Broad Beans
French *or* Runner Beans	Celery
Peas	Tomato

Additional ingredients:

Butter	Seasoning
Stock	Chopped Parsley

Method:

1. Prepare vegetables according to kind. Slice, place in pan or casserole in layers with butter and seasoning.
2. Add water or stock to come about halfway up vegetables. Cook gently till almost tender, about 1 hour. The time will depend on size to which vegetables are cut.
3. Add sliced tomato and cook for another 5–10 minutes.
4. Sprinkle with chopped parsley.

83. ROASTED VEGETABLES

Ingredients – any of the following vegetables are suitable for roasting, on their own or used in combinations:

Carrots	Parsnips
Aubergines	Turnips
Courgettes	Onions
Peppers	Beetroots
Tomatoes	Sweet Potatoes *or* Yams
Celery	Fennel

Additional ingredients:

Salt and Pepper	3–4 tablespoons Olive Oil
2 Garlic cloves	Basil leaves (optional)

Time: 30–40 minutes

Oven Temperature: 200ºC, No. 6

Position in Oven: Near the top

Method:

1. Prepare vegetables according to kind and cut into even-sized pieces. Place in a roasting tin.
2. Chop garlic finely and sprinkle over vegetables.

3. Chop the basil leaves and mix with the oil.
4. Coat the vegetables with the oil and basil mixture and season with salt and pepper.
5. Roast in the oven till tender.

SALADS AND DRESSINGS

SALADS

SALAD DRESSINGS

SALADS

Salads are a popular accompaniment to a meal and may be served with hot or cold dishes. They vary from one salad plant served alone to a combination of different fruits and vegetables. Combined with a protein food they form an appetising main course.

1. ROOT OR OTHER VEGETABLES SUITABLE FOR SALADS

The following may be combined with green salad plants to make mixed salads

Vegetable	Preparation
Carrots	Wash, peel and grate
Beetroot	Wash, cook, peel and grate; or use cold, pickled beetroot
Celeriac	Remove root fibres, wash and peel thinly
Parsnips	Wash, peel and grate
Turnips	Wash, peel thickly and grate
Radish	Wash well, and slice or leave whole, if small
Onions, Shallots	Peel, and cut into thin slices
Spring Onions	Peel, if small serve whole, if large slice
Garlic	Use sparingly. Peel and crush well, or use cut clove to rub round salad bowl to give a milder flavour. Crush and use in dressings
Tomatoes	Wash. Peel if liked: cut a cross in the bottom of the tomato. Scald tomato in boiling water for 30 seconds to 1 minute. Then plunge into cold water. Skin should come away easily. Alternatively hold tomato over a gas flame on fork, turn gently until skin splits. Peel
Potatoes (New)	Choose small potatoes, boil with skins on, and serve hot or cold

2. PREPARATION OF GREEN VEGETABLES FOR SALADS

Vegetable	Preparation
Lettuce and Salad Leaves	Remove any withered or bruised leaves. Wash leaves under cold running water and shake well in clean tea towel or in a salad basket to dry. If necessary tear larger leaves before using
Endive	Remove darker outside leaves as they may have a bitter taste. Wash other leaves well in cold water. May be used instead of lettuce in winter
Chicory	Makes a good salad on its own or combined with other vegetables. Halve or quarter head lengthwise and wash thoroughly
Sea Kale	Trim off root and wash heads under running water
Celery	Separate stalks and remove leaves. Wash thoroughly, scrubbing if necessary

Watercress	Remove discoloured leaves and end of stalks. Wash thoroughly in cold salted water
Fine Cress	Wash cress thoroughly to remove seed casings and earth, either under running water or in large bowl of cold water. Shake well in a colander
Cabbage	Use the heart for salads (keeping the coarse leaves for cooking). Quarter the heart and remove centre stalk. Wash leaves, shake dry. Shred finely
Cauliflower	Sprig and wash well. Use either as small sprigs or grated
Broccoli	Remove tough stem and wash florets in cold water. Use small sprigs
Cucumber	Cut in thin slices. May be peeled first if liked
Courgettes	Wash and grate or cut into thin strips
Avocado	Cut in half lengthwise, remove stone and peel. Slice or chop
Sweet Pepper	Remove stalk and seeds. Slice or chop

3. FRUITS SUITABLE FOR SALADS

Fruits and vegetables may be combined to make an attractive salad

Fruit	Preparation
Oranges	Peel and slice thinly, or remove all pith and skin and divide into segments
Grapefruit	Peel and divide into segments
Apples	Peel only if liked. Slice thinly and sprinkle with lemon juice to keep the flesh white
Pears	Peel, dice and sprinkle with lemon juice
Plums	Stone
Dates	Stone
Prunes	Soak and stone or, if tough, stew
Raisins	None required
Grapes	Wash and stone
Peaches or Nectarines	Skin, stone and slice
Pineapple	Peel, core and cut into rings or cubes

4. GREEN SALADS

These can be made with any of the following vegetables and salad leaves: lettuce, endive, rocket, celery, chicory, sea kale, fine cress, watercress, cabbage, spinach.

Green salads should be prepared just before serving as they become soft and wilted if allowed to stand. They should be dressed immediately before serving. Vinaigrette or French dressing (page 219) is generally used.

5. FRENCH SALAD

Ingredients:

Salad Leaves   Basic Vinaigrette (page 219)

Method:

1. Prepare salad leaves and dry carefully. Thorough drying of the leaves is important as the dressing will not adhere if the leaves are wet.
2. Put the salad leaves into a large bowl, sprinkle over vinaigrette. Then, using two spoons, toss the lettuce until each leaf is coated with the dressing. Use a large enough bowl to allow room for tossing the leaves.

Note: This method will produce a salad which is lightly and evenly dressed.

6. COLESLAW OR RAW CABBAGE SALAD

Ingredients:

¼ Cabbage heart (shredded)   1 tablespoonful finely-chopped Onion
¾ cupful Thousand Island Dressing   *or* a little Shallot
   (page 221) *or* Mayonnaise (page 220)

Method:

1. Wash and dry cabbage heart, shred finely.
2. Toss cabbage and onion in dressing or mayonnaise and serve very cold.

Alternative method:

1. Shred cabbage finely and blanch.
2. Toss in vinegar dressing.

Vinegar dressing:

1 tablespoonful Vinegar   1 teaspoonful Salt
1 tablespoonful Water   1 teaspoonful Sugar

Add seasonings to vinegar and water and mix well.

7. CUCUMBER SALAD

Ingredients:

Cucumber   Basic Vinaigrette (page 219)
Salt and Pepper   Chives (chopped)

Method:

1. Wash the cucumber and slice thinly. Sprinkle with salt and pepper.
2. Arrange in layers in salad bowl. Pour over vinaigrette dressing. Sprinkle with chopped chives.

8. TOMATO SALAD (1)

Ingredients:

4 Tomatoes   Salt and Pepper
Parsley *or* Basil (chopped)   Pinch Cayenne (if liked)
1 tablespoonful Salad Oil   1 tablespoonful chopped Shallot (if liked)
1 dessertspoonful Vinegar

Method:

1. Prepare and slice tomatoes. Sprinkle over a little chopped parsley or basil.
2. Prepare the dressing of oil, vinegar and seasonings and pour over tomatoes. If liked, chopped shallot or onion may be sprinkled over tomatoes.

9. TOMATO SALAD (2)

Ingredients:

4 Tomatoes	Lettuce
1 Egg (hard-boiled, finely chopped)	Salad Dressing (1) (page 219)
1 dessertspoonful Spring Onion	Fine Cress
(finely chopped)	Salt and Pepper

Method:

1. Wash tomatoes and cut a small slice off top of each. Scoop out pulp.
2. Mix hard-boiled egg and chopped onion together.
3. Season tomatoes. Fill with egg mixture; replace tops.
4. Toss prepared lettuce in salad dressing and arrange on dish with tomatoes.
5. Garnish with fine cress.

10. MIXED VEGETABLE SALAD

Ingredients:

Tomatoes	Fine Cress *or* Watercress
Lettuce	Parsley *or* Mint
Cucumber	Hard-boiled Eggs
Radishes	Cooked Dressing (page 220)
Spring Onions	

Method:

1. Prepare tomatoes and slice or cut into quarters.
2. Prepare lettuce and tear into suitable-sized pieces.
3. Slice cucumber, slice radishes.
4. Prepare spring onions (slice or leave whole) and cress.
5. Slice hard-boiled eggs.
6. Arrange lettuce in salad bowl.
7. Put tomatoes, cucumber, radishes, spring onions and hard-boiled egg in rows or groups on the lettuce.
8. Arrange the cress in small bunches, sprinkle with chopped parsley or mint and serve with cooked dressing.

11. ENGLISH SALAD

Ingredients:

200 g firm Tomatoes	2 Eggs (hard-boiled)
1 Lettuce	Salad Dressing (1) (page 219)
Watercress	

Method:

1. Prepare tomatoes and cut into slices or quarters.
2. Prepare lettuce. Tear into suitable-sized pieces. Arrange in a salad bowl.
3. Slice the eggs or cut into quarters.
4. Put tomatoes and eggs with the lettuce and garnish with watercress.

12. RAW WINTER SALAD

Any green and root vegetables may be combined:
the green vegetable is usually winter cabbage

Method:

1. Prepare the vegetables according to kind.
2. Arrange in sections on a salad dish.
3. Serve with cooked salad dressing (page 220); dressing separate from salad.

The following combinations of vegetables may be used:

1. Shredded cabbage or Brussels sprouts, grated carrot, turnip and beetroot sprinkled with chopped parsley.
2. Shredded cabbage, celery, tomatoes, cauliflower sprigs.

13. FRUIT AND VEGETABLE SALAD

Ingredients:

Dates *or* Prunes	Nuts
Cream Cheese	Lettuce
1 Orange	Fine Cress
Grated Carrot	Mint
Spring Onions	Salad Dressing (1) (page 219)

Method:

1. Stone the dates or prunes and fill with cream cheese.
2. Prepare orange, carrots and spring onions. Slice.
3. Chop the nuts roughly or leave whole.
4. Arrange prepared lettuce in a salad bowl. Place the other ingredients in groups with the cress in small bundles. Sprinkle with chopped mint.
5. Serve with salad dressing.

Note: This type of salad is suitable to serve on individual plates.

14. TOMATO AND CELERY SALAD

Ingredients:

4–6 Tomatoes	Salad Dressing (1) (page 219)
½ head Celery	Chopped Parsley

Method:

1. Prepare and slice tomatoes.
2. Prepare the celery, cut into strips.
3. Arrange the tomatoes in a salad bowl and pile the celery in the centre. Sprinkle with chopped parsley.

15. CELERY, NUT AND APPLE SALAD

Ingredients:

2 dessert Apples	Lettuce
1 small head Celery	Fine Cress
50 g Walnuts	French *or* Salad Dressing (pages 219–220)
50 g Dates	

Method:

1. Wash the apples but do not peel. Cut into dice. Wash and dice celery.
2. Chop the walnuts and dates roughly.
3. Mix all together with dressing or if preferred some orange juice.
4. Pile into a salad bowl and garnish with crisp lettuce leaves and fine cress.

Alternative method:

1. Halve the apples or cut off tops, scoop out the inside and chop along with walnuts, dates and celery. Add dressing and mix well.
2. Fill up apple cases with mixture, replace tops and serve on lettuce leaves. Garnish with cress.

16. ORANGE SALAD

Ingredients:

Oranges	Sugar
Salad Dressing (1) (page 219)	

Method:

1. Prepare and slice oranges, sprinkle with sugar; place in a flat salad dish.
2. Pour the dressing over and chill until required.

Note: Usually served as an accompaniment to wild duck.

17. POTATO SALAD

Waxy potatoes are best for this salad

Ingredients:

Freshly boiled Potatoes		Salad Dressing (1) (page 219)
Mint or Chives (chopped)	*or*	Mayonnaise (page 220)

Method:

1. Dice the potatoes while hot and pour the dressing over; in this way the dressing will penetrate the potatoes and give a good flavour. Leave till cold.
2. Arrange piled up on a salad dish and sprinkle with chopped mint or chives.

Note: Cold, left-over potatoes may be used, but the flavour is not so good.

18. WINTER SALAD

A salad of mixed cooked vegetables

Any combination of the following ingredients:

Potatoes, Carrots, Beetroot, Cauliflower, French Beans, Green Peas, Celery

To these should be added:

French Dressing (page 219) or Mayonnaise (page 220)

Parsley and Mint (chopped)

Method:

1. Cut the vegetables into small dice or strips. Mix well.
2. Add enough mayonnaise to bind them together. The pieces of vegetable should not be broken.
3. Pile up in a salad bowl and sprinkle with chopped parsley or mint.

19. MAIN DISH SALADS

When a salad is to form the main dish in a meal, a protein food should be included along with the vegetables and fruit:

Allow per person:

50 g Cheese	1 ½ Eggs
50 g Cold Meats and Chicken	50 g Sardines, Salmon, etc

These foods may be served alone with a salad or may be combined to give variety, e.g. cheese and ham salad (page 218). When foods are combined, less of each is required. Nuts may be used to supply or supplement the protein. As side dishes, a small portion of potato salad (page 216), chilled pasta or rice with a dressing, bread, or a baked potato could be served to make a meal well-balanced in protein and carbohydrate.

20. RUSSIAN SALAD

Any combination of the following ingredients:

Cooked Vegetables (e.g. cooked Potato, Peas, Carrots)

Cold Cooked Chicken *or* Ham, *or* Tongue *or* Smoked Fish

To these should be added:

Cooked Dressing (page 220) *or* Mayonnaise (page 220)

Method:

1. Dice the cooked vegetables. The meat should be shredded, the fish flaked.
2. Combine with enough mayonnaise to bind them together.

21. FISH SALAD

Ingredients:

Cold Fish such as Turbot *or* Halibut	A little chopped Shallot
Shrimps	Mayonnaise (page 220)
Hard-boiled Eggs	Lettuce
Beetroot (cooked)	Cucumber
Gherkins	Tomatoes
Capers	Watercress

Method:

1. Flake fish. Chop shrimps, hard-boiled eggs, gherkins, capers. Dice cooked beetroot. Mix with a little chopped shallot and mayonnaise.

2. Pile the mixture in a salad bowl. Put lettuce and sliced cucumber round and garnish with tomatoes, watercress and beetroot.

22. CHEESE AND HAM SALAD

Ingredients:

100 g Cheddar Cheese
100 g cooked Ham – cut thick
1 head Celery
1 small Onion

Lettuce
French *or* Salad Dressing (pages 219–220)
Paprika (if liked)

Servings: 4

Method:

1. Dice the cheese and ham neatly.
2. Wash the celery and dice. Chop the onion finely.
3. Mix all together with salad dressing.
4. Pile the salad high, sprinkle with paprika and garnish with crisp lettuce leaves.

23. CHEESE AND FRUIT SALAD

Ingredients:

150 g Cheddar Cheese
50 g Mixed Nuts
50 g Sultanas
Salad Dressing (1) (page 219)

or

1 small tin Peach slices
1 small tin Pineapple pieces
Lettuce
Chives (chopped)

Servings: 4

Method:

1. Grate or dice cheese.
2. Chop nuts. Drain and chop fruit.
3. Mix all ingredients together with salad dressing.
4. Arrange crisp lettuce leaves in a bowl and serve salad on top. Sprinkle with chopped chives.

24. CHICKEN SALAD

Ingredients:

Cold Chicken
Lettuce
Celery

Salt and Pepper
Mayonnaise (page 220)

Method:

1. Remove skin, bone and tendons from chicken and dice. Season.
2. Prepare lettuce and tear into small pieces.
3. Cut the celery into thin strips.
4. Mix the chicken, lettuce and celery with a little mayonnaise.
5. Garnish with the small inside leaves of the lettuce, and celery tops.

SALAD DRESSINGS

Salad dressings are vital to the success of any salad. Many different dressings can be made using a basic vinaigrette type of mixture or a mayonnaise. A salad dressing is an emulsion made by whisking an oil with an acidic liquid such as vinegar or citrus juice. The ingredients may also be placed in a screw-top jar and shaken vigorously. The recommended proportion of oil to vinegar or citrus juice in vinaigrette is 3:1.

The flavour of the dressing can be varied using different types of oil, vinegars and citric juices. Other flavouring ingredients, such as herbs and spices and flavoured vinegars, can also be added to give variety. The following table gives some suggestions.

Oils	Vinegars	Flavourings
Olive Oil	Wine Vinegar	Mustard, e.g. Dijon
Sunflower Oil	Malt Vinegar	Garlic
Grapeseed Oil	Balsamic Vinegar	Fresh Herbs
Rapeseed Oil	Cider Vinegar	Chilli
Walnut Oil	Sherry Vinegar	
Hazelnut Oil	Flavoured Vinegars: e.g. tarragon, garlic, raspberry, chilli.	
	Note: Lemon, lime and orange juice may be used instead of vinegar	

25. BASIC VINAIGRETTE OR FRENCH DRESSING

Ingredients:

3 tablespoonfuls Oil   ½ teaspoonful Dijon Mustard
1 tablespoonful Vinegar   Salt and Pepper

Method

Place all the ingredients into a bowl and whisk together (or shake in a screw-top jar) until emulsified and thickened.

26. SALAD DRESSING (1)

Ingredients:

1 tablespoonful Salad Oil   Pinch Cayenne
1 teaspoonful Lemon Juice   Pinch Salt and Pepper
1 teaspoonful Vinegar (Wine *or* Tarragon)   Onion *or* Garlic to flavour

Method:

1. Rub bowl with cut onion or garlic.
2. Mix oil and seasonings, then gradually add lemon juice and vinegar, beat well.
Note: This quantity is sufficient for one head of lettuce. This dressing may be used with lettuce, tomatoes, cold meat, potato salad and to marinade chicken, prawns, lobster and crab where they are to be used for salads.

27. SALAD DRESSING (2)

Ingredients:

2 tablespoonfuls Salad Oil
2 tablespoonfuls Tarragon Vinegar
Salt and Pepper

½ teaspoonful chopped Parsley
1 small teaspoonful chopped Shallots
1 teaspoonful chopped Gherkins

Method:

1. Mix oil, salt and pepper together, then gradually add the vinegar.
2. When well mixed, stir in other ingredients.

28. COOKED DRESSING

May be used instead of mayonnaise if you want to avoid eating raw eggs.
Ideal for potato or pasta salads

Ingredients:

1 level tablespoonful Flour
1 level teaspoonful Mustard
1 level teaspoonful Sugar
½ level teaspoonful Salt
1 Egg

100 ml Milk
100 ml Water
50 ml Vinegar
10–25 g Butter
Single cream

Method:

1. Mix dry ingredients in pan. Beat egg and work in smoothly. Gradually add liquids, stirring all the time.
2. Bring to the boil over a medium high heat, stirring all the time.
3. Remove from heat and beat in butter.
4. Allow to cool, stirring occasionally.
5. Add a little cream before use if necessary.

29. ENGLISH DRESSING

Ingredients:

Yolks of 2 hard-boiled Eggs
1 level teaspoonful Castor Sugar
1 level teaspoonful Mustard

1–2 tablespoonfuls Vinegar (Wine *or* Tarragon)
125 ml Salad Oil
Seasoning

Method:

1. Mix egg yolks, seasonings, and sugar together.
2. Gradually add the vinegar, stirring vigorously, and finally the oil slowly.

30. MAYONNAISE

Ingredients:

1 Egg Yolk
½ level teaspoonful Salt
½ level teaspoonful Mustard
½ level teaspoonful Sugar
Pinch Cayenne

125–150 ml light Salad Oil
1 tablespoonful Lemon Juice
1 tablespoonful Vinegar
  (Tarragon if liked)
1 tablespoonful thick Cream

Method:

1. Mix egg yolk, sugar and seasonings together in a small bowl.
2. Gradually add the oil – drop by drop to begin with – and beat constantly with a whisk or wooden spoon until thick.
3. Stir in a little of the lemon juice or vinegar.
4. Add more oil and beat again until stiff.
5. Continue adding oil and vinegar and lemon juice until all are used. The result should be a thick, smooth cream that will keep its shape and not run off the end of a spoon.
6. Lastly, stir in cream.

Note: Should the mayonnaise curdle, add mayonnaise very gradually to another egg yolk and it should return to its smooth consistency.

Mayonnaise can be made in a liquidiser using the whole egg.

31. THOUSAND ISLAND DRESSING

Ingredients:

1 cupful Mayonnaise (page 220)	½ Onion
2 level teaspoonfuls Paprika	¼ cupful finely diced Celery
¼ cupful Sweet Chilli Sauce	2 Eggs (hard-boiled)
2 tablespoonfuls Wine Vinegar	

Method:

1. Chop onion and hard-boiled eggs finely.
2. Mix all ingredients well, chill and serve.

32. CREAM DRESSING

Ingredients:

75 ml Cream	Pinch Cayenne Pepper
Seasoning	1 tablespoonful Lemon Juice
	or Vinegar

Method:

Add seasonings to cream and half whip. Stir in lemon juice or vinegar.

33. SOUR CREAM DRESSING

Ingredients:

125–150 ml Sour Cream	3 tablespoonfuls Lemon Juice
½ teaspoonful Sugar	*or* Vinegar
Seasoning	2–3 tablespoonfuls Cream

Method:

1. Beat sugar and seasoning into sour cream.
2. Gradually add lemon juice or vinegar and cream. Chill before serving.

Note: A tablespoonful of finely chopped chives or parsley or a pinch of garlic salt may be added to vary the flavour.

34. YOGHURT DRESSING

Ingredients:

125–150 ml plain Yoghurt   1 teaspoonful Vinegar
125–150 ml Salad Cream *or* Mayonnaise

Method:

Add salad cream or mayonnaise gradually to yoghurt. Beat well then mix in vinegar. Add chopped fresh herbs that are complementary to the food to be served with the dressing.

35. LOW-CALORIE YOGHURT DRESSING

Ingredients:

125–150 ml low-fat plain Yoghurt   ½ teaspoonful chopped fresh Herbs,
1 teaspoonful Lemon Juice   e.g. Chives and Parsley
Seasoning   Pinch Paprika
Pinch dry Mustard

Method:

Mix all ingredients well together.
Note: A teaspoonful of curry powder could be added to vary flavour.

HOT PUDDINGS

MILK PUDDINGS

CUSTARD PUDDINGS

STEWED FRUIT AND FRUIT PUDDINGS

SUET PUDDINGS

PUDDINGS USING PASTRY

CAKE MIXTURE PUDDINGS

HOT SOUFFLÉS

MILK PUDDINGS

I. CLASSES OF GRAIN FOR MILK PUDDINGS

I. Whole-Grain.—Rice, Barley.

2. Medium- or Partially Ground-Grain.—Semolina, Ground Rice, Sago, Tapioca.

3. Fine- or Powdered-Grain.— Cornflour, Custard Powder, Arrowroot.

Average Proportions:

40 g Grain to 500 ml Milk

2. BAKED RICE OR OTHER WHOLE-GRAIN PUDDINGS

Ingredients:

40 g Pudding Rice	25 g Sugar
500 ml Milk	Grated Nutmeg *or* Cinnamon

Servings: 3–4

Time: 3 hours

Oven Temperature: 150°C, No. 2

Position in Oven: Middle shelf

Method:

1. Wash rice.
2. Put all ingredients into greased ovenproof dish.
3. Grate nutmeg or sprinkle cinnamon on top.
4. Stir the pudding once or twice during the first hour.
5. Bake until creamy in a slow oven.

3. BOILED RICE PUDDING

Ingredients:

40 g Pudding Rice	25 g Sugar
500 ml Milk	

Servings: 3–4

Time: 1–1 ½ hours

Method:

1. Wash rice and put in pan with milk.
2. Bring to boiling point.
3. Simmer very slowly with lid on till tender.
4. Add sugar and serve either hot or cold.

Note: A beaten egg may be mixed into the cooked pudding and then baked in a moderate oven till brown on top.

Sultanas or raisins may be added 20 minutes before serving.

4. SEMOLINA OR OTHER MEDIUM-GRAIN PUDDINGS

Ingredients:

40 g Semolina   25 g Sugar
500 ml Milk   1 Egg (optional, see alternative methods
                                 1, 2 and 3 below)

Servings: 3–4
Time: 20 minutes
Oven Temperature: 190–200°C, No. 5–6
Position in Oven: Middle shelf

Method:

1. Heat the milk, sprinkle in the semolina and, stirring all the time, bring slowly to boiling point.
2. Continue stirring at simmering point till grain is soft. Time, about 10 minutes.
3. Remove from heat, add sugar.
4. Pour into a serving dish.

Note: The pudding can be enriched by adding 1 egg to 500 ml pudding.

Method (1):

Make pudding. Remove from heat and add beaten egg.
Reheat without boiling, or pour into an ovenproof dish and bake in a moderate oven till brown on top.

Method (2):

Separate egg yolk and white.
Stir yolk into pudding.
Beat white and fold in. Bake as above.

Method (3):

Add egg yolk to pudding, pour into an ovenproof dish.
Beat white stiffly, fold in 40–50 g sugar and pile on top. Bake, 170°C, No. 3, until meringue is firm.

5. FAROLA PUDDING

Make as semolina pudding, above.

6. GROUND RICE PUDDING

Make as semolina pudding, above.

7. SAGO PUDDING

Make as semolina pudding; cook for 20 minutes, till grain is clear.

8. TAPIOCA PUDDING

Make as sago pudding.

9. BIRD'S NEST PUDDING

Ingredients:

1–2 Apples according to size of dish (peeled and cored)
Pinch Salt   15 g Butter
40 g Sago   500 ml Milk
25 g Sugar

Servings: 3–4
Time: 1 hour 30 minutes
Oven Temperature: 170°C, No. 3
Position in Oven: Middle shelf

Method:

1. Place the prepared apples in an ovenproof dish.
2. Fill centres with sugar, then add sago, salt, butter and milk to the dish.
3. Bake until set, stirring once or twice during first hour.

10. CORNFLOUR OR OTHER FINE-GRAIN PUDDINGS (BAKED)

Ingredients:

40 g Cornflour   25 g Sugar
500 ml Milk   Flavouring as desired
Pinch Salt   1 Egg

Servings: 3–4
Time: 20 minutes
Oven Temperature: 190°–200°C, No. 5–6
Position in Oven: Middle shelf

Method:

1. Blend cornflour with some of the milk, add pinch of salt.
2. Heat the milk and pour onto blended cornflour.
3. Return to pan, stir until boiling, boil 3 minutes.
4. Add sugar and flavouring.
5. Separate egg, add yolk to mixture and fold in stiffly beaten white; or add beaten egg whole.
6. Pour into a greased ovenproof dish and bake until set.

11. CORNFLOUR PUDDING (SET)

Ingredients:

40 g Cornflour   25 g Sugar
500 ml Milk   Flavouring as desired
Pinch Salt   Colouring as desired

Servings: 3–4

Method:

1. Blend cornflour with some of the milk, add pinch of salt.
2. Heat rest of milk and pour onto blended cornflour.
3. Return to pan, stir until boiling, boil 3 minutes.

4. Add sugar, flavouring and colouring.
5. Pour into serving dish and leave till set, or pour into a wetted mould, leave till set and turn out.

12. CHOCOLATE CORNFLOUR PUDDING

Ingredients:

40 g Cornflour	Pinch Salt
15 g Cocoa *or* 25 g Drinking Chocolate	25–50 g Sugar
500 ml Milk	1 teaspoonful Vanilla Essence

Servings: 3–4

Method:

1. Blend the cornflour and cocoa or chocolate with some of the cold milk.
2. Make as for cornflour pudding (page 227).

CUSTARD PUDDINGS

Custard is made from milk, eggs, sugar and sometimes cornflour or plain flour. It is usually flavoured with vanilla but other flavours could be substituted. The thickness of the custard depends on the proportion of eggs or egg yolks to milk – the more yolks the thicker the custard.

For custard sauce *see* Sauces section (page 299).

Proportions:

Steamed Custards.—1 Egg to 250 ml Milk
Baked Custards.—1 Egg to 250 ml Milk
Custards with solids (i.e. as an ingredient).—1 Egg to 250–500 ml Milk

13. STEAMED CUSTARD

Ingredients:

250 ml Milk	1 Egg
Sugar to taste	Flavouring as desired

Servings: 1–2
Time: 20 minutes small, 40 minutes large

Method:

1. Heat milk and sugar, stir to dissolve.
2. Beat the egg.
3. Pour the milk slowly over beaten egg. Whisk with a balloon whisk.
4. Pour into greased moulds.
5. Cover with greased paper and place in pan of boiling water.
6. The water should come halfway up mould.
7. On a low- to medium-heat allow the water to simmer gently.
8. When the custard is firm, serve either hot or cold.

Note: If the custard is to be turned out of the moulds, reduce the quantity of milk.

14. **BAKED CUSTARD**

Ingredients:

1 Egg	250 ml Milk
Sugar to taste	Little Nutmeg

Servings: 2
Time: 45 minutes
Oven Temperature: 170°C, No. 3
Position in Oven: Middle shelf

Method:

1. Heat the milk in a pan until it steams.
2. Lightly beat egg and sugar in a bowl.
3. Pour the heated milk slowly onto the egg. Whisk with a balloon whisk.
4. Pour into a greased ovenproof dish.
5. Grate a little nutmeg on top, and bake till set.

15. **CARAMEL CUSTARDS**

Ingredients:

Custard	Caramel
250 ml Milk	2 tablespoonfuls Water
2 Eggs	1 tablespoonful Lemon Juice
1 level tablespoonful Sugar	50 g Sugar
Vanilla Extract	

Servings: 2–3
Time: 20–40 minutes
Oven Temperature: 170°C, No. 3
Position in Oven: Middle shelf

Method:

1. Make a caramel of golden brown colour, using water, lemon juice and sugar (pages 300, 423).
2. Pour into a warmed mould or pie dish to cover the bottom and allow to harden.
3. Make a custard. Heat the milk till it steams. Whisk the eggs and sugar in a bowl. Pour the hot milk over the eggs and whisk. Return to the pan and gently heat, stirring continuously with a wooden spoon till thick.
4. Add vanilla. Stir and pour custard into mould.
5. Cover with greased paper and place in a pan of water, just under boiling point, sufficient to come halfway up the mould.
6. Steam gently or poach in the oven in a roasting tin half-filled with water until set, 170°C, No. 3.
7. Allow to shrink well before turning out.
8. Serve hot or cold.
9. Add 4 tablespoonfuls water to remaining caramel. Dissolve and pour round the base of the custard and serve.

16. BREAD AND BUTTER PUDDING

Ingredients:

1 Egg	2 thin slices Bread and Butter
500 ml Milk	25 g Currants
25 g Sugar	Chopped Peel (if liked)

Servings: 3–4
Time: 30–40 minutes
Oven Temperature: 190°C, No. 5
Position in Oven: Middle shelf

Method:

1. Make a custard. Heat the milk till it steams. Whisk the eggs and sugar in a bowl. Pour the hot milk over the egg mixture, and whisk. Return to the pan and gently heat, stirring continuously with a wooden spoon till it thickens.
2. Cut the bread and butter into small squares, and place in a buttered oven-proof dish.
3. Sprinkle currants between, adding chopped peel, if liked.
4. Pour custard over and allow to soak into bread for 30 minutes.
5. Bake until pudding has risen and set.

17. CABINET PUDDING

Ingredients:

250 ml Milk	Almond Essence
25 g Sugar	Glacé Cherries to decorate
2 Eggs	1 Sponge Round

Servings: 4
Time: 1 hour

Method:

1. Grease a plain pudding basin with butter. Line the bottom with paper and butter thickly. Decorate with cherries.
2. Cut a round of sponge slightly smaller than bottom of tin. Cut the remaining sponge into fingers and arrange round the side of the tin. Press sponge round into bottom of tin.
3. Make a custard. Heat the milk till it steams. Whisk the eggs and sugar in a bowl. Pour the hot milk over the eggs and whisk. Add essence. Return to the pan and gently heat, stirring continuously with a wooden spoon till it thickens.
4. Fill pudding basin with custard and soak for 15 minutes.
5. Cover with greased paper and place in a pan of water, sufficient to come halfway up the basin.
6. Steam steadily for 1 hour.
7. Allow to shrink slightly then turn out. Remove paper. Serve with jam sauce (page 301).

18. VIENNOISE PUDDING

Ingredients:

1 level tablespoonful Sugar
  (to make caramel)
250 ml Milk
50 g Bread (no crusts)
25 g chopped Peel
50 g Sultanas

50 g Sugar
Rind of ½ Lemon
2 tablespoonfuls Sherry *or* Orange Juice
2 Eggs (beaten)
4 tablespoonfuls Cream *or*
  Evaporated Milk

Servings: 4
Time: 45 minutes

Method:

1. Make caramel with sugar and a little water (page 300, 423), and cool slightly.
2. Add milk to caramel and heat to dissolve it.
3. Cut bread into tiny squares.
4. Grease a pudding basin or ovenproof dish with butter.
5. Place bread in pudding basin with the chopped peel, sultanas, 50 g sugar, grated lemon rind and sherry.
6. Pour milk with dissolved caramel over the beaten eggs, add cream. Strain over the bread mixture. Cover, allow to stand 30 minutes.
7. Cover with a greased paper, steam steadily, cooking it rather quickly for the first 10 minutes.
8. Allow to shrink, then turn out.
9. Serve with a custard or sabayon sauce (pages 299, 300).

19. QUEEN OF PUDDINGS

Ingredients:

250 ml Milk
Small piece Butter
50 g Breadcrumbs
A little grated Lemon Rind
1 level tablespoonful Sugar

1–2 Eggs (separated)
40–50 g Castor Sugar for each Egg White
  (for Meringue)
2–3 tablespoonfuls Jam

Servings: 3–4
Time: 45 minutes–1 hour approx.
Oven Temperature: 180°C, No. 4; then 140–150°C, No. 1–2
Position in Oven: Middle shelf

Method:

1. Mix together breadcrumbs, sugar and lemon rind.
2. Heat the milk and butter. Pour over breadcrumbs, sugar and grated lemon rind. Add beaten egg yolks and mix well.
3. Pour into a well-greased ovenproof dish and bake till set for 30–40 minutes.
4. Remove from oven, spread with jam.
5. Beat the egg whites very stiffly, fold in castor sugar, and pile on top of pudding. Sprinkle a little sugar on top.
6. Bake in a cool oven, 140–150°C, No. 1–2, for 15–20 minutes till pale brown.

20. COCONUT PUDDING

Ingredients:

250 ml Milk
25 g Butter
50 g Breadcrumbs
25 g Sugar
25 g Coconut (dessicated)

A little grated Orange *or* Lemon Rind
1–2 Eggs (separated)
40–50 g Castor Sugar for each Egg White
(for Meringue)

Servings: 3–4
Time: 45 minutes–1 hour approx.
Oven Temperature: 180°C, No. 4; then 140–150°C, No. 1–2
Position in Oven: Middle shelf

Method:

1. Mix together breadcrumbs, sugar, coconut and lemon rind.
2. Heat the milk and butter. Pour over breadcrumbs, sugar, coconut and lemon rind. Add beaten egg yolks and mix well.
3. Pour into a well-greased ovenproof dish and bake till set in a moderate oven for 30–40 minutes.
4. Beat the egg whites very stiffly, fold in castor sugar, and pile on top of pudding. Sprinkle a little sugar on top.
5. Bake in a cool oven, 140–150°C, No. 1–2, for 15–20 minutes till pale brown.

21. BAKED CHOCOLATE PUDDING

Ingredients:

250 ml Milk
35 g Drinking Chocolate
15 g Butter
50 g Breadcrumbs
1 level tablespoonful Sugar

1 teaspoonful Vanilla Essence
1–2 Eggs (separated)
40–50 g Castor Sugar for each Egg White
(for Meringue)

Servings: 3–4
Time: 45 minutes–1 hour approx.
Oven Temperature: 180°C, No. 4; then 140–150°C, No. 1–2
Position in Oven: Middle shelf

Method:

1. Heat the milk, chocolate and butter. Pour over breadcrumbs, sugar and vanilla essence. Add beaten egg yolks and mix well.
2. Pour into a well-greased ovenproof dish and bake till set in a moderate oven for 30–40 minutes.
3. Beat the egg whites very stiffly, fold in the castor sugar, and pile on top of pudding. Sprinkle a little sugar on top.
4. Bake in a cool oven, 140–150°C, No. 1–2, for 15–20 minutes till a pale brown.

22. LEMON MERINGUE PUDDING

Ingredients:

250 ml Milk	1–2 Eggs (separated)
25 g Butter	1 Lemon (Rind and Juice)
75 g Breadcrumbs	40–50 g Castor Sugar for each Egg White
75 g Sugar	(for Meringue)

Servings: 3–4

Time: 45 minutes–1 hour approx.

Oven Temperature: 180°C, No. 4; then 140–150°C, No. 1–2

Position in Oven: Middle shelf

Method:

1. Heat milk and butter and pour over breadcrumbs, sugar and lemon rind. Add lemon juice and beaten egg yolks and mix well. Cover and leave to soak for 30 minutes.
2. Pour into a well-greased ovenproof dish and bake till set in a moderate oven for 30–40 minutes.
3. Beat egg whites stiffly, fold in castor sugar and pile on top of pudding; sprinkle with sugar.
4. Bake in a cool oven, 140–150°C, No. 1–2, for 15–20 minutes till pale brown.
5. Serve hot or cold.

23. PINEAPPLE PUDDING

Ingredients:

50 g Butter	2 Eggs (separated)
50 g Flour	1 small tin Pineapple Pieces
250 ml Milk	75 g Castor Sugar
25 g Sugar	(for Meringue)

Servings: 3–4

Time: 20 minutes approx.

Oven Temperature: 150°C, No. 2

Position in Oven: Middle shelf

Method:

1. Melt butter, stir in flour, add milk and boil up.
2. Add sugar, pineapple juice and egg yolks, return to the heat and stir till mixture thickens.
3. Stir in pineapple pieces, and pour into a greased ovenproof dish.
4. Beat up egg whites stiffly, fold in castor sugar and pile on top of mixture.
5. Bake in a cool oven for 15–20 minutes till crisp.

24. **RICE AND APRICOT PUDDING**

Ingredients:

50 g Rice	2 Eggs
500 ml Milk	100 g ready to eat dried Apricots
Pinch Salt	*or* 1 small tin Apricots (drained)
25 g Sugar	75 g Castor Sugar (for Meringue)

Servings: 4–5

Oven Temperature: 180°C, No. 4;
then 140–150°C, No. 1–2

Time: 20–30 minutes for rice (or cook in pan instead);
15–20 minutes for meringue

Position: Middle shelf

Method:

1. Wash the rice and put in a pan with milk and salt. Cook slowly till thick, then remove from heat.
2. Add sugar and egg yolks. Mix well. Pour into a greased ovenproof dish and bake till set, in a moderate oven. Or reheat in pan till mixture thickens, without boiling.
3. Spread the apricots on top.
4. Beat egg whites stiffly, fold in castor sugar and pile on top of the pudding, sprinkle with sugar.
5. Bake in a cool oven, 140–150°C, No. 1–2, for 15–20 minutes till pale brown.

Note: Other fruits may be substituted for apricots.

STEWED FRUIT AND FRUIT PUDDINGS

25. **STEWED FRUIT (FRESH)**

Average proportions to stew fresh fruit:

500 g Fruit	125–250 ml Water
75–100 g Sugar	(depending on fruit)

Method (1):

1. Prepare fruit, put with sugar and water in a pan and cook gently till soft. The quantity of water depends on fruit, e.g. rhubarb requires 125 ml, less juicy fruits may require 250 ml.
2. Fruit may be stewed in a casserole in a moderate oven when longer time is required.

Method (2):

1. Dissolve sugar in the water, bring to the boil, simmer 2 minutes.
2. Add fruit and cook gently till tender. This method is recommended for fruits which break down readily in cooking.

26. **STEWED FRUIT (DRIED)**

Average proportions to stew dried fruit, e.g. Prunes, Apricots, Figs:

500 g Dried Fruit   500 ml Water
50 g Sugar   Strip of Lemon Rind (if liked)

Method:

1. Wash and soak the fruit in measured water overnight.
2. Cook in the same water, making sure that the fruit is nearly covered. Add lemon rind and simmer for 15–20 minutes or till fruit is tender.
3. Add sugar and cook for another 10 minutes.
4. Serve hot or cold.

Note: Dried fruit may be cooked in a casserole in the oven, but a longer time must be allowed.

27. **BAKED APPLES**

Ingredients:

Apples   Dates *or* Sultanas
Sugar, Honey *or* Syrup

Time: 20–30 minutes
Oven Temperature: 180°C, No. 4
Position in Oven: Middle shelf

Method:

1. Wash apples and core; slit the skin with a sharp knife, making a ring round the middle.
2. Put on a baking tray or ovenproof dish with a little water.
3. Fill centre with sugar, honey or syrup, adding dates or sultanas, if liked.
4. Bake till tender, time varying according to size and type of apple.

28. **SWISS PUDDING**

Ingredients:

500 g Apples (peeled and sliced)   100 g Brown Sugar
50 g Suet *or* Butter   Small pieces Butter
100 g Breadcrumbs

Servings: 3–4
Time: 30 minutes
Oven Temperature: 190°C, No. 5
Position in Oven: Middle shelf

Method:

1. Stew the apples till tender.
2. Chop the suet finely, or cut butter into small pieces, and mix with the breadcrumbs and sugar.
3. Grease an ovenproof dish. Put half the breadcrumb mixture at the bottom, then put in stewed apples. Cover with the rest of the mixture. Dot with butter.
4. Bake for 30 minutes in a moderate oven.

29. **APPLE CRUMBLE**

Ingredients:

500 g Apples (peeled and sliced)   50 g Butter
150 g Sugar   100 g Flour

Servings: 3–4
Time: 35–40 minutes
Oven Temperature: 190°C, No. 5
Position in Oven: Middle shelf

Method:

1. Prepare the apples, slice and put in a greased ovenproof dish in layers with 100 g of the sugar.
2. Rub butter into flour.
3. Add 50 g sugar and rub into mixture.
4. Spread evenly over apples.
5. Bake for first 15 minutes at 190°C, No. 5, and then continue cooking for remainder of time at 180°C, No. 4.
6. Serve with custard sauce (page 299).

30. **APPLE CHARLOTTE**

Ingredients:

500 g Apples (peeled and sliced)   1 Lemon
100 g Sugar   Thin slices Bread
A little Water   50 g Butter
                                        Castor Sugar (for sifting)

Servings: 3–4
Time: 30 minutes
Oven Temperature: 200°C, No. 6
Position in Oven: Middle shelf
Size of Cake Tin: 10 cms diameter approx.

Method:

1. Stew apples in sugar and a little water till tender and turned into a thick pulp.
2. Add lemon juice.
3. Cut bread in strips, with rounds for top and bottom of a small round cake tin.
4. Dip one side of bread in melted butter and line bottom and sides of cake tin, with butter side next to tin.
5. Pour in apple pulp, and place other round of bread, dipped in melted butter, on top.
6. Bake for 30 minutes until brown and crisp.
7. Turn out and sift some sugar over.

SUET PUDDINGS

31. FOUNDATION SUET PUDDING RECIPE

Shredded suet is now available in a vegetable-fat version which can be substituted for beef suet

Ingredients:

or 200 g Flour + 2 level teaspoonfuls Baking Powder } White Pudding
200 g Self-Raising Flour

200 g Flour + 1 level teaspoonful Bicarbonate of Soda } Brown Pudding
+ 1 level teaspoonful Spices

75–100 g Suet (Vegetable *or* Beef)
50–100 g Sugar
Milk to mix

Servings: 5–6
Time: 1½–2 hours

General method:

1. Chop suet very finely or use shredded suet.
2. Mix all dry ingredients together and mix to a soft consistency with milk.
3. Put mixture into a greased pudding basin or heatproof bowl, cover.
4. Steam 1½–2 hours.
5. Turn out and serve with syrup (page 302) or jam sauce (page 301).

Note: The pudding may be boiled in a scalded floured cloth.

Variations:

75 g dried fruit can be added.
Breadcrumbs can be substituted for half the flour.
Syrup, treacle or jam can be substituted for half the sugar.
1–2 eggs could be added.

32. TREACLE PUDDING (1)

Ingredients:

200 g Flour	1 Egg (beaten)
1 level teaspoonful Bicarbonate of Soda	50 g Treacle *or* Golden Syrup
75 g Suet (Vegetable *or* Beef)	125 ml Milk
50 g Sugar	Pinch Salt
2 level teaspoonfuls ground Ginger	

Servings: 5–6
Time: 1½–2 hours

Method:

1. Chop suet finely or use shredded suet.
2. Mix all the dry ingredients together.
3. Add the beaten egg, treacle or syrup, and milk.
4. Mix to a soft consistency and pour into a greased pudding basin.
5. Cover with a greased paper and steam 1½–2 hours.
6. Serve with a treacle or syrup sauce (page 302).

237

33. TREACLE PUDDING (2)

Ingredients:

100 g Flour

100 g Breadcrumbs

100 g Suet (Vegetable *or* Beef)

50 g Currants

50 g Sugar

Grated Rind and Juice 1 Lemon

1 level teaspoonful Bicarbonate of Soda

2 Eggs (beaten)

Milk

2 tablespoonfuls Treacle *or* Golden Syrup

Servings: 5–6

Time: 1½–2 hours

Method:

1. Chop the suet very finely, or use shredded suet.
2. Mix all the dry ingredients together.
3. Add the beaten eggs, milk, and treacle or syrup.
4. Mix to a soft consistency, turn into a greased pudding basin and steam 1½–2 hours.
5. Turn out and serve with syrup or custard sauce (pages 302, 299).

34. SEVEN-CUP PUDDING

Ingredients:

1 cupful Flour

1 cupful Breadcrumbs

1 cupful Suet (Vegetable *or* Beef)

1 cupful Sugar

1 cupful Raisins

1 cupful Currants

1 cupful Milk

1 level teaspoonful Bicarbonate of Soda

2 level teaspoonfuls ground Cinnamon

1 Egg (beaten)

Servings: 5–6

Time: 1½–2 hours

Method:

Make as treacle pudding, above.

35. BROWN PUDDING

Ingredients:

50 g Flour

50 g Wholemeal Flour

50 g Breadcrumbs

50 g Suet (Vegetable *or* Beef)

25 g Raisins

25 g Mixed Peel

25 g Brown Sugar

Pinch of Salt

1 level teaspoonful Spice

1 level teaspoonful Bicarbonate of Soda

Grated Carrot (small)

1 teaspoonful Syrup

Milk

Servings: 5–6

Time: 1½–2 hours

Method:

1. Chop suet very finely. Chop raisins and peel.
2. Mix all the dry ingredients together, including grated carrot.
3. Add syrup and milk and mix to a soft consistency.
4. Pour into a greased pudding basin and steam 1½–2 hours.
5. Turn out, serve with jam or custard sauce (pages 301, 299).

36. FIG PUDDING

Ingredients:

100 g Flour	1 level teaspoonful Bicarbonate of Soda
100 g Breadcrumbs	2 level teaspoonfuls Cream of Tartar
100 g Figs	Pinch Salt
50 g Sugar	2 Eggs (beaten)
100 g Suet (Vegetable *or* Beef)	A little Milk

Servings: 5–6

Time: 1½–2 hours

Method:

1. Wash the figs and chop them along with sugar.
3. Mix all the dry ingredients including suet.
4. Add the beaten eggs and enough milk to mix to a soft consistency.
5. Turn into a greased pudding basin, cover with greased paper and steam for 1½–2 hours.
6. Serve with fig sauce (page 302).

37. DATE PUDDING

Make as fig pudding, above, substituting dates for figs.

38. STEAMED GROUND RICE PUDDING

Ingredients:

50 g Flour	50 g Brown Sugar
50 g Ground Rice	Pinch Salt
50 g Suet (Vegetable *or* Beef) *or* Butter	1 level teaspoonful Bicarbonate of Soda
50 g Raisins	125 ml Milk

Servings: 3–4

Time: 2 hours

Method:

1. Chop the suet finely, wash the raisins.
2. Mix all the dry ingredients well together.
3. Add the milk, making the mixture very moist.
4. Pour into a greased pudding basin.
5. Cover with a greased paper and steam for 2 hours.
6. Turn out and serve with jam or custard sauce (pages 301, 299).

Note: If butter is used, rub into dry ingredients.

39. PLUM PUDDING

Ingredients:

100 g Flour	I Lemon (rind and juice)
100 g Breadcrumbs	Grated Nutmeg
100 g Suet (Vegetable *or* Beef)	½ level teaspoonful Salt
100 g Currants	½ Cooking Apple (grated)
100 g Sultanas	I Egg (beaten)
100 g Raisins	I tablespoonful Treacle
25 g Mixed Peel	A little Milk, 125 ml approx.
25 g Almonds (blanched)	I tablespoonful Brandy *or* Rum (optional)
100 g Demerara Sugar	

Time: 6 hours

Method:

1. Chop suet finely.
2. Wash fruit.
3. Chop raisins, almonds and peel roughly.
4. Mix all dry ingredients and grated lemon rind.
5. Add grated apple, lemon juice, beaten egg, treacle, milk and brandy or rum.
6. Mix well and press down into greased pudding basin.
7. Cover with greased paper and steam for 6 hours.
8. Store for a few weeks.
9. Steam for I hour or longer before using.

40. RICH PLUM PUDDING

Ingredients:

150 g Breadcrumbs	50 g Almonds (blanched)
150 g Suet (Vegetable *or* Beef)	I level teaspoonful Salt
300 g Raisins	75 g Brown Sugar
25 g Mixed Peel	4 Eggs (beaten)
100 g Currants	½ glass Brandy

Servings: 6–7

Time: 6 hours

Method:

1. Chop suet very finely, mix with breadcrumbs.
2. Wash dried fruit, chop peel and almonds.
3. Mix all the dry ingredients together.
4. Add the beaten eggs and brandy and mix well.
5. Pour into greased pudding basin.
6. Cover with greased paper and steam for 6 hours.
7. This pudding is improved if made several weeks before being used. After cooking, remove paper, cool and cover with fresh greaseproof paper or food wrap. Store in a cool place.
8. Steam for I hour before using.
9. Serve with brandy butter (page 303).

41. **CLOOTIE DUMPLING**

Ingredients:

250–300 g Flour	2 level teaspoonfuls Bicarbonate
100 g Suet (Vegetable *or* Beef)	of Soda
50 g Orange Peel (*or* grated	200 g Currants
rind 1 Orange)	100 g Sultanas
4 level teaspoonfuls Cinnamon	150 g Sugar
2 level teaspoonfuls Ginger	Some grated Nutmeg
½ level teaspoonful Salt	Milk to mix (about a cup)

Time: 4–5 hours

Equipment: A muslin cloth and a large pot

Method:

1. Add all dry ingredients to the flour and mix well with some milk.
2. Scald centre of cloth with boiling water and dust with flour.
3. Put mixture in centre and tie up, leaving room for mixture to swell.
4. Place on top of an inverted plate in a large pot with a lid. Fill with boiling water and boil for 4–5 hours. Do not allow pot to boil dry.

PUDDINGS USING PASTRY

42. **ROLY-POLY PUDDING**

Ingredients:

100 g Suet Pastry (page 307)	4 tablespoonfuls Jam

Servings: 3–4

Time: 1½–2 hours

Method:

1. Roll the pastry into an oblong 15 x 30 cm approx.
2. Spread with jam almost to the edge.
3. Wet edge, roll up and place in a greased, straight-sided jar.
4. Cover with greased paper and steam 1½–2 hours.
5. Turn out and serve with a custard or jam sauce.

Note: The roly-poly pudding may be boiled in a pudding cloth which has been scalded in boiling water and floured well. Tie securely at ends and cook for 2 hours. The pudding may be baked. Place pudding in an ovenproof dish and add 125 ml of milk. Bake in a moderate oven for 1 hour approximately.

43. **JAM LAYER PUDDING**

Ingredients:

100 g Suet Pastry (page 307)	Some Jam *or* Syrup

Servings: 3–4

Time: 1½–2 hours

Method:

1. Make the suet pastry and divide into four pieces, graded in size. Roll out to fit a pudding basin or ovenproof bowl.
2. Fill a greased pudding basin with alternate layers of pastry and jam or syrup, finishing with pastry.
3. Cover with greased paper and steam for 2 hours.
4. Turn out and serve with a suitable sauce.

44. DELAWARE PUDDING

Ingredients:

100 g Suet Pastry (page 307)	1 medium Apple
1 tablespoonful Syrup	25 g Mixed Peel
50 g Demerara *or* Soft Brown Sugar	A level teaspoonful Mixed Spice
25 g Currants	Grated rind ½ Lemon

Servings: 4–5
Time: 1½–2 hours

Method:

1. Prepare filling; mix syrup, sugar, currants, chopped apple and mixed peel, spice and grated lemon rind.
2. Make the suet pastry and divide into four pieces, graded in size. Roll out to fit a pudding basin or ovenproof bowl.
3. Fill a greased pudding basin with alternate layers of pastry and filling, finishing with pastry.
4. Cover with greased paper and steam for 1½–2 hours.
5. Turn out and serve with a suitable sauce.

45. STEAMED FRUIT DUMPLING

Ingredients:

100 g Suet Pastry (page 307)	75 g Sugar
250 g Any Fruit in season (for filling)	A little Water

Servings: 3–4
Time: 1½–2 hours

Method:

1. Prepare the fruit according to its kind.
2. Make pastry, cut off a third for the lid.
3. Roll out remainder of the pastry and line a greased pudding basin or ovenproof bowl with the pastry.
4. Put in half the fruit, add sugar and remainder of fruit.
5. Turn edge of pastry onto the fruit, wet the edge.
6. Roll remaining pastry to fit the top of the pudding basin. Press on firmly.
7. Cover with greased paper and steam 1½–2 hours.

46. JAM TART

Ingredients:

100 g Short Pastry (page 307)   Jam
Servings: 3–4
Time: 20 minutes
Oven Temperature: 200°C, No. 6
Position in Oven: Middle shelf
Size of Plate: 15–17 cm

Method:

1. Roll out pastry a size larger than tart plate.
2. Put on plate and turn extra pastry under to make a double edge.
or Cut off a strip to fit rim of plate. Wet rim and place on strip of pastry. Wet the strip. Roll remainder of pastry to fit plate. Place on pastry, press the edge and trim.
3. Fill centre with jam.
4. Decorate with narrow strips of pastry from trimmings, arranged in a trellis pattern.
5. Bake for 20 minutes, reducing the heat after 15 minutes, if necessary.

47. SYRUP TART

Ingredients:

100 g Short Pastry (page 307)   Grated Rind and Juice of
100 g Syrup   Lemon
40–50 g Breadcrumbs
Servings: 3–4
Time: 30 minutes
Oven Temperature: 200°C, No. 6
Position in Oven: Middle shelf
Size of Plate: 15–17 cm

Method:

1. Make Pastry.
2. Mix syrup, breadcrumbs, lemon rind and juice.
3. Roll out pastry and prepare as for jam tart.
4. Spread on filling and bake, reducing the heat after 15 minutes if necessary.

48. JAM TURNOVERS

Ingredients:

or 100 g Short Pastry   Jam
Scraps of Short Pastry
Time: 20 minutes
Oven Temperature: 200°C, No. 6
Position in Oven: One-third from top

243

Method:

1. Roll out pastry, cut out in rounds.
2. Put a teaspoonful of jam in the centre of each round.
3. Wet the edges, fold over and press edges together.
4. Bake 20 minutes.

49. APPLE BALLS

Ingredients:

Apples	50 g Short Pastry for each
Sugar	Apple (page 307)

Time: 30–45 minutes
Oven Temperature: 190–200°C, No. 5–6
Position in Oven: One-third from top

Method:

1. Make pastry.
2. Core and peel the apples.
3. Divide the pastry according to the number of apples.
4. Place an apple on each piece and work the pastry round.
5. Fill up the hole in the apple with sugar and one clove, if liked.
6. Join the edges of the pastry over the apple – there must be no cracks.
7. Place on a greased baking tin.
8. Bake from ½–¾ hour according to size of apples.
9. To test for readiness insert a skewer through middle of the apple.

50. FRUIT PIE

Ingredients:

125 g Short Pastry (page 307)	A little Water for less
500 g seasonable Fruit	juicy Fruits
75–100 g Sugar	Castor Sugar (for dredging)

Servings: 4–5
Time: 30–40 minutes
Oven Temperature: 200°C, No. 6
Position in Oven: Middle shelf
Size of Pie Dish: 500 ml (deep, wide-rimmed)

Method:

1. Make pastry and lay aside.
2. Mix fruit and sugar together. Fill pie dish with prepared fruit.
3. Roll out the pastry to a size larger than a deep pie dish.
4. Cut off a continuous strip of pastry the width of the rim of the pie dish. Wet edges of pie rim and lay the strip of pastry over the top (to double the thickness of the pie rim).
5. Wet this strip of pastry too, and then cover the pie with the remainder of the pastry.

6. Trim edges and mark with a fork.
7. Bake 30–40 minutes reducing temperature to 180°C, or No. 4, after 15 minutes.
8. When cooked, make a slit with a knife at either end to allow steam to escape at the same time testing the fruit.
9. Dredge top with castor sugar.

51. FRUIT TART

Ingredients:

150 g Short Pastry (page 307)	100 g Sugar
500 g Fruit	Castor Sugar (for dredging)

Servings: 4–5
Time: 30 minutes
Oven Temperature: 200°C, No. 6
Position in Oven: Middle shelf
Size of Tart Plate: 15–17 cm

Method:

1. Divide pastry in two, keeping rather more than half for the top.
2. Roll out the smaller portion to fit the plate.
3. Wet the rim of plate and place on pastry.
4. Put prepared fruit and sugar on pastry, having sugar in the middle of the fruit.
5. Roll out remaining pastry to cover, and put on top, first wetting the edge of pastry lining the plate.
6. Press edges well together and trim.
7. Mark edge with a fork. Bake.
8. When the pastry is set after 10–15 minutes, reduce heat to 180°C, No. 4, and continue cooking.
9. On removal from oven make two small slits in tart to allow steam to escape.
10. Dredge with castor sugar.

52. SPICED APPLE TART

Ingredients:

300 g Apples	1½ level teaspoonfuls ground Cinnamon
100 g Dates *or* Prunes (stoned)	A little Water
50 g Sugar	100 g Spiced Short Pastry (page 308)
	Icing Sugar (for dredging)

Servings: 4–5
Time: 30 minutes
Oven Temperature: 200°C, No. 6
Position in Oven: One-third from top
Size of Flan Ring or Dish: 15 cm

Method:

1. Prepare the apples, cut up dates or prunes, stew with the sugar, cinnamon and water until tender.
2. Spread mixture on a plate and leave till cold.
3. Make the pastry, cut off one-third for the lid and roll out thinly, cut with flan ring.
4. Lay the flan ring on a baking sheet, roll out remaining pastry and line the flan ring.
5. Pack fruit mixture in tightly and turn edge of pastry over fruit.
6. Damp this edge and lay the lid on top.
7. Press down evenly, bake until set and a golden brown colour.
8. Serve hot, thickly dredged with icing sugar, or cold, with glacé icing.

53. SWISS TART

Ingredients:

100 g Biscuit Pastry (page 309)	2 Egg Whites
500 g Apples (peeled and quartered)	100 g Castor Sugar (for Meringue)
2 tablespoonfuls Water	
75–100 g Sugar	

Servings: 4
Time: 15–20 minutes for pastry; 20–30 minutes for meringue
Oven Temperature: 190–200°C, No. 5–6
Position in Oven: One-third from top
Size of Flan Ring or Plate: 15–17 cm

Method:

1. Make a syrup with the water and sugar. Stew the apples in the syrup, being careful not to break them. Cool.
2. Put a greased flan ring on a baking tray.
3. Roll out the pastry a little bigger than the flan ring. Line the ring, prick the base. Place a piece of greaseproof paper in pastry case to cover bottom and sides.
4. Bake blind till pale brown at 190–200°C, No. 5–6 for 5–10 minutes, reducing the heat to 180°C, No. 4 for a further 5–10 minutes approx.
5. When pastry is set, remove the paper and crisp flan case in oven for 5 minutes. Cool. Remove flan ring.
6. Fill the case with stewed apples.
7. Put egg whites and sugar in a pudding basin and beat over hot water until stiff. Pipe on top. Bake at 150°C, No. 2, for 20–30 minutes.

54. APPLE AMBER PUDDING

Ingredients:

500 g Apples	2 Eggs (separated)
50–75 g Sugar	100 g Short Pastry (page 307)
Little Water	80 g Castor Sugar (for Meringue)
Rind and Juice ½ Lemon	

Servings: 3–4
Time: 10–15 minutes for pastry; 30 minutes for filling; 15–20 minutes for meringue
Oven Temperature: 190–200°C, No. 5–6
Position in Oven: One-third from top
Size of Flan Ring or Plate: 15–17 cm

Method:

1. Stew apples with sugar, water and lemon rind till soft. Sieve or mash.
2. Add egg yolks and lemon juice, mix well.
3. Line the plate with pastry, decorate edge, brush with egg; or line a flan ring. Fork base and bake blind till pale brown at 190°–200°C, No. 5–6 for 10–15 minutes.
4. Pour in the filling mixture, bake for 20–30 minutes, reducing the heat after 15 minutes to 180°C, No. 4.
5. Beat egg whites stiffly, fold in castor sugar.
6. Place meringue on top of pudding and bake for 15–20 minutes in a cool oven, 150°C, No. 2, till pale brown.

55. MANCHESTER PUDDING

Ingredients:

100 g Short *or* Flaky Pastry (pages 307, 310)	Small piece Butter
250 ml Milk	1–2 Eggs (separated)
Grated rind ½ Lemon	Raspberry Jam
50 g Breadcrumbs	40–80g Castor Sugar for Meringue
25 g Castor Sugar	Glacé Cherries (for decoration)
	Angelica (for decoration)

Servings: 3–4
Time: 10–15 minutes for pastry; 30 minutes for filling; 15–20 minutes for meringue
Oven Temperature: 190–200°C, No. 5–6
Position in Oven: One-third from top
Size of Flan Ring or Plate: 15–17 cm

Method:

1. For the filling, heat the milk with the lemon rind. Remove rind and pour the milk over the breadcrumbs. Add sugar, butter and beaten egg yolks. Mix well and leave to cool.
2. Line the plate or flan ring with pastry, decorate edge, brush with egg; prick base and bake blind till pale brown at 190–200°C, No. 5–6 for about 10–15 minutes.
3. Spread a layer of jam on the bottom and pour in the filling mixture.
4. Bake for half an hour, reducing heat to 180°C, No. 4 after 10 minutes.
5. Whisk egg whites stiffly, fold in castor sugar. Pile on top of pudding and bake in a cool oven, 150°C, No. 2, for 15–20 minutes or till set and lightly browned.
6. Decorate with glacé cherries and angelica.

56. MADEIRA PUDDING

Ingredients:

100 g Short Pastry (page 307)   100 g Butter or Block Margarine
2 tablespoonfuls Raspberry Jam   100 g Castor Sugar
100 g Flour and   3 Eggs
  1 level teaspoonful Baking Powder   1 teaspoonful Vanilla Essence
or 100 g Self-raising Flour

Servings: 6–7
Time: 30–40 minutes
Oven Temperature: 200°C, No. 6; 180°C, No. 4, after 10 minutes
Position in Oven: Middle shelf
Size of Flan Ring or Deep Plate: 15–17 cm

Method:

1. Line a deep plate with pastry, decorate the edges, or line flan ring. Spread jam on the bottom.
2. Cream the butter or margarine and sugar, add egg a little at a time, beating well.
3. Stir in sieved flour and baking powder, and add vanilla essence.
4. Put mixture in the lined plate and bake, reducing the heat to 180°C, No. 4, after 10 minutes.

57. LEMON MERINGUE PIE

Ingredients:

100 g Short Pastry (page 307)   25 g Butter
25 g Cornflour   2 Eggs
125 ml Water   80 g Castor Sugar (for Meringue)
50–75 g Castor Sugar   1 Lemon (juice and rind)

Servings: 4
Time: 10–15 minutes for pastry; 15–20 minutes for meringue
Oven Temperature: 190–200°C, No. 5–6
Position in Oven: One-third from top
Size of Flan Ring or Plate: 15–17 cm

Method:

1. Roll out pastry and line plate; decorate the edges and brush with egg; or line a flan ring. Prick base with a fork. Bake blind till pale brown, at 190–200°C, No. 5–6 reducing heat to 180°C, No. 4, after 10 minutes.
2. For the filling, blend the cornflour, add water, sugar and lemon juice. Bring to the boil, stirring all the time.
3. Add grated lemon rind, butter and egg yolks. If mixture goes thin reheat till thickens without boiling.
4. Spread filling mixture onto the pastry case.
5. Whisk egg whites stiffly, fold in castor sugar and pile on top of mixture.
6. Bake in a cool oven, 150°C, No. 2, for 15–20 minutes until set and lightly browned.

58. **BUTTERSCOTCH TART**

Ingredients:

100 g Short Pastry (page 307)	25 g Butter
75 g Brown Sugar	1 teaspoonful Vanilla Essence
25 g Flour	1 Egg (separated)
3 tablespoonfuls Water	40–50 g Castor Sugar for Meringue
125 ml Milk	

Servings: 4

Time: 10–15 minutes for pastry; 15–20 minutes for meringue

Oven Temperature: 190–200°C, No. 5–6

Position in Oven: One-third from top

Size of Flan Ring or Plate: 15–17 cm

Method:

1. Roll out pastry and line plate, decorate edge and brush with egg, or line a flan tin. Prick base with a fork. Bake blind till pale brown, reducing heat to 180°C, No. 4, after about 10 minutes.
3. Mix sugar and flour and blend with the water. Heat the milk and pour over, add butter and mix well.
4. Cook slowly till thick. Take from the heat and add flavouring and egg yolk. If mixture goes thin reheat till it thickens without boiling. Pour mixture into pastry case.
5. Make meringue by whisking the egg white till stiff and folding in the castor sugar.
6. Pile on top of mixture and bake in a cool oven, 150°C, No. 2, till set and lightly browned, about 20 minutes.

59. **BAKEWELL TART**

Ingredients:

or 100 g Short Pastry (page 307)	40–50 g Cake Crumbs
Rich Short Pastry (page 308)	25 g Ground Almonds
40–50 g Butter or Block Margarine	½ teaspoonful Almond Essence
50 g Castor Sugar	Raspberry Jam
1 Egg (beaten)	

Servings: 4

Time: 30–40 minutes

Oven Temperature: 190–200°C, No. 5–6

Position in Oven: One-third from top

Size of Flan Ring or Plate: 15–17 cm

Method:

1. Roll out pastry and line plate; decorate the edges and brush with egg; or line a flan ring.
2. Cream butter and sugar, add egg gradually and stir in the other ingredients.
3. Spread base of pastry with jam and spread the mixture over.
4. Bake for 30–40 minutes, lowering the heat as required.

60. **CUSTARD TART**

Ingredients:

100 g Short Pastry (page 307)	150 ml Milk
1 Egg	20 g Sugar
	Little Nutmeg (if liked)

Servings: 4
Time: 30–40 minutes
Oven Temperature: 180°C, No. 4
Position in Oven: Middle shelf
Size of Flan Ring or Plate: 15–17 cm

Method:

1. Line flan ring or deep pie plate with pastry. Bake blind at 200°C, No. 6, for about 10 minutes.
2. Make custard with egg, milk and sugar (page 229). Pour into baked flan.
3. Sprinkle with nutmeg if liked and bake for 20–30 minutes at 180°C, No. 4.

61. **MINCE PIES**

Ingredients:

Short, Rough Puff *or* Flaky Pastry (pages 307, 309, 310)
Mincemeat (page 456)

Servings: 100 g short pastry will make 6–8 pies
100 g rough puff or flaky pastry will make 8–10 pies
Time: 20–30 minutes
Oven Temperature: 220°C, No. 7
Position in Oven: One-third from top

Method:

1. Roll out the pastry thinly. Cut into rounds a little larger than the top of the patty tins to be used.
2. Line the tins, then put in mincemeat to two-thirds fill them.
3. Cut out rounds of pastry for the top, dampen the edges, place on top of mincemeat. Join the edges and press together.
4. Brush with beaten egg, if a flaky pastry; make two slits on top. Put on baking tray.
5. Place in a hot oven and bake for 20–30 minutes till golden brown.
6. Turn out and dredge with castor or icing sugar.

Second method – mince pies made without using patty tins:

1. Roll out pastry and cut in rounds one half slightly larger than the other.
2. Put the smaller rounds on baking tray, pile mincemeat in centre. Cover with larger rounds of pastry, pressing edges well together.
3. Bake as for first method.

CAKE MIXTURE PUDDINGS

62. PLAIN CAKE MIXTURE PUDDINGS

Foundation recipe
Ingredients:

or
200 g Flour and
   3 level teaspoonfuls Baking Powder
200 g Self-raising Flour
100 g Butter

75 g Castor Sugar
2 Eggs
A little Milk or Water

Servings: 6–8
Time: 1 hour 30 minutes

Method:

1. Sieve the flour and baking powder. Rub in fat and add sugar.
2. Beat the eggs, add to the flour with enough milk or water to make a dropping consistency.
3. Put into a greased pudding basin.
4. Cover with greased paper and steam steadily.
5. Turn out.

Note: For half quantity, steam 45 minutes to 1 hour.

Variations

Leicester Pudding.—Put some jam in pudding basin before adding mixture.
Syrup Pudding.—Use syrup instead of jam
Sultana Pudding.—Add 100 g sultanas to mixture.
Cherry Pudding.—Add 75 g cherries.
Black Cap Pudding.—Line bottom of pudding basin with cooked prunes.

63. RICH CAKE MIXTURE PUDDINGS

Foundation recipe
Ingredients:

2 Eggs
100 g Butter
100 g Sugar

or
Little Milk *or* Water
125 g Flour and 1 level teaspoonful
   Baking Powder
125 g Self-raising Flour

Servings: 6–7
Time: 30 minutes small: 1 hour large

Method:

1. Cream the butter and sugar.
2. Add the beaten eggs a little at a time.
3. Stir in sieved flour and baking powder. If necessary add a little milk or water.
4. Mix well. Put in greased dariole moulds or a greased pudding basin and put in a pan with boiling water to come halfway up moulds.
5. Cover with greased paper and steam steadily.

6. Allow to shrink before turning out.

7. Serve with a suitable sauce.

Note: If preferred the mixture may be baked in a moderate oven, in small moulds, 190°C, No. 5, for approximately 20 minutes, 40–50 minutes in large moulds.

Variations

Castle Pudding.—Add grated rind of a lemon, serve with lemon sauce.

Orange Pudding.—Add grated rind of an orange, serve with orange sauce.

Chocolate Pudding.—Add 25 g drinking chocolate and 1 teaspoonful vanilla essence, serve with chocolate sauce.

Sultana Pudding.—Add 50 g sultanas, serve with lemon sauce.

Cherry Pudding.—Add 25 g chopped glacé cherries, serve with jam sauce.

Upside Down Pudding.—Cream 40 g butter with 60 g soft brown sugar. Spread on bottom of greased 18–20 cm cake tin. Add layer of tinned fruit, e.g. pineapple. Top with basic mixture. Bake.

Eve's Pudding.—Slice 300 g apples into a greased ovenproof dish, top with ½ the basic mixture. Bake.

64. EVE'S PUDDING

See above for an alternative method of making Eve's Pudding
based on Rich Cake Mixture Pudding

Ingredients:

300 g Apples	50 g Butter *or* Block Margarine
50 g Sugar	40 g Sugar
75 g Flour	1 Egg (beaten)
1 ½ level teaspoonfuls Baking Powder	100 ml Milk

Servings: 4–5

Time: 30 minutes

Oven Temperature: 190°C, No. 5

Position in Oven: Middle shelf

Size of Pie dish: 500 ml

Method:

1. Stew apples with sugar and a little water.

2. Sieve flour and baking powder; rub butter or block margarine into flour, add sugar, beaten egg and milk, and mix to a soft consistency.

3. Pour hot apples into a greased ovenproof dish and pour the mixture on top.

4. Bake till sponge is firm and lightly browned.

65. LEMON OR ORANGE PUDDING

Ingredients:

	25 g Butter or Block Margarine	25 g Flour
	100 g Castor Sugar	Pinch of Salt
or	Rind and Juice of 1 Lemon	2 Eggs (separated)
	Rind and Juice of 1 Orange	125 ml Milk

Servings: 3–4
Time: 45 minutes
Oven Temperature: 180°C, No. 4
Position in Oven: Middle shelf
Size of Pie dish: 500 ml

Method:

1. Cream the butter or block margarine and sugar.
2. Add lemon or orange juice and grated rind.
3. Beat in the flour and egg yolks alternately.
4. Stir in the milk. Fold in the stiffly-beaten egg whites. Pour into greased ovenproof dish.
5. Place in a roasting tin with water and bake.
6. Dredge with castor sugar and serve.

66. STEAMED CHOCOLATE PUDDING

Ingredients:

50 g Butter	40–50 g Sugar
50 g block Chocolate	Vanilla Essence
2 tablespoonfuls Milk	2 Eggs (separated)
50 g Cake Crumbs	Chocolate Sauce (pages 300, 301)

Servings: 4
Time: 1 hour

Method:

1. Heat butter, chocolate and milk together; stir in cake crumbs. Stir till mixture thickens and leaves the sides of the pan.
2. Remove from heat, add sugar, vanilla essence and egg yolks.
3. Fold in stiffly beaten egg whites.
4. Pour into a greased pudding basin. Cover with greased paper and steam gently 1 hour.
5. Turn out and coat with chocolate sauce.

HOT SOUFFLÉS

67. FOUNDATION RECIPE FOR SOUFFLÉS

Panada (page 292):

25 g Butter
25 g Flour
125 ml Liquid

Raising agents:

2 Egg Yolks
2 Egg Whites

Distinctive ingredients:
Liquids:

1 teaspoonful to 1 tablespoonful according to strength and nature of liquid used.

Solids:

    50–75 g finely divided Preserved Fruits.

Seasonings:

    For Sweet Soufflés add 25 g Sugar. For Savoury Soufflés add Salt and Pepper.
    Note: Soufflés take their names from the distinctive ingredients used, e.g. Vanilla,
    Cherry, Chocolate.

68. BAKED SOUFFLÉ

Servings: 3–4
Time: 20 minutes
Oven Temperature: 200–220°C, No. 6–7
Position in Oven: Middle shelf

Method:

1. Melt the butter, add the flour and cook slightly.
2. Gradually blend with the liquid and cook thoroughly to make panada (page 292).
3. Add the distinctive ingredients (flavourings etc.), sugar and egg yolks. Mix well.
4. Fold in the stiffly beaten egg whites.
5. Pour into a greased and sugared ovenproof dish; or into a soufflé case with a double band of greaseproof paper coming 5 cm above the top of case.
6. Bake till well-risen and browned, and serve with a suitable sauce.

69. STEAMED SOUFFLÉ

Time: 25–30 minutes

Method:

1. Make as for baked soufflé (above).
2. Pour into a greased soufflé tin, with a double band of greased paper coming 5 cm above the top of the tin. Place in a pot of hot water (water coming up no further than halfway up the soufflé tin).
3. Cover with a greased paper and steam very gently, 25–30 minutes.
4. Allow to shrink, turn out carefully and serve with a suitable sauce.

Variations:

    Vanilla.—Add 1 teaspoon vanilla essence.
    Chocolate.—Dissolve 40–50 g chocolate in the milk.
    Banana.—Add 1 mashed banana to panada.
    Coffee.—Add 2 teaspoonfuls coffee essence.
    Pineapple.—Make panada with ½ milk and ½ pineapple juice and add 50–75 g finely chopped pineapple.
    Cherry.—Add 50 g chopped cherries, and a few drops almond essence.

70. DINNER PANCAKES

Ingredients:

    250 ml Yorkshire Pudding Batter (1) (page 475)

Cooking Fat *or* Oil for frying   Lemon Juice
Sugar

Method:

1. Melt fat in a frying pan (a small piece about the size of a nut, or a tablespoon oil).
2. When it is hot, pour in just enough batter to cover the bottom of the pan.
3. When the batter is set, shake it loose.
4. When brown toss or turn and brown the other side.
5. Turn onto a sugared paper or plate, sprinkle with sugar and add a squeeze of lemon juice.
6. Roll up and keep hot while rest of pancakes are being fried. Serve very hot.

Note: Jam or marmalade, stewed fruit or a savoury filling may be used instead of lemon and sugar.

71. APPLES IN BATTER

Ingredients:

250 ml Yorkshire Pudding   200 g Apples
Batter (page 475)   50 g Sugar

Servings: 3–4
Time: 30–40 minutes
Oven Temperature: 220°C, No. 7
Position in Oven: One-third from top

Method:

1. Peel, quarter and core the apples.
2. Place in a greased ovenproof dish.
3. Add sugar to the batter and pour over apples.
4. Bake until set.

72. APPLE FRITTERS

Ingredients:

2 Apples   Coating Batter (page 474)
Castor Sugar   Oil for deep-frying

Method:

1. Peel, core and slice the apples.
2. Dip in batter and deep-fry in hot oil until golden brown.
3. Drain, toss in castor sugar. Serve.

Variations:

Orange Fritters.—Peel orange and remove pith. Cut in thick slices. Proceed as for apple fritters.

Banana Fritters.—Peel and cut bananas in two, lengthwise, then across, giving four pieces. Proceed as for apple fritters.

Pineapple Fritters.—Use tinned pineapple rings, draining them well before dipping in batter.

73. SPANISH PUFFS

Ingredients:

Choux Pastry (page 312)
125 ml Jam Sauce (page 301)

Method:

1. Drop choux pastry carefully in teaspoonfuls into a pan of hot oil.
2. Deep-fry slowly and thoroughly. Drain well.
3. Place on serving dish, dredge with castor sugar and serve with jam sauce.

74. SAVARIN

Ingredients:

10 g Yeast	1 Egg
1 level teaspoonful Sugar	A few Almonds
3–4 tablespoonfuls lukewarm	25 g Butter
Milk and Water	2 level teaspoonfuls Castor
100 g Flour	Sugar
½ level teaspoonful Salt	Rum Syrup (page 303)

Servings: 3–4
Time: 20 minutes
Oven Temperature: 200°C, No. 6
Position in Oven: Middle shelf
Tin: 12–15 cm Timbale Mould or 10–12 cm Cake Tin

Method:

1. Sieve flour and salt into a warm bowl.
2. Grease tin and line with blanched shredded almonds.
3. Add yeast to 2 tablespoonfuls lukewarm milk and water. Add 1 level teaspoonful sugar. Pour into the centre of the flour, lightly cover with flour and set aside in a warm place for about 10 minutes.
4. When yeast cracks through flour, add beaten egg, remainder of liquid, melted butter and sugar.
5. Beat for 10 minutes till of a thick batter consistency.
6. Turn into prepared cake tin.
7. Leave in a warm place, to rise to double its size.
8. Bake in a hot oven for 20 minutes if mixture is in a timbale mould; if a cake tin is used, bake at 180–190°C, No. 4–5, for 40 minutes.
9. Turn out, fork, pour rum syrup over. Serve hot.
10. Alternatively serve cold with fruit and cream.

Rum syrup
Ingredients:

150 g Sugar	500 ml Water
Rum *or* Rum Essence	

Method:

Boil sugar and water until reduced to half original quantity. Add rum or essence according to taste.

75. **BABAS**

Ingredients:

100 g Flour	1 tablespoonful Milk
25 g Sugar	25 g Mixed Dried Fruit (chopped)
1 Egg (beaten)	A few shredded Almonds
25 g Butter	Rum Syrup (page 303)
10 g Yeast	

Servings: 3–4
Time: 10 minutes
Oven Temperature: 200°C, No. 6

Method:

1. Sieve flour into warm bowl.
2. Grease boat-shaped or dariole moulds and line with shredded almonds.
3. Add yeast to 1 tablespoonful of lukewarm milk and 1 level teaspoonful sugar. Pour into the centre of the flour and set aside in a warm place for about 10 minutes.
4. When yeast cracks through flour add beaten egg, melted butter, sugar.
5. Beat well for 10 minutes. Add chopped dried fruit.
6. Half-fill prepared moulds with the mixture and leave to rise to top of moulds.
7. Bake for 10 minutes.
8. Turn out. Fork and soak in rum syrup. Serve hot or cold.

COLD PUDDINGS

COLD PUDDINGS

1. CURDS AND CREAM OR JUNKET

Ingredients:

500 ml Milk	2 teaspoonfuls Rennet
2 teaspoonfuls Sugar	Single Cream

Servings: 3–4

Method:

1. Warm milk to blood heat, add sugar and pour into a glass dish.
2. Stir in rennet and allow to set at room temperature for around 30 minutes.
3. Serve with cream.

Note: Proportion of rennet stated on the bottle should be adhered to. Vegetarian rennet is available in some health food stores and supermarkets and also online.

2. CARAMEL CORNFLOUR MOULD

Ingredients:

100 g Sugar	} Caramel	1 Egg (beaten)
4 tablespoonfuls Water		25 g Sugar
500 ml Milk		Vanilla Essence
40 g Cornflour		

Servings: 3–4

Method:

1. Dissolve sugar in water and boil until a golden brown caramel is formed. Cool.
2. Add milk to caramel and stir until dissolved.
3. Blend cornflour, add milk, stir over heat until boiling.
4. Remove from heat, add sugar, beaten egg and vanilla essence.
5. Pour into a serving dish or mould and turn out when cold.

3. TAPIOCA OR SAGO CREAM

Ingredients:

40 g Tapioca *or* Sago	Some Ratafias
500 ml Milk	A little Sherry
25 g Sugar	125 ml Cream
Almond Essence	

Servings: 3–4

Method:

1. Simmer tapioca or sago in milk till clear and creamy. Add sugar and a little almond essence.
2. Stir occasionally till cold, add sherry and half-whisked cream.
3. Soak the ratafias in a glass dish with a little sherry. Pour the tapioca or sago over.
4. Decorate with some ratafias and serve.

4. **COMPÔTE OF FRUIT**

Ingredients:

500 ml Water	200–250 g Fresh Fruit
200 g Sugar	Colouring (if liked)
200–250 g Dried Fruit	Flavouring (if liked)

Servings: 4

Method:

1. Wash and soak dried fruit in measured water.
2. Cook till fruit begins to soften, add sugar and dissolve.
3. Add prepared fresh fruit and continue cooking, simmer till all the fruit is cooked but not broken.
4. Put into a serving dish, reduce the syrup if necessary and pour over.

5. **FRUIT SALAD**

Ingredients:

250 ml Water	1 tin Fruit
100 g Sugar	1 Apple
Piece Cinnamon Stick ⎱ Fruit Syrup	1 Orange
Rind and Juice ½ Lemon	1 Pear
Little Sherry or Brandy (if liked)	1 Banana
Nuts and Dates (if liked)	50–100 g Grapes

Servings: 3–4

Method:

1. Put water, sugar, cinnamon stick and strip of lemon rind in a pan.
2. Add sugar and dissolve. Bring to boiling point. Boil quickly till mixture takes on an oily consistency.
3. Add lemon juice, syrup from tinned fruit, strain, add sherry and cool.
4. Prepare fruit, slice and soak in the syrup. Serve in a glass dish. There should be sufficient syrup to cover the fruit.

6. **GOOSEBERRY FOOL**

Ingredients:

1 kg Gooseberries	200 g Sugar
125 ml Water	250 ml Cream or Custard,
	or a Mixture of both

Servings: 4–6

Method:

1. Stew fruit till soft, sweeten and sieve, or liquidise.
2. Cool, then mix with the half-whipped cream or custard.
3. Colour pale green if necessary and serve cold.

Note: Any fresh fruit can be treated similarly.

7. SAGO OR TAPIOCA AND RHUBARB MOULD

Ingredients:

500 g Rhubarb
125 ml Water
75 g Sago *or* Tapioca
Custard Sauce (page 299)

Strips Lemon Rind
50–75 g Sugar
A little Colouring (if necessary)

Servings: 6–8

Method:

1. Cut up rhubarb and cook for five minutes with the water.
2. Add sago and lemon rind, simmer for 30 minutes taking care it does not burn.
3. Remove rind, add sugar and colouring. Stir till dissolved and pour into a mould.
4. When set, turn out and serve with custard.

8. SAGO OR TAPIOCA AND GOOSEBERRY MOULD

Use gooseberries instead of rhubarb with 250 ml of water. Sieve before adding sago.

9. COLD FRUIT PUDDING

Ingredients:

200–250 g Raspberries
200–250 g Redcurrants } 250 ml Purée
250 ml Water

40 g Cornflour
100 g Sugar

Servings: 4

Method:

1. Stew the fruit and sugar together till soft. Sieve.
2. Blend the cornflour with the water and add to the fruit (make up to 500 ml if necessary).
3. Boil for a few minutes. Pour into a dish or wetted mould.
4. Allow to set, then turn out.

10. BEN RHYDDING PUDDING

Ingredients:

500 g juicy Summer Fruit
Sugar to sweeten
1 Sponge Round

or

250 ml Whipped Cream
250 ml Custard and Cream mixed
Glacé cherries (if liked)

Servings: 4

Method:

1. Stew the fruit with enough sugar to sweeten.
2. Cut the sponge in thin slices and line a bowl; cut a round for the top.
3. Put in stewed fruit and any scraps of sponge until the bowl is filled up. Finish off with the sponge round.
4. Put a plate with a weight on top and allow to stand in the refrigerator for several hours.

5. Turn out and coat with whipped cream or a mixture of cream and custard.
6. Decorate with glacé cherries.

11. SUMMER PUDDING

Make as Ben Rhydding pudding (page 263) but use bread instead of sponge to make a plain pudding.

Fruits suitable:

Rhubarb, redcurrants or raspberries.

12. APPLE SNOW

Ingredients:

1 Sponge

Custard:

250 ml Milk
Strip of Lemon Rind
2 Egg Yolks (beaten)
25 g Castor Sugar

Snow:

2 Baked Apples
2 Egg Whites
50 g Castor Sugar
Juice 1 Lemon

Servings: 3–4

Method:

1. Heat the milk and lemon rind, pour over beaten egg yolks and add sugar.
2. Return to pan and stir over a very low heat till custard thickens. Cool, stirring occasionally. Remove lemon rind.
3. Cut the sponge into slices and lay in a glass dish. Soak with the cold custard.
4. Skin and core apples and beat apple pulp until smooth. Add lemon juice.
5. Whisk the whites very stiffly and alternately add sugar and apple pulp, whisking well.
6. Pile on top of sponge and decorate with cherries and angelica.

13. TRIFLE

Ingredients:

1 Sponge Round
Raspberry *or* Apricot Jam
A few Ratafias (optional)
or 6 tablespoonfuls Sherry
125 ml Fruit Juice

Tinned Fruit (optional)
250 ml Custard Sauce (page 299)
125 ml Cream
½ teaspoonful Vanilla Essence
Sugar to sweeten Cream

Servings: 4
Size of Dish: 1 litre

Method:

1. Slice sponge, spread with jam and place in the bottom of a suitable dish. Add sliced tinned fruit and ratafias.
2. Pour sherry or fruit juice over sponge and fruit.
3. Make custard sauce. Cool. Pour over sponge and fruit and allow to soak.

4. Flavour with vanilla essence, sweeten and whip the cream.

5. Pipe on top of custard and decorate as liked.

14. GATEAU

Ingredients:

or 1 4-egg Genoese Sponge (page 398)   2 level teaspoonfuls Cornflour or ⎫
     1 2-egg Victoria Sandwich (page 391)   Arrowroot   ⎬ Glaze
     Fruit (tinned)   125 ml Fruit Juice (from tin) ⎭
     Cream (lightly whipped)
     Nuts (finely chopped), coconut (grated),
         cornflakes (crushed)

Method:

1. Drain fruit. Keep juice. Put a little fruit aside for decoration and chop remainder. Whip cream and add 1 tablespoonful to chopped fruit.

2. Sandwich sponge together with fruit and cream mixture.

3. Spread cream round the sides and dip in finely chopped nuts, coconut or crushed cornflakes.

4. Spread cream on top. Decorate with fruit as desired.

5. Blend arrowroot with fruit juice, bring to the boil. Glaze fruit, cool.

6. Pipe with cream.

15. SPONGE FLAN

Ingredients:

Cream Sponge (page 397)   125 ml Fruit Juice (from tin)   ⎫
Peaches, Pears or other Fruits (tinned)   2 level teaspoonfuls Cornflour or ⎬ Glaze
125 ml Cream   Arrowroot   ⎭

Servings: 5–6
Time: 20 minutes
Oven Temperature: 190°C, No. 5
Position in Oven: One-third from top
Size of Tin: 22-cm sponge flan tin

Method:

1. Make sponge mixture and pour into greased and floured sponge flan tin.

2. Bake, turn out and cool.

3. Drain fruit. Fill flan with fruit.

4. Blend arrowroot with fruit juice, bring to the boil and boil 1–2 minutes. Cool slightly.

5. Pour over fruit, allow to set and cool.

6. Whip cream and pipe on top of fruit.

Note: A circle of greased paper can be put in the bottom of the tin to make turning out easier.

16. FRUIT FLAN

Ingredients:

100 g Rich Short Pastry (page 308)
Apricots *or* other Fruits (tinned)
125 ml Sweetened Cream

2 level teaspoonfuls Arrowroot *or* ⎫
    Cornflour   ⎬ Glaze
125 ml Fruit Juice (from tin) ⎭

Servings: 4
Time: 20–30 minutes
Oven Temperature: 200°C, No. 6
Position in Oven: One-third from top
Size of Flan Ring: 15 cm

Method:

1. Put flan ring on a baking tray.
2. Roll out pastry and line flan ring.
3. Place a piece of greased greaseproof paper in pastry case.
4. Bake blind, reducing heat to 180°C, No. 4, after 10–15 minutes.
5. When pastry is set, remove paper and crisp flan case in oven for a few minutes more.
6. When cold, fill flan case with fruit.
7. Blend arrowroot with fruit juice, bring to the boil and boil for 1–2 minutes.
8. Cool slightly.
9. Pour over fruit, allow to set.
10. Whip cream and pipe over top of fruit.

17. VOL-AU-VENT OF FRUIT

Ingredients:

150 g Puff Pastry (page 310)
Whipped Cream

Mixed Fresh Fruit

Servings: 4
Time: 25–30 minutes
Oven Temperature: 230°C, No. 8
Position in Oven: Middle shelf
Size of Cutter: 15–16 cm vol-au-vent Cutter

Method:

1. Cut out and bake vol-au-vent case (page 311).
2. Fill case with fruit and cream mixture and decorate with whipped cream.

18. WHIPPED JELLY CREAM

Ingredients:

1 packet Table Jelly (any flavour)
½–¾ of the quantity of Water
    stated on Jelly packet

250 ml Evaporated Milk
Cream for decorating

Servings: 6

Method:

1. Dissolve jelly in ½–¾ of the boiling water that it states on packet. Cool.
2. Whip evaporated milk until it becomes thick.
3. Whisk cooled jelly into milk gradually.
4. Pour or pile up in serving dish.

Note: Fruit juice can be used instead of water and chopped fruit added to the mixture.

19. CARAMEL WHIP

Ingredients:

50 g Granulated Sugar ⎫ Caramel
3 tablespoonfuls Water ⎰
125 ml Water
250 ml Evaporated Milk

Vanilla Essence
30 g Castor Sugar
5 g Gelatine

Servings: 3–4

Method:

1. Make a golden caramel with sugar and water, cool. Add water and dissolve caramel.
2. Put caramel syrup, sugar and gelatine in a pan. Heat to dissolve gelatine. Cool.
3. Whip evaporated milk, add vanilla essence.
4. Pour caramel mixture onto whipped evaporated milk and beat until on point of setting.
5. Pour into a glass dish or mould.
6. Unmould when set and decorate as desired.

20. CHOCOLATE WHIP

Ingredients:

or   50 g Drinking Chocolate
25 g Cocoa
200 ml Water

40 g Sugar
500 ml Evaporated Milk
10 g Gelatine

Servings: 5–6

Method:

1. Put water, chocolate and gelatine in a pan, stir over heat until dissolved. Cool.
2. Whisk evaporated milk, whisk in chocolate mixture.
3. When setting pour into a glass dish or mould.

21. RHUBARB MOULD

Ingredients:

500 g Rhubarb ⎫
1 tablespoonful Water ⎬ 500 ml Pulp
Juice 1 Lemon ⎭

10 g Gelatine
2–3 tablespoonfuls Water
75 g Sugar

Servings: 4–6

Method:

1. Wash and cut up the rhubarb. Add water and stew to a pulp. Add lemon juice. Measure and make up to 500 ml.
2. Dissolve the gelatine in the water and mix it with the still-warm rhubarb.
3. Add sugar and stir well till dissolved. Pour into mould or serving dish.
4. Allow to set, turn out and serve with custard or cream.

Variations:

Gooseberry Mould
Raspberry Mould
Plum or Damson Mould

22. PRUNE MOULD

Ingredients:

100 g Prunes	50 g Sugar
250 ml Water	10 g Gelatine
Slice of Lemon Rind	1 Banana (if liked)
Piece of Cinnamon Stick	Carmine Colouring

Servings: 3–4

Method:

1. Soak prunes in measured water. Stew, adding lemon rind and cinnamon stick.
2. Stone prunes, then sieve or chop, and make up pulp to 500 ml with prune juice, lemon juice and extra water.
3. Add sugar and gelatine to prune pulp, and heat to dissolve gelatine.
4. Add colour if necessary and sliced banana if liked. Stir till beginning to show signs of setting.
5. Pour into mould. Turn out when set.

23. APRICOT MOULD

Make as prune mould, above, but using apricots instead. Tinned apricots can be used instead of dried, in which case soaking will not be necessary.

24. ORANGE JELLY

Ingredients:

Juice 2 Oranges		100 g Sugar
Juice 2 Lemons	} 500 ml	15 g Gelatine
Water		

Servings: 4

Method:

1. Put the liquid, sugar, gelatine and the juice of 2 oranges and 1 lemon in a pan.
2. Heat to dissolve gelatine and sugar.
3. Strain jelly.
4. When cool, pour into a serving dish or wetted mould. Turn out mould when set.

25. **RASPBERRY JELLY**

Ingredients:

> 200–250 g Raspberries (to give 250 ml Raspberry Juice)
> 100 g Sugar   15 g Gelatine
> Juice 1 Lemon   250 ml Water

Servings: 4

Method:

1. To obtain juice, squeeze the fresh raspberries in a clean cloth.
2. Make as for orange jelly. Tinned or frozen raspberries may be used.

26. **FRUIT IN JELLY (1)**

Make as orange jelly (page 268) using 20 g gelatine. If using tinned fruit, use fruit juice from the tin in place of water.

Add tinned fruit to jelly when cool or set in layers.

Note: Clear Lemon Jelly gives a more sparkling result.

27. **CLEAR JELLIES**

Average proportions:

> 30 g Gelatine to 1 litre Liquid
> (In very hot weather use generous measure of Gelatine)
> 200 g Sugar
> 2 Egg Whites and washed Shells of Eggs

For setting fruit:

> 40 g Gelatine to 1 litre Liquid

For chopping:

> 50 g Gelatine to 1 litre

28. **LEMON JELLY**

Ingredients:

> Rind 4 Lemons   750 ml Water
> 30 g Gelatine (or according to use)   250 ml Lemon Juice
> 200 g Sugar (Demerara if liked)   2 tablespoonfuls Sherry (optional)
> 2 Cloves   Whites and washed Shells of 2 Eggs

Servings: 6–8

Method:

1. Scald a pan large enough to allow room for jelly to boil up.
2. Wash the lemons and put the thinly peeled rind, sugar, cloves, egg whites, washed and crushed egg shells, water, lemon juice and gelatine into the scalded pan.

3. Whisk well till almost at boiling point. Bring to boiling point undisturbed.
4. Allow to boil up 3 times. Simmer gently 10 minutes, having pan covered with a plate.
5. Pour jelly through a scalded jelly bag or towel.
6. Pour the sherry through the bag into the jelly.
7. Allow to cool, then pour into a wetted mould. Allow to set, pass mould through hot water and turn out.

Note: If no sherry is used, substitute same quantity of water.

29. RASPBERRY JELLY (CLEAR)

Ingredients:

Water	100–150 g Sugar
Juice 1 Lemon	500 ml juice 2 Egg Whites and washed
500 g Raspberries (juiced)	Shells of 2 Eggs
30 g Gelatine	

Servings: 4

Method:

To obtain raspberry juice, squeeze fresh raspberries in a clean cloth. Frozen or tinned raspberries may be used in which case less sugar is required. Make as lemon jelly.

30. FRUIT IN JELLY (2)

Ingredients:

1 litre Lemon Jelly (using 40 g Gelatine)	2 Bananas
50–100 g White Grapes	2 Tangerine Oranges
50–100 g Black Grapes	*or* Any Mixed Fruit

Servings: 4–6

Method:

1. Set 1 cm jelly in the bottom of a scalded mould.
2. Prepare the fruit according to kind and cut into neat pieces.
3. Put a layer of fruit in mould and set with a little jelly; when fruit is set, pour in jelly to cover. Allow to set.
4. Put in another layer of fruit and jelly and continue until the mould is filled, finishing with a layer of jelly. Set aside.
5. When set, unmould by passing the mould through warm water.
6. Decorate with fruits or whipped cream if liked.

Note: Individual moulds can be made in the same way.

31. HONEYCOMB MOULD

Ingredients:

500 ml Milk   10 g Gelatine
125 ml Water   2–3 Eggs (separated)
50 g Sugar   1 teaspoonful Vanilla Essence

Servings: 4

Method:

1. Put milk, water, sugar, gelatine, and beaten egg yolks in a pan.
2. Stir till boiling.
3. Pour immediately over stiffly-beaten egg whites.
4. Add vanilla essence and whisk the mixture a little to mix well.
5. Pour into serving dish. Decorate with whipped cream if desired.

Note: When raw eggs are an ingredient it is best not to serve the dish to children, the elderly, the infirm or pregnant women.

32. NORWEGIAN CREAM

Ingredients:

3 Eggs (separated)   Vanilla Essence
50–75 g Castor Sugar   2 tablespoonfuls Raspberry Jam
250 ml Milk   125 ml Cream (lightly whipped)
10 g Gelatine

Servings: 4–6

Method:

1. Separate eggs.
2. Put yolks and sugar in a pan, beat lightly, add milk and gelatine.
3. Stir until thickens (do not boil), add vanilla and leave till cold but not set.
4. Beat whites till stiff and fold through custard.
5. Pour into serving dish and leave to set.
6. Spread with jam and pour over lightly beaten cream.

Note: When raw eggs are an ingredient it is best not to serve the dish to children, the elderly, the infirm or pregnant women.

33. ORANGE OR LEMON SOUFFLÉ

Ingredients:

2 Eggs (separated)   5 g Gelatine
1 Lemon *or* 1 Orange   2 tablespoonfuls Water
50 g Castor Sugar   Cream to decorate

Servings: 3

Method:

1. Separate the eggs.
2. Whisk yolks, grated lemon or orange rind and sugar until thick and creamy.
3. Add strained juice, a little at a time, and whisk until creamy again.
4. Whisk up whites; dissolve gelatine in warm water.

5. Add dissolved gelatine to egg yolk mixture and carefully fold in the stiffly-beaten whites.
6. Pour into a No. 5 soufflé case prepared by tying a band of paper round, allowing 3 cm above top of case.
7. When set, remove the paper and decorate.

Note: Alternatively, soufflé mixture may be poured into a glass dish.

When raw eggs are an ingredient it is best not to serve the dish to children, the elderly, the infirm or pregnant women.

34. MILANAISE SOUFFLÉ

Ingredients:

2 Eggs (separated)	10 g Gelatine
1 Lemon	2 tablespoonfuls Water
75 g Castor Sugar	Cream to decorate
125 ml Cream (lightly whipped)	

Servings: 3–4

Method:

1. Separate the eggs. Whisk yolks, grated lemon rind and sugar till thick and creamy.
2. Add strained lemon juice gradually, again whisk till creamy. Add the whipped cream.
3. Dissolve gelatine in warm water and add to the mixture; fold in stiffly beaten whites.
4. Pour into No. 4 soufflé case, prepared by tying a band of paper around, allowing 3 cm above top of case.
5. When set, remove paper and decorate.

Note: When raw eggs are an ingredient it is best not to serve the dish to children, the elderly, the infirm or pregnant women.

35. STRAWBERRY SOUFFLÉ

Ingredients:

2 Eggs (separated)	10 g Gelatine
50 g Castor Sugar	2 tablespoonfuls Water
125 ml Strawberry Purée	Cream to decorate
125 ml Cream (lightly whipped)	

Servings: 3–4

Method:

1. Separate the eggs. Whisk yolks and sugar till thick and creamy.
2. Add strawberry purée and lightly whipped cream.
3. Dissolve gelatine in water and add to the mixture. Fold in stiffly beaten whites.
4. Pour into No. 4 soufflé case prepared by tying a band of paper round, allowing 3 cm above top of case. Alternatively pour into a glass dish.
5. When set, remove paper, and decorate.

Note: When raw eggs are an ingredient it is best not to serve the dish to children, the elderly, the infirm or pregnant women.

Variations:

Raspberry Soufflé
Gooseberry Soufflé

36. CHOCOLATE SOUFFLÉ

Ingredients:

3 Eggs (separated)	10 g Gelatine
50 g Castor Sugar	2 tablespoonfuls Water
75 g Chocolate	Cream to decorate
125 ml Cream (lightly whipped)	

Servings: 3–4

Method:

1. Separate the eggs. Whisk yolks and sugar till thick and creamy.
2. Add melted chocolate and lightly whipped cream; dissolve gelatine in water and add to mixture. Fold in stiffly beaten whites.
3. Pour into a No. 4 soufflé case prepared by tying a band of paper round, allowing 3 cm above top of case.
4. When set, remove paper and decorate.

Note: When raw eggs are an ingredient it is best not to serve the dish to children, the elderly, the infirm or pregnant women.

37. CREAM PUDDING

This is a rich pudding set with gelatine. There are three types:

1. **Full Creams.**—Cream only.
2. **Custard Creams.**—Equal quantities custard and cream.
3. **Fruit Creams.**—Equal quantities fruit purée and cream.

38. VANILLA CREAM

Ingredients:

250 ml Milk ⎫	250 ml Cream
2 Eggs ⎬ Custard	10 g Gelatine
25–30 g Sugar ⎭	2 tablespoonfuls Water
	1 teaspoonful Vanilla Essence

Servings: 4

Method:

1. Make custard from milk, eggs and sugar (page 229). Cool. Add flavouring and half-whisked cream.
2. Dissolve gelatine in the water and add to the mixture.
3. Stir till it shows signs of setting and pour into a mould.
4. Unmould when set and decorate as desired.

Variations:

Coffee Cream.—1 tablespoonful coffee essence.
Almond Cream.— Few drops almond essence.
Caramel Cream.— 75 g granulated sugar made into caramel and dissolved in milk used for custard, and 2 tablespoonfuls brandy.

39. STRAWBERRY CREAM

Ingredients:

500 g Strawberries		250 ml Cream
50–100 g Sugar	} 250 ml Purée	10 g Gelatine
Colouring (if required)		2 tablespoonfuls Water

Servings: 4

Method:

1. Add the sugar to the fruit and sieve or liquidise (tinned fruit, omit sugar).
2. Add colouring to make purée deeper in colour than required, as cream lessens colour when added.
3. Stir half-whisked cream into the fruit purée.
4. Dissolve gelatine in warm water and add to the purée.
5. Continue stirring till just setting.
6. Set in jelly-lined mould in which decorations may be set if liked. Unmould when set, or pour into a serving dish.

Variations:

Suitable Fruits:
Raspberry.—250 ml raspberry purée and 1 teaspoonful redcurrant jelly.
Apricot.—250 ml apricot purée, a drop of almond essence.

40. CHARLOTTE RUSSE

Ingredients:

250 ml Vanilla Cream (page 273)	Pistachio Nuts (unsalted, chopped)
Sponge Fingers	Cream for decorating
Jelly	

Servings: 4

Method:

1. Set a thin layer of jelly in the bottom of the mould.
2. Line the tin with split sponge fingers, having edges dipped in liquid jelly.
3. Fill with cream, nearly setting.
4. When set, trim sponges evenly.
5. Turn out and decorate as desired.
Note: Cream can be used instead of custard and cream.

41. FRUIT CHARLOTTE

Make as charlotte russe, above, using 250 ml of any fruit cream (page 237, recipe 37).

42. **CHARTREUSE OF BANANA**

Ingredients:

250 ml Lemon Jelly (Fruit in Jelly page 270)
4–5 Bananas (some cut, 125 ml as purée)
Pistachio Nuts (unsalted, chopped)
25 g Castor Sugar

Lemon Juice
125 ml Cream
5 g Gelatine
2 tablespoonfuls Water

Servings: 3–4

Method:

1. Line a plain mould with lemon jelly. Decorate with rounds of banana dipped in jelly, filling up the spaces with chopped pistachio nuts.
2. Mask again with cold liquid jelly.
3. Add sugar, lemon juice and banana pulp to half-whipped cream; add gelatine dissolved in a little warm water.
4. Stir until beginning to set and pour into mould immediately.
5. When set, turn out and decorate the base with cream or chopped jelly.

43. **CHARTREUSE OF ORANGES**

Ingredients:

250 ml Orange *or* Lemon Jelly
   (Fruit in Jelly page 270)
5 g Gelatine
2 tablespoonfuls Water

25 g Sugar Cubes
3–4 Oranges
Pistachio Nuts (unsalted, chopped)
250 ml Cream

Servings: 3–4

Method:

1. Line a plain mould with jelly.
2. Put one orange aside for the cream. Peel other oranges and cut in thin slices.
3. Dip each slice in jelly and use to line mould. Fill spaces with chopped pistachio nuts. Re-line with jelly.
4. Rub the sugar on the orange rind. Dissolve it in the juice of one orange.
5. Dissolve gelatine in the water.
6. Half whisk the cream. Mix gelatine and orange syrup. Add to the cream and stir till setting. Pour into the prepared mould.
7. When set dip in warm water and turn out.

44. **ALMOND PEACHES**

Ingredients:

3 Peach halves (tinned)
3 Sponge Rounds
125 ml Lemon Jelly
125 ml Cream
Cream for Piping
A little peach juice

1 teaspoonful ground Almonds
A little Sugar
Maraschino
Apricot Jam
Chopped Nuts

Servings: 3

Method:

1. Cut rounds of sponge slightly larger than peach. Dip edge in jam and nuts.
2. Mix almonds, sugar and maraschino and bind with peach juice.
3. Put a little of the mixture in the centre of each sponge.
4. Dry rounded surface of peaches and put on cooling tray.
5. Mix cream with cold jelly, colour pale pink and stir till setting.
6. Coat peaches with mixture (once or twice).
7. Lift carefully onto a sponge and pipe cream round the edge.

45. PROFITEROLES

Ingredients:

2-Egg quantity Choux Pastry (page 312)   125 ml Cream
Chocolate Sauce (page 300)   A few browned flaked Almonds

Servings: 4–5 **Time:** 20 minutes
Oven Temperature: 200°C, No. 6
Position in Oven: A third from top

Method:

1. Make choux pastry and put in teaspoonfuls on a greased baking tin.
2. Bake.
3. Cool and fill with cream.
4. Pile up on serving dish and pour chocolate sauce over. Sprinkle with flaked almonds.

46. MERINGUES

Eggs for meringues should be as fresh as possible.
The glass bowl in which they are whisked must be completely clean and grease free

Proportions:

50 g Castor Sugar to 1 Egg White

Time: 2–2½ hours
Oven Temperature: 130°C, No. ½
Position in Oven: Middle shelf

Method:

1. Whisk the whites stiffly, gradually add one half of the sugar, whisking well between each addition till the mixture will stand in points.
2. Fold in all remaining sugar at once.
3. To shape, pipe the mixture with a plain or star pipe onto a greased, floured baking tin or use 2 dessertspoons dipped in cold water; take a spoonful of the meringue mixture and with other spoon round off onto a greased floured baking tin. Sift lightly with castor sugar.
4. Bake in a cool oven until dry and easily removed from tin.
5. When quite cold, fill with sweetened cream and decorate.

47. COOKED MERINGUE

This meringue does not absorb moisture so readily and is suitable for meringue baskets

Proportions:

50 g Castor Sugar to 1 Egg White

Method:

1. Put whites and sugar in a bowl and beat over hot water until stiff.
2. Use as required.

48. MERINGUE BASKET

Ingredients:

3 Egg Whites   150 g Castor Sugar
125 ml Cream

Servings: 4–5
Time: 1 hour 30 minutes
Oven Temperature: 140°–150°C, No. 1–2

Method:

1. Mark a circle 10 cm in diameter on a piece of greaseproof paper. Put on a baking tin and lightly brush with oil.
2. Make cooked meringue, as above.
3. Spread layer of meringue over the circle and pipe stars round the edge to give three rows in height and bake.
4. When cool, fill with fruit and cream. Pipe cream on top and decorate.

Note: Individual baskets are made similarly.

49. NUT MERINGUES

Ingredients:

2 Egg Whites   75 g Castor Sugar
50 g Nuts (finely chopped)

Method:

Make as meringues, fold in nuts.

Note: Use for meringues or grease and line two 10 cm sandwich tins spread with mixture and bake till firm and dry. Sandwich with cream or cream and fruit.

50. PAVLOVA CAKE

Ingredients:

3 Egg Whites   Fruit, e.g. Peaches
150 g Castor Sugar   125 ml Cream
10–15 g Cornflour
2 small teaspoonfuls Vinegar

Servings: 4
Oven Temperature: 150°C, No. 2
Position in Oven: Middle

Method:

1. Draw a circle 16–20 cm in diameter on a piece of greaseproof paper and put onto a baking sheet. Grease.
2. Whisk egg whites till stiff. Mix sugar and cornflour, and whisk in half of mixture. Fold in remaining mixture and vinegar.
3. Spread to an even depth over prepared circle and bake for 1 hour.
4. When cooked, remove paper and allow to cool. Cover with cream and fruit as desired.

Note: A piece of oiled greaseproof paper may be put round meringue mixture before baking if desired. This meringue can also be cooked on a greased ovenproof plate.

ICES

ICES MADE IN A MACHINE

ICES MADE USING A FREEZER

ICES MADE IN A MACHINE

1. ICE-CREAM MAKERS

Ice-cream makers are now readily available and relatively affordable, however, it is perfectly possible to make ice-cream in a domestic freezer. The recipes and instructions for using a domestic freezer follow on page 284. The recipes below work best in an ice-cream maker. Please follow your machine's manufacturer's instructions. Ensure that all the parts of the machine that can be removed and cleaned have been thoroughly scalded before use.

Ice-cream using an old-fashioned churn-freezer

These recipes also work in an old-fashioned, ice-cream churn-freezer that must be turned by hand. Old-fashioned ice-cream makers are now very rare but, should you ever get the opportunity to use one, the directions for using one are as follows:

The freezer:	The freezer must be perfectly clean; the can, spatula and lid should be scalded. The can must be properly adjusted on the pivot and the crank working smoothly before placing in the freezing mixture or mixture to be frozen.
Freezing mixture:	Ice and bay salt are used in proportion of two parts ice to one part bay salt. The ice should be chipped finely.
Packing the freezer:	Pack well round the can with ice and salt before placing in the mixture to be frozen, being careful that no salt touches lid or rim of can.
Proportions:	Observe accurate proportions, especially with sugar; average proportion is 75 g sugar to 500 ml liquid. Remember to slightly over-sweeten and over-colour, as flavour and colour are both reduced in freezing, but if too sweet, the mixture will not freeze. If not sufficiently sweet, it will be hard and rocky.
Filling the can:	Fill the can two-thirds full with ice-cream mixture; never put in more mixture than this as room must be allowed for the spatula and for the mixture to expand. Place in the spatula, and put on the lid. The mixture must be cold when placed in the can.
Turning the handle:	Turn the handle steadily and evenly till the mixture is frozen – about 20 minutes. If necessary, scrape down the mixture from the sides of the can occasionally, taking care to wipe the lid when removing it, as salt would spoil the mixture.
Ripening:	When the mixture is sufficiently frozen, remove the spatula. Place a piece of greased paper over the top of the can, then the lid. Cover with a blanket and leave to "ripen". As the ice melts, the water must be drained away and the can kept continually well-packed with ice and salt.

2. CLASSES OF ICES

1. Custard Ice.— i.e. custard plus cream.
2. Fruit Ice.— i.e. fruit purée plus cream.

3. PLAIN VANILLA ICE

Ingredients:

10–15 g Cornflour *or* Custard Powder   75 g Sugar
500 ml Milk   Vanilla Essence
1 Egg (beaten)   125 ml Cream *or* Evaporated Milk

Method:

1. Blend cornflour with a little of the milk. Heat remainder of milk and pour over blended cornflour. Return to heat and boil up.
2. Add sugar, flavouring and beaten egg. Return to the heat but do not boil.
3. Cool custard and add lightly beaten cream before freezing.
4. Pour into ice-cream maker. Freeze in machine till of correct consistency.

4. VANILLA ICE

Ingredients:

500 ml Milk   75 g Sugar
3 Egg Yolks   Vanilla Essence
1 whole Egg   250 ml Cream (whipped)

Method:

1. Make custard with milk, egg and yolks and sugar (page 299). Allow to cool.
2. Add vanilla essence. Add the whipped cream.
3. Pour into ice-cream maker. Freeze in machine till of correct consistency.

5. STRAWBERRY ICE

Ingredients:

250 ml Purée from about 500 g Strawberries   250 ml Cream (slightly whipped)
75 g Castor Sugar   *or* { 125 ml Cream (slightly whipped)
Squeeze Lemon Juice   and 125 ml Custard (page 299)

Method:

1. Crush the strawberries and sieve. Add sugar and lemon juice to the purée.
2. Add whipped cream (or cream and custard) and flavouring.
3. Pour into ice-cream maker. Freeze in machine till of correct consistency.
Note: Any tinned or frozen fruit with a distinctive flavour may be used instead of fresh, but less sugar will be required. A little lemon juice added to fruit ices enhances the flavour.

6. CHOCOLATE ICE

Ingredients:

100 g Chocolate   2 Eggs and 2 Yolks
500 ml Milk   *or*   3 whole Eggs
50–75 g Sugar   125–250 ml Cream (whipped)

Method:

1. Melt chocolate in milk. Make custard with chocolate-milk and eggs (page 299) and add sugar.

2. When cold add to the whipped cream.

3. Pour into ice-cream maker. Freeze in machine till of correct consistency.

7. COFFEE ICE

Make as chocolate ice (page 282) omitting chocolate, and adding sufficient coffee (1 tablespoonful approx.) or coffee essence to custard to give a distinctive flavour.

8. PEACH MELBA

Ingredients:

250 ml Vanilla Ice-Cream (page 282)   Cream (whipped)
4 Peach halves   Ice-Cream wafers
125 ml Melba Sauce (page 303)

Method:

1. Put a portion of ice-cream in sundae glasses. Place a half peach on each.

2. Glaze with melba sauce. Decorate with cream and ice-cream wafers.

9. PEAR BELLE HÉLÈNE

Ingredients:

250 ml Vanilla Ice-Cream   Cream for decorating
4 Pear halves   Ice-cream Wafers
Chocolate Sauce (page 300)

Method:

1. Put a portion of ice-cream in a sundae glass. Put a half pear on each.

2. Pour chocolate sauce over. Decorate with cream and ice-cream wafers.

10. BAKED ALASKA

Ingredients:

1 block of Ice-Cream   3 Egg Whites
1 piece Sponge (same size as block   150 g Castor Sugar
   of Ice-Cream)   1 small tin Fruit (slices)

Servings: 6–8
Time: 2–3 minutes
Oven Temperature: 240°C, No. 9
Position in Oven: Top shelf

Method:

1. Put sponge cake in an ovenproof serving dish.

2. Put block of ice-cream on top.

3. Cover with fruit slices.

4. Whip egg whites, beat in half sugar, fold in remainder.

5. Completely cover ice and sponge with meringue mixture.

6. Bake in a very hot oven for 2–3 minutes.

11. LEMON WATER ICE

Ingredients:

500 ml Water	Juice 4 Lemons
Thin rind of 1 Lemon	2 Egg Whites
200 g Granulated Sugar	

Method:

1. Put water, lemon rind and sugar in a pan and boil for 10 minutes.
2. Strain the juice which should measure 125 ml; it may take more than 4 lemons to give this quantity.
3. When syrup is cold, strain, add lemon juice and freeze.
4. When half-frozen, add the beaten whites of two eggs. Continue freezing till firm.

12. ORANGE WATER ICE

Ingredients:

500 ml Water	Juice 3 Oranges
Thin rinds of 1 Orange	Juice 1 Lemon
150 g granulated Sugar	2 Egg Whites

Method:

Make as for lemon water ice, above.

ICES MADE USING A FREEZER

Ices can be successfully made in the fast-freezesection of a freezer, but the finished result does not give the smooth velvet texture got from using an ice-cream machine.

Ingredients: Plain ices have generally a solid base of cornflour or flour while the richer type have an egg custard.

Gelatine: This is added to give smoothness to the ice and help prevent the formation of crystals.

Sugar: Excess sugar tends to cause the formation of crystals. Castor and icing sugar are more suitable than granulated because of quicker dissolving.

Cream: Should be beaten until of the same consistency as the foundation mixture in order to get a uniform mixture. Evaporated milk can take the place of cream and should be chilled before using.

Fruit: If this is added it should be sieved or chopped finely.

Beating: Most freezer ice-cream requires beating during the process of freezing. This is to break down any crystals and incorporate air.

Method used in making ice-cream in the freezer:

1. Use the fast-freeze section of your freezer.
2. Empty and dry a freezer tray, pour in mixture.

3. When half-frozen remove to a bowl and beat until broken down but not soft.
4. Return to tray and finish freezing.
5. If necessary whisk again to break down ice crystals.
6. When fully frozen, store covered in a normal section of your freezer.

13. PLAIN VANILLA ICE

Ingredients:

10 g Cornflour	Small tin Evaporated Milk
40 g Castor Sugar	1 teaspoonful Vanilla Essence
500 ml Milk	

Time: 1½–2 hours

Method:

1. Mix cornflour and sugar, blend with a little milk till smooth.
2. Combine with rest of milk. Bring to the boil, and boil 3 minutes. Cool.
3. Beat chilled evaporated milk until stiff.
4. Add cornflour and milk, gradually, to beaten evaporated milk, beating well.
5. Add vanilla, pour into tray – freeze without disturbing.

14. VANILLA ICE

Ingredients:

250 ml Milk	Pinch Salt
1 level teaspoonful Gelatine	1 Egg (separated)
75 g Castor Sugar	250 ml Evaporated Milk
1 level teaspoonful Flour	1 teaspoonful Vanilla Essence

Time: 2 hours

Method:

1. Mix sugar, flour and salt, and blend with a little milk till smooth.
2. Dissolve gelatine in remainder of milk and add blended flour.
3. Bring to boil and boil 2–3 minutes, remove from heat.
4. Beat egg yolk in a bowl. Pour mixture over egg yolk and whisk together.
5. Allow to cool, pour into ice-tray.
6. When half-frozen remove and beat.
7. Beat evaporated milk till stiff. Beat egg white until stiff. Then fold together.
8. Fold through ice mixture, add vanilla.
9. Freeze until set for 2 hours.

15. CHOCOLATE ICE

Ingredients:

25 g Chocolate	2 Eggs (separated)
250 ml Milk	125 ml Cream
40–50 g Sugar	1 teaspoonful Vanilla Essence

Time: 20–25 minutes

Method:

1. Flake chocolate, add milk and sugar and heat until dissolved; cool.
2. Beat yolks until creamy.
3. Beat in cold chocolate mixture.
4. Whip cream, add to mixture along with vanilla.
5. Pour into freezing tray, freeze in the fast-freeze section of the freezer for 40 minutes or until firm.
6. Remove to bowl, add stiffly beaten whites and beat until smooth.
7. Return to freezing tray, freeze for 20–25 minutes.

16. COFFEE ICE

Ingredients:

1 level teaspoonful Gelatine	50 g Castor Sugar
2 tablespoonfuls strong Coffee	Pinch Salt
250 ml Milk	125 ml Cream
2 Egg Yolks	

Method:

1. Add gelatine to coffee and about 2 tablespoonfuls milk, and heat to dissolve gelatine. Add rest of milk. Heat till almost boiling.
2. Beat egg yolks in a bowl. Pour coffee and milk mixture over beaten yolks.
3. Cook over a low heat to make a custard (page 299). Add sugar and salt.
4. When cool, pour into freezing tray.
5. When half-frozen remove to bowl, beat until light.
6. Add cream and beat it well into coffee mixture.
7. Re-freeze.

Note: This may be made using 1 rounded teaspoonful of instant coffee.

17. RASPBERRY ICE

Ingredients:

or 250 g Raspberries	1 tablespoonful cold Water
1 carton Frozen Raspberries	125 ml Cream
50 g Icing Sugar	1 White of Egg
1 level teaspoonful Gelatine	

Method:

1. Sieve raspberries, add sugar.
2. Dissolve gelatine in water.
3. Add to raspberry purée, chill 30 minutes.
4. Beat cream with lemon juice.
5. Add stiffly beaten white of egg and purée, beat again.
6. Pour into ice-tray, freeze undisturbed.

Note: If frozen raspberries are used, halve sugar proportion. Any soft fruit may be used in this recipe.

18. **LEMON WATER ICE**

Ingredients:

200 g Granulated Sugar   Juice 4 Lemons (125 ml)
500 ml Water   2 Egg Whites (beaten till stiff)

Method:

1. Put sugar and water in a pan, boil 10 minutes.
2. Strain lemon juice and make up to 125 ml with water if necessary.
3. When syrup is cold, strain, add lemon juice and freeze.
4. When half-frozen add stiffly beaten egg whites.
5. Pour into ice-tray, freeze until firm.

19. **STRAWBERRY WATER ICE**

Ingredients:

250 g Strawberries   3 tablespoonfuls cold Water
2 tablespoonfuls Lemon Juice   100 g Castor Sugar

Method:

1. Crush the strawberries, add lemon juice and sieve.
2. Add water and sugar.
3. Pour into freezing tray.
4. Freeze until half-frozen or firm round edges.
5. Turn into bowl, beat well until light.
6. Return to ice-tray, freeze until firm.

20. **SAUCES TO SERVE WITH ICES**

Caramel Sauce (page 300)
Butterscotch Sauce (page 302)
Chocolate Sauce (page 300, 301)
Fruit Sauce (page 303)
Melba Sauce (page 303)

SAUCES

WHITE SAUCES

RICH WHITE SAUCES

BROWN SAUCES

CHAUDFROID SAUCES

MISCELLANEOUS

SWEET SAUCES

WHITE SAUCES

I. FOUNDATION WHITE SAUCE

Ingredients:

For Binding	For Coating	For Pouring
25 g Butter 25 g Flour 125 ml Liquid (*milk or water, or mixture; or fish or meat stock) Salt and Pepper	25 g Butter 25 g Flour 250 ml Liquid (see *) Salt and Pepper	25 g Butter 25g Flour 500 ml Liquid (see *) Salt and Pepper

Method (1): Make a roux

1. Melt the butter, add the flour and cook for a few minutes without discolouring. Remove from heat.
2. Add liquid (stock or milk) gradually, beating well. Add salt and pepper to taste.
3. Stir till boiling, cook 2 minutes.

Method (2):

1. Put all ingredients into pan.
2. Stir constantly over a gentle heat until boiling. Cook 2 minutes.

2. VARIATIONS FOR 250 ML FOUNDATION WHITE SAUCE

The following variations are made by adding ingredients after cooking foundation sauce.

Anchovy Sauce	I teaspoonful Anchovy Essence
Caper Sauce	I tablespoonful Capers, I teaspoonful Caper Vinegar
Cheese Sauce	50–75 g grated Cheese, ½ teaspoonful dried Mustard
Egg Sauce	I hard-boiled Egg (chopped)
Fish Sauce	Fish Stock and Milk as the Foundation Sauce's liquid
Mustard Sauce	I teaspoonful dried Mustard
Onion Sauce	2 large Onions (chopped, boiled and drained) Sauté chopped onions in measured butter till soft but not coloured Add flour and liquid as in basic sauce. Adjust salt and pepper to taste
Parsley Sauce	I tablespoonful chopped Parsley
Cucumber Sauce	2 tablespoonfuls finely chopped Cucumber, I teaspoonful Vinegar Add chopped cucumber to sauce, simmer 5 minutes Add vinegar and salt and pepper to taste
Sweet Sauce	250 ml pouring White Sauce, Sugar to sweeten, Flavouring as liked
Ginger Sauce	250 ml pouring White Sauce, and I level teaspoonful ground Ginger moistened in Water, Sugar to taste

3. MUSHROOM SAUCE

Ingredients:

250 ml Foundation White Sauce   Milk
(page 291, made using   50 g Mushrooms
mushroom liquor)   125 ml Water
Seasoning

Method:

1. Clean and chop mushrooms.
2. Stew in water for 10 minutes, strain.
3. Add milk to this cooking liquor to make 250 ml white sauce (page 291).
4. Add chopped, cooked mushrooms.

RICH WHITE SAUCES

4. BÉCHAMEL SAUCE

Ingredients:

1 small Onion   25 g Butter
Small piece Carrot   25 g Flour
Small piece Turnip   Salt and Pepper
¼ blade Mace   2 tablespoonfuls Cream
250 ml Milk

Method:

1. Simmer vegetables and mace in the milk for 15 minutes.
2. Strain and use this liquid to make white sauce (page 291).
3. Season with salt and pepper and add cream.

5. PANADA

A binding sauce

Ingredients:

25 g Butter   125 ml Liquid (Milk *or* Stock)
25 g Plain Flour

Method:

1. Melt butter, add flour and cook about 1 minute.
2. Add the liquid and beat well over the heat. Cook for 1–2 minutes.

6. VELOUTÉ SAUCE

Make as béchamel sauce, above, except using white stock instead of flavoured milk. Fish stock is used when the sauce is for fish dishes.

7. VARIATIONS FOR 250 ML BÉCHAMEL OR VELOUTÉ SAUCE

Maître d'Hôtel Sauce	I tablespoonful finely chopped Parsley, 2 teaspoonfuls Lemon Juice
Dutch Sauce	I–2 Egg Yolks, I tablespoonful Vinegar or I–2 tablespoonfuls Lemon Juice, Cayenne, I tablespoonful Cream Add egg and vinegar or lemon juice to the cooked sauce; add salt and pepper to taste. Add cream, reheat but do not boil
Tartare Sauce (Hot)	250 ml Dutch Sauce, I tablespoonful chopped Capers, I tablespoonful chopped Gherkins Add chopped gherkins and capers to Dutch Sauce and reheat
Soubise Sauce (Onion)	Purée made from 4 boiled Onions, 2 tablespoonfuls Cream Add onion purée and cream to sauce and reheat
Horseradish Sauce (Hot)	2 tablespoonfuls grated Horseradish, I tablespoonful Vinegar, 2 tablespoonfuls Cream, 2 level teaspoonfuls Sugar Add horseradish to the cooked sauce. Add cream, vinegar and sugar and reheat
Lobster Sauce	2 tablespoonfuls Lobster Meat, 2 tablespoonfuls Cream, 2 teaspoonfuls Lemon Juice Cut lobster in small pieces, add to sauce with lemon juice and cream. Colour with coral butter (page 46). Reheat
Shrimp Sauce	2 tablespoonfuls Shrimps, 2 teaspoonfuls Lemon Juice, 2 tablespoonfuls Cream Add chopped shrimps to sauce with lemon juice, cream and seasoning. Reheat

BROWN SAUCES

8. BROWN SAUCE

A brown sauce is so called because of its brown meat-stock base

Ingredients:

I Onion
25 g Butter
15 g Flour
250 ml Stock *or* Water and Meat Extract

Salt and Pepper
or I small Tomato
Piece of Carrot

Method:

1. Cut onion into rings and fry in butter till golden brown.
2. Add flour, stir well, add stock and salt and pepper. Bring to the boil.
3. Add tomato or carrot, and simmer for 30 minutes. Strain.

9. ESPAGNOLE SAUCE

Espagnole sauce forms the basis from which many other sauces can be made

Ingredients:

25 g Bacon		500 ml Brown Stock	
25 g Butter		2 tablespoons Tomato Pulp	
1 small Carrot	} Mirepoix	*or* 1 Tomato	
1 Onion		3 Mushrooms	
Bouquet of Herbs		*or* Mushroom Trimmings	
25 g Flour		Salt and Pepper	
		2 tablespoonfuls Sherry	

Method:

1. Cut up the bacon and fry lightly in the butter.
2. Add the vegetables cut up roughly and fry 5 minutes.
3. Add the flour and cook very slowly till a golden brown colour.
4. Add the stock, tomato pulp, herbs, mushrooms or trimmings. Simmer gently for 30–40 minutes.
5. Add the sherry, bring to boiling point, skim and strain. Add salt and pepper to taste.

10. VARIATIONS FOR 250 ML ESPAGNOLE SAUCE

Bigarade Sauce (for Wild Duck)	Juice of 1 Orange and 1 Lemon, 1 Shallot, 125 ml Port Wine or Claret, Pinch Castor Sugar Chop shallot very finely, add shallot, orange and lemon juice, wine and sugar to the sauce. Boil well for 5 minutes, strain and serve
Chasseur Sauce	1 tablespoonful Redcurrant Jelly, 1 teaspoonful Meat Extract Few drops Lemon Juice, 125 ml Port Wine, Pinch Cayenne Add to sauce and boil till reduced to 250 ml. Strain and serve
Poivrade Sauce	Juice of 2 Lemons, or 125 ml Vinegar, Few Peppercorns Boil the peppercorns in the vinegar until reduced to half quantity. Add to sauce and strain
Reform Sauce	250 ml Poivrade Sauce, 2 teaspoonfuls Redcurrant Jelly 2 tablespoonfuls Port Wine, Cayenne Pepper Add jelly, wine and pepper to sauce. Boil for a few minutes and strain

11. BÉARNAISE SAUCE

A sauce traditionally served with steak

Ingredients:

2 Shallots *or* 1 Onion   3 Egg Yolks
2 tablespoonfuls Tarragon Vinegar   75 g Butter
2 tablespoonfuls White Vinegar   Chopped Parsley
125 ml White Sauce (page 291)   Salt and Pepper

Method:

1. Chop shallots or onion. Boil with vinegars and reduce to 1 tablespoonful.
2. Strain, add to white sauce and mix well.
3. Put in a double saucepan and whisk in egg yolks one at a time till mixture thickens.
4. Whisk in butter in small pieces. Add parsley.

12. HOLLANDAISE SAUCE

This sauce is used in Eggs Benedict (page 321) and is also served with green or white asparagus

Ingredients:

3 tablespoonfuls White Vinegar   50 g Butter
2 Egg Yolks (beaten)   Salt and Pepper

Method:

1. Boil vinegar and reduce to 1 tablespoonful.
2. Add to beaten egg yolks.
3. Melt half the butter and pour into a small bowl. Add egg mixture.
4. Put bowl over a pan of hot water; stir till thick. Remove from heat.
5. Whisk in the remainder of the butter in small pieces. If it is too thick, add a little hot water.

CHAUDFROID SAUCES

Chaudfroid sauces are served cold. Their use is as a coating for cold fish and meats or as a base (e.g. in a mould) upon which these could be presented.

13. WHITE CHAUDFROID SAUCE

Ingredients:

250 ml Béchamel *or* Velouté Sauce (page 292)   2 tablespoonfuls Cream
250 ml Aspic Jelly (packet Aspic)   Salt and Pepper

Method:

1. Add liquid aspic to sauce while both are still warm. Add cream and salt and pepper to taste.
2. Stir till beginning to set and use immediately.

14. BROWN CHAUDFROID SAUCE

Ingredients:

250 ml Espagnole Sauce (page 294)   250 ml Aspic Jelly (packet)

Method:

1. Add the warm liquid aspic to the warm sauce.
2. Stir till beginning to set and use immediately.

15. TOMATO CHAUDFROID SAUCE

Ingredients:

125 ml Béchamel Sauce (page 292)   250 ml Aspic Jelly (packet)
125 ml Tomato Sauce   2 tablespoonfuls Cream

Method:

1. Mix two sauces, add warm aspic jelly.
2. Stir in cream, allow to cool, use before setting.

MISCELLANEOUS

16. APPLE SAUCE

Traditionally served with pork

Ingredients:

4 large Cooking Apples   25 g Butter
1–2 tablespoonfuls Water   3 Cloves
50 g Sugar   Squeeze Lemon Juice

Method:

1. Pare, core and quarter apples.
2. Stew with water and cloves until soft.
3. Add sugar, stir until dissolved, remove cloves.
4. Beat butter and lemon juice thoroughly through.

17. BREAD SAUCE

Traditionally served with turkey

Ingredients:

½ Onion   50 g soft white Breadcrumbs
6 Peppercorns   15–25 g Butter
¼ blade Mace   Salt and Pepper
2 Cloves   2 tablespoonfuls Cream (optional)
250 ml Milk

Method:

1. Simmer onion, peppercorns, cloves, and mace in milk.
2. When well-flavoured, strain, add breadcrumbs, butter and salt and pepper.
3. Cook slowly until bread has absorbed milk, add cream, if liked.

18. **CRANBERRY SAUCE**

Traditionally served with turkey

Ingredients:

200 g Cranberries
75 g Sugar
150 ml Water

2 level teaspoonfuls Cornflour
Pinch Cinnamon

Method:

1. Boil cranberries in water until soft, sieve.
2. Add sugar, reheat.
3. Mix cornflour and cinnamon, blend with water.
4. Add cornflour to cranberry purée, boil for 5 minutes.

19. **TOMATO SAUCE (1)**

Ingredients:

or

150 ml tinned Tomatoes
100 g Fresh Tomatoes
25 g Bacon
1 small Onion
Small piece Butter

2 level teaspoonfuls Cornflour
150 ml Stock or Water
Pinch Sugar
Salt and Pepper

Method:

1. Slice tomatoes, bacon and onion, sauté in melted butter for 10 minutes.
2. Add stock, simmer until onion is soft.
3. Sieve, thicken with blended cornflour. Add salt and pepper to taste.

20. **TOMATO SAUCE (2)**

Ingredients:

250 ml Tomato Juice
1 small Onion (chopped)

1 level tablespoonful Cornflour
Salt and Pepper

Method:

1. Heat tomato juice, add chopped onion. Simmer 10 minutes.
2. Blend cornflour with water, add to tomato, stir until boiling.
3. Strain, add a pinch of sugar, if necessary, and add salt and pepper to taste.

21. **CURRY SAUCE**

Ingredients:

1 tablespoonful dried Coconut
250 ml Stock
1 small Onion
1 small Apple
25 g Butter
3 level teaspoonfuls Curry Powder
1 level teaspoonful Curry Paste

1 level tablespoonful Flour
2 level teaspoonfuls Chutney
25 g Sultanas
Salt
1 teaspoonful Lemon Juice
1 tablespoonful Milk

Method:

1. Soak the coconut in stock.
2. Chop the onion and the apple and fry till brown in butter.
3. Add the curry powder and paste, and cook gently for 20 minutes.
4. Add flour and gradually the coconut stock. Stir till boiling; add chutney and sultanas. Simmer 20 minutes longer. Add salt if necessary.
5. Add lemon juice and milk before serving.

22. **HORSERADISH SAUCE**

Traditionally served with beef

Ingredients:

1 Horseradish root	About 150 ml stiffly whisked Cream
1 level teaspoonful Mustard	1 ½ tablespoonfuls Vinegar
2 level teaspoonfuls Castor Sugar	
Pinch Salt	

Method:

1. Let the horseradish lie in water till firm. Scrub well. Peel and grate finely (the released oils can sting the eyes and nose so it might be preferable to use a food processor for grating the root).
2. Mix mustard, sugar and salt; gradually add the cream and vinegar, then the horseradish.

23. **TARTARE SAUCE**

Traditionally served with fried fish or seafood

Ingredients:

250 ml Mayonnaise (page 220) *or* use ready-made Mayonnaise
1 tablespoonful chopped Gherkins
1 tablespoonful chopped Capers

Method:

Add chopped gherkins and capers to mayonnaise.

24. **MINT SAUCE**

Traditionally served with lamb

Ingredients:

2 tablespoonfuls Brown Vinegar	2 level teaspoonfuls Sugar
2 tablespoonfuls boiling Water	4 tablespoonfuls chopped Mint

Method:

Add sugar to the finely chopped mint. Add water and, when cold, the vinegar.

SWEET SAUCES

25. CORNFLOUR OR CUSTARD POWDER SAUCE

Ingredients:

or

| 1 level tablespoonful Cornflour | 250 ml Milk |
| 1 level tablespoonful Custard Powder | Sugar (to taste) and Flavouring |

Method:

1. Blend powder with some of the milk.
2. Heat remainder and pour over, return to the pan.
3. Stir till boiling and cook for 1 minute.
4. Sweeten and add flavouring.

26. CUSTARD SAUCE (1)

Ingredients:

1 level tablespoonful Cornflour	2 teaspoonfuls Sugar
250 ml Milk	Flavouring (if liked)
1 Egg (beaten)	

Method:

1. Blend the cornflour with a little cold milk.
2. Heat remainder of milk, pour over the blended cornflour and return to the pan. Stir till boiling and cook for 1 minute.
3. Cool slightly, pour over the well-beaten egg. Return to the pan and stir over heat until the mixture thickens, do not boil.
4. Add sugar and flavouring. Serve hot or cold. If serving cold, cover tightly while cooling to avoid a skin forming.

Note: The addition of cornflour makes the mixture thicken more easily, more stable and less likely to curdle.

27. CUSTARD SAUCE (2)

Ingredients:

| 250 ml Milk | 15–25 g Sugar |
| 2 Egg Yolks *or* Whole Eggs | Vanilla Essence |

Method:

1. Heat the milk and pour over the beaten eggs; strain.
2. Stir over a gentle heat till sauce thickens, do not boil; add sugar.
3. Add vanilla essence. Serve hot or cold. If serving cold, cover tightly while cooling to avoid a skin forming.

Note: If custard curdles or is lumpy it has been allowed to boil.

If it is too thin it has not been cooked sufficiently.

28. VARIATIONS FOR 250 ML CUSTARD SAUCE I AND 2

Coffee.—Dissolve 2 teaspoonfuls instant coffee in milk and add.
Caramel.—Dissolve 50 g sugar in 150 ml water, bring to the boil and boil till pale caramel colour. Add to hot custard sauce No. 1 and dissolve.

29. SABAYON OR WHIPPED-EGG SAUCE

Also known in Italian cookery as zabaglione when made with Marsala wine

Ingredients:

1 Egg Yolk	2 tablespoonfuls Sherry
2 level teaspoonfuls Castor Sugar	75 ml Double cream (softly whipped, optional)

Method:

1. Whisk egg, sugar and sherry over a low heat in a shallow pan till quite frothy and warm.
2. Fold in the cream if you are using it.

30. CARAMEL SAUCE (1)

Ingredients:

50 g Sugar	Extra Sugar to taste
150 ml Water	

Method:

1. Dissolve sugar in half the water, bring to the boil, and boil without stirring till a pale caramel colour.
2. Add remaining water and dissolve the caramel. Add extra sugar to taste.

31. CARAMEL SAUCE (2)

Ingredients:

100 g Granulated Sugar	Squeeze Lemon Juice
2 tablespoonfuls Water	250 ml Water

Method:

1. Dissolve sugar in 2 tablespoonfuls water and lemon juice until a golden syrup forms.
2. Add remaining water, dissolve caramel and cook until of a syrupy consistency.

32. CHOCOLATE SAUCE (1)

Ingredients:

25 g Butter	30 g Sugar
25 g Flour	1 level tablespoonful Cocoa
250 ml Milk	Vanilla Essence

Method:

1. Mix sugar and cocoa and blend with a little milk.
2. Melt butter, add flour, then the milk gradually. Add cocoa mixture.
3. Stir till boiling and cook for a few minutes. Add essence to taste.

33. CHOCOLATE SAUCE (2)

Ingredients:

50 g Icing Sugar   2 level teaspoonfuls Arrowroot
200 ml Water   ½ teaspoonful Vanilla Essence
50 g block Chocolate

Method:

1. Boil sugar and water. Reduce heat and add broken chocolate. Melt and blend throroughly. Pour over blended arrowroot.
2. Return to pan and boil for 1 minute. Add essence.

34. CHOCOLATE SAUCE (3)

Ingredients:

100 g Plain Chocolate   1 teaspoonful Vanilla Essence
125 ml Water   2 tablespoonfuls Cream
1 tablespoonful Sugar   Small piece Butter

Method:

1. Flake chocolate, dissolve in water.
2. Add sugar and vanilla.
3. Cook very slowly for 15–20 minutes.
4. Add cream and butter.

35. JAM SAUCE (1)

Ingredients:

1 tablespoonful Jam   250 ml Water
2 level teaspoonfuls Cornflour

Method:

1. Blend cornflour with some of the measured water.
2. Bring remaining water and jam to boil and pour over blended cornflour.
3. Return to pan, stir till boiling, boil for 1 minute and strain.

36. JAM SAUCE (2)

Ingredients:

2 tablespoonfuls Jam   250 ml Water
50 g Sugar   Few drops Lemon Juice

Method:

1. Boil sugar, water and jam together rapidly for about 5 minutes until syrupy.
2. Add lemon juice, strain and serve.

37. MARMALADE SAUCE

Make as jam sauce (1), using marmalade instead of jam.

301

38. SYRUP SAUCE (1)

Ingredients:

2 tablespoonfuls Syrup *or* Treacle   Few drops Lemon Juice
150 ml Water

Method:

Boil together until syrupy (about 5 minutes).

39. SYRUP SAUCE (2)

Make as jam sauce (1), page 301, using syrup instead of jam.

40. ORANGE SAUCE (THICKENED)

Ingredients:

or   2 level teaspoonfuls Arrowroot   Juice of 1 Orange
    3 level teaspoonfuls Cornflour   150 ml Water
    A little Sugar

Method:

1. Mix arrowroot with a little of the measured water. Boil remainder of water and pour over blended arrowroot.
2. Add orange juice, and sugar to taste; return to the pan and boil for 1 minute.

41. LEMON SAUCE

Ingredients:

100 g Granulated Sugar   Rind and Juice 1 Lemon
250 ml Water

Method:

1. Place sugar and water in pan. Simmer till reduced to half the original quantity.
2. Peel the lemon thinly, cut rind into shreds 2½ cm long.
3. When the syrup has reduced add the strained lemon juice and shreds, boil for a few minutes.

Variations:

Orange Sauce.—Substitute 1 orange for 1 lemon.
Fig Sauce.—4 chopped figs instead of 1 lemon.
Date Sauce.—4 chopped dates instead of 1 lemon.
Sultana Sauce.—1 tablespoonful sultanas instead of 1 lemon.

42. BUTTERSCOTCH SAUCE

Ingredients:

100 g Brown Sugar   50 g Butter
1 tablespoonful Syrup   2 tablespoonfuls Milk

Method:

1. Boil sugar, syrup and butter together. Test by dropping a little of the mixture

into a cupful of cold water. If sufficiently cooked it will roll into a soft ball between the finger and thumb (page 423).

2. Cool and beat in milk.

43. BRANDY BUTTER OR HARD SAUCE

Ingredients:

100 g fresh Butter	I tablespoonful Sherry
25 g ground Almonds	½ tablespoonful Brandy
50 g Castor Sugar	

Method:

1. Cream butter and sugar and beat in almonds.
2. Add sherry and brandy just before serving.
3. Pile up on a small dish and serve with plum pudding.

44. FRUIT SAUCE

Ingredients:

125 ml Pineapple *or* other Fruit Juice	Squeeze Lemon Juice
I level teaspoonful Arrowroot	I teaspoonful Sugar

Method:

1. Blend arrowroot with fruit juice.
2. Pour into pan, bring to the boil, boil for I minute.
3. Add lemon juice and sugar, colour if desired.

45. MELBA SAUCE

Ingredients:

100 g Raspberries	4 tablespoonfuls Water
or 125 ml tinned Raspberries	2 level teaspoonfuls Cornflour
1–2 teaspoonfuls Lemon Juice	Sugar

Method:

1. Blend cornflour with water and add other ingredients.
2. Cook gently till boiling.
3. Strain, cool and use as required.

Note: Add sugar to taste, if fresh raspberries used.

46. RUM SYRUP

Ingredients:

150 g Sugar	500 ml Water
Rum *or* Rum Essence	

Method:

Boil sugar and water until reduced to half original quantity. Add rum or rum essence according to taste.

303

PASTRY

PASTRY

Pastry benefits from having all ingredients cold, e.g. ice cold water. Once mixed, pastry should be "rested" in the refrigerator for at least 30 minutes. Resting allows fats to solidify and the gluten in the pastry to relax. If made by hand, hands should be cold.

I. SUET PASTRY

Ingredients:

or

200 g Flour and
  2 level teaspoonfuls Baking Powder
200 g Self-raising Flour
I level teaspoonful Salt

75–100 g Packet Suet (Vegetable *or*
  Beef suet are available)
125 ml cold Water (approx.)

Method:

1. Mix dry ingredients; add cold water to make an elastic consistency.
2. Use as required; may be boiled, steamed or baked.

Note: If butcher's suet is used, remove skin and chop very finely.

2. SAVOURY BALLS

Ingredients:

or

75 g Flour and
  I level teaspoonful Baking Powder
75 g Self-raising Flour
25 g Suet (chopped, Vegetable *or* Beef)
I tablespoonful chopped Onion

I teaspoonful chopped Parsley
Pinch Herbs
Salt and Pepper
Cold Water to mix

Method:

1. Mix dry ingredients together. Make into a light dough with cold water.
2. Divide into 6 pieces. Roll each lightly into balls in flour.
3. Cook for 30 minutes in stews, mince, casseroles etc.

Note: Savoury balls can be served with boiled beef (page 89), mince (page 99) and sea pie (page 94).

3. SHORT PASTRY

Ingredients:

200 g Flour
½ level teaspoonful Salt
Cold Water (75–100 ml approx.)

100 g Shortening – Butter, Block
  Margarine, Cooking Fat, *or* a mixture
  of Block Margarine and Cooking Fat

Method:

1. Cut fat into flour or shred if hard. Rub till like fine breadcrumbs. Add salt.
2. Add cold water and mix to a very stiff consistency. Work till smooth.
3. Rest. Roll out, and use as required.

Note: Self-raising flour may be used instead of plain but pastry will not stay crisp. For sweet dishes add I level tablespoonful of castor sugar to the above recipe.

4. FORK-MIX PASTRY

Ingredients:

200 g Flour	½ level teaspoonful Salt
100 g Soft Margarine	2 tablespoonfuls cold Water

Method:

1. Put all ingredients together in mixing bowl.
2. Work together with a fork.
3. Work out cracks on a lightly floured surface. Use as short pastry (page 307).

5. FLAN CASE

Ingredients:

100 g Short Pastry (page 307)

Oven Temperature: 200°C, No. 6
Size of Flan Ring or Sandwich Tin: 15–17 cm
Position in Oven: Middle shelf

Method:

1. Roll out pastry and line flan ring or sandwich tin. Prick base with a fork. Cover bottom and sides of case with greased paper.
2. Bake for 15 minutes. Remove paper. Brush base and side with beaten egg to seal pastry. This helps to keep the base crisp when adding liquid ingredients, e.g. when making cheese flan (page 343) or quiche Lorraine (page 344).
3. Return flan to the oven for 5–10 minutes to dry the base, reducing heat to 180°C, No. 4.

Note: For a savoury flan case, 25 g grated cheese can be added to the dry ingredients.

6. RICH SHORT PASTRY

Ingredients:

200 g Flour	Pinch Salt
125 g Butter *or* Block Margarine	1 Egg Yolk
25 g Castor Sugar (for sweet dishes)	Cold Water

Method:

1. Rub fat into flour, add sugar and salt.
2. Mix egg yolk with a little cold water and use to mix to a stiff consistency. If no water is used pastry is very brittle.
3. Rest then roll out and use as required.

7. SPICED SHORT PASTRY

Ingredients:

200 g Flour		2 level teaspoonfuls Cinnamon
100 g Butter *or* Block Margarine	*or*	1 Egg Yolk and little cold Water
25 g Castor Sugar		1 Whole Egg

Method:

1. Rub fat into flour. Add sugar and cinnamon.
2. Mix with egg yolk and cold water to make a stiff consistency. If whole egg is used, the pastry is less crisp.
3. Rest, then roll out and use as required.

8. BISCUIT PASTRY

Ingredients:

200 g Flour	Pinch Salt
125 g Butter *or* Block Margarine	Egg, if necessary
40 g Castor Sugar	

Method:

1. Cream fat and sugar, work in flour and, if necessary, sufficient beaten egg to form a stiff paste.
2. Rest, then roll out and use as required.

9. ROUGH PUFF PASTRY

Ingredients:

200 g Flour	I level teaspoonful Salt
125–150 g Shortening – Butter, Block Margarine	125 ml cold Water (approx.)
or A mixture of Block Margarine and Cooking Fat	A few drops Lemon Juice

Method:

1. Mix the dry ingredients.
2. Cut fat into fairly large pieces and put into flour.
3. Add lemon juice to water and mix to an elastic consistency.
4. Turn out and work lightly.
5. Roll into an oblong strip, flour lightly, fold in three, seal edges, quarter turn, roll out again.
6. Repeat this for a second and third, and if necessary a fourth time, till fat is evenly distributed.
7. Rest before using as required.

10. FLAKY PASTRY

See illustration on page 310

Ingredients:

200 g Flour	125 ml cold Water (approx.)
150 g Butter, Block Margarine	A few drops Lemon Juice
or A mixture of Block Margarine and Cooking Fat	Pinch Salt

Method:

1. Divide fat into four equal portions. (Fats may be softened if very hard.)
2. Add salt to flour and rub one quarter of fat into flour.

3. Add lemon juice to water, add to flour and mix to an elastic consistency.
4. Turn out and work lightly. Roll into an oblong and place one quarter of the fat in small pieces on two-thirds of the pastry (A).
5. Fold up one-third (B) and down one-third (C), having dough and fat in alternate layers.
6. Seal edges. Quarter turn. Roll out again.
7. Proceed similarly with remainder of fat.
8. Set the pastry aside for a short time in a cool place.
9. Roll out twice more, giving five rollings in all.
10. Set aside for 30 minutes in refrigerator or cool place before using.

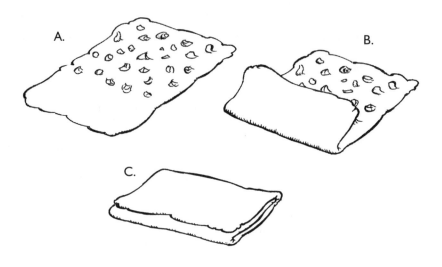

A.   B.   C.

11. **PUFF PASTRY**

See illustration on page 311

Ingredients:

200 g Flour   250 ml cold Water
200 g Butter *or* Block Margarine   A few drops Lemon Juice
Pinch Salt

Method:

1. Add salt to flour and rub a small piece of the fat into the flour (about 10 g).
2. Add lemon juice to water, add to flour and mix to an elastic consistency.
3. Turn out and work lightly until smooth.
4. Soften butter to same consistency as dough.
5. Roll dough into a square. Put a square pat of butter in the centre (A) and fold dough evenly over fat.
6. Press lightly and roll into a long strip (B). Flour lightly and fold in three (C). Quarter turn pastry.

7. Repeat steps 5 and 6, as above, six times, giving seven foldings in all. Leave aside for 15–20 minutes between each two or three rollings.

Alternative method:

Roll dough thinly into a square, place a square pat of butter in the centre, fold both ends to meet in the centre. Fold in two forming four layers. Roll out and fold in a similar manner five times.

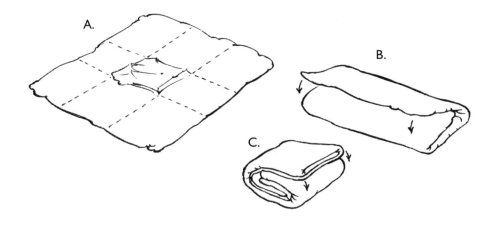

12. PATTY CASES OR VOL-AU-VENTS

Ingredients:

200 g Puff Pastry (page 310)

Servings: 8 patties cut with a 6–7 cm cutter

Time: 45 minutes

Oven Temperature: 240°C, No. 9; 230°C, No. 8; and 190°C, No. 5

Position in Oven: One-third from the top

Method:

1. Roll pastry 1 cm thick.
2. Dip the cutter in water and cut out rounds without twisting.
3. Turn rounds upside down onto a heavy baking tin which has been sprinkled with cold water.
4. Mark the top of the patties with a cutter two sizes smaller, which has been dipped in water. Do not cut through. Brush outer ring with egg.
5. Wrap in cling film or greaseproof paper and allow to rest for 15 minutes in refrigerator. Roll scraps of pastry thinner. Using the smaller cutter, cut out a top for each case.
6. Bake in an oven which has been heated at 240°C, No. 9, for 30 minutes, the temperature being reduced to 230°C, No. 8, when the patty cases and tops are put in and to 190°C, No. 5, after 15 minutes.
7. Scoop out any soft dough from inside of case and put back in the oven for a few minutes to dry off.

13. **VOL-AU-VENT CASE (LARGE)**

Ingredients:

> 200 g Puff Pastry (page 310)
>> **Servings:** 1 case cut with a 15–16 cm cutter
>> **Time:** 40–45 minutes
>> **Oven Temperature:** 240°C, No. 9; 230°C, No. 8;
>> and 190°C, No. 5
>> **Position in Oven:** One-third from the top

Method:

> Follow instructions for small patty cases (page 311).

Alternative method:

1. Roll out pastry twice size of larger cutter.
2. Cut two ovals, removing the middle from one, using a cutter two sizes smaller.
3. Brush edge of larger oval with egg and put rim in position.
4. Prick through at intervals with a skewer.
5. Use small cut-out piece for lid.
6. Leave aside in refrigerator or cool place for at least half an hour.
7. Brush lid and rim with egg.
8. Bake as for patties, about 40 minutes.

Note: If ready prepared pastry is used for patty or vol-au-vent cases, it should be rolled more thinly.

14. **HOT WATER PASTRY OR RAISED PIE CRUST**

Ingredients:

300 g Flour	125 ml Milk *or* Water
100 g Lard *or* Cooking Fat	1½ level teaspoonfuls Salt

Method:

1. Add salt to flour.
2. Bring milk and lard or cooking fat to the boil and stir in the flour.
3. Knead well until smooth and allow to stand for a short time if too soft for moulding.
4. Keep warm and use for raised meat, game or fruit pies.

15. **CHOUX PASTRY**

Ingredients:

70 g Flour	Pinch Salt
25 g Butter *or* Block Margarine	2 small Eggs (beaten)
125 ml Water	

Method:

1. Bring the water and butter or block margarine to the boil.
2. Sieve the flour and salt onto a paper and gradually add to boiling liquid.
3. Beat well until smooth and cook for half a minute.

4. Allow to cool slightly and add the beaten eggs gradually, beating well
   between each addition.
5. Use as required.

16. CHEESE PASTRY

Ingredients:

100 g Flour
50 g Butter *or* Block Margarine
Salt and Pepper
Cayenne Pepper

100 g Cheese (grated, mixture of
   Cheddar and Parmesan)
A little cold Water
1 Egg Yolk

Method:

1. Sieve flour and add salt and pepper.
2. Rub in butter or block margarine, add grated cheese, egg yolk and a little
   water to make a stiff paste.

Note: All the cheese used may be Cheddar, and it should be finely grated; this is
more easily done if the cheese is dry.

17. OATMEAL PASTRY

Ingredients:

100 g Flour
100 g Oatmeal
Pinch Salt

75–100 g Butter, Block Margarine *or*
   Cooking Fat
Cold Water to mix

Method:

1. Sieve flour and mix with oatmeal.
2. Rub butter, block margarine or cooking fat into flour and oatmeal.
3. Add salt and mix to a very stiff consistency with cold water.
4. Work lightly until smooth.
5. Roll out and use as required.

18. POTATO PASTRY

Ingredients:

100 g Flour
½ level teaspoonful Salt
75 g Butter *or* Block Margarine

2 level teaspoonfuls Baking Powder
100 g Potatoes (cooked, sieved)
A little cold Water (to mix)

Method:

1. Rub butter or block margarine into sieved flour and baking powder.
2. Mix in the sieved potatoes.
3. Add water to make a stiff dough.
4. Roll out and use as you would short pastry (page 307).

Note: Self-raising flour may be used.

BREAKFASTS

BREAKFASTS

1. TEA

Allow one small teaspoonful for each person and one over, if for a small number. If catering for a large number the proportion is less. ¼ kg tea should give 100 cups.

Method:

1. Thoroughly heat the teapot.
2. Add tea, and pour on freshly boiled water.

2. COFFEE

Allow 40–50 g freshly ground coffee to 500 ml water

Method:

1. Heat a coffee pot or cafétière.
2. Add ground coffee, pour on boiling water.
3. Stand in a warm place 5–10 minutes.
4. Plunge cafétière and pour into cups, or decant from coffee pot and pour through fine strainer.
5. Serve with cream and sugar if liked.

3. COCOA

Ingredients:

1–2 level teaspoonfuls Cocoa
1 teacupful Milk *or* Milk and Water mixed
Sugar to taste

Method:

1. Mix cocoa and sugar and blend with a little of the cold liquid.
2. Boil remaining liquid and pour it over the cocoa. Stir briskly.

4. PORRIDGE

Ingredients:

1 litre Water   1 level teaspoonful Salt
100 g Oatmeal

Method:

1. Boil water, add salt, sprinkle in oatmeal, stirring.
2. Bring to the boil and put on the lid.
3. Simmer 20–30 minutes, stirring frequently.

Note: To shorten the cooking time, oatmeal may be soaked overnight in the water, or rolled oats can be used which need only be boiled for 5 minutes.

5. MUESLI

Ingredients:

100 g Rolled Oats	25 g Sultanas
25 g Raisins	25 g Nuts (chopped, optional)
25 g Brown Sugar	1 Eating Apple (grated, optional)
Fresh *or* Canned Fruit (chopped)	Milk, Cream *or* Yoghurt to mix

Servings: 4

Method:

1. Combine oats, dried fruit and sugar.
2. Add fresh or canned fruit if used.
3. Serve with milk, cream or yoghurt to mix to a creamy consistency.
4. Serve as a breakfast cereal or dessert.

6. BOILED EGG (HARD)

Method:

1. Put egg into cold water; bring to boil; boil slowly for 10 minutes.
2. Cool in cold water to prevent yolk discolouring.

Note: To help keep yolk in centre of egg, stir water for a few moments after adding egg.

7. BOILED EGG (SOFT)

Method:

Proceed as for hard-boiled egg, cooking 3 minutes, or 4–5 minutes if new-laid.

8. SCRAMBLED EGG

Ingredients:

½ slice Toast	1 tablespoonful Milk
Small piece Butter	Seasoning
1 Egg	

Method:

1. Beat egg, add milk and seasoning.
2. In a small pan, melt butter, add egg, stir slowly until set and creamy.
3. Place on hot buttered toast.

Note: Cheese may be added to the mixture before cooking, in the proportion of 25 g grated cheese per egg.

9. POACHED EGG

Ingredients:

1 slice Toast	Water (enough to float egg)
1 Egg	Vinegar
Salt	

Method:

    1. Butter toast and keep hot.

    2. Break egg into a cup.

    3. Add salt and teaspoonful vinegar to water.

    4. Boil water, reduce heat, slip in egg carefully.

    5. When set, remove with draining spoon. Serve on toast.

10. BACON AND EGG

Ingredients:

    2 Bacon rashers   1 Egg

Method:

    1. Remove rind from bacon.

    2. Cook slowly on both sides till fat is clear and crisp.

    3. Drop egg carefully into hot fat.

    4. Baste with the hot fat until lightly set.

    5. Serve with the bacon.

11. BACON AND TOMATO

Ingredients:

    2 Bacon rashers   Seasoning

    1 Tomato

Method:

    1. Remove rind from bacon and cook slowly on both sides till fat is clear and crisp.

    2. Remove bacon and keep hot.

    3. Cut tomato in thick slices or halves, fry, season, arrange around bacon.

    Note: Mushrooms may be treated in the same way. Bacon and tomato may also be grilled.

12. BACON, SAUSAGE AND APPLE

Ingredients:

    4 Bacon rashers   2 Sausages

    1 Apple

Method:

    1. Remove rind from bacon, prick sausages, skin, core and slice apple into rings.

    2. Cook sausages slowly for 4 minutes turning frequently.

    3. Add bacon and cook till fat is clear and crisp. Remove from pan.

    4. Fry apple rings till soft.

    5. Serve with bacon and sausages.

    Note: Can also be grilled, putting the sliced apple in the bottom of the grill pan at the beginning.

13. **LIVER, BACON AND TOMATO**

Ingredients:

1 rasher Fat Bacon   1 Tomato
50 g Calf's Liver (sliced)

Method:

1. Remove rind from bacon and cook slowly on both sides till fat is clear and crisp; remove cooked bacon and keep warm.
2. Wash liver, fry on both sides in bacon fat, 5–6 minutes in all.
3. Halve tomato, fry cut side down, turn and cook until soft but not collapsed.
4. Serve with liver and bacon.

14. **BEANS AND BACON**

Ingredients:

50 g cooked Haricot Beans *or* tinned Butter Beans
2 Bacon rashers

Method:

1. Cook bacon slowly on both sides till fat is clear and crisp.
2. Remove bacon, and fry beans in the fat.
3. Place on a plate with bacon surrounding.

15. **BACON FRITTERS**

Ingredients:

25 ml Oil   Salt and Pepper
4 Bacon rashers   3 tablespoonfuls Milk
75 g Self-raising Flour

Method:

1. Chop bacon, fry until crisp.
2. Put fried bacon, flour, seasoning and milk in a bowl, beat well.
3. Heat oil in the frying pan. Drop spoonfuls of batter into pan, flatten.
4. Fry untill golden brown on both sides.

16. **FRENCH TOAST**

Ingredients:

Fingers of White Bread   Seasoning
1 Egg   Butter *or* Oil

Method:

1. Beat egg, season.
2. Dip bread fingers into egg.
3. Heat fat and fry till golden brown on both sides. Serve with bacon.
Note: French toast can also be served with a jam sauce (page 301).

17. **WELSH RAREBIT (1)**

Ingredients:

10 g Butter	Salt and Pepper
50 g Cheese (grated)	Pinch Mustard
125 ml Milk	Buttered Toast

Method:

1. Put butter, cheese, milk, seasoning and mustard in a pan, mix.
2. Heat through, stirring.
3. Spread on toast and grill until golden brown.

18. **WELSH RAREBIT (2)**

Ingredients:

20 g Butter	Salt, Pepper and Mustard
20 g Flour	75 g Cheese (grated)
125 ml Milk	Buttered Toast

Method:

1. Melt butter, add flour and milk, beat until smooth. Stir till boiling.
2. Add seasoning, mustard and cheese and stir well.
3. Spread on toast and grill until golden brown.

19. **BUCK RAREBIT**

Make as Wesh Rarebit, above, with the addition of a poached egg served on top.

20. **SAVOURY HADDOCK ON TOAST**

Ingredients:

1 medium fillet Haddock	25 g Butter
125 ml Milk	Seasoning
15 g Flour	Buttered Toast

Method:

1. Simmer fish in milk and butter for 7 minutes, skin and flake.
2. Blend flour with cold water, add to milk and stir till boiling. Season.
3. Add fish and serve on slices of buttered toast.

21. **EGGS BENEDICT**

Ingredients:

1 Poached Egg (page 318)	½ Muffin (page 373, toasted)
1 Bacon rasher	Hollandaise Sauce (page 295)

Servings: 1 person

Method:

1. Make Hollandaise sauce.
2. Remove rind from bacon and grill or fry.
3. Poach egg. Toast muffin while egg is poaching.
4. Butter muffin and place bacon on top. Place poached egg on bacon and serve with a spoonful of Hollandaise sauce.

OMELETTES

OMELETTES

I. GENERAL POINTS

1. Use the correct size of pan, approx. 15 cm for 2 eggs.
2. If possible, use pan for omelettes only. If using a frying pan, heat a little oil in it and rub round with paper to form a skin.
3. Omelette pans should be non-stick.

2. PLAIN OMELETTE

Ingredients:

2 Eggs   10 g Butter *or* I teaspoonful Oil
I tablespoonful Water   Seasoning

Servings: I person

Method:

1. Eggs should be beaten until yolk and white are lightly mixed, add water and seasoning.
2. Melt butter till sizzling, pour in egg mixture; with a spatula push mixture from side of pan, allowing unset egg to run onto hot pan.
3. Continue until all the egg is very lightly set, taking about 2 minutes.
4. Fold omelette in half.
5. Turn out and serve very hot.

Variations:

Savoury Omelette.—Add I level teaspoonful chopped parsley or herbs to egg mixture.
Cheese Omelette.—Add I tablespoonful grated cheese to egg mixture.
Sweet Omelette.—Add 2 level teaspoonfuls sugar to egg mixture.

3. STUFFED OMELETTES

Suggested Stuffings:

Bacon   Tuna Fish
Tomato   Mushroom
Shrimp or Prawn   Asparagus
Cheese (grated)

Stuffing must be cooked beforehand, with the exception of grated cheese which may be sprinkled on while omelette is setting.

Ingredients:

Stuffing of choice   I tablespoonful Water
2 Eggs   25 g Butter
Seasoning

Servings: I person

Method:

1. Melt half the butter in a small pan and cook the stuffing ingredient.
3. Beat eggs, water and seasoning lightly.
4. Melt remaining butter in omelette pan until sizzling.
5. Pour in egg mixture. With a spatula, push mixture from side of pan, allowing unset egg to run onto hot pan.
6. Continue until all the egg is very lightly set, taking about 2 minutes.
7. Leave undisturbed until egg is almost dry on top.
8. Place hot stuffing in centre of omelette.
9. Fold in half, or roll over, enclosing stuffing.

4. KIDNEY OMELETTE

Ingredients:

1 Sheep's Kidney	1 tablespoonful Water
2 Eggs	25 g Butter
Seasoning	

Servings: 1 person

Method:

1. Skin, core and wash kidney, cut in small pieces.
2. Melt half the butter in a small pan, fry kidney till cooked.
3. Beat eggs, water and seasoning lightly.
4. Melt remaining butter in omelette pan until sizzling.
5. Pour in egg mixture. With a spatula push mixture from side of pan, allowing unset egg to run onto hot pan.
6. Continue until all the egg is very lightly set, taking about 2 minutes.
7. Leave undisturbed until egg is almost dry on top.
8. Place hot kidneys in centre of omelette.
9. Fold in half, or roll over, enclosing kidney.

5. OMELETTE SOUFFLÉ

Ingredients:

2 Eggs		10 g Butter
2 level teaspoonfuls Castor Sugar	or	1 teaspoonful Vegetable Oil
Jam		

Method:

1. Separate the eggs, add sugar to the yolks and beat well.
2. Whisk whites stiffly and lightly fold yolks and whites together.
3. Melt the butter in an omelette pan. Pour in the mixture and cook lightly till set and browned on underside.
4. Cook the top under a moderate grill or in a moderate oven.
5. Turn onto a sugared paper. Make an incision in the centre and put in 2 teaspoonfuls of warmed jam.
6. Fold over, dredge castor sugar on top and serve at once.

Note:

1. Other fillings may be used instead of jam, e.g. stewed or tinned fruit.
2. The mixture may be poured into an ovenproof dish and baked in a hot oven, 230°C, No. 8, for 5 minutes.

Savoury Omelette Soufflé:

Omit sugar, add seasoning and fill with a savoury filling.

6. SPANISH OMELETTE

Ingredients:

4 Eggs	Cooked *or* raw Potato
I tablespoonful Water	Any left-over diced Vegetables
I Onion	*or* Tomato *or* Peppers (sliced)
Seasoning	
Oil for frying	

Servings: 3–4

Method:

1. Slice onion (and potatoes if raw).
2. Heat oil in a frying pan, add onion and potato and cook gently till soft.
3. Add other vegetables.
4. Mix eggs, water, seasoning and pour over vegetables.
5. Cook gently till set and lightly brown on underside, brown under the grill or turn carefully.
6. Serve cut in wedges.

SAVOURY DISHES

SAVOURY DISHES

1. MACARONI CHEESE (1)

Ingredients:

50 g Macaroni   250 ml Cheese Sauce (page 291)
25 g Cheese (grated)

Servings: 3

Method:

1. Cook pasta in boiling salted water till al dente (follow cooking time on packet).
2. Strain, add to cheese sauce.
3. Put into an ovenproof baking dish, sprinkle with grated cheese.
4. Bake or brown under grill.

2. MACARONI CHEESE (2)

Ingredients:

40 g Macaroni   ½ teaspoonful made Mustard
75 g Cheese (grated)   1 Egg
Salt and Pepper   250 ml Milk

Servings: 3
Time: 45–60 minutes
Oven Temperature: 170°C, No. 3
Position in Oven: Middle shelf

Method:

1. Cook pasta in boiling salted water till al dente (follow cooking time on packet).
2. Strain, add 50 g cheese, mustard and seasoning.
3. Put into an ovenproof baking dish.
4. Beat egg, add milk, season.
5. Strain custard mixture over macaroni, stir through, sprinkle with the rest of the grated cheese.
6. Bake.

3. SAVOURY MACARONI

Ingredients:

2 Tomatoes (skinned, page 202)   100 g Cheese (grated)
50 g Macaroni   1 tablespoonful chopped Parsley
1 Onion   Salt and Pepper
25 g Butter   500 ml Milk
50 g Breadcrumbs

Servings: 3–4
Time: 30 minutes
Oven Temperature: 190°C, No. 5
Position in Oven: Middle shelf

Method:

1. Parboil onion and chop finely. Cook macaroni (follow cooking time on packet). Rub butter into breadcrumbs. Arrange pasta, onions, tomatoes, breadcrumbs then cheese in layers in an ovenproof dish. Reserve 1 tablespoonful cheese.
2. Pour milk over, allow to stand 10 minutes.
3. Sprinkle with remaining grated cheese.
4. Bake. Serve sprinkled with chopped parsley.

4. SAVOURY SPAGHETTI

Ingredients:

150 g Spaghetti	5 Bacon rashers
75 g Cheese	1 small tin Tomato Soup
5 Mushrooms	

Method:

1. Cook pasta in boiling salted water till soft (follow cooking time on packet). Drain.
2. Grill bacon and mushrooms, chop up, and add to cooked spaghetti.
3. Add soup and heat.
4. Pour into a casserole, sprinkle cheese on top. Grill until golden brown.

5. RAVIOLI

Ingredients:

200 g Flour	2–3 tablespoonfuls Water
1 Egg	

Method:

1. Place flour in a bowl with a pinch salt.
2. Drop in egg and enough water to make a stiff dough.
3. Knead until smooth, stand 30 minutes before using.
4. Divide dough in two, roll out till very thin.
5. Place filling (see below) on one piece of dough in teaspoonfuls about 5 cm apart.
6. Cover with remaining dough, cut in rounds with a small cutter or into squares with a knife. Seal edges.
7. Cook in boiling salted water for 15 minutes.
8. Drain, serve with Parmesan cheese and tomato sauce (page 297), or toss in melted butter.

Cheese filling

Ingredients:

125 g Cream Cheese	50 g Parmesan Cheese
25 g Butter	1 tablespoonful chopped Parsley
1 Egg Yolk	Salt and Pepper

Method:

1. Beat cream cheese with butter until soft.
2. Beat in egg yolk, Parmesan cheese, parsley and seasoning.

Chicken filling
Ingredients:

125 g cooked Chicken
50 g Parmesan Cheese (grated)
2 teaspoonfuls chopped Parsley
Salt and Pepper

I tablespoonful Spinach *or* other
   vegetable Purée
I Egg

Method:

1. Chop chicken.
2. Mix all ingredients, bind with egg.

6. SAVOURY RICE

Ingredients:

100 g Rice
25 g Butter
I Onion (chopped)
Salt and Pepper

500 ml Stock
3 Tomatoes (skinned, page 202)
50 g Mushrooms (skinned)
100 g Cheese (grated)

Servings: 2–3
Time: 20–30 minutes

Method:

1. Wash rice. Fry onion lightly, add washed rice and stir till buttered.
2. Add seasoning and a third of the stock.
3. Cook slowly until stock is almost absorbed, then add other two-thirds in the same way.
4. Add tomatoes and mushrooms, skinned and sliced.
5. Cook slowly for 10 minutes. Add half the cheese.
6. Mound on a serving dish, sprinkle with cheese, grill.

7. RISOTTO

Ingredients:

25 g Butter
I clove Garlic *or* small Onion
150 g Arborio Rice
2 Tomatoes *or* a small tin

500 ml Stock
Salt and Pepper
50 g grated hard Cheese

Servings: 3–4

Method:

1. Heat butter, fry chopped onion or garlic.
2. Add washed rice and stir until fat is absorbed.
3. Add tomatoes and one-third of stock.
4. Simmer and stir until liquid is absorbed.
5. Add more stock and continue cooking and stirring until rice is soft but still moist.
6. Season, serve sprinkled with cheese.

8. POTATO STEW

Ingredients:

500g Potatoes
2 Onions
150 ml Water
Salt and Pepper

150 ml Milk
100–150 g Cheese (grated)
Chopped Parsley

Method:

1. Peel and slice potatoes, chop onions.
2. Put potatoes, onions and seasoning in layers in a stewpan.
3. Add water, stew gently 15 minutes.
4. Add milk and stew 20 minutes longer until everything is cooked.
5. Place on a serving dish and sprinkle with grated cheese. Brown under grill.
6. Serve with chopped parsley sprinkled on top.

9. CHEESE POTATOES

Ingredients:

500g boiled Potatoes
Small piece Butter
2 tablespoonfuls Milk

Salt and Pepper
50–100 g Cheese (grated)

Method:

1. Mash potatoes smoothly, add butter and milk, beat well, season.
2. Beat two-thirds of cheese into potatoes.
3. Put into a baking dish, sprinkle remaining cheese on top.
4. Brown under grill.

10. CHEESE PUDDING

Ingredients:

50 g Breadcrumbs
50 g Cheese (grated)
250 ml Milk
25 g Butter

Seasoning
¼ teaspoonful Mustard
1–2 Eggs

Servings: 2–3
Time: 30–40 minutes
Oven temperature: 180°C, No. 4
Position in Oven: Middle shelf

Method:

1. Mix breadcrumbs, cheese, seasoning and mustard.
2. Heat milk and butter, pour over crumbs.
3. Beat egg, add to mixture.
4. Put in a greased baking dish. Bake.

11. BAKED RAREBIT

Ingredients:

50 g Butter	2 Eggs
50 g Breadcrumbs	2 tablespoonfuls Milk
100 g Cheese	Salt and Pepper

Servings: 2
Time: 10–15 minutes
Oven temperature: 180°C. No. 4
Position in Oven: Middle shelf

Method:

1. Melt butter, mix through breadcrumbs, season.
2. Cut cheese in thin slices.
3. Put crumbs in a thin layer on an ovenproof dish.
4. Cover with cheese slices, repeat layers, finishing with cheese.
5. Beat eggs lightly, add milk, pour over cheese mixture.
6. Bake.

12. CHEESE CUSTARD

Ingredients:

3 level teaspoonfuls Cornflour	2 Eggs (beaten)
500 ml Milk	Salt and Pepper
100 g Cheese (grated)	½ teaspoonful Mustard

Servings: 3–4
Time: 45 minutes
Oven Temperature: 170°C, No. 3
Position in Oven: Middle shelf

Method:

1. Blend cornflour with beaten eggs.
2. Add milk, cheese and seasonings.
3. Pour into an ovenproof dish and bake in a moderate oven.

13. CHEESE AND HADDOCK SAVOURY

Ingredients:

25 g Flour	2 Eggs (beaten)
250 ml Milk	1 cooked Findon Haddock
50 g Cheese (grated)	2 Tomatoes
Salt and Pepper	

Servings: 3

Method:

1. Flake haddock, skin and slice tomatoes, place in ovenproof dish, season.
2. Blend flour with a little milk, add remainder and stir till boiling.
3. Boil sauce for 3 minutes, add cheese, beaten eggs and reheat till it thickens without boiling.

4. Pour sauce over fish and tomato.

5. Reheat if necessary. Serve.

14. CHEESE CUTLETS

Ingredients:

25 g Butter

25 g Flour

125 ml Milk

25 g Macaroni (cooked)

75 g Cheese (grated)

Salt and Pepper

Egg and Breadcrumbs for coating

Oil for frying

Servings: 4

Method:

1. Melt butter, add flour and milk, cook until a thick sauce is formed.

2. Chop cooked macaroni, add along with cheese.

3. Season, spread on a plate to cool.

4. When cold, divide into equal portions, shape into cutlets or cakes; egg and crumb.

5. Fry till golden brown in hot oil.

15. LENTIL AND CHEESE CUTLETS

Ingredients:

100 g Lentils

100 g Potatoes (cooked)

Salt and Pepper

100 g Cheese (grated)

25 g Butter

1 Egg Yolk and 1 whole Egg (beaten)

Breadcrumbs for coating

Oil for frying

Servings: 3–4

Method:

1. Boil lentils, drain and dry thoroughly over a gentle heat.

2. Mash lentils and potatoes together.

3. Mix in cheese, butter and seasoning. Bind with egg yolk. Cool.

4. Form into cutlets or cakes.

5. Coat with egg and breadcrumbs, twice, fry till golden brown.

16. CHEESE EGGS

Ingredients:

3 Eggs (hard-boiled)

250 ml Cheese Sauce (page 291)

25 g Cheese (grated)

Servings: 2

Method:

1. Shell and slice eggs, put into a greased ovenproof dish.

2. Coat with cheese sauce, sprinkle with cheese.

3. Brown under grill.

17. CHEESE AND POTATO EGGS

Ingredients:

500 g Potatoes (cooked)	125 ml Milk
25 g Butter	3 Eggs (hard-boiled)
75 g Cheese (grated)	Salt and Pepper

Servings: 4

Method:

1. Mash potatoes over heat.
2. Add cheese, butter, milk and seasoning, and beat.
3. Place sliced eggs in the bottom of a baking dish, cover with potatoes.
4. Sprinkle with grated cheese, brown in oven or under grill.

18. BAKED EGG IN POTATO

Ingredients:

1 large Potato	Seasoning
1 Egg	1 tablespoonful Cheese (grated)
A little Milk	

Servings: 1
Time: 1–1½ hours
Temperature: 190°C, No. 5

Method:

1. Scrub potato. Bake 190°C, No. 5 for 1–1¼ hours, depending upon size.
2. Cut slice from flat side of potato. Scoop out potato carefully.
3. Mash potato with a little milk, season, and add to potato case, to quarter fill.
4. Drop egg on top of potato, season.
5. Sprinkle with cheese, bake until set.

Variations for Stuffed Baked Potato:

Cold Meat or Chicken.—Prepare as above. Mix meat, finely chopped and well seasoned, with creamed potato. Replace cheese with butter.

Shrimp or Prawn.—As above.

Smoked Haddock.—Or other cooked fish, flaked and mixed with potato.

Fried Bacon or **Fried Kidney.**—Chopped.

19. CAULIFLOWER AU GRATIN

Ingredients:

1 Cauliflower	25 g Cheese (grated)
250 ml Cheese Sauce (page 291)	Salt and Pepper

Method:

1. Prepare and cook cauliflower (page 185).
2. Drain well and coat with cheese sauce.
3. Sprinkle cheese on top and brown under the grill.

Note: Cauliflower may be broken into sprigs before cooking, so reducing the cooking time. Other vegetables suitable for au gratin: celery, leeks, onions, potatoes.

20. CELERY AND HAM PIE

Ingredients:

Small head Celery	100 g Ham (cooked, chopped)
25 g Butter	1 Egg
25 g Flour	25 g Cheese
250 ml Water (in which celery was cooked) and Milk	25 g Breadcrumbs
	Seasoning

Serving: 3

Time: 20–30 minutes

Oven Temperature: 180°C, No. 5

Position in Oven: One-third from top

Method:

1. Cut celery in 5 cm lengths, cook in boiling salted water. Drain and reserve liquid.
2. Melt butter, add flour. Add water and milk gradually, mix well, boil.
3. Take off heat. Beat egg and add to sauce.
4. Add celery and ham to sauce. Mix well.
5. Put into an ovenproof dish. Cover with breadcrumbs and cheese mixed together.
6. Bake.

21. CONVENT EGGS

Ingredients:

1 small Onion	250 ml Milk
15 g Butter	Seasoning
25 g Flour	2 Eggs (hard-boiled)

Servings: 2

Method:

1. Slice onion thinly, fry in butter until soft, without browning.
2. Add flour, then milk gradually, season.
3. Stir until boiling then simmer for 3 minutes.
4. Halve shelled eggs, heat in sauce.
5. Lift out eggs, place on serving dish, pour sauce over. Garnish with toasted bread.

22. SPANISH EGGS

Ingredients:

3 large Eggs	25 g Cheese (grated)
250 ml Cheese Sauce (page 291)	

Servings: 2–3

Time: 7–10 minutes

Oven Temperature: 200°C, No. 6

Position in Oven: Middle shelf

Method:

1. Heat a flat ovenproof baking dish; grease it.
2. Drop eggs whole onto hot dish.
3. Coat with sauce, sprinkle with cheese.
4. Bake.

23. CREAMED CORN EGGS

Ingredients:

1 tin Sweetcorn	1 tablespoonful Cream
25 g Butter	3 poached Eggs
Seasoning	Paprika

Servings: 3

Method:

1. Drain sweetcorn.
2. Melt butter, add corn, seasoning and cream.
3. Heat through, place on shallow serving dish.
4. Arrange eggs on top, sprinkle with paprika.

24. CURRIED EGGS

Ingredients:

4 Eggs (hard-boiled)	100 g Rice
250 ml Curry Sauce (page 297)	

Servings: 2–3
Time: 10–15 minutes

Method:

1. Halve eggs and place in hot sauce.
2. Simmer slowly until heated through.
3. Serve with boiled rice (page 475).

25. SCOTCH EGGS

Ingredients:

3 Eggs (hard-boiled)	Egg (beaten, for coating)
125 g Sausagemeat	Breadcrumbs (fresh, or dried
Oil for deep-frying	page 477)

Servings: 3
Time: 7–10 minutes

Method:

1. Remove shell from eggs, roll in flour.
2. Completely cover with sausagemeat.
3. Coat in beaten egg and dip in breadcrumbs and deep-fry in hot oil until golden brown.
4. Serve hot with a sauce or cold with salad.

26. EGG CUTLETS

Ingredients:

25 g Butter	25 g Ham (cooked, chopped)
25 g Flour	2 Eggs (hard-boiled)
125 ml Milk	3 Mushrooms
Salt and Pepper	Egg
Oil for deep-frying	Breadcrumbs

Servings: 3

Method:

1. Melt butter, add flour and milk and boil until thick; season.
2. Finely chop ham, eggs, mushrooms. Season and add to sauce.
3. Spread on plate and allow to cool.
4. Divide into 4 or 6 portions. Shape into cutlets, cakes or croquettes.
5. Dip in beaten egg and coat in breadcrumbs. Deep-fry in hot oil.

27. EGG MAYONNAISE

Ingredients:

3 Eggs (hard-boiled)	Tomato
Lettuce hearts	Watercress
Mayonnaise (page 220)	

Servings: 2

Method:

1. Shell and dry eggs. Cut in halves.
2. Arrange prepared lettuce on serving dish.
3. Place eggs on top.
4. Coat with mayonnaise.
5. Decorate with watercress and slices of tomato.

28. FINDON HADDOCK AND POACHED EGG

Ingredients:

1 Findon Haddock *or* smoked Fillet	1 level tablespoonful Flour
150 ml Milk	2 Poached Eggs (page 318)
15 g Butter	2 Bacon rashers

Servings: 2

Time: 10 minutes

Method:

1. Skin fish, cut in pieces.
2. Add to milk and simmer gently.
3. Remove to serving dish, keep hot.
4. Blend flour till smooth with a little milk. Add to rest of milk and boil.
5. Pour over the fish and sprinkle with chopped parsley.
6. Serve with poached eggs or grilled bacon.

Note: This method may be carried out in a baking dish, in the oven for 20 minutes, at 180°C, No. 4.

29. **STUFFED PEPPERS OR AUBERGINES**

Ingredients:

4 Green *or* Red Peppers *or* 2 Aubergines
Tomato Sauce (page 297)

Stuffing:

50 g Macaroni	25 g Breadcrumbs
100 g Cheese (grated)	½ teaspoonful Worcester Sauce
2 tablespoons Tomato Purée	Salt and Pepper

Servings: 4
Time: 30 minutes
Oven Temperature: 180°C, No. 4
Position in Oven: Middle shelf

Method:

1. Boil macaroni till al dente (follow cooking time on packet).
2. Wash the peppers and cut a slice from the top or cut lengthwise, remove the seeds.
   or For aubergines, cut lengthwise and remove some of the pulp. Pulp can then be added to the stuffing.
3. Mix together the ingredients for the stuffing.
4. Fill the peppers or aubergines.
5. Place in a greased ovenproof dish and bake in a moderate oven, 180°C, No. 4, for 30 minutes.
6. Serve with tomato sauce.

Note: An alternative stuffing could be savoury rice (page 333).

30. **STUFFED CUCUMBERS**

Ingredients:

1 Cucumber	250 ml Tomato Sauce (page 297)

Forcemeat:

200 g Sausagemeat	1 teaspoonful Onion (finely chopped)
25 g Breadcrumbs	Seasoning

Method:

1. Mix all the ingredients for the forcemeat together.
2. Wash the cucumber and cut in 5-cm lengths.
3. Scoop out the inside carefully, almost to the bottom.
4. Mix ingredients for forcemeat, add chopped cucumber pulp, fill the cucumber.
5. Cook in tomato sauce about 30 minutes.
6. Serve with tomato sauce poured round.

31. STUFFED VEGETABLE MARROW

Ingredients:

1 Marrow

or Tomato Sauce (page 297)
Brown Sauce (page 293)

Stuffing:

150–200 g Sausagemeat
100 g Breadcrumbs
1 Onion (parboiled)
Pinch Sage

Pinch ground Ginger
Egg to bind
Seasoning

Time: 45 minutes approx.
Oven Temperature: 180°C, No. 4
Position in Oven: Middle shelf

Method:

1. Chop onion, add other ingredients, bind with beaten egg.
2. Peel the marrow, split lengthwise and scoop out the inside.
3. Blanch.
4. Stuff both halves of the marrow with forcemeat.
5. Poach in a covered baking dish or tin with 2.5 cm water, in a moderate oven until tender.
6. Serve with tomato or brown sauce.

Note: Marrow may be cut crosswise into thick rings. Scoop out seeds, not quite to the bottom, and stuff. Savoury rice may be used as an alternative stuffing (page 333). Cook for 20 minutes.

32. STUFFED TOMATOES

Ingredients:

4 large Tomatoes
25 g Butter
½ small Onion (chopped)

100 g lean Bacon (chopped)
4 level tablespoonfuls Breadcrumbs
Salt and Pepper

Servings: 2
Time: 10–15 minutes
Oven Temperature: 180°C, No. 4
Position in Oven: Middle shelf

Method:

1. Wash tomatoes, cut thick slice from rounded end.
2. Remove seeds and centre from tomato.
3. Melt butter, fry chopped onion without browning.
4. Add chopped bacon, cook for 5 minutes.
5. Add tomato pulp, breadcrumbs and seasoning.
6. Fill tomatoes, do not pack tightly.
7. Replace tops, put in baking dish, bake.

33. STUFFED ONIONS

Ingredients:

4 Onions (medium)   Seasoning
100 g Sausagemeat   Cooking Oil

Servings: 2–4
Time: 30–45 minutes
Oven Temperature: 180°C, No. 4
Position in Oven: Middle shelf

Method:

1. Parboil the onions to soften them so that the centres can be removed.
2. Chop the parts from the centres and mix with the sausagemeat and seasoning.
3. Fill the cavities with the sausagemeat mixture.
4. Heat a little cooking oil in a baking tin, put in the onions. Baste well and bake. Baste the onions several times during cooking.
5. Drain well and serve with tomato sauce (page 297) or brown sauce (page 293).

34. CHEESE AND EGG PIE

Ingredients:

100 g Flaky *or* Short Pastry (pages 309, 307) 3 Eggs
150 g Cream Cheese   1 teaspoonful chopped Mint
Seasoning

Servings: 3
Time: 20 minutes
Oven Temperature: 200°C, No. 6
Position in Oven: Middle shelf

Method:

1. Spread cheese on the bottom of a deep ovenproof pie plate.
2. Crack the eggs, drop on top, season.
3. Sprinkle with chopped mint.
4. Roll pastry to cover top. Bake.
Note: May be served cold with salad.

35. CHEESE FLAN

Ingredients:

100 g Short Pastry (page 307)   125 ml Milk
2 level teaspoonfuls Cornflour   50–60 g Cheese (grated)
1 Egg (beaten)   Seasoning

Servings: 3
Time: 20–30 minutes
Oven Temperature: 180°C, No. 4
Position in Oven: Middle shelf
Size of Flan Ring or Deep Pie Plate: 15 cm

Method:

1. Line flan ring or deep pie plate with pastry. Bake for 10 minutes at 200°C, No. 6.
2. Mix cornflour and beaten egg.
3. Add milk and cheese, season.
4. Pour into baked flan case, sprinkle with cheese. Bake for 20 minutes.

36. QUICHE LORRAINE

Quiche Lorraine is made by adding 50 g diced, cooked ham to the above recipe.

37. VEGETABLE FLAN

Ingredients:

Savoury Flan Case (page 308)   Vegetable Filling
250 ml Cheese Sauce (page 291)   25 g Cheese (grated)

Servings: 3–4

Method:

1. Prepare flan case.
2. Fill with suitable vegetable filling (see below).
3. Coat with 250 ml cheese sauce.
4. Sprinkle cheese on top and grill or bake.

Filling variations:

Cauliflower.—1 small cauliflower (cooked and sprigged).
Tomato and Celery.—2 tomatoes (sliced), ½ head celery (cooked).
Tomato and Egg.—2 tomatoes (sliced), 2 hard-boiled eggs (sliced).

38. KIDNEY AND TOMATO FLAN

Ingredients:

Savoury Flan Case (page 308)   150 ml Stock *or* Water
3 Sheep's Kidneys   2 Tomatoes
1 small Onion   25 g seasoned Flour
25 g Butter   Chopped Parsley

Servings: 3–4

Time: 30 minutes stewing, 10–15 minutes baking

Oven Temperature: 180°C, No. 4

Position in Oven: Middle shelf

Method:

1. Prepare flan case.
2. Skin, core and quarter kidneys, dip in flour.
3. Slice onion, fry with kidneys in hot fat.
4. Add stock, stew gently until tender, season.
5. Skin and slice tomatoes, put in flan case, add kidney.
6. Thicken gravy with remainder of the flour blended.
7. Strain over kidneys, heat through in oven. Serve sprinkled with parsley.

39. **CUMBERLAND PIE**

Ingredients:

150 g Short *or* Flaky Pastry (pages 307, 309)   1 Tomato
75 g Bacon   Seasoning
2 Eggs (beaten)

Servings: 4
Time: 30 minutes
Oven Temperature: 220°C, No. 7
Position in Oven: Middle shelf
Size of Flan Ring or Sandwich Tin: 15-cm

Method:

1. Line a sandwich tin or flan ring with half the pastry.
2. Cut bacon into small pieces. Skin tomato (page 202) and slice. Put in flan case.
3. Beat eggs, season and pour over bacon and tomato.
4. Cover with remaining pastry, brush with beaten egg or milk. Bake.

40. **VEGETABLE PIE**

Ingredients:

500 g mixture of seasonable   125 ml Stock *or* Cheese Sauce
   Vegetables, including Peas *or* Beans   Few slices lean Bacon
Tomatoes   150 g Short *or* Oatmeal Pastry
Seasoning   (pages 307, 313)

Time: 30–40 minutes
Oven Temperature: 200°C, No. 6
Position in Oven: Middle shelf

Method:

1. Parboil the vegetables except the tomatoes.
2. Slice the vegetables and put in layers with seasoning and bacon into a pie dish, add a little stock or cheese sauce.
3. Cover with pastry as for steak and kidney pie (page 171).
4. Bake in a hot oven, 200°C, No. 6.

Alternative method using 500 g creamed potatoes instead of pastry:

1. Place potato mixture on top of the vegetables, sprinkle with grated cheese.
2. Bake in a hot oven, 200°C, No. 6, for approximately 30 minutes.

41. SAVOURY PATTIES

Ingredients:

100 g Flaky *or* Rough Puff Pastry (page 309)   1 Egg (beaten)

Fillings:

Russian Fish Pie filling.— (page 69).
Salmon.—1 small tin salmon, 125 ml white sauce (page 291).
Scrambled Egg and Tomato.—3 eggs, 1 tomato.
Mince.— 1 small tin mince, 1 tomato, thicken with 1 teaspoonful cornflour.

Time: 20 minutes
Oven Temperature: 220°C, No. 7
Position in Oven: One-third from top

Method:

1. Prepare filling and cool. Roll pastry thinly and cut rounds and lids to fit patty tins.
2. Line tins, put in filling.
3. Wet edge of pastry and fit on lid.
4. Brush with beaten egg, make a small hole in the centre.
5. Bake for 20 minutes.
6. Serve hot or cold.

42. CHEESE SOUFFLÉ (1)

Ingredients:

250 ml Milk   25 g Butter
25 g Semolina   Salt and Pepper
100 g Cheese (grated)   Mustard
2 Eggs (separated)

Servings: 3
Time: 20–30 minutes
Oven Temperature: 220°C, No. 7
Position in Oven: Middle shelf
Size of Dish: 500 ml

Method:

1. Heat milk, sprinkle in semolina, stir till boiling, simmer for 5 minutes.
2. Add grated cheese, butter, salt, pepper and mustard and egg yolks.
3. Beat whites until stiff and fold through mixture.
4. Put into a deep ovenproof baking dish.
5. Bake till risen and well browned.

43. CHEESE SOUFFLÉ (2)

Ingredients:

10 g Butter	2 Eggs (separated)
10 g Flour ⎱ Panada	50 g Cheese (grated)
125 ml Milk – good measure ⎰	Salt, Pepper, Cayenne

Servings: 2–3
Time: 20 minutes
Oven Temperature: 220°C, No. 7
Position in Oven: Middle shelf
Size of Dish: 500 ml

Method:

1. Melt butter, add flour.
2. Slowly add milk and cook thoroughly.
3. Add egg yolks, seasoning and grated cheese.
4. Fold in stiffly beaten egg whites.
5. Pour into prepared soufflé case or greased ovenproof dish and bake.
6. Serve at once as it falls quickly.

44. CAULIFLOWER AND TOMATO SOUFFLÉ

Ingredients:

25 g Butter	100 g Cheese (grated)
25 g Flour	1 small Cauliflower (cooked)
250 ml Milk	2 small Tomatoes
2 Eggs	Seasoning

Servings: 3–4
Time: 20–30 minutes
Oven Temperature: 220°C, No. 7
Position in Oven: Middle shelf
Size of Dish: 1 litre

Method:

1. Skin and slice tomatoes, sprig cauliflower.
2. Melt butter, add flour, cook a few minutes. Add milk gradually; bring to the boil.
3. Add egg yolks, seasoning, vegetables and two-thirds of the cheese.
4. Fold in stiffly beaten whites.
5. Pour into deep baking dish; sprinkle with remainder of cheese.
6. Bake, serve immediately.

45. SPINACH SOUFFLÉ

Ingredients:

25 g Butter	Seasoning
25 g Flour ⎱ Panada	2 Egg Yolks
125 ml Spinach Purée ⎰	3 Egg Whites

Servings: 3
Time: 20–30 minutes
Oven Temperature: 220°C, No. 7
Position in Oven: Middle shelf

Method:

1. Melt butter, add flour, then gradually add spinach purée.
2. Cook until thick.
3. Beat in egg yolks, fold in stiffly beaten whites.
4. Put into a greased ovenproof dish.
5. Bake until well risen and firm on top.

46. HAM BALLS

Ingredients:

200 g Potatoes	Seasoning
100 g Ham (cooked, chopped)	Breadcrumbs
25 g Butter	2 Eggs (beaten)

Servings: 2–3

Method:

1. Boil and mash potatoes.
2. Add butter, chopped ham and seasoning. Beat.
3. Add half of beaten egg. Mix well.
4. Roll into balls. Dip in rest of beaten egg and coat in breadcrumbs. Fry in hot fat until golden brown.

47. STUFFED HAM SLICES

Ingredients:

50 g Mushrooms	1 Egg (hard-boiled, chopped)
15 g Butter	1 teaspoonful chopped Parsley
1 level tablespoonful Flour	4 thin slices Ham (cooked)
125 ml Milk *or* Stock	250 ml Cheese Sauce (page 291)
Seasoning	

Servings: 3–4
Time: 15 minutes
Oven Temperature: 180°C, No. 4
Position in Oven: Middle shelf

Method:

1. Wash and chop mushrooms.
2. Melt butter, fry mushrooms slowly until soft.
3. Add flour, stir through, add milk, boil.
4. Season, add chopped egg, and parsley.
5. Place some mixture on ham slices, roll up.
6. Put on a baking dish.
7. Pour cheese sauce over. Bake 15 minutes.

---

48. **NUT ROLL**

Ingredients:

150 g ground Nuts
100 g Breadcrumbs
1 small Onion (chopped)
Pinch Herbs

Seasoning
50 g Butter (melted)
1 Egg (beaten)

Method:

1. Mix all dry ingredients including chopped onion.
2. Add melted butter and beaten egg.
3. Pack into a greased, rimless jar or cocoa tin.
4. Steam for 1 hour 30 minutes. Serve hot with a suitable sauce, or cold with salad.

---

49. **MOUSSAKA**

Ingredients:

250 g Mince
Seasoning
Worcester Sauce *or* Tomato Purée
1 Onion
Fat for frying

1 medium Aubergine (sliced)
125 g Potatoes (raw *or* parboiled, sliced)
250 ml Cheese Sauce (page 291)
1 tablespoonful Cheese (grated)

Servings: 3–4
Time: 40–60 minutes
Oven Temperature: 180°C, No. 4
Position in Oven: Middle shelf

Method:

1. Fry sliced aubergine lightly.
2. Chop onion, fry and add mince, brown in frying pan for 10 minutes. Add 1–2 teaspoonfuls Worcester sauce or tomato purée.
3. Put mince, potatoes, and aubergine in alternate layers in an ovenproof casserole.
4. Pour cheese sauce over, sprinkle a little grated cheese on top and put in oven.

---

50. **SPAGHETTI BOLOGNESE**

Ingredients:

250 g Mince
25 g Butter *or* 1 dessertspoonful Oil
75 g Mushrooms (sliced)
25 g Parmesan Cheese (grated)
25 g Bacon (chopped)
400 g tinned Tomatoes
Seasoning

1 Onion (chopped)
1 shredded Carrot (optional)
1 clove Garlic (crushed)
250 ml Stock
Pinch Mixed Herbs
1 tablespoonful Tomato Purée
150 g Spaghetti

Servings: 3–4

Method:

1. Melt butter and fry onion, carrot and mushrooms gently for 4–5 minutes.
2. Add mince and chopped bacon and brown thoroughly.
3. Add tomato purée, tinned tomatoes, crushed garlic, stock, seasonings. Simmer for 30 minutes to 1 hour. Stir occasionally.
4. Cook spaghetti in boiling, salted water for 10–15 minutes. Drain.
5. Put spaghetti on a hot dish and pour the sauce on top. Sprinkle with Parmesan cheese.

51. **PIZZA PIE**

Yeast base (1)
Ingredients:

200 g Flour	125 ml lukewarm Water (approx.)
15 g Yeast *or* 7 g Dried Yeast (page 363)	
1 level teaspoonful Sugar	1 level teaspoonful Salt

Pizzas: 2
Time: 20 minutes
Oven Temperature: 230°C, No. 8
Position in Oven: One-third from top

Method:

1. Add salt to flour. Warm.
2. Dissolve sugar in lukewarm liquid. Sprinkle in yeast and leave to froth. (See page 363 for use of dried yeast.)
3. Add to flour along with any remaining liquid and knead until smooth.
4. Put to rise in a warm place to double size.
5. Topping: prepare as necessary.
6. Turn out dough and knead well. Cut in half and roll into 2 circles 1 cm thick, put well apart on a greased baking tray.
7. Put to rise 10 minutes.
8. Cover with topping.
9. Bake in a hot oven, 230°C, No. 8 for 20 minutes.

Scone base (2)
Ingredients:

200 g self-raising Flour
½ level teaspoonful Salt
50 g Butter
125 ml Milk

Pizzas: 2
Time: 20 minutes
Oven Temperature: 220°C, No. 7
Position in Oven: One-third from top

Method:

1. Prepare topping.
2. Rub butter into flour and salt.

3. Mix to an elastic consistency with milk.

4. Divide into two and roll out into 2 rounds 1 cm thick.

5. Cover with topping.

6. Bake for 20 minutes.

Toppings
Ingredients:

Medium tin Tomatoes (drained)   1 teaspoonful Herbs
100–150 g thick sliced *or* grated Cheese
Arrange topping and cover dough to give an even distribution.

Additions:

A few olives or capers, kipper fillets, sardines, anchovies, ham, fried onions, fried mushrooms, garlic.

52. TOAD-IN-A-HOLE

Ingredients:

200 g Sausages *or* cold Meat   250 ml Yorkshire Pudding Batter (page 475)
Seasoning   Oil *or* Dripping to coat bottom of tin

Servings: 3
Time: 30 minutes approx.
Oven Temperature: 220°C, No. 7
Position in Oven: Middle shelf

Method:

1. Preheat a roasting tin with oil or dripping in it till fat is smoking.

2. Skin sausages or chop meat. Place in bottom of roasting tin. Return to oven and allow sausages to colour.

3. Remove. Pour batter over, bake till puffed up and golden brown.

Note: To remove excess fat, place sausages in cold water and bring to the boil before skinning.

53. SAUSAGE IN CUSTARD

Ingredients:

250 g Sausages   500 ml Milk
2–3 Eggs   Seasoning

Servings: 3
Time: 45 minutes
Oven Temperature: 180°C, No. 4
Position in Oven: Middle shelf

Method:

1. Put sausages in a greased ovenproof dish.

2. Heat milk slightly, pour over beaten egg, season and strain over sausages.

3. Bake till set and brown.

Note: To remove excess fat, place sausages in cold water and bring to the boil before skinning.

54. **PAN HAGGIS OR SKIRLIE**

Ingredients:

100 g Suet (Vegetable *or* Beef)	200 g Oatmeal
1 Onion (chopped)	Seasoning

Method:

1. Chop suet finely, melt slowly in a saucepan.
2. Add onion, fry lightly.
3. Add oatmeal and seasoning, cover pan.
4. Cook slowly for 20 minutes, stirring occasionally.

Note: Can be served with mince, poached egg, Findon haddock, etc.

55. **WHITE PUDDINGS**

Ingredients:

Pudding Skins	1 Onion
100 g Suet	Seasoning
200 g Oatmeal	

Time: 2 hours

Method:

1. Thoroughly cleanse skins by washing in cold water, turning outside in, rinsing and leaving overnight in cold water.
2. Chop suet finely, add to oatmeal and grated onion. Season.
3. Cut skins into suitable lengths and fill two-thirds full; tie in circles.
4. Prick well and cook in boiling water for 2 hours.

Note: If liked the mixture may be pressed into a bowl and steamed.

SANDWICHES

SANDWICH FILLINGS

TYPES OF SANDWICHES

SANDWICHES

Bread for sandwiches should be as fresh as possible.

A sliced loaf gives approximately 26 slices and requires 150 g of butter to spread.

Brown bread is more suitable for sweet fillings. Rough brown bread should be avoided as it crumbles when thinly cut.

If crusts are to be removed, this is best done when sandwiches have been made and several layers piled on top of one another.

Butter should always be softened before spreading and all fillings should be of a spreading consistency.

If sandwiches are to be made up some time beforehand, wrap in foil, a clean damp cloth or place in a polythene bag, and leave in refrigerator.

SANDWICH FILLINGS

Suitable for Bread, or Rolls

1. CHEESE AND EGG

Ingredients:

25 g Cheese	1 teaspoonful made Mustard
1 Egg (hard-boiled)	Salt and Pepper
25 g Butter	1 tablespoonful Chopped Parsley

Method:

1. Grate cheese.
2. Pound egg with a fork until fine.
3. Soften butter, mix in all ingredients.

2. CREAM CHEESE AND CELERY

Ingredients:

3 tablespoonfuls Cream Cheese	2 stalks Celery
3 Walnut halves (finely chopped)	Salt and Pepper
2 tablespoonfuls Cream	

Method:

1. Mix cheese and walnuts, add cream, beat.
2. Season, add finely chopped celery.

3. CUCUMBER SANDWICHES

Ingredients:

Piece of Cucumber   Salt
Mayonnaise

Method:

1. Slice cucumber very thinly.
2. Spread bread with butter, then mayonnaise.
3. Cover with cucumber; sprinkle with salt.

4. SALMON AND CUCUMBER

Ingredients:

or 125 g Cooked Salmon   1 teaspoonful Mint Jelly (optional)
1 tin Salmon   Salt and Pepper
Piece of Cucumber   Mayonnaise (page 220) to bind

Method:

1. Pound salmon. If tinned, drain, remove bones and pound.
2. Chop cucumber finely.
3. Mix all ingredients, beat until smooth.

5. EGG AND TOMATO

Ingredients:

25 g Butter   Salt and Pepper
1 Egg (hard-boiled)   1 large Tomato (skinned)

Method:

1. Soften butter.
2. Break down egg, using a fork.
3. Skin tomato, remove seeds, chop.
4. Beat egg and tomato well into butter. Season.

6. SARDINE AND EGG

Ingredients:

1 tin Sardines   ½ teaspoonful Worcester
1 Egg (hard-boiled)   Sauce
Salt and Pepper

Method:

1. Remove tail and bone from sardines.
2. Break egg down finely with a fork.
3. Mix sardines and egg, add seasoning and sauce.

7. HAM AND MAYONNAISE

Ingredients:

100 g cooked Gammon *or* tinned Luncheon Meat
1 large Tomato

Mayonnaise (page 220) to bind
Salt and Pepper

Method:

1. Chop luncheon meat finely.
2. Skin tomato, de-seed and chop.
3. Mix luncheon meat and tomato; season. Add mayonnaise to bind.

8. SHRIMP AND TOMATO

Ingredients:

or 100 g cooked Shrimps
1 tin Shrimps
2 Tomatoes (skinned)

25 g Butter
Salt and Pepper

Method:

1. Chop shrimps and tomatoes finely.
2. Cream butter, beat in shrimps, tomato and seasoning.

9. CRABS AND CRESS

Ingredients:

1 tin Crab Meat
1 punnet Fine Cress

2 tablespoonfuls Cream
Salt and Pepper

Method:

1. Drain and chop crab, chop cress.
2. Beat cream until thick, almost butter consistency.
3. Fold in cress, crab and seasoning.

10. OTHER SUGGESTED FILLINGS

Savoury fillings:

Hard-boiled Egg and Cress
Scrambled Egg and Grated Cheese
Scrambled Egg with Chopped Shrimp
Chopped Cooked Gammon, Hard-boiled Egg and Mayonnaise
Lettuce and Tomato
Tongue and Cucumber
Sardine and Cliced Tomato
Cream Cheese, chopped Apple and Walnut
Grated Cheese, Chutney and chopped Celery

Sweet fillings (best for brown bread):

Chopped Dates, preserved Ginger and grated Apple
Chopped Dates, mashed Bananas

Lemon Curd, grated Apple, Brown Sugar
Chopped hard-boiled Egg, Banana and Walnut
Cream Cheese with Blackcurrant Jam and chopped Walnut
Chopped preserved Ginger and whipped Cream

TYPES OF SANDWICHES

11. LAYERED SANDWICHES

These may be made using brown and white bread in four alternate layers with filling. Press well together. They may be cut into small triangles or squares.

12. BRIDGE ROLL SANDWICHES

Any suitable filling may be used.
They may be closed or open. If open, spread filling liberally on halved rolls. Decorate with parsley, cucumber etc.

13. ROLLED SANDWICHES

1. Cut bread thinly, remove crust, roll lightly with a rolling pin to prevent cracking.
2. Spread with creamed butter.
3. Spread filling thinly on buttered side of bread, roll up tightly.
4. Keep in a damp muslin or polythene bag.
5. If a large loaf is used, rolls may require to be cut in half.
Note: Fillings on page 357, recipe 10, are equally suitable for rolled sandwiches.

14. ASPARAGUS ROLLS

Ingredients:

1 tin Asparagus Tips	1 tablespoonful Mayonnaise (page 220)
(or boiled, fresh Asparagus Tips)	50 g Butter

Method:

1. Drain asparagus.
2. Cream butter, work in mayonnaise.
3. Cut bread thinly, remove crust, roll lightly with a rolling pin to prevent cracking.
4. Spread with creamed butter.
5. Put one or two tips on edge of bread, roll up tightly.
6. Keep in a damp muslin or polythene bag.
7. If large loaf is used, rolls may require to be cut in half.
Note: Fillings on page 357, recipe 10, are equally suitable for rolled sandwiches.

15. **PINWHEEL SANDWICHES**

1. Make as for rolled sandwiches (page 358).
2. Bread should be soft and cut thinly lengthwise.
3. Spread filling over the buttered bread.
4. Roll tightly then place in a damp cloth and leave for 30 minutes.
5. Cut in slices.
6. Hold together with cocktail sticks.

16. **TOASTED SANDWICHES**

Bread should be thin and fillings previously cooked.

Mushroom and Bacon
Ingredients:

4 Bacon rashers	Pinch Mustard
50 g Mushrooms	Seasoning

Method:

1. Chop bacon and mushrooms, fry.
2. Mix with mustard and seasoning.
3. Put between buttered bread.
4. Place under the grill and toast on both sides.

Other suitable fillings:

Scrambled Egg and Cheese
Scrambled Egg and Cooked Fish
Flaked Kipper, Tomato and Mustard
Findon Haddock and grated Cheese
Slices of Cheese and Tomato (not previously cooked)
Tinned Sardine and Chopped Gherkin (not previously cooked)

17. **OPEN SANDWICHES**

An open sandwich is a breakfast, supper or snack dish that can consist of 1 slice of bread, half a bagel, half a roll, or half a muffin, with a topping. It is usually eaten with a knife and fork. For this reason, soft bread rather than crusty is best for open sandwiches.

Typical toppings:

Cooked Meat
Sliced Cheese
Prawn Marie Rose
Sliced Hard-boiled Eggs
Sliced Tomato
Salad Leaves

BAKING

YEAST MIXTURES

SCONES

CAKES

SMALL CAKES

BISCUITS

YEAST MIXTURES

In the recipes below, where yeast is indicated in the ingredients this is compressed fresh yeast. This may be difficult to find, though it is possible if you ask for some at the bakery section of your local supermarket.

Fresh yeast can be successfully substituted with dried active yeast. With dried yeast, half the amount of the weight of the fresh yeast indicated in the recipe is the usual proportion, however as different brands of yeast vary in how quick-acting they are and how they are activated, please follow the manufacturer's instructions on the tin or packet.

In the recipes below, each yeast mixture's method, step 2, refers to the activation of fresh yeast. When using dried yeast, substitute the manufacturer's instructions for step 2 of the method. This is because of some differences in the activation of dried yeast. Dried yeast may need the temperature of the liquid in which it is activated to be slightly higher than the liquid which will activate fresh yeast (just above body temperature). In addition, some "easy-blend" or "fast-action" dried yeasts may simply be added to the dry ingredients without the need for activation with warm liquid and sugar.

To test if ready, tip out onto a gloved hand and tap. The bread shold sound hollow.

1. WHITE BREAD

Ingredients:

500 g Strong *or* Bread Flour	1 level teaspoonful Sugar
2 level teaspoonfuls Salt	250 ml lukewarm Water (approx.)

15 g fresh Yeast *or* 7 g Dried Yeast (see note on dried yeast, above)

Time: 30–40 minutes

Oven Temperature: 230°C, No. 8

Position in Oven: Middle shelf

Method:

1. Add salt to flour, warm in a low oven.
2. Dissolve sugar in half the warm liquid. Sprinkle in yeast and leave to froth. (See note on use of dried yeast, above.)
3. Add to flour along with the remaining liquid, to make an elastic dough. Knead well until smooth and leaves sides of bowl.
4. Cover bowl with a plate or put dough in a plastic bag; put in a warm place to rise for 1 hour, or until double the size.
5. Turn out and knead well.
6. Shape into 2 loaves, place in warm greased bread tins, three-quarters full, or one large bread tin three-quarters full.
7. Cover again; leave to prove (i.e. rise) until at top of tin.
8. Place in hot oven. Then reduce heat to 190°C, No. 5 and bake for 30–40 minutes , or 1 hour if one tin, until brown and crisp

Note: The addition of 25 g cooking fat or butter rubbed into each 500 g flour makes the bread keep moist for a longer time.

2. BROWN BREAD

Ingredients:

400 g Wholemeal Flour
100 g Strong *or* Bread Flour
2 level teaspoonfuls Salt
15 g Cooking Fat

15 g fresh Yeast *or* 7 g Dried Yeast
   (see note on dried yeast, page 363)
1 level teaspoonful Sugar
250 ml lukewarm Water *or* Milk and
   Water, mixed (approx.)

Time: 30–40 minutes
Oven Temperature: 230°C, No. 8
Position in Oven: Middle shelf

Method:

Make as for white bread (page 363).

3. BROWN BREAD (ONE RISING)

Ingredients:

400 g Wholemeal Flour
100 g Flour
15 g Cooking Fat
250 ml lukewarm Water *or* Milk and
   Water, mixed (approx.)

15 g Yeast *or* 7 g Dried Yeast (see
   note on dried yeast, page 363)
1 level teaspoonful Sugar
2 level teaspoonfuls Salt

Time: 30–40 minutes
Oven Temperature: 230°C, No. 8
Position in Oven: Middle shelf

Method:

1. Mix flours, add salt, warm in a low oven.
2. Rub in cooking fat.
3. Dissolve sugar in half the warm liquid. Sprinkle in yeast and leave to froth. (See note on use of dried yeast, page 363.)
4. Add to flour along with remaining liquid to make an elastic dough. Knead well until smooth.
5. Shape into 2 loaves, place in warm greased bread tins, three-quarters full.
6. Cover and leave to prove until dough reaches top of tin.
7. Place in a hot oven. Reduce heat to 190°C, No. 5 and bake until brown and crisp on top.

4. FRENCH BREAD (1)

Ingredients:

500 g Strong *or* Bread Flour
2 level teaspoonfuls Salt
2 level teaspoonfuls Sugar
50 g Butter

15 g fresh Yeast *or* 7 g Dried Yeast (see
   note on dried yeast, page 363)
250 ml lukewarm Milk (approx.)

Time: 45–60 minutes
Oven Temperature: 220°C, No. 7; 180°C, No. 4
Position in Oven: Middle shelf

Method:

1. Add salt to flour, warm in a low oven.
2. Dissolve sugar in half the warm milk. Sprinkle in yeast and leave to froth. (See note on use of dried yeast, page 363.)
3. Rub in butter.
4. Add to flour along with remaining milk to make an elastic dough, knead well.
5. Cover, put to rise.
6. Re-knead, put into greased warm tin, three-quarters full.
7. Prove until dough fills tin.
8. Place in a hot oven. Reduce heat to 180°C, No. 4 and bake until brown and crisp on top.

5. FRENCH BREAD (2)

Ingredients:

500 g Strong *or* Bread Flour
2 level teaspoonfuls Salt
25 g Butter
15 g Yeast *or* 7 g Dried Yeast (see note on dried yeast, page 363)

2 level teaspoonfuls Sugar
250 ml Milk (approx.)
1 Egg (beaten)

Time: 20–30 minutes
Oven Temperature: 220°C, No. 7
Position in Oven: Middle shelf

Method:

1. Add salt to flour; warm in a low oven.
2. Warm milk and butter to blood heat, add sugar and sprinkle in yeast. Leave to froth. (See note on use of dried yeast, page 363.)
3. Add liquid to beaten egg, add to flour and mix to elastic dough, knead well.
4. Cover, allow to rise until double the size.
5. Knead, shape into two round loaves or plaits.
6. Put on greased tin, make cut across top of loaves.
7. Prove for 10 minutes, brush with beaten egg.
8. Bake in a hot oven for 15–20 minutes.

6. YORKSHIRE TEA CAKES

Ingredients:

Dough as for French Bread (2)

Quantity: 6 Cakes
Time: 12–15 minutes
Oven Temperature: 220°C, No. 7
Position in Oven: One-third from top

Method:
1. Make dough and put to rise.
2. Knead until smooth, divide into six.
3. Shape into 6 flat, round tea cakes, put on greased tin.
4. Prove for 10 minutes then bake in a hot oven until brown and crisp on top.
5. While hot, rub tops with a buttered paper.

Note: 25 g currants may be added to the dough while kneading.

7. **DINNER ROLLS**

Ingredients:

Dough as for French Bread (1)

Quantity: 6 rolls
Time: 10–15 minutes
Oven Temperature: 220°C, No. 7
Position in Oven: One-third from top

Method:
1. Make dough and put to rise.
2. Knead until smooth, roll out 1 cm thick.
3. Cut into rounds or form into shapes, prove on greased tin.
4. Bake in a hot oven till brown and crisp on top.
5. While hot, rub tops with a buttered paper or brush with egg before baking.

8. **CHELSEA BUNS**

Ingredients:

250 g Strong *or* Bread Flour	1 level teaspoonful Salt
40 g Butter	1 level teaspoonful Sugar
125 ml Milk (approx.)	15 g Yeast *or* 7 g Dried Yeast (see note on dried yeast, page 363)

Filling:

40 g Sugar	40 g Currants

Quantity: 8–10 buns
Time: 15 minutes
Oven Temperature: 220°C, No. 7
Position in Oven: One-third from top

Method:
1. Add salt to flour, warm in a low oven.
2. Warm milk and butter to blood heat, add sugar and sprinkle in yeast. Leave to froth. (See note on use of dried yeast, page 363.)
3. Add to flour, mix to elastic dough, knead.
4. Allow to rise until double in size.
5. Knead, roll into a square 1 cm thick.
6. Sprinkle with sugar and currants, roll up, cut in pieces 3 cm thick.
7. Stand on greased tin, cut side up.
8. Prove for 10 minutes, brush with egg, bake for 15 minutes.

9. DOUGHNUTS (YEAST)

Ingredients:

250 g Strong *or* Bread Flour	I level teaspoonful Salt
25 g Sugar	25 g Butter
125 ml Milk and I Egg (beaten)	Oil for Deep-frying
15 g Yeast *or* 7 g Dried Yeast	Castor Sugar and a little Cinnamon

Quantity: 8–10 doughnuts

Time: Around 5–6 minutes

Method:

1. Add salt to flour, warm in a low oven.
2. Warm milk to blood heat, add sugar and sprinkle in yeast. Leave to froth. (See note on use of dried yeast, page 363.)
3. Rub butter into flour.
4. Add milk and yeast to beaten egg, add to flour and mix to an elastic dough.
5. Knead until smooth, put to rise.
6. Knead, roll out I cm thick, cut into rings.
7. Put on a warmed greased tin, prove for 10 minutes.
8. Deep-fry in hot oil for 5–6 minutes or until golden brown.
9. Drain, toss in castor sugar and a little cinnamon.

10. HOT CROSS BUNS

Ingredients:

250 g Dough, as Yeast Doughnuts	I level teaspoonful Spice
25 g Short Pastry, rolled out very thinly (page 307)	

Quantity: 8–10 buns   **Time:** 15 minutes

Oven Temperature: 220°C, No. 7

Position in Oven: One-third from top

Method:

1. Make dough as for yeast doughnuts, adding I teaspoon spice, and put to rise.
2. Knead until smooth, form into buns.
3. Place buns on a warmed, greased tin, prove for 10 minutes.
4. Brush with egg and place a cross of uncooked pastry on top.
5. Bake in a hot oven for 15 minutes.

11. SALLY LUNN

Ingredients:

300 g Strong *or* Bread Flour	2 level teaspoonfuls Sugar
I level teaspoonful Salt	15 g Yeast *or* 7 g Dried Yeast (see note on dried yeast, page 363)
50 g Butter	
I Egg (beaten)	125 ml Lukewarm Milk

Glazing syrup:

I tablespoonful Sugar ⎫ Dissolve and bring to boiling point,
I tablespoonful Milk ⎭ then remove from the heat.

Time: 20 minutes
Oven Temperature: 220°C, No. 7
Position in Oven: One-third from top
Size of Tins: Two 15-cm tins

Method:

1. Add salt to flour, warm in a low oven.
2. Warm milk and butter to blood heat, add sugar and sprinkle in yeast. Leave to froth. (See note on use of dried yeast, page 363.)
3. Add liquid to beaten egg, add to flour and mix to an elastic dough and knead well.
4. Divide dough in two, put into well-greased tins.
5. Set to rise for 1 hour, bake in hot oven for 20–30 minutes.
6. Brush with glazing syrup.

Note: 50 g mixed dried fruit may be added.

12. YEAST RING

Ingredients:

250 g Dough as for French Bread (2)
Time: 20 minutes
Oven Temperature: 220°C, No. 7
Position in Oven: One-third from top

Method:

1. Make dough and put to rise. Knead and form into a roll, wet the ends and stick together to form a ring.
2. Place on a greased tin, allow to rise well for 10 minutes.
3. Bake in a hot oven for 20–30 minutes. Glaze with glazing syrup (see Sally Lunn Bread, page 367).

Note: Before proving, the ring may be snipped in a slanting direction, with scissors, at intervals of about 4 cm. Alternatively, it may be brushed over with butter and sprinkled with cinnamon or chopped nuts.

13. CROISSANTS

Ingredients:

250 g Flour	150 ml Milk
½ level teaspoonful Salt	1 Egg (beaten)
15g Yeast *or* 7 g Dried Yeast (see note on dried yeast, page 363)	30 g Butter
	Apricot Jam (optional)
25g Sugar	Icing Sugar for dredging (optional)

Quantity: 12 croissants
Time: 15 minutes
Oven Temperature: 220°C, No. 7, lowering to 190°C, No. 5
Position in Oven: One-third from top

Method:

1. Warm flour and salt and 20 g of sugar in a low oven.
2. Warm milk, add 5 g sugar and sprinkle in yeast. Leave to froth. (See note on use of dried yeast, page 363.)
3. Pour liquid over half of beaten egg, add to flour, knead well and put to rise.
4. Re-knead and roll into a strip.
5. Divide butter into three and, using one-third, cover two-thirds of the strip with small pats of butter (A).
5. Fold in three (B), quarter turn and roll out. Repeat twice using remaining two-thirds of the butter.
6. Cover and place in fridge for 1 hour.
7. Roll into a strip and cut into triangles (C). Wet corners and roll up from wide edge to point (D and E).
8. Shape into croissants (F); place on a warmed, greased baking tray and prove for 10 minutes. Brush with rest of beaten egg.
9. Bake in a hot oven for 5 minutes and then lower to 190°C, No. 5, for 10 minutes.

Note: May be brushed with warm apricot jam and then dredged with icing sugar.

A.   B.

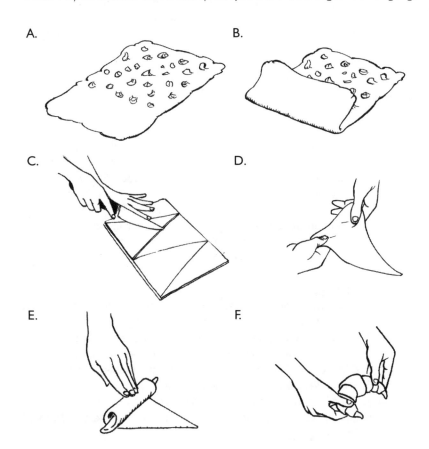

C.   D.

E.   F.

14. GRISSINI BREAD

Ingredients:

500 g Strong *or* Bread Flour	1 level teaspoonful Sugar
2 level teaspoonfuls Salt	3–4 tablespoonfuls Milk
25 g Butter	Lukewarm Water to mix

15 g Yeast *or* 7 g Dried Yeast (see note on dried yeast, page 363)

Time: 15–20 minutes
Oven Temperature: 190°C, No. 5
Position in Oven: One-third from top

Method:

1. Add salt to flour, warm in a low oven.
2. Warm milk, add sugar and sprinkle in yeast. Leave to froth. (See note on use of dried yeast, page 363.)
3. Rub butter into flour.
4. Add yeast mixture to flour along with lukewarm water to make a stiff dough. Knead.
5. Cover and allow to rise 1 hour 30 minutes.
6. Knead. Divide into pieces and roll out into long thin sticks.
7. Bake at once in a moderate oven till crisp.

Note: Salt sticks are made similarly – brush with milk and sprinkle with salt.

15. YULE CAKE

Ingredients:

500 g Strong *or* White Flour	250 ml Milk
1 level teaspoonful Salt	1 Egg
100 g Butter	20g Yeast *or* 10 g Dried Yeast (see
100g Sugar	note on dried yeast, page 363)
½ level teaspoonful Nutmeg	300–350 g Sultanas
50 g Candied Peel	

Time: 50–60 minutes
Oven Temperature: 200°C, No. 6; lowering to 180°C, No. 4
Position in Oven: Middle shelf
Size of Tin: 20 cm

Method:

1. Beat egg.
2. Warm milk, add one teaspoonful of sugar, sprinkle in yeast. Leave to froth. (See note on use of dried yeast, page 363.)
3. Sieve flour and salt, rub in butter, add remainder of sugar.
4. Pour liquid over beaten egg, add to flour and knead well.
5. Allow to rise from 50–60 minutes or until double in size.
6. Knead well, work in fruit and nutmeg.
7. Place in greased tin and allow to prove.
8. Bake in a hot oven until lightly browned, reduce heat to 180°C, No. 4 and finish cooking.

16. **CRUMPETS (YEAST)**

Ingredients:

100 g Strong *or* Bread Flour   I level teaspoonful Sugar
½ level teaspoonful Salt   125 ml Milk – short measure
15 g Butter   I Egg
10 g yeast *or* 5 g Dried Yeast (see note on dried yeast, page 363)

Method:

1. Add salt to flour, warm.
2. Warm milk to blood heat, add sugar, sprinkle in yeast. Leave to froth. (See note on use of dried yeast, page 363.)
3. Rub butter into flour and add yeast liquid to egg.
4. Add gradually to flour, beat well.
5. Allow to stand for 40 minutes in a warm place.
6. Drop the mixture onto a hot girdle or non-stick frying pan.
7. Bake on both sides until lightly browned.

SCONES

17. **AVERAGE PROPORTIONS**

1.   400 g Self-raising Flour
   or $\begin{cases} 400 \text{ g Flour} \\ 6 \text{ level teaspoonfuls Baking Powder} \end{cases}$
   Milk

2.   400 g Flour
   2 level teaspoonfuls Bicarbonate of Soda
   4 level teaspoonfuls Cream of Tartar
   Milk

3.   400 g Flour
   2 level teaspoonfuls Bicarbonate of Soda
   2 level teaspoonfuls Cream of Tartar
   Buttermilk

To the above, butter and fruits in the proportion of 50–100 g to each 400 g of flour may be used.

18. **MILK ROLLS**

Ingredients:

200 g Self-raising Flour   I level teaspoonful Salt
25 g Butter *or* Block Margarine   Milk

Time: 15 minutes
Oven Temperature: 220°C, No. 7
Position in Oven: One-third from top

Method:

1. Sieve dry ingredients and rub in butter.
2. Add milk and mix to a light, elastic dough.
3. Shape into rolls.
4. Bake in a hot oven for 15 minutes.

19. SODA BREAD

Ingredients:

200 g Self-raising Flour	1 level teaspoonful Salt
or { 200 g Flour 1 level teaspoonful Bicarbonate of Soda 2 level teaspoonfuls Cream of Tartar	125 ml Milk

Time: 30 minutes
Oven Temperature: 190°C, No. 5
Position in Oven: Middle shelf

Method:

1. Sieve all dry ingredients. Add milk and mix to a light, elastic dough.
2. Shape into a round and place on a greased tin. Make two cuts on top.
3. Bake in a moderate oven for 30–40 minutes.

20. GIRDLE SCONES

Ingredients:

200 g Self-raising Flour	1 level teaspoonful Salt
or { 200 g Flour 1 level teaspoonful Bicarbonate of Soda 2 level teaspoonfuls Cream of Tartar	125 ml Milk (or if using Buttermilk use 1 level teaspoonful Cream of Tartar)

Time: 6–8 minutes

Method:

1. Heat the girdle, or a heavy-based, non-stick frying pan, slowly.
2. Sieve dry ingredients, add milk and mix to a light, elastic dough. Divide dough into two pieces.
3. Roll out thinly into a circle on a floured board. Cut into four.
4. Cook on a fairly hot girdle or a non-stick frying pan, allowing 3–4 minutes per side.
5. Cool in a towel.

Note: 25–50 g butter or block margarine may be rubbed into the ingredients if liked.

21. **MUFFINS**

Ingredients:

200 g Self-raising Flour   25 g Sugar
or { 200 g Flour   50 g Butter *or* Block Margarine
       1 level teaspoonful Bicarbonate of Soda   (melted)
       2 level teaspoonfuls Cream of Tartar   1 Egg (beaten)
½ level teaspoonful Salt   Milk to mix

Time: 8–10 minutes

Method:

1. Sieve dry ingredients.
2. Add beaten egg and butter.
3. Add milk and mix to a light, elastic dough.
4. Roll out 1 cm thick, cut in rounds.
5. Cook on heated girdle, for 4–5 minutes each side.

22. **SWEET MILK SCONES**

Ingredients:

200 g Self-raising Flour   25–50 g Sugar
or { 200 g Flour   25–50 g Butter *or* Block Margarine
       1 level teaspoonful Bicarbonate of Soda   125 ml Milk
       2 level teaspoonfuls Cream of Tartar
1 level teaspoonful Salt

Time: 8–10 minutes
Oven Temperature: 230°C, No. 8
Position in Oven: One-third from top

Method:

1. Sieve dry ingredients.
2. Rub in butter, add milk and mix to a light, elastic dough.
3. Turn onto a floured surface, work lightly.
4. Roll out 2 cm thick.
5. Cut out, place on baking tray.
6. Bake in a hot oven for 8–10 minutes.

Note: Scones may be dusted with flour before baking or glazed with egg or milk.

23. **SULTANA SCONES**

To make sultana scones, follow the sweet milk scones recipe, above, to which 25–50 g sultanas can be added after the butter or block margarine has been rubbed in.

24. **WHEATEN SCONES**

Ingredients:

150 g Wholemeal Flour	I level teaspoonful Salt
50 g Flour	25 g Sugar
I level teaspoonful Bicarbonate of Soda	25 g Butter *or* Block Margarine
2 level teaspoonfuls Cream of Tartar	125 ml Milk

Time: 8–10 minutes

Method:

1. Mix dry ingredients and continue as sweet milk scones (page 373).

25. **WHOLEMEAL BREAD**

Ingredients:

150 g Wholemeal Flour	I level teaspoonful Salt
50 g Flour	25 g Butter *or* Block Margarine
3 level teaspoonfuls Baking Powder	I dessertspoonful Golden Syrup
or {I level teaspoonful Bicarbonate of Soda	Milk to mix
{2 level teaspoonfuls Cream of Tartar	

Time: 20–30 minutes

Oven Temperature: 190°C, No. 5

Position in Oven: Middle shelf

Method:

1. Mix dry ingredients.
2. Rub in butter, add syrup and milk to make an elastic dough.
3. Put into a well-greased cylindrical tin or bread tin. Cover with a lid or baking tin.
4. Bake in a moderate oven for 20–30 minutes. Remove from tin.

26. **TREACLE SCONES**

Ingredients:

200 g Self-raising Flour	I level teaspoonful Salt
{200 g Flour	25 g Sugar
or {I level teaspoonful Bicarbonate of Soda	25 g Butter *or* Block Margarine
{2 level teaspoonfuls Cream of Tartar	I tablespoonful Treacle
I level teaspoonful Cinnamon	Milk to mix
I level teaspoonful Mixed Spice	

Time: 8–10 minutes

Oven Temperature: 230°C, No. 8

Position in Oven: One-third from top

Method:

1. Sieve dry ingredients.
2. Rub in butter, add treacle and milk to make a light, elastic dough.
3. Turn onto floured surface, work lightly until smooth.
4. Roll 2 cm thick, cut out, put on baking tin.
5. Bake in a hot oven for 8–10 minutes.

27. CHEESE SCONES

Ingredients:

200 g Self-raising Flour   Shake of Pepper

or { 200 g Flour / 1 level teaspoonful Bicarbonate of Soda / 2 level teaspoonfuls Cream of Tartar }   25 g Butter *or* Block Margarine / 75–100 g Grated Cheese / 125 ml Milk

1 level teaspoonful Salt

Time: 8–10 minutes

Oven Temperature: 230°C, No. 8

Position in Oven: One-third from top

Method:

1. Sieve dry ingredients.
2. Rub in butter and add grated cheese.
3. Add milk and mix to a light, elastic dough.
4. Turn out and roll into a strip 2 cm thick.
5. Place on a floured or greased baking tray, and cut into fingers.
6. Brush with beaten egg or milk and bake in a hot oven for 8–10 minutes.

28. DROPPED SCONES OR SCOTCH PANCAKES

Ingredients:

200 g Self-raising Flour   25 g Sugar

or { 200 g Flour / 1 level teaspoonful Bicarbonate of Soda / 2 level teaspoonfuls Cream of Tartar }   1 dessertspoonful Syrup / 1 large Egg / 250 ml Milk (approx.)

1 level teaspoonful Salt

Time: 1–2 minutes each side

Method:

1. Sieve dry ingredients.
2. Add egg, syrup and sufficient milk to give a thick batter consistency.
3. Drop mixture in spoonfuls, onto a fairly hot girdle or non-stick frying pan.
4. Cook until lightly browned, turn, brown second side.
5. Cool in a tea towel.

Note: If iron girdle is used, grease beforehand.

29. CRUMPETS

Ingredients:

200 g Self-raising Flour   25 g Butter *or* Block Margarine

or { 200 g Flour / 1 level teaspoonful Bicarbonate of Soda / 2 level teaspoonfuls Cream of Tartar }   25 g Sugar / 2 Eggs (beaten) / 250 ml Milk

1 level teaspoonful Salt

Method:

1. Sieve dry ingredients.
2. Rub in butter.
3. Mix with beaten egg and milk slowly until smooth.
4. Cook in spoonfuls on a hot girdle or non-stick frying pan.
5. When brown on one side turn and brown on other side.
6. Cool in a tea towel.

30. POTATO SCONES

Ingredients:

200 g Potatoes (cooked)	I level teaspoonful Salt
Small piece Butter	Pinch Baking Powder
About 50 g Flour	

Method:

1. Mash potatoes, while hot, with butter and salt.
2. Mix baking powder with flour.
3. Work into the potatoes as much flour as will make a pliable dough.
4. Roll out very thinly. Cut into four or six scones, fork, and place on a hot girdle.
5. Cook for 3 minutes on each side. Cool in a towel.

Note: Oatmeal may be used instead of flour.

31. OATCAKES (1)

Ingredients:

200 g Oatmeal	I level teaspoonful Salt
10–15 g Dripping or Cooking Fat (melted)	Hot Water
Pinch Bicarbonate of Soda	

Method:

1. Add salt and bicarbonate of soda to oatmeal, pour in melted fat.
2. Add enough hot water to make a rather soft consistency. Divide in two.
3. Knead well, work mixture into a round on a board sprinkled with oatmeal.
4. Roll out into a circle as thinly as possible and cut into four.
5. Rub with dry oatmeal to whiten.
6. Cook on a fairly hot girdle.
7. When cooked on one side, dry off in cool oven or under grill.

32. OATCAKES (2)

Ingredients:

As Oatcakes (1)

Method:

1. Add salt and bicarbonate of soda to oatmeal, rub in fat.
2. Add enough cold water to make a slightly stiffer consistency than oatcakes (1).
3. Finish as oatcakes (1).

33. **OATMEAL BANNOCKS**

Ingredients:

150 g fine Oatmeal	Pinch Bicarbonate of Soda
50 g Self-raising Flour	½ level teaspoonful Salt
50 g Butter	Warm water to mix

Method:

1. Rub fat into dry ingredients.
2. Mix with warm water to a stiff consistency. Divide into two.
3. Turn out onto a board sprinkled with oatmeal, and work mixture into a round.
4. Roll out and cut into desired shape.
5. Cook on a girdle or non-stick frying pan for 5 minutes on one side and finish either in oven or under grill.
6. Alternatively, place on a baking tray and cook in the oven at 150°C, No. 2, for 45 minutes.

CAKES

34. **PLAIN CAKES**

Foundation Proportions:

Ingredients:	Example:
	For 400 g Flour:
⅓–½ Fat to Flour	150–200 g Fat
½ Sugar to Flour	150–200 g Sugar
1–2 Eggs to 200 g Flour	2–4 Eggs
2 level teaspoonfuls Baking Powder to 200 g Flour	4 level teaspoonfuls Baking Powder or use Self-raising Flour
½–1½ Fruit to Flour	200–600 g Fruit
	Milk

Preparation of Fruit:	Dried Fruit: If fruit is not already prepared, remove any stalks, wash and dry. Cherries: If sticky, wash in warm water, dry and halve. Coat the fruit with a little of the measured flour before adding to the cake mixture
Method:	Rubbing in: The fat is cut and rubbed into the flour
Consistency:	Buns: Stiff consistency Large Cakes: Soft, dropping consistency

Approximate Size of Cake Tin:	200 g flour plus small amount of fruit: 15 cm diameter 200 g flour plus large amount of fruit: 17 cm diameter
Preparation of Tin:	Grease, or grease and flour
Oven Temperature:	The plainer the mixture the hotter the oven Buns: 220°C, No. 7. Large Cakes: 180°C, No. 4
Position in Oven:	Buns: One-third from top Large Cakes: Middle
Test for Readiness:	Cakes should be lightly browned and firm to the touch. Large cakes should be tested by inserting a warm skewer into the centre of the cake. The skewer should come out without any mixture adhering
Storing:	Cakes should be cold before storing in an air-tight tin

35. ROCK BUNS

Ingredients:

200 g Self-raising Flour	50–75 g Sugar
or { 200 g Flour	25 g Mixed Peel
2 level teaspoonfuls Baking Powder	50 g Currants
75 g Butter *or* Block Margarine	1 Egg (beaten)
Pinch of Salt	Little Milk

Quantity: Approx. 14 buns
Time: 15 minutes
Oven Temperature: 220°C, No. 7
Position in Oven: One-third from top

Method:

1. Sieve flour, baking powder and salt. Rub in the butter.
2. Add sugar, peel and washed currants.
3. Mix well. Add egg and mix to a stiff consistency, adding milk if necessary.
4. Put the mixture in rough heaps on a greased baking sheet.
5. Bake in a hot oven for about 15 minutes.

36. COCONUT BUNS

Ingredients:

200 g Self-raising Flour	75 g Sugar
or { 200 g Flour	50 g Coconut
2 level teaspoonfuls Baking Powder	1 Egg (beaten)
Pinch of Salt	Little Milk
75 g Butter *or* Block Margarine	

Time: 15 minutes
Oven Temperature: 220°C, No. 7
Position in Oven: One-third from top

Method:

1. Sieve flour, baking powder and salt. Rub in the butter, add sugar and coconut. Mix well.
2. Add beaten egg and enough milk to make a stiff consistency.
3. Put mixture in rough heaps on greased baking sheet.
4. Bake in a hot oven for about 15 minutes.

37. RASPBERRY BUNS

Ingredients:

125 g Self-raising Flour

or { 125 g Flour
2 level teaspoonfuls Baking Powder

75 g Ground Rice

Pinch of Salt

50 g Butter *or* Block Margarine

75 g Sugar

2 Eggs (beaten)

Raspberry Jam

Time: 15 minutes
Oven Temperature: 220°C, No. 7
Position in Oven: One-third from top

Method:

1. Sieve flour, baking powder and salt, add ground rice, rub in butter and add sugar.
2. Mix to a stiff consistency with most of the beaten eggs.
3. Form into balls, make a hole in the centre, put in a little jam, close up the opening and brush over with remaining beaten egg.
4. Bake in a hot oven for 15 minutes, or according to size.

Note: 200 g flour can be used instead of 125 g flour and 75 g ground rice.

38. LONDON BUNS

Ingredients:

200 g Self-raising Flour

or { 200 g Flour
2 level teaspoonfuls Baking Powder

75 g Butter *or* Block Margarine

50 g Sugar

25 g Peel

Little grated Lemon Rind

Pinch of Salt

1 Egg

Milk to mix

Time: 15 minutes
Oven Temperature: 220°C, No. 7
Position in Oven: One-third from top

Method:

1. Sieve flour and baking powder, rub in the butter and add the dry ingredients.
2. Mix to a light dough with most of the beaten egg and milk.
3. Shape into balls. Put on a greased baking sheet.
4. Brush with remaining egg, sprinkle with sugar.
5. Bake in a hot oven for 15 minutes.

39. DOUGHNUTS (WITHOUT YEAST)

Ingredients:

200 g Self-raising Flour

or { 200 g Flour

2 level teaspoonfuls Baking Powder

Pinch of Salt

50–75 g Butter *or* Block Margarine

50 g Sugar

1 Egg (beaten) and Milk to mix

Oil for deep-frying

Method:

1. Sieve flour, baking powder and salt.
2. Rub in the butter, add sugar.
3. Add egg and sufficient milk to give a light dough.
4. Roll out and cut into rings.
5. Deep-fry in hot oil until a deep golden brown.
6. Drain and toss in sugar.

40. COFFEE BUNS

Ingredients:

200 g Self-raising Flour

100 g Butter *or* Block Margarine

100 g Soft Brown Sugar

1 Egg (beaten)

75 g Currants

Time: 15 minutes

Oven Temperature: 190°C, No. 5

Position in Oven: One-third from top

Method:

1. Cream butter and sugar till soft.
2. Add most of the egg and work in the flour.
3. Add currants and form into balls.
4. Put in a greased baking sheet and brush with beaten egg.

Note: These buns are so-called as they are normally served with coffee.

41. DATE AND WALNUT BREAD

Ingredients:

200 g Flour

100–150 g Dates (stoned, soaked)

100 g Sugar

50 g Butter *or* Block Margarine

1 Egg (beaten)

1 level teaspoonful Bicarbonate of Soda

1 level teaspoonful of Baking Powder

25–50 g Walnuts (chopped)

250 ml Water (short measure)

Time: 1 hour

Oven Temperature: 180–190°C, Nos. 4–5

Position in Oven: Middle shelf

Size of Tin: 2 tins 10–15 cm

Method:

1. Chop dates and sprinkle with bicarbonate of soda. Add boiling water and leave for 30 minutes.

2. Cream butter and sugar, add egg, soaked dates, chopped walnuts and flour alternately. Add baking powder and mix to a soft dough.

3. Put into a greased, floured tin and bake.

42. ORANGE BREAD

Ingredients:

200 g Self-raising Flour	Grated rind 1 Orange
50 g Butter *or* Block Margarine	2 tablespoonfuls Orange Juice
150 g Castor Sugar	2–3 tablespoonfuls Milk
1 Egg	1 level teaspoonful Salt

Time: 30 minutes

Oven Temperature: 180–190ºC, Nos. 4–5

Position in Oven: Middle shelf

Size of Tin: 10–15 cm

Method:

1. Cream butter and sugar, beat in egg.
2. Stir in the orange juice, rind and milk.
3. Sieve the flour and add salt and fold into the mixture. Put into a greased, floured tin and bake.

43. BANANA TEA BREAD

Ingredients:

200 g Self-raising Flour	50 g Sultanas
1 level teaspoonful Salt	25–50 g Walnuts (chopped)
Pinch Spice	25–50 g Glacé Cherries
100 g Butter *or* Block Margarine	400 g Ripe Bananas (weight with skin on)
150 g Sugar	2 Eggs (beaten)

Time: 1½–1¾ hours

Oven Temperature: 180ºC, No. 4, for first hour; 170ºC, No. 3, for remainder of time

Position in Oven: Middle shelf

Size of Tin: 2 tins, 10–15 cm

Method:

1. Sieve flour, salt and spice, rub in butter. Add mashed banana and all other ingredients. Beat well.
2. Put into prepared tins and bake.

44. PLAIN WHITE CAKE

Ingredients:

200 g Self-raising Flour	75–100 g Butter *or* Block Margarine
or { 200 g Flour	75–100 g Sugar
2 level teaspoonfuls Baking Powder	2 Eggs (beaten)
Milk	

Time: 45–60 minutes
Oven Temperature: 180°C, No. 4
Position in Oven: Middle shelf
Size of Tin: 15 cm diameter

Method:

1. Sieve flour and baking powder.
2. Rub in butter and add sugar.
3. Mix to a dropping consistency with beaten eggs and milk.
4. Put into a greased tin, bake in a moderate oven.

Variations:

Sultana Cake.—150–200 g sultanas.
Cherry Cake.—75–100 g cherries.
Ginger Cake.—50–100 g preserved ginger.
Fruit Cake.—200–250 g mixed fruit.
Seed Cake.—25 g caraway seed.

45. FRUIT CAKE

Ingredients:

200 g Self-raising Flour	100 g Sultanas
or { 200 g Flour	100 g Currants
{ 2 level teaspoonfuls Baking Powder	50 g Peel
Pinch of Salt	Few drops Almond Essence (optional)
100 g Sugar	2 Eggs
100 g Butter *or* Block Margarine	Milk

Time: 1–1¼ hours
Oven Temperature: 180°C, No. 4
Position in Oven: Middle shelf
Size of Tin: 15 cm diameter

Method:

1. Prepare dried fruit (page 384).
2. Sieve flour, salt and baking powder.
3. Rub in butter, add sugar and fruit.
4. Beat egg, add essence.
5. Add to flour along with enough milk to make a dropping consistency.
6. Put into a greased tin, and bake in a moderate oven, for around 1 hour.

46. LUNCH CAKE

Ingredients:

300 g Flour	50 g Butter *or* Block Margarine
½ level teaspoonful Ground Cloves	100 g Currants
2 level teaspoonfuls Mixed Spice	75 g Raisins

2 level teaspoonfuls Cinnamon   50 g Peel
1 ½ level teaspoonfuls Bicarbonate of Soda   150 g Sugar
½ level teaspoonful Cream of Tartar   2 Eggs (beaten)
Pinch Salt   Milk to mix
75 g Cooking Fat

Time: 2 hours
Oven Temperature: 180°C, No. 4
Position in Oven: Middle shelf
Size of Tin: 18 cm diameter

Method:

1. Prepare fruit (page 384).
2. Sieve flour, spices, raising agents and salt
3. Rub in fats.
4. Add remaining dry ingredients.
5. Mix to a rather soft consistency with beaten eggs and milk.
6. Put into a greased tin and bake in a moderate oven for 2 hours, reducing the heat after the cake is set.

47. VINEGAR CAKE

Ingredients:

200 g Flour   ½ teaspoonful Almond Essence
75 g Butter *or* Block Margarine   1 dessertspoonful Golden Syrup *or*
100 g Brown Sugar   Treacle
200 g Sultanas   125 ml Milk
100 g Currants   1 Egg (beaten)
50 g Peel   1 level teaspoonful Bicarbonate of
1 level teaspoonful Mixed   Soda
   Spice   2 teaspoonfuls Vinegar

Time: 1 hour 30 minutes
Oven Temperature: 180°C, No. 4
Position in Oven: Middle shelf
Size of Tin: 17–18 cm diameter

Method:

1. Prepare fruit (page 384).
2. Rub butter into flour, mix dry ingredients except soda.
3. Mix in fruit.
4. Mix essence, egg and syrup mixed with milk.
5. Mix with dry ingredients except soda.
5. Add soda mixed with vinegar, mix well.
6. Put into a greased tin, bake in moderate oven for
   1 hour 30 minutes.

48. RICH CAKES

Foundation Proportions:

Ingredients:	Example: for 400 g Flour
½–equal quantities Fat to Flour	200–400 g Fat
½–equal quantities Sugar to Flour	200–400 g Castor Sugar
3–4 Eggs to 200 g Flour	6–8 Eggs
As Eggs increase Baking Powder decreases	2–0 level teaspoonfuls Baking Powder
½–3 times Fruit to Flour	Up to 1200 g Fruit

Preparation of Fruit:	Dried Fruit: If fruit is not already prepared, remove any stalks, wash and dry. Cherries: If sticky wash in warm water, dry and halve. When baking a cake, coat the fruit with a little of the measured flour before adding to the cake mixture
Method:	Creaming: The fat and sugar are creamed. For a spongy-textured cake add the eggs gradually to the creamed mixture and lightly stir in the flour. For a close-textured cake add the eggs and flour alternately
Consistency:	Stiff dropping
Approximate Size of Cake Tin:	200–250 g flour plus small amount of fruit: 15 cm 200–250 g flour plus larger amount of fruit: 16–18 cm
Preparation of Tins:	Large Cakes: Line the sides and bottom of the tin with greaseproof paper. It is not necessary to grease it. (See the diagram opposite.) If the cake requires several hours cooking, tie 2–3 layers of brown paper round the outside of the tin Sandwich Cakes: Grease and flour, or the bottom of the tin can be lined with greaseproof paper. Grease paper
Oven Temperature:	The richer the mixture the cooler the oven Sandwich Cakes and Small Cakes: 190°C, No. 5 Large Cakes: 170–180°C, Nos. 3–4
Position in Oven:	Sandwich Cakes and Small Cakes: Middle to one-third from top Large Cakes: Middle to lower third

Test for Readiness:	Cakes should be lightly browned and firm to the touch. Large cakes can be tested by inserting a warm skewer into the centre of the cake. The skewer should come out without any mixture adhering
Storing:	Cakes should be cold before storing in an airtight tin

How to line a cake tin:

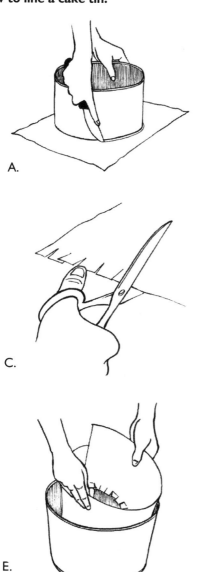

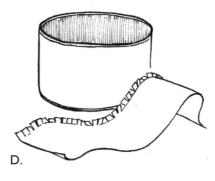

A.

B.

C.

D.

E.

A. Cut out a circle of paper to fit bottom of tin.
B. Cut a strip of paper to go around tin, 5 cm wider than the tin.
C. Snip along edge of paper.
D. Fold in this edge.
E. Line sides then insert circle of paper to fit the bottom of the tin.

49. **WHITE CAKE**

Ingredients:

250 g Flour	1 ½ level teaspoonfuls Baking Powder
200 g Butter *or* Soft Cake Margarine	3–4 Eggs (according to size)
150 g Castor Sugar	1 teaspoonful flavouring if liked e.g. Vanilla, Almond, Orange, Coffee

Time: 1–1 ½ hours
Oven Temperature: 180°C, No. 4
Position in Oven: One-third from bottom
Size of Tin: 15–18 cm

Method:

1. Cream butter and sugar. Beat eggs and add alternately with sieved flour and baking powder.
2. Flavour, put into prepared tin and bake.

Variations:

Sultana Cake.—250–275 g sultanas.
Fruit Cake.—200–275 g mixed fruit.
Cherry Cake.—125 g glacé cherries.
Ginger Cake.—100–125 g preserved ginger.
Coconut Cake.—50 g coconut.
Madeira Cake.—Grated rind of half a lemon. Put a strip of citron peel on top of cake after half an hour in the oven.

50. **SULTANA CAKE**

Ingredients:

200 g Flour	1 level teaspoonful Baking Powder
100 g Butter *or* Soft Margarine	Pinch Salt
100 g Castor Sugar	100–150 g Sultanas
2–3 Eggs (beaten)	50 g Peel
A little Milk	Grated Rind ½ Lemon

Time: 1–1 ¼ hours
Oven Temperature: 180°C, No. 4
Position in Oven: Below middle
Size of Tin: 15 cm

Method:

1. Prepare fruit (page 384).
2. Cream butter and sugar, add beaten egg gradually.
3. Stir in sieved flour, salt, baking powder. Add milk to give a dropping consistency.
4. Add fruit and lemon rind.
5. Put into a prepared tin (page 385) and bake in a moderate oven.

51. **DUNDEE CAKE**

Ingredients:

200 g Flour	10 g Almonds (blanched)
150 g Butter *or* Soft Margarine	25 g Mixed Peel (chopped)
125 g Castor Sugar	75 g Currants
4 Eggs (beaten)	75 g Raisins
1 level teaspoonful Baking Powder	75 g Sultanas

Time: 1 hour 30 minutes
Oven Temperature: 180°C, No. 4
Position in Oven: Below middle
Size of Tin: 15–18 cm

Method:

1. Prepare fruit (page 384).
2. Cream butter and sugar.
3. Add beaten egg, alternately with sieved flour and baking powder.
4. Mix in fruit, put in a prepared tin (page 385).
5. Bake for 15 minutes, lay split almonds on top, cook for the required time.

52. **GENOA CAKE**

Ingredients:

250 g Flour	1 level teaspoonful Baking Powder
200 g Butter *or* Soft Cake Margarine	250 g Sultanas
150 g Castor Sugar	50–75 g Cherries
4 Eggs (beaten)	50 g Mixed Peel

Time: 1½–2 hours
Oven Temperature: 180°C, No. 4
Position in Oven: Below middle
Size of Tin: 18 cm

Method:

1. Prepare fruit (page 384).
2. Cream butter and sugar.
3. Add beaten egg alternately with sieved flour and baking powder, mix in fruit.
4. Put in a prepared tin (page 385). Bake in a moderate oven.

53. **PLUM CAKE**

Ingredients:

200 g Flour	1½ level teaspoonfuls Ginger
150 g Butter *or* Soft Cake Margarine	¾ level teaspoonful Mixed Spice
150 g Castor Sugar	150 g Raisins
4 Eggs (beaten)	150 g Currants
1 level teaspoonful Baking Powder	50 g Almonds
1 level teaspoonful Cinnamon	50 g Mixed Peel

Time: 2 hours
Oven Temperature: 180°C, No. 4 lowering to 170°C, No. 3
Position in Oven: One-third from bottom
Size of Tin: 18–20 cm diameter

Method:

1. Prepare fruit.
2. Cream butter and sugar.
3. Add beaten egg alternately with sieved dry ingredients.
4. Mix fruit thoroughly through mixture.
5. Put into a prepared tin (page 385). Bake in a slow oven.

54. CHRISTMAS CAKE

Ingredients:

250 g Flour plus pinch Baking Powder	200 g Currants
200 g Butter *or* Soft Cake Margarine	250 g Raisins
200 g Sugar – Castor *or* Brown	100 g Sultanas
4 Eggs (beaten)	50 g Cherries
25 g Ground Almonds	25 g Almonds
2 level teaspoonfuls Mixed Spice	25 g Mixed Peel
1 tablespoonful Treacle	

Time: 2 ½–3 hours
Oven Temperature: 170°C, No. 3
Position in Oven: One-third from bottom
Size of Tin: 18–20 cm diameter

Method:

1. Prepare fruit (page 384). Blanch almonds and chop.
2. Cream butter and sugar.
3. Add beaten egg alternately with sieved dry ingredients and mix well.
4. Stir in fruit and other ingredients and put into a prepared tin (page 385).
5. Bake for about 3 hours.

Icing:

Almond Paste (page 419)
Royal Icing (page 418)

Method:

1. Divide almond paste in two.
2. Roll one half into a strip the depth of the cake and sufficient to go round it.
3. Brush strip with warm apricot jam and cover side of cake.
4. Roll other half of almond paste to the size of the top of cake. Brush with warm apricot jam and press firmly on top of cake.
5. Cover with royal icing and draw out in points.

55. SIMNEL CAKE

Ingredients:

200 g Flour	3 Eggs (beaten)
1 level teaspoonful Baking Powder	150 g Sultanas
	150 g Raisins
½ level teaspoonful Mixed Spice	75 g Currants
	50 g Peel
Grating of Nutmeg	25 g Almonds
150 g Butter *or* Soft Cake Margarine	A little Milk if necessary
150 g Castor Sugar	200 g Almond Paste (page 419)

Time: 2½–3 hours

Oven Temperature: 180°C, No. 4

Position in Oven: Below the middle

Size of Tin: 18–20 cm diameter

Method:

1. Prepare fruit (page 384). Make almond paste and wrap in greaseproof paper.
2. Cream butter and sugar. Add beaten egg alternately with sieved dry ingredients. Mix in prepared fruit.
3. Put half of the mixture into a prepared tin (page 385). Roll a circle out of a third of the almond paste and put on top of mixture.
4. Cover with remaining cake mixture. Bake for 1 hour at 180°C, No. 4, then lower to 170°C, No. 3, until cooked. Cool.
5. Roll out half of the remaining almond paste to fit the top of the cake. Brush with warm apricot jam. Press firmly on top of cake.
6. Make 11 balls with the remaining almond paste and put round edge of cake.
7. Brush with a little of the warm apricot jam and brown lightly under the grill.
8. Decorate centre as desired.

56. SCOTCH CURRANT BUN

Ingredients—lining:

200 g Flour	75 g Butter *or* Block Margarine
1 level teaspoonful Baking Powder	Cold Water

Method:

1. Rub butter or block margarine into sieved flour, and baking powder.
2. Mix with water to make a stiff paste.

Mixture:

150 g Flour	2 level teaspoonfuls Ground Ginger
500 g Blue Raisins	2 level teaspoonfuls Ground Cinnamon
750 g Currants	½ level teaspoonful Black Pepper
100 g Almonds	½ level teaspoonful Bicarbonate of Soda
100 g Sugar	½ level teaspoonful Cream of Tartar
2 level teaspoonfuls Allspice	
250 ml (approx.) Milk	

Time: 2½–3 hours
Oven Temperature: 180°C, No. 4
Position in Oven: One-third from bottom
Size of Tin: 18 cm square

Method:

1. Line tin with two-third dough, leaving one-third to make a lid.
2. Prepare fruit, mix all ingredients, moisten with milk.
3. Pack tightly into pastry-lined tin, place on lid.
4. Seal edges firmly, fork all over, brush with egg.
5. Bake in moderate oven.

57. CHOCOLATE LUMP CAKE

Ingredients:

100 g Self-raising Flour	50 g Drinking Chocolate
or { 100 g Flour	25–50 g Walnuts (chopped)
{ 1 level teaspoonful Baking Powder	1 dessertspoonful Coffee Essence
100 g Butter or Soft Cake Margarine	100 g niblets of Broken Chocolate *or*
100 g Castor Sugar	Chocolate Drops
2 Eggs (beaten)	

Time: 50 minutes
Oven Temperature: 180–190°C, No. 4–5
Position in Oven: Middle shelf
Size of Tin: 15 cm

Method:

1. Cream the butter and sugar.
2. Add beaten eggs gradually, beating well.
3. Stir in sieved dry ingredients, coffee essence and a little water if necessary. Fold in nuts and chocolate.
4. Put in a prepared tin (page 385) and bake.

58. CHOCOLATE CAKE

Ingredients:

150 g Flour	150 g Castor Sugar
50 g Ground Rice	4 Eggs (beaten)
100 g Chocolate (block)	2 level teaspoonfuls Baking Powder
2 tablespoonfuls Milk *or* Water	Vanilla Essence
150 g Butter *or* Soft Cake Margarine	

25 g Chocolate Butter Icing (page 418)
200 g Chocolate Water Icing (page 417)
Time: 1–1¼ hours in 1 tin, or 30–40 minutes in 2 tins
Oven Temperature: 180°C, No. 4
Position in Oven: Middle shelf
Size of Tin: 18 cm, or two 18 cm sandwich tins

Method:

1. Dissolve chocolate in liquid.
2. Cream butter and sugar, add chocolate, beaten egg gradually, then add sieved baking powder and flour, ground rice and vanilla essence.
3. Put in a prepared tin (page 385). Bake.
4. When cold, split and fill with chocolate butter icing, coat with chocolate water icing.

59. ORANGE CAKE

Ingredients:

100 g Self-raising Flour	Grated rind and juice of ½ Orange
or { 100 g Flour	Orange Water Icing using remainder of
1 level teaspoonful Baking Powder	juice (page 417)
100 g Butter or Soft Cake Margarine	Orange Filling (page 420)
100 g Castor Sugar	2 Eggs (beaten)

Time: 35–40 minutes in 1 tin,
20 minutes in 2 tins
Oven Temperature: 180–190°C, No. 4–5
Position in Oven: Middle shelf
Size of Tin: 15–17 cm cake tin or two 15–17 cm sandwich tins

Method:

1. Cream the butter and sugar. Gradually add beaten egg.
2. Stir in sieved flour and baking powder, orange juice and rind. Turn into prepared cake tin.
3. Bake in a moderate oven.
4. When cool, split and spread with orange filling, coat with orange water icing and decorate as desired.

60. WALNUT CAKE

Ingredients:

As for Orange Cake but Omit Orange and add:

25 g Walnuts (chopped)	or	Seven Minute Frosting (page 419)
Walnut Filling (page 420)		Feather Icing (page 418)

Method:

Make as for Orange Cake.

61. VICTORIA SANDWICH

Ingredients:

100 g Self-raising Flour	100 g Butter or Soft Cake Margarine
or { 100 g Flour	100 g Castor Sugar
1½ level teaspoonfuls Baking Powder	2 Eggs (beaten)
Icing Sugar	Jam

Time: 20 minutes
Oven Temperature: 190°C, No. 5
Position in Oven: Middle shelf
Size of Tins: Two 15 cm sandwich tins

Method:

1. Grease tins and line bottom with greaseproof paper.
2. Cream butter or soft cake margarine and sugar, add beaten eggs gradually, beating well.
3. Stir in sieved flour adding a little water if necessary.
4. Put in prepared tins in a moderate oven.
5. When cold, sandwich with jam and dredge with icing sugar.

Note: 150 g Self-raising flour can be used. If baked in one tin, allow 45–50 minutes.

62. ICED VICTORIA SANDWICH

Ingredients:

As for Victoria Sandwich recipe (above) plus
50 g Butter Icing (page 418)
200 g Water Icing (page 417)

Method:

1. Sandwich cakes together with butter icing, filling in any gaps with more butter icing to give smooth sides.
2. Make water icing to a thick pouring consistency.
3. Pour water icing onto the centre of the cake. It should run to the edge and down the sides. A hot, dry knife can be used on the sides, joining icing to icing, if necessary.
4. Decorate as desired.

Note: If top only to be iced use half quantity water icing.

63. VICTORIA SANDWICH (QUICK METHOD)

Ingredients:

As Victoria Sandwich (page 391) using well-softened Butter or Soft Cake Margarine.

Method:

1. Grease tins and line bottoms with greaseproof paper.
2. Sieve flour.
3. Put all the ingredients in a bowl, and beat thoroughly till well mixed, for 1–2 minutes.
4. Divide mixture between sandwich tins.
5. Bake in a moderate oven.
6. When cold, sandwich with jam and dredge with icing sugar.

Note: 150 g Self-raising Flour
       ½ level teaspoonful Baking Powder } Can be used instead of 100 g flour to
       2 tablespoonfuls Water } give a larger cake

64. CHOCOLATE SANDWICH CAKE

Ingredients:

100 g Self-raising Flour
2 level tablespoonfuls Cocoa
100 g Butter *or* Soft Cake margarine
100 g Castor Sugar
25–50 g Chocolate Butter Icing (page 418)
200 g Chocolate Water Icing (page 417)

25 g Syrup
2 Eggs (beaten)
½ teaspoonful Vanilla Essence
1 tablespoonful Milk

Time: 20 minutes
Oven Temperature: 190°C, No. 5
Position in Oven: Middle shelf
Size of Tin: Two 15–18 cm sandwich tins

Method:

1. Grease tins and line bottoms with greaseproof paper.
2. Cream butter and sugar, syrup and essence, add beaten egg gradually, beating well.
3. Stir in sieved flour, cocoa and milk if necessary.
4. Bake in prepared tins in a moderate oven.
5. When cold, sandwich with chocolate butter icing and ice with chocolate icing.

65. BATTENBERG CAKE

Ingredients:

Victoria Sandwich Mixture (page 391)
Pink colouring
Jam

Almond Paste:
100 g Ground Almonds
100 g Castor Sugar
100 g Icing Sugar
Egg to bind

Time: 20 minutes
Oven Temperature: 190°C, No. 5
Position in Oven: Middle shelf
Size of Tin: 16–24 cm square tin

Method:

1. Line tin with paper, grease. Put a division of paper down the centre.
2. Halve mixture and put in one half of tin. Colour remainder pink and put into other half of tin. Bake.
3. When cold, cut each half in two by the length and sandwich together alternately with jam.
4. Press well together.
5. Make almond paste. Mix all dry ingredients thoroughly and bind with egg.
6. Roll out thinly into an oblong sufficient to cover the whole cake. Spread with jam.
7. Lay cake along one edge and carefully cover with the almond paste.

66. GINGERBREADS

Foundation Proportions:

Ingredients:	Example for 400 g Flour:
¼–½ Fat to Flour	100–200 g Butter or Block Margarine
¼–½ Sugar to Flour	100–200 g Sugar
¼–½ Treacle to Flour	100–200 g Treacle
I level teaspoonful Bicarbonate of Soda to 200 g Flour	2 level teaspoonfuls Bicarbonate of Soda
1–2 Eggs to 200 g Flour	2–4 Eggs

Method:	Melting: The fat, sugar and treacle are melted
Consistency:	Soft
Approximate Size of Tin:	200 g Flour: 15 cm diameter
Preparation of Tin:	Grease or grease and flour Rich Gingerbreads: line with greaseproof paper (page 385)
Approximate Position in Oven:	Middle to lower third
Approximate Oven Temperature:	170–180°C, Nos. 3–4

67. GINGERBREAD (PLAIN)

Ingredients:

50 g Butter *or* Block Margarine
50 g Sugar
120 g Treacle
2–3 level teaspoonfuls Ground Ginger
I level teaspoonful Mixed Spice
I level teaspoonful Ground Cinnamon
200 g Flour
I level teaspoonful Bicarbonate of Soda
I Egg (beaten)
Milk to mix

Time: 30–40 minutes
Oven Temperature: 180°C, No. 4
Position in Oven: Middle shelf
Size of Tin: Roasting tin, 20–25 cm

Method:

1. Melt butter or block margarine, sugar and treacle.
2. Sieve all dry ingredients.
3. Add treacle mixture, then egg and enough milk to make a soft consistency.
4. Put into a greased tin, bake in a moderate oven.

68. GINGERBREAD (SPONGY)

Ingredients:

200 g Flour	50 g Sugar
2 level teaspoonfuls Ground Ginger	1 tablespoonful Treacle
1 level teaspoonful Cinnamon	2 tablespoonfuls Syrup
1 level teaspoonful Bicarbonate of Soda	1 Egg (beaten)
Pinch Salt	A little warm Water
50 g Butter *or* Block Margarine	50 g Sultanas *or* Raisins (optional)

Time: 1 ¼ hours

Oven Temperature: 180°C, No. 4

Position in Oven: Middle shelf

Size of Tin: 15 cm

Method:

1. Sieve dry ingredients.
2. Rub butter or block margarine into mixture, add sugar.
3. Melt treacle and syrup, add beaten egg.
4. Pour into dry ingredients along with warm water to make a soft consistency.
5. Put into a prepared tin and bake in a moderate oven.

69. GINGERBREAD (RICH)

Ingredients:

250 g Flour	100 g Treacle
150 g Butter *or* Soft Cake Margarine	2 Eggs (beaten)
150 g Brown Sugar	75 g Almonds
1 ½ level teaspoonfuls Bicarbonate of Soda	150 g Sultanas
3 level teaspoonfuls Ground Ginger	Little warm Milk
3 level teaspoonfuls Cinnamon	50 g Crystallised Ginger

Time: 2 hours

Oven Temperature: 180°C, No. 4

Position in Oven: Below middle

Size of Tin: 16–17 cm

Method:

1. Cream the butter or soft cake margarine and the sugar.
2. Add sieved dry ingredients, treacle and beaten eggs.
3. Add fruit, nuts and a little milk to give a soft dropping consistency.
4. Put in a greased tin and bake for about 2 hours; reduce heat to 150°C, No. 3, after 20 minutes.

70. SPONGES

Foundation Proportions:

Ingredients:	1 Egg 25–50 g Castor Sugar 25–50 g Flour
Method:	Whisking The eggs and sugar are whisked together and the flour is folded in
Consistency:	Thick pouring
Approximate Size of Tin:	Sponge Sandwich: Two 15 cm sandwich tins. Swiss Roll: 20–30 cm baking tin
Preparation of Tin:	Grease and dredge with flour or flour and castor sugar mixed If liked, the bottom of the tin may be lined with non-stick greaseproof baking paper
Oven Temperature:	Cakes: 180°C, No. 4 Swiss Roll: 220–230°C, No. 7–8
Position in Oven:	Cakes: Middle Swiss Roll: One-third from top
Test for Readiness:	Well risen, lightly browned and firm to the touch

71. SWISS ROLL

Ingredients:

75 g Self-raising Flour   3 Eggs (beaten)
or {75 g Flour   75 g Castor Sugar
{1 level teaspoonful Baking Powder   Flavouring as liked
Hot Jam

Time: 6–8 minutes
Oven Temperature: 220–230°C, Nos. 7–8
Position in Oven: Top shelf
Size of Tin: 20–30 cm

Method:

1. Beat eggs and sugar until thick, add flavouring.
2. Sieve flour and baking powder.
3. Lightly fold into egg mixture.
4. Put into a lined, greased tin, bake.
5. When firm and golden brown turn onto sugared paper.
6. Trim edges and spread with warm jam, roll up tightly.
Note: 2 eggs and 2 tablespoonfuls warm water can be used instead of 3 eggs.

72. **SPONGE CAKE**

Ingredients:

100 g Flour	
3–4 Eggs (beaten)	*or* Some grated Lemon Rind / Lemon Essence
100 g Castor Sugar	

Time: 15–20 minutes for sandwich tins; 1 hour for 15 cm tin
Oven Temperature: 180°C, No. 4
Position in Oven: Middle shelf
Size of Tins: Two 15 cm sandwich tins, or one tin, 15 cm diameter

Method:

1. Grease tin and dredge thickly with a teaspoonful flour and a teaspoonful sugar mixed or cut out a circle of non-stick greaseproof baking paper to fit the bottom, still greasing and dredging the sides.
2. Beat eggs and sugar over hot water till thick and creamy.
3. Fold sieved flour, lemon rind or essence into the beaten eggs.
4. Turn into tin or tins and bake.

73. **CREAM SPONGE**

Ingredients:

100 g Self-raising Flour	2 Eggs (beaten)
or { 100 g Flour / 1 level teaspoonful Baking Powder	100 g Castor Sugar / 3 tablespoonfuls warm Water
125 ml Cream	

Time: 20 minutes **Oven Temperature:** 180°C, No. 4
Position in Oven: Middle shelf
Size of Tins: Two 15 cm sandwich tins – prepared as for Sponge Cake

Method:

1. Sieve flour and baking powder.
2. Whisk eggs and sugar till thick and creamy – this can be done over hot water.
3. Remove from heat, lightly fold in flour and water.
4. Bake in a moderate oven for 20 minutes.
5. When cold, sandwich with cream and dredge with icing sugar.

74. **MOCHA CAKE**

Ingredients:

3 Eggs (beaten)	50 g Coffee Butter Icing (page 418)
100 g Flour	100 g Castor Sugar
100 g Coffee Water Icing (page 417)	Walnuts (chopped)
1 teaspoonful Coffee Essence (optional)	Coffee Butter Icing (page 418)

Time: 20–30 minutes
Oven Temperature: 180°C, No. 4
Position in Oven: Middle shelf
Size of Tins: Two 15 cm sandwich tins

Method:

1. Grease tins and line the bottoms with non-stick greaseproof baking paper.
2. Whisk eggs and sugar until thick and creamy. Add coffee essence.
3. Lightly fold in flour.
4. Put into prepared sandwich tins and bake.
5. When cold, sandwich with coffee butter icing.
6. Spread sides with butter icing, roll in chopped walnuts.
7. Coat top with coffee water icing.
8. Decorate with walnuts or butter icing.

75. GENOESE SPONGE

Ingredients:

75 g Flour   75 g Castor Sugar (good measure)
4 Eggs (beaten)   50 g Butter

Time: 40 minutes for 18–20 cm tin; 15–20 minutes for 20–30 cm tin
Oven Temperature: 180°C, No. 4, for 18–20 cm tin; 190°C, No. 5, for 20–30 cm tin
Position in Oven: Middle shelf
Size of Tins: 18–20 cm, or 20–30 cm shallow tin

Method:

1. Line tin with non-stick greaseproof baking paper. Grease.
2. Beat the eggs and sugar over hot water till thick and creamy.
3. Melt the butter: have it and the flour at the same temperature as the egg mixture.
4. Add half the sieved flour and half the butter, and fold in lightly.
5. Fold in the remainder of the flour and butter.
6. Turn into the prepared tin and bake in a moderate oven.

To Ice:

Split and spread with butter icing (page 418).
Coat with water icing (page 417) and decorate as desired.
Can be cut into fingers or squares if baked in a shallow tin.
These can be iced and decorated.

SMALL CAKES

76. LEMON CURD TARTLETS

Ingredients:

Biscuit Pastry to line patty tins (page 309)
Lemon Curd (page 420)

Time: 15–20 minutes
Oven Temperature: 190°C, No. 5
Position in Oven: One-third from top

Method:

    1. Line patty tins with pastry, prick bottom.

    2. Bake in a moderate oven until lightly browned and crisp.

    3. When cold fill with lemon curd.

77. JAM TARTLETS

Make as above using jam in place of lemon curd or half-fill with jam before baking.

78. STRAWBERRY TARTLETS

Ingredients:

or 200 g Biscuit Pastry (page 309)	125 ml Fruit Juice
Rich Short Pastry (page 308)	Colouring if required
or 200 g fresh Strawberries	*or* 2 level teaspoonfuls Arrowroot
1 pkt. frozen Strawberries	Sachet of quick setting gel
125 ml Cream	

Time: 15–20 minutes

Oven Temperature: 190°C, No. 5

Position in Oven: One-third from top

Method:

    1. To make fruit juice: soak fresh strawberries with 1 tablespoonful sugar until juice flows. Make up if necessary to 125 ml with water.

    2. Line patty tins with pastry, fork the base.

    3. Bake until a very pale brown. Cool.

    4. Fill up cases with prepared fruit – halved if necessary.

    5. Thicken the fruit juice with blended arrowroot and cook for 1–2 minutes or use a sachet of quick setting gel.

    6. Glaze fruit, allow to cool and decorate with whipped cream.

Note: A little cream spread on bottom of case helps to prevent the pastry softening.

79. PINEAPPLE TARTLETS

Ingredients:

200 g Biscuit *or* Rich Short Pastry (pages 309, 308)	Crushed Pineapple
	Yellow Colouring
Cream	

100 g Water Icing (page 417, recipe 1, using pineapple flavouring, or recipe 2 using Pineapple Juice instead of Orange Juice)

Time: 15–20 minutes

Oven Temperature: 190°C, No. 5

Position in Oven: One-third from top

Method:

    1. Line patty tins with pastry, fork the base and bake till pale brown.

2. Drain pineapple well and half-fill patty case.
3. Beat cream and spread over pineapple.
4. Make water icing, using strained, heated pineapple juice. Colour.
5. Cover cream with icing.

80. RASPBERRY TARTLETS

Raspberry jam can be used instead of pineapple and icing coloured pink.

81. ECCLES CAKES

Ingredients:

200 g Flaky Pastry (page 309)

Filling:

100 g Currants   Grated Nutmeg
25 g Peel   25 g Butter *or* Block Margarine
50 g Sugar   White of 1 Egg
                                  Icing Sugar (for dredging)

Time: 15–20 minutes
Oven Temperature: 220°C, No. 7
Position in Oven: Middle shelf

Method:

1. Mix fruit, sugar, nutmeg and butter or block margarine.
2. Roll pastry out, 1 cm thick, cut in rounds with cutter.
3. Place a spoonful of mixture on each round.
4. Gather up edges, seal firmly.
5. Turn over, roll out until fruit shows through.
6. Mark lightly in diamonds with a knife. Brush with white of egg, dredge with icing sugar.
7. Bake in a hot oven for 10–15 minutes then reduce heat to 180°C, No. 4.
8. Test for readiness: pastry should be crisp and lightly browned.

Alternative method:

Cut in squares instead of rounds and continue as directed.

82. FRUIT CAKES OR SLICES

Ingredients:

200 g Puff *or* Flaky Pastry (pages 310, 309)   50 g Sugar
200 g Currants   2 level teaspoonfuls Mixed Spice
1 Apple   25 g Chopped Peel
25 g Melted Butter

Time: 20–30 minutes
Oven Temperature: 220°C, No. 7
Position in Oven: One-third from top

Method:

1. Pare and chop apple finely, mix with currants, sugar, peel, spice and butter.
2. Halve pastry, rolling out thinly two oblongs or squares.
3. Place mixture on one half, wet edges, lay other half on top and press edges together; brush with egg, mark into squares.
4. Bake in a hot oven for 10–15 minutes, remove to lower shelf for 10–15 minutes.
5. Test for readiness. Pastry should be crisp and lightly browned.
6. Cut into squares, cool.

Note: The filling may be cooked for 5 minutes and cooled before using.

83. VANILLA SLICES

Ingredients:

100 g Puff Pastry (page 310)

Time: 15 minutes
Oven Temperature: 220°C, No. 7
Position in Oven: One-third from top

Method:

1. Roll out pastry as thinly as possible, cut into strips 8–10 cm wide.
2. Prick and bake.
3. Sandwich together with confectioner's custard (page 419) or jam and cream.
4. Ice with water icing and cut into fingers.

Note: Pastry may be cut into fingers before baking.

84. COBURG CAKES (1)

Ingredients:

125 g Flour	50 g Butter *or* Block Margarine
50 g Sugar	2 teaspoonfuls Syrup
Grating of Nutmeg	1 teaspoonful Treacle
1 level teaspoonful Cinnamon	1 Egg and a little Milk (beaten)
1 level teaspoonful Bicarbonate of Soda	Almonds (split)

Makes: 14 Cakes
Time: 15 minutes
Oven temperature: 180–190°C, Nos. 4–5
Position in Oven: Middle shelf

Method:

1. Mix all dry ingredients.
2. Melt butter or block margarine, syrup and treacle.
3. Beat egg and add a little milk.
4. Add butter mixture and egg to dry ingredients and mix to a soft consistency.
5. Put half an almond in the bottom of greased patty tins and half fill tins with mixture.
6. Bake till well risen and firm to the touch.

85. **COBURG CAKES (2)**

Ingredients:

125 g Flour
50 g Butter *or* Block Margarine
50 g Castor Sugar
1 Egg (beaten)
1 level teaspoonful Cinnamon
Grating of Nutmeg

1 level teaspoonful Bicarbonate of
   Soda
1 level teaspoonful Treacle
1 level teaspoonful Syrup
Milk
Almonds (split)

Makes: 14 Cakes
Time: 15 minutes
Oven Temperature: 180°C, No. 4
Position in Oven: Middle shelf

Method:

1. Cream butter or block margarine and sugar, add beaten egg.
2. Sieve dry ingredients and stir into butter mixture.
3. Add syrup and treacle and sufficient milk to make a dropping consistency.
4. Put half an almond in the bottom of each greased patty tin.
5. Three-quarter fill tins, bake till well risen and firm to the touch.

86. **QUEEN CAKES**

Ingredients:

150 g Self-raising Flour
or { 150 g Flour
       { 2 level teaspoonfuls Baking Powder
100 g Butter or Soft Cake Margarine
100 g Castor Sugar

2 Eggs (beaten)
25 g Currants
1 teaspoonful grated Lemon Rind
1 tablespoonful Milk or Water (approx.)

Makes: 10–12 Cakes
Time: 15 minutes
Oven Temperature: 190°C, No. 5
Position in Oven: Middle shelf

Method:

1. Cream butter or soft cake margarine and sugar.
2. Add beaten eggs gradually.
3. Stir in sieved flour, currants and lemon rind, add milk to give a soft dropping consistency.
4. Three-quarter fill greased patty tins. Bake till well risen, golden brown and firm to the touch.

87. **BUTTERFLY CAKES**

Ingredients:

Queen Cakes, omitting currants
1 level teaspoonful Castor Sugar

125 ml Cream
Few drops Vanilla Essence

Makes: 12 Cakes
Time: 15 minutes
Oven Temperature: 190°C, No. 5
Position in Oven: Middle shelf

Method:

1. Cut slice from top of cake, cut across centre.
2. Beat cream, add sugar and vanilla.
3. Place a small teaspoonful cream on top of each cake.
4. Place cut tops on cream to form wings, dust with icing sugar.

Note: A small circle can be cut from the centre of the cake and cream added.
Dredge with icing sugar. Brush top of circle with jam and place on top of cream.

88. CHOCOLATE CAKES

Ingredients:

75 g Flour	2 Eggs (separated)
75 g Butter *or* Soft Cake Margarine	50 g Chocolate
75 g Castor Sugar	1 tablespoonful Water

Makes: 8–10 Cakes
Time: 20 minutes
Oven Temperature: 180°C, No. 4
Position in Oven: Middle shelf

Method:

1. Cream butter and sugar, add egg yolks and flour.
2. Dissolve chocolate in water, cool, add to mixture.
3. Beat whites until stiff, fold lightly through mixture.
4. Three-quarter fill greased patty tins. Bake till well risen and firm to the touch.
5. If liked, cakes may be coated with chocolate water icing (page 417).

89. ADELAIDE CAKES

Ingredients:

100 g Flour	50 g Cornflour
100 g Butter *or* Soft Cake Margarine	2 level teaspoonfuls Baking Powder
100 g Castor Sugar	1 tablespoonful Milk (if necessary)
50 g Cherries (chopped)	
25 g Almonds (chopped)	
3 Eggs (beaten)	

Makes: 12–14 Cakes
Time: 15–20 minutes
Oven Temperature: 190°C, No. 5
Position in Oven: Middle shelf

Method:

    1. Cream butter and sugar.

    2. Add beaten eggs gradually, beating well.

    3. Mix flours and baking powder, stir into butter mixture. Add cherries and almonds.

    4. Add milk if necessary, to make a fairly soft consistency.

    5. Three-quarter fill greased patty tins. Bake till well risen, golden brown and firm to the touch.

90. WELSH CHEESE CAKES

Ingredients:

100 g Short or Flaky Pastry (pages 307, 309)	50 g Butter or Soft Cake Margarine
50 g Self-raising Flour	50 g Castor Sugar
or { 50 g Flour	1 Egg (beaten)
{ ½ level teaspoonful Baking Powder	Jam

Makes: 10–12 Cakes

Time: 15–20 minutes

Oven Temperature: 190°C, No. 5

Position in Oven: One-third from top

Method:

    1. Line patty tins with pastry, and put in a very little jam.

    2. Cream butter or soft cake margarine and sugar, add beaten egg.

    3. Stir in sieved flour and baking powder.

    4. Three-quarter fill tins with mixture.

    5. Bake in a moderate oven.

    6. Test for readiness: risen, golden brown and firm to the touch.

    7. Remove from tins. If pastry on bottom is soft, return cakes to oven until crisp.

91. MACAROON CHEESE CAKES

Ingredients:

100 g Short or Flaky Pastry (pages 307, 309)	1 Egg (beaten)
Little Jam	50 g Ground Almonds
20 g Castor Sugar	Almond Essence
50 g Butter or Soft Cake Margarine	

Makes: 10–12 Cakes

Time: 20 minutes

Oven Temperature: 190°C, No. 5

Position in Oven: One-third from top

Method:

    1. Line patty tins with pastry, put in a little jam.

    2. Cream butter or soft cake margarine and sugar, add beaten egg slowly.

    3. Stir in ground almonds and a few drops essence.

    4. Three-quarters fill tins with almond mixture.

    5. Bake in a moderate oven.

    6. Test for readiness: lightly browned and cracked on top.

92. **ALMOND MACAROONS**

Ingredients:

100 g Rich Short Pastry (page 308)	75 g Castor Sugar
2 Egg Whites (beaten)	Almond Essence
50 g Ground Almonds	Raspberry Jam

Makes: 10–12 Cakes
Time: 20–30 minutes
Oven Temperature: 180°C, No. 4
Position in Oven: Middle shelf

Method:

1. Line patty tins with pastry, put in a little jam.
2. Beat egg whites, mix in almonds, sugar and essence.
3. Three-quarter fill lined tins.
4. Bake for 20–30 minutes.
5. Test for readiness: pastry should be crisp and macaroon mixture firm on top.

93. **MASERINES**

Ingredients, Pastry:

100 g Flour	25 g Ground Almonds
2 teaspoonfuls Castor Sugar	1 Egg Yolk
50 g Butter *or* Block Margarine	Raspberry Jam

Mixture:

1 Egg White	50 g Almonds (roughly-chopped)
100 g Granulated Sugar	2 teaspoonfuls Chocolate (grated)

Time: 25–30 minutes
Oven Temperature: 180–190°C, Nos. 4–5
Position in Oven: Middle shelf

Method:

1. Cream butter and sugar, add flour, ground almonds and egg yolk, mix to a stiff paste.
2. Roll out into two strips, 8–10 cm wide, 20–30 cm long.
3. Cut a 1-cm wide strip from each long side and place on top of pastry side to form a raised edge.
4. Half cook in moderate oven 10–15 minutes.
5. Remove from oven, spread with jam.
6. Make filling mixture by beating egg white until frothy, then add sugar, chocolate and nuts.
7. Stir over heat until boiling, pour on top of pastry.
8. Cook for 15–20 minutes, 170°C, No. 3.
9. Test for readiness: top should be firm and glossy.
10. Cut into fingers while hot.

94. ALMOND RING CAKES

Ingredients:

Biscuit mixture: **Almond mixture:**

100 g Self-raising Flour	2 Egg Whites (whisked)
25 g Castor Sugar	50 g Castor Sugar
50 g Butter *or* Block Margarine	100 g Ground Almonds
Little Egg Yolk	Few drops Almond Essence

Makes: 14 Cakes

Time: 15 minutes

Oven Temperature: 180–190°C, Nos. 4–5

Position in Oven: Middle shelf

Method:

1. Cream butter and sugar.
2. Add sieved flour and enough egg to form a stiff dough.
3. Roll out and cut in rounds.
4. Whisk whites until stiff, mix in sugar, almonds and essence.
5. Pipe almond mixture round each biscuit using a star pipe.
6. Bake in a moderate oven until lightly browned.
7. When cold put a little jam or jelly in centre of each.

95. MACAROONS

Ingredients:

100 g Ground Almonds	½ teaspoonful Vanilla Essence
200 g Castor Sugar	Rice Paper
3 Egg Whites	Few shredded Almonds
3 level teaspoonfuls Rice Flour	

Time: 20 minutes

Oven Temperature: 180°C, No. 4

Position in Oven: Middle shelf

Method:

1. Beat well together almonds, sugar, egg whites, rice flour and vanilla essence.
2. Pipe 3 cm apart onto rice paper in 3 cm rounds, using a plain pipe.
3. Sprinkle with shredded almonds.
4. Bake in a moderate oven for about 20 minutes.
5. Test for readiness: firm to touch.

96. COCONUT PYRAMIDS (12)

Ingredients:

200 g Coconut	1 large Egg White
50 g Castor Sugar	½ teaspoonful Vanilla Essence
25 g Rice Flour	

Makes: 12
Time: 20 minutes
Oven Temperature: 150°C, No. 2
Position in Oven: Middle shelf

Method:

1. Mix all dry ingredients.
2. Beat egg white until stiff, stir in dry ingredients.
3. Add vanilla, place in small heaps on greased tin.
4. Bake until lightly browned.

97. CREAM BUNS

Ingredients:

Choux Pastry (page 312)

Filling:

125 ml Cream   Sugar to taste
Few drops Vanilla

Makes: 10–12 Buns
Time: 20 minutes
Oven Temperature: 200°C, No. 6
Position in Oven: One-third from top

Method:

1. Make the pastry.
2. Drop in teaspoonfuls or pipe onto a greased tray.
3. Bake in fairly hot oven till well risen and dry.
4. Split and remove any soft part inside.
5. Fill with whipped cream and dredge with icing sugar.

98. CHOCOLATE ECLAIRS

Ingredients:

Choux Pastry (page 312)
Whipped Cream *or* Confectioner's Custard (page 419)
150 g Chocolate Water Icing (page 417)

Makes: 10–12 Eclairs
Time: 20 minutes
Oven Temperature: 200°C, No. 6
Position in Oven: One-third from top

Method:

1. Pipe pastry in finger lengths onto greased tin.
2. Bake until risen and dry.
3. Cool, split, remove any soft mixture from centre.
4. Fill with sweetened cream or confectioner's custard.
5. Ice with chocolate icing.

99. BRANDY SNAPS

Ingredients:

100 g Flour	100 g Syrup
100 g Butter	½ level teaspoonful Ginger
100 g Sugar	Juice ½ Lemon

Makes: 36 Snaps

Time: About 10 minutes

Oven Temperature: 180°C, No. 4

Position in Oven: Middle shelf

Method:

1. Put all in a pan and heat till just warm.
2. Put on well-greased tin in teaspoonfuls, six inches apart
3. Bake till golden brown.
4. Allow to cool a second, turn over and roll up round the greased handle of a wooden spoon. These may be stored in tins.
5. Cream may be piped inside just before serving.

BISCUITS

100. OATMEAL BISCUITS

Ingredients:

150 g Self-raising Flour	75 g Cooking Fat
or { 150 g Plain Flour	Pinch Salt
2 level teaspoonfuls Baking Powder	Milk to bind
150 g Oatmeal	25 g Sugar, if liked

Time: 10–12 minutes

Oven Temperature: 180°C, No. 4

Position in Oven: Middle shelf

Method:

1. Mix dry ingredients, rub in fat.
2. Add milk to give a very stiff mixture.
3. Sprinkle board with oatmeal, roll out thinly and fork.
4. Cut into rounds, bake on a greased tin.

101. PARKINS

Ingredients:

100 g Oatmeal	Pinch Salt
100 g Flour	50 g Cooking Fat
1 ½ level teaspoonfuls Bicarbonate of Soda	75 g Syrup
75 g Sugar	½ Egg
½ level teaspoonful Mixed Spice	Few Almonds
1 level teaspoonful Cinnamon	1 level teaspoonful Ginger

Time: 15–20 minutes
Oven Temperature: 170°C, No. 3
Position in Oven: Middle shelf

Method:

1. Mix dry ingredients, rub in fat.
2. Mix egg and syrup, add to flour to give a stiff dough.
3. Roll into small balls, place well apart on greased tin.
4. Press half almond on top of each. Bake.

102. GINGER SNAPS

Ingredients:

100 g Self-raising Flour	25 g Sugar
or {100 g Flour	50 g Cooking Fat
1 level teaspoonful Baking Powder	50 g Syrup
2 level teaspoonfuls Ginger	A little Egg if necessary

Time: 15 minutes
Oven Temperature: 170–180°C, Nos. 3–4
Position in Oven: Middle shelf

Method:

1. Sieve flour, baking powder and ginger, add sugar.
2. Melt lard and syrup, add to flour.
3. Mix to a stiff paste with egg.
4. Roll into walnut-sized balls.
5. Place well apart on a greased baking tin.
6. Bake in a moderate oven for 15 minutes.

103. ABERNETHY BISCUITS

Ingredients:

200 g Flour	50 g Cooking Fat
1 level teaspoonful Cream of Tartar	40 g Sugar
½ level teaspoonful Bicarbonate of Soda	1 tablespoonful Milk
50 g Butter *or* Block Margarine	Pinch Salt

Time: 20 minutes
Oven Temperature: 180°C, No. 4
Position in Oven: Middle shelf

Method:

1. Sieve flour and raising agent.
2. Rub in the fats.
3. Melt sugar in milk and add to dry ingredients.
4. Make a stiff dough and roll out 5 mm thick.
5. Cut into biscuits. Prick with a fork.
6. Bake in moderate oven for 20 minutes.

104. SHREWSBURY BISCUITS

Ingredients:

150 g Flour

100 g Butter *or* Block Margarine

75 g Castor Sugar

1 Egg (beaten), if necessary

or 2 level teaspoonfuls Caraway Seeds

1 level teaspoonful Cinnamon

Time: 15 minutes

Oven Temperature: 170–180°C, No. 3–4

Position in Oven: Middle shelf

Method:

1. Cream the butter or block margarine and sugar.
2. Add the dry ingredients and mix to a stiff consistency with egg if required.
3. Roll out, fork and cut into biscuits.
4. Place on a greased tin and bake in a moderate oven.

105. SHORTBREAD

Ingredients:

200 g Flour

or { 150 g Flour
       50 g Rice Flour

100 g Butter

50 g Castor Sugar

Time: 30–40 minutes

Oven Temperature: 170°C, No. 3

Position in Oven: Middle shelf

Method:

1. Mix flour and sugar.
2. Work flour and sugar gradually into butter, using the hand.
3. Knead well, shape into cakes, or roll into strips.
4. Place on baking tin, pinch edges, prick the top with a fork.
5. Bake a pale brown.
6. Allow to cool short time before moving.
7. If a strip, cut into fingers before cold.

Note: Butter and sugar can be creamed and the flour worked in.

Variations:

Pitcaithly Bannocks.—add 50 g blanched chopped almonds and chopped citron peel.

Ginger Biscuits.—add 25–50 g chopped crystalised ginger.

Cherry Biscuits.—add 50 g chopped cherries.

106. IMPERIAL BISCUITS

Ingredients:

200 g Flour

100 g Butter *or* Block Margarine

100 g Castor Sugar

1 level teaspoonful Baking Powder

1 level teaspoonful Ground Cinnamon (if liked)

Egg (beaten, to bind)

Jam

Water Icing (page 417)

Time: 15–20 minutes
Oven Temperature: 170–180°C, No. 3–4
Position in Oven: Middle shelf

Method:

1. Cream butter or block margarine and sugar.
2. Mix flour, baking powder and cinnamon.
3. Add flour to creamed mixture, bind with egg, keeping mixture very stiff.
4. Knead well, roll 5 mm thick, fork, cut into biscuits.
5. Bake, cool, spread with jam; sandwich two biscuits together.
6. Ice with water icing. Decorate each biscuit with half a glacé cherry if liked.

107. VANILLA BISCUITS

Ingredients:

75 g Flour	50 g Cooking Fat
100 g Flaked Oats	75 g Sugar
2 level teaspoonfuls Baking Powder	1 teaspoonful Syrup
1 level teaspoonful Bicarbonate of Soda	3 teaspoonfuls Boiling Water
50 g Butter	1 teaspoonful Vanilla
50 g Butter Icing (page 418)	

Time: 20 minutes
Oven Temperature: 170–180°C, No. 3–4
Position in Oven: Middle shelf

Method:

1. Mix flour, oats and raising agent.
2. Cream fat and sugar, adding dry ingredients, mix well.
3. Add syrup melted in boiling water and vanilla.
4. Knead, roll out about 5 mm thick, cut in rounds.
5. Place on greased baking tin. Bake.
6. When cool, sandwich together with butter icing.

108. CHOCOLATE BISCUITS

Ingredients:

100 g Butter *or* Block Margarine	1 Egg (beaten)
100 g Castor Sugar	50 g Chocolate Butter Icing (page 418)
125 g Flour	100 g Chocolate Water Icing (page 417)
25 g Cocoa	

Time: 15–20 minutes
Oven Temperature: 170–180°C, No. 3–4
Position in Oven: Middle shelf

Method:

1. Cream butter or block margarine and sugar, mix flour and cocoa.
2. Add beaten egg and sieved flour alternately.
3. Knead, roll out 5 mm thick, fork, cut in rounds.

4. Bake, cool, sandwich with butter icing.

5. Coat with chocolate icing, decorate with walnut or flaked chocolate.

109. COFFEE WALNUT BISCUITS

Ingredients:

150 g Flour   25 g Walnuts (chopped)
100 g Butter *or* Block Margarine   50 g Butter Icing (page 418)
50 g Castor Sugar   100 g Coffee Water Icing (page 417)

Time: 15 minutes
Oven Temperature: 180°C, No. 4
Position in Oven: Middle shelf

Method:

1. Cream butter or block margarine with the sugar. Gradually work in flour and add chopped walnuts.
2. Roll out 5 mm thick and cut into biscuits.
3. Bake for 15 minutes. Cool.
4. Sandwich two biscuits together with butter icing.
5. Ice the top with coffee water icing and decorate with a small piece of walnut.

110. NAPOLEON FINGERS

Ingredients:

100 g Flour   25 g Ground Almonds
75 g Butter *or* Block Margarine   1 Egg Yolk
50 g Castor Sugar   Raspberry Jam
Pinch Salt

Time: 10–15 minutes
Oven Temperature: 170–180°C, No. 3–4
Position in Oven: Middle shelf

Method:

1. Rub butter or block margarine into flour. Add sugar and salt and ground almonds and mix well.
2. Add enough egg yolk to make a stiff paste and lay aside to firm if necessary.
3. Roll out into two thin strips.
4. Bake until pale brown in a moderate oven.
5. Spread one biscuit with jam, lay another on top. Cut into fingers while hot and dredge with icing sugar.

111. **TANTALLON BISCUITS**

Ingredients:

200 g Flour
100 g Butter
2 Egg Yolks
Chopped Almonds *or* Coconut

½ level teaspoonful Baking Powder
50 g Castor Sugar
Royal Icing: 1-Egg quantity (page 418)

Time: 10–15 minutes
Oven Temperature: 170°C, No. 3
Position in Oven: Middle shelf

Method:

1. Mix flour and baking powder, rub in butter.
2. Add sugar, mix with yolks to a stiff paste.
3. Knead well until smooth, roll out 5 mm thick.
4. Cut into strips 8 cm wide, place on baking tin.
5. Make royal icing to give a spreading consistency.
6. Spread icing thinly over strips, decorate edges with almonds or coconut.
7. Cut into fingers, leave 15 minutes to firm.
8. Bake until golden brown.

112. **VIENNESE BISCUITS**

Ingredients:

200 g Self-raising Flour
200 g Butter *or* Block Margarine
50 g Icing Sugar

Time: 15 minutes
Oven Temperature: 180°C, No. 4
Position in Oven: Middle shelf

Method:

1. Cream butter or block margarine with sugar. Work in flour.
2. Pipe in fingers onto a greased tin. Bake for 15 minutes.
3. Cool.

Variations:

1. Sandwich together with butter icing, and dip ends in melted chocolate.
2. Pipe into rounds and put cherry or chopped nuts into centre.
3. Pipe into paper cases with cherry in the middle. When cool, dredge with icing sugar.

ICINGS AND FILLINGS

ICINGS AND FILLINGS

1. **WATER ICING**

Ingredients:

200 g Icing Sugar (sieved) Flavouring as desired, e.g.
2–3 tablespoonfuls warm Water   Vanilla, Coffee, Raspberry

Method:

1. Gradually add water to icing sugar, beat well between additions until the desired consistency has been reached.
2. Add flavouring, mix well. Check consistency – if too soft add a little more icing sugar.

2. **ORANGE WATER ICING**

Ingredients:

200 g Icing Sugar (sieved) 2–3 tablespoonfuls fresh Orange Juice (warmed)

Method:

Gradually add orange juice to icing sugar, beat well between additions until desired consistency has been reached.

3. **CHOCOLATE WATER ICING (1)**

Ingredients:

200 g Icing Sugar (sieved) 2 tablespoonfuls hot Water
50–75 g Chocolate (Plain, Milk or White) 1 teaspoonful Vanilla Essence

Method:

1. Dissolve chocolate in water, allow to cool.
2. Gradually add to sugar beating well between additions until desired consistency has been reached.
3. Add vanilla. Check consistency.

4. **CHOCOLATE WATER ICING (2)**

Ingredients:

200 g Icing Sugar (sieved) 2–3 tablespoonfuls warm Water
20–25 g Cocoa 1 teaspoonful Vanilla Essence
or
35–40 g Chocolate Powder

Method:

1. Dissolve cocoa or chocolate powder in water.
2. Gradually add to icing sugar beating well between additions until desired consistency has been reached.
3. Add vanilla. Check consistency.

5. BUTTER ICING

Ingredients:

150–200 g Icing Sugar (sieved)	100 g soft Butter
Flavouring	Colouring

Method:

1. Cream the butter; gradually add icing sugar and beat till light and creamy.
2. Add flavouring and colouring as desired.

Suitable flavourings:

1 teaspoonful Vanilla Essence	2 drops Almond Essence
Rind and Juice ½ Orange	1 level tablespoonful Instant Coffee (dissolved)

6. CHOCOLATE BUTTER ICING

Ingredients:

150–200 g Icing Sugar (sieved)   100 g soft Butter
75 g grated Chocolate *or* 40 g Chocolate Powder *or* 25 g Cocoa

Method:

1. Cream butter, gradually add icing sugar, beat well.
2. Melt chocolate over hot water, allow to cool but not set, or mix chocolate powder or cocoa with 2 tablespoonfuls of boiling water.
3. Beat into creamed mixture.

7. ROYAL ICING

Ingredients:

200 g Icing Sugar (sieved)	2 Egg Whites
2–3 drops Lemon Juice	

Method:

1. Slightly whisk egg whites.
2. Add icing sugar gradually to egg whites beating well between each addition,
3. Add lemon juice. Beat very well. Check consistency.

Note: Icing should be soft and spreadable but not runny.

8. FEATHER ICING

Ingredients:

200 g Granulated Sugar	Pinch Cream of Tartar
4 tablespoonfuls Water	Egg White

Method:

1. Dissolve sugar slowly in water, boil, add cream of tartar.
2. Allow to boil until 116°C is reached or until the syrup forms a soft ball when tested in cold water.
3. Whisk egg lightly, gradually add syrup.
4. Beat well, continue beating until icing begins to thicken.
5. Immediately pour over cake.

Note: This icing may be coloured if desired.

9. SEVEN MINUTE FROSTING

Ingredients:

150 g Granulated Sugar
1 Egg White (unbeaten)
2 tablespoonfuls cold Water

½ level teaspoonful Baking Powder
1 level teaspoonful Flavouring (*or* as
    desired)

Method:

1. Put all the ingredients except baking powder, into the top of a double boiler or a bowl.
2. Put bowl in a pan over boiling water and whisk for 7 minutes.
3. Add flavouring and baking powder, beat.
4. Spread on cake.

10. ALMOND PASTE OR MARZIPAN

Ingredients:

200 g Ground Almonds
200 g Icing Sugar (sieved)

Few drops Almond Essence and Vanilla
1 large Egg *or* 2 Yolks

Method:

1. Mix icing sugar and ground almonds, add essence.
2. Add sufficient beaten eggs, to form a stiff paste.

Note: Sugar may be half castor and half icing; equal quantities ground almonds, castor and icing sugar may be used.

11. CONFECTIONERS' CUSTARD

Ingredients:

250 ml Milk
25 g Cornflour (*or* 35 g Flour)
30–40 g Sugar

2 Egg Yolks
Vanilla Essence

Method:

1. Heat milk till boiling.
2. Mix other ingredients thoroughly. Pour boiling milk over mixed ingredients, stirring all the time.
3. Return to pan and cook till mixture thickens. Cool and use as required.

12. ALMOND FILLING

Ingredients:

1–2 tablespoonfuls Apricot Jam
1 teaspoonful Maraschino *or* Sherry

75 g Ground Almonds

Method:

1. Sieve jam.
2. Mix all together.

Note: If being used immediately, the addition of 2 tablespoonfuls whipped cream is an improvement.

13. ORANGE FILLING

Ingredients:

25 g Cornflour　　　　　　　　Water
Juice 1 Orange　　　　　　　　1 Egg Yolk
1 tablespoonful Lemon Juice　　25 g Sugar
10 g Fresh Butter

Method:

1. Grate rind of orange.
2. Squeeze orange, make juice up to 250 ml (short measure) with water.
3. Blend cornflour with liquids, adding gradually. Put in a pan and bring to boil.
4. Remove from heat, add beaten yolk and sugar.
5. Beat butter through mixture. Cool before using.

14. WALNUT FILLING

Ingredients:

3 tablespoonfuls Apricot Jam　　　1 tablespoonful Walnuts (chopped)
3 tablespoonfuls Ground Almonds　1 teaspoonful Vanilla Essence

Method:

1. Sieve jam.
2. Mix all together.

15. LEMON CURD

Ingredients:

50 g Butter　　　　　2 Lemons (juice and grated rind)
150 g Sugar　　　　　4 Egg Yolks *or* 2 whole Eggs

Method:

1. Melt butter and pour into a bowl, add sugar and grated lemon rind.
2. Add lemon juice and egg yolks.
3. Put the bowl in a pan of hot water (not touching the water), stir over the heat till the mixture thickens.
4. Put into a jar and use as required.

Note: Instead of grating, the lemon rind may be peeled thinly and removed when the curd is thick.

SIMPLE CONFECTIONERY

SIMPLE CONFECTIONERY

I. RULES

General rules	1. Use a strong, thick pan of a size to allow contents to boil up 2. Always dissolve sugar in the water or milk before allowing it to boil 3. At boiling point, add cream of tartar or glucose, this prevents granulation 4. Brush round sides of pan constantly with a pastry brush dipped in warm water to remove sugar crystals 5. Keep thermometer in a pan of hot water at side of the cooker 6. When testing syrup, read thermometer in upright position, eye on a level with top of the mercury
To Test Syrup without a Thermometer	Dip a teaspoon in cold water, then in the boiling syrup, and drop a little syrup into cold water. The degree to which the syrup has been boiled can be judged by its hardness
Soft Ball:	Heat till 114–118°C, 238–245°F *or* Drop a little syrup into cold water, leave for a few minutes. Pick up between finger and thumb, when it should roll into a small soft ball
Hard Ball:	Heat till 120–130°C, 248–265°F *or* Test as above when syrup should roll into a hard ball
Crack:	Heat till 135–148°C, 275–300°F *or* Test as above when thread of syrup should break sharply
Caramel:	Heat till 155–175°C, 310°F *or* When the syrup begins to colour, caramel stage is reached. Although the term caramel is used, there are various stages of this from light golden brown to a dark brown colour. Care should be taken to avoid making it too dark as the taste will be bitter

2. FAMILY TOFFEE

Ingredients:

500 g Granulated Sugar   30 g Golden Syrup
125 ml Milk   25 g Butter

Method:

1. Put all ingredients into a pan and heat gently, stirring occasionally till sugar is dissolved.
2. Boil to 125°C (hard ball); do not stir.
3. Pour into a greased tin, around 15–20 cm.
4. Mark in squares when firm.

3. CLEAR TOFFEE

Ingredients:

500 g Granulated Sugar   125 ml Water
25 g Butter   Pinch Cream of Tartar

Method:

1. Put all ingredients into a pan over a low heat. Stir only occasionally, till sugar is dissolved.
2. Boil to 125°C (hard ball); do not stir.
3. Pour into a greased tin, around 15–20 cm in size.
4. Mark in squares when firm.

4. TREACLE TOFFEE

Ingredients:

500 g Demerara Sugar   Large pinch Cream of Tartar
250 ml Water   50 g Treacle
50 g Butter   2 teaspoonfuls Vinegar

Method:

1. Dissolve sugar in water, stirring occasionally.
2. Add butter, cream of tartar, treacle and vinegar and boil up.
3. Boil to 138°C (crack).
4. Allow to settle.
5. Pour into greased tin, around 15–20 cm in size.
6. Mark in squares when firm.
7. Wrap each piece in waxed paper.

5. EVERTON TOFFEE

Ingredients:

500 g Granulated Sugar   50 g Golden Syrup
250 ml cold Water   Pinch Cream of Tartar
75–100 g Butter   Lemon Essence to taste

Method:

1. Dissolve sugar in water, stirring gently.
2. Add half butter, the syrup and cream of tartar.
3. Boil fairly rapidly, with occasional stirring to 125°C (hard ball).
4. Add rest of butter and boil to 148°C (crack).
5. Add lemon, allow to settle.
6. Pour quickly into a greased tin, around 15–20 cm in size.
7. When beginning to firm, mark into squares.
8. Break up when cold, wrap in waxed paper.

Note: Treacle may be used instead of syrup to give a dark toffee.

6. **RUSSIAN TOFFEE**

Ingredients:

500 g Granulated Sugar	200 ml Condensed Milk
250 ml Water	3 tablespoonfuls Golden Syrup
100 g Butter	Little Vanilla Essence

Method:

1. Dissolve sugar in water, stirring gently.
2. Add a third of the butter, condensed milk and syrup.
3. Boil to 118°C (soft ball), stirring gently all the time.
4. Add remainder of butter, small pieces at a time.
5. Add essence and boil to 125°C (hard ball).
6. Allow to settle, pour into greased tin, around 15–20 cm in size.
7. When nearly firm mark in oblong shapes.
8. Cut when cold and wrap in waxed paper.

7. **CREAM CARAMELS**

Ingredients:

500 g granulated Sugar	25 g Butter
250 ml Water	125 ml Double Cream
100 g Glucose	Vanilla Essence

Method:

1. Dissolve sugar in water, stirring gently.
2. Add glucose and boil to 118°C (soft ball).
3. Add butter in slices.
4. Add cream and vanilla.
5. Boil to 122°C (firm ball), stirring gently.
6. Pour into greased tin, around 15–20 cm in size.
7. Mark in squares when firm.
8. Wrap each caramel in waxed paper.

8. **PULLED MOLASSES**

Ingredients:

200 g Demerara Sugar	25 g Butter
1 tablespoonful Syrup	Pinch Cream of Tartar
125 ml Water	

Method:

1. Put ingredients into pan and stir gently. Dissolve sugar, before allowing to boil.
2. Boil to 142°C (crack).
3. Turn onto oiled slab or ashet.
4. Fold over from sides with an oiled scraper or knife.
5. Pull with oiled hands when cool enough to handle.
6. Cut into pieces with oiled scissors and wrap in waxed paper.

Note: Chopped walnuts or peppermint essence may be added when on slab.

9. VANILLA TABLET

Ingredients:

500 g Granulated Sugar   1 tablespoonful Golden Syrup
50 g Butter   Vanilla Essence
250 ml Milk

Method:

1. Put sugar, butter, milk and syrup in a pan. Stir gently to dissolve sugar.
2. Bring slowly to boiling point.
3. Boil to 115°C (soft ball), stirring all the time.
4. Remove from heat, add vanilla.
5. Beat till beginning to grain.
6. Pour into greased tin, around 15–20 cm in size, and cut when cold.

10. WALNUT TABLET

Ingredients:

500 g Granulated Sugar   1 tablespoonful Golden Syrup
50 g Butter   75 g Walnuts
250 ml Milk

Method:

Make as for vanilla tablet, above, adding chopped walnuts before beating, step 5.

11. CHOCOLATE TABLET

Ingredients:

50 g Chocolate (grated)   50 g Glacé Cherries (chopped)

Method:

Make as vanilla tablet, above, adding chocolate to step 1, and cherries before beating, step 5.

12. HELENSBURGH TOFFEE

Ingredients:

500 g Granulated Sugar   1 dessertspoonful Golden Syrup
125 ml Milk *or* Water   200 ml Condensed Milk
50 g Butter   Vanilla Essence

Method:

1. Melt butter with water or milk. Stir gently.
2. Add sugar and syrup; continue stirring and, when dissolved, add condensed milk.
3. Stir gently all the time, boil to 118°C (soft ball).
4. Remove from heat, allow to settle, add essence.
5. Beat till beginning to grain; quickly pour into greased tin, 15–20 cm in size.
6. When set, cut in squares.

13. **COCONUT TABLET**

Ingredients:

500 g Granulated Sugar   50 g Desiccated Coconut
125 ml Milk   Colouring, if liked
Small piece Butter

Method:

1. Dissolve sugar in milk, stirring gently. Bring gradually to the boil.
2. At boiling point add butter and coconut.
3. Boil to 115°C (soft ball), stirring all the time.
4. Beat till creamy and thick and beginning to grain.
5. Pour into greased tin, around 15–20 cm in size.
6. When set, cut in squares.

14. **COCONUT ICE**

Ingredients:

500 g Granulated Sugar   50 g Desiccated Coconut
125 ml Water   2 Egg Whites

Method:

1. Dissolve sugar in water stirring gently, Boil to 114°C (soft ball).
2. Stir in coconut and cook for a few minutes.
3. Beat egg whites and add; cook a few minutes.
4. Pour into greased tin, around 15–20 cm in size.
5. When cold, cut in squares.

15. **VANILLA FUDGE**

Ingredients:

400 g Granulated Sugar   1 tablespoonful Golden Syrup
100 g Butter   1 teaspoonful Vanilla Essence
170 ml Evaporated Milk

Method:

1. Put milk, sugar, butter and syrup in pan and heat gently, stirring, until sugar dissolved.
2. Boil to 118°C (soft ball), stirring all the time.
3. Cool slightly, add vanilla and beat till thick.
4. Pour at once into greased tin, around 15–20 cm in size.
5. When set, cut in squares.

16. **TURKISH DELIGHT**

Ingredients:

500 g Granulated Sugar   20 g powdered Gelatine
1 Lemon   125 ml Water
1 Orange   Pink Colouring

Method:

1. Put lemon and orange rind, juice, sugar, gelatine and water in a pan.
2. Stir to dissolve sugar before bringing to the boil.
3. Add colouring and strain into wetted dish.
4. Leave 12 hours till set.
5. Cut into squares, toss in icing sugar.
6. Leave exposed to air till a skin is formed.

Note: 50 g almonds and pistachio nuts may be added when syrup is on the point of setting.

17. MARSHMALLOWS

Ingredients:

250 g Granulated Sugar
15 g powdered Gelatine
125 ml Water and Orange-Flower
    Water mixed

125 ml Water
1 dessertspoonful Glucose
1 Egg White

Method:

1. Melt gelatine in water and orange-flower water in fairly large pan.
2. Dissolve sugar and glucose in water in another pan and boil to 127°C (hard ball).
3. Pour onto gelatine mixture, beating briskly with a whisk for a minute or two.
4. Add stiffly-beaten egg white.
5. Continue whisking till white and stiff.
6. Pour into tin greased and dredged with icing sugar.
7. When set, rub over with icing sugar.
8. Cut into squares with scissors.
9. Toss squares in icing sugar.

Note: Various flavourings can be used.

18. PEPPERMINT CREAMS

Ingredients:

500 g Icing Sugar (sieved)
2 Eggs Whites

Peppermint Essence *or* Oil of Peppermint

Method:

1. Slightly whisk whites.
2. Gradually stir in sugar till stiff consistency.
3. Add peppermint flavouring and knead well.
4. Roll out on board with icing sugar.
5. Cut into small rounds and leave overnight to dry on waxed paper.

19. **CHOCOLATE TRUFFLES**

Ingredients:

75 g Butter
200 g sweetened Chocolate Powder
1 teaspoonful Vanilla Essence

50 g Chocolate Vermicelli
or Cocoa

Method:

1. Cream butter.
2. Gradually work in chocolate powder and vanilla essence.
3. Roll into balls and toss in chocolate vermicelli or cocoa.
4. Put in paper cases when firm.

Note: 25 g finely chopped glacé cherries and chopped nuts can be added.

20. **MARZIPAN**

Ingredients:

200 g Granulated Sugar
125 ml Water
Pinch Cream of Tartar

150 g Ground Almonds
1 Egg White (whisked)
1–2 tablespoonfuls Icing Sugar

Method:

1. Dissolve sugar in water, stirring gently. Bring to the boil.
2. At boiling point, add cream of tartar.
3. Boil to 115°C (soft ball).
4. Add almonds, stir well.
5. Add egg white gradually, and cook a few minutes over a gentle heat.
6. Pour onto an oiled slab or board, cool slightly.
7. Work till smooth with icing sugar.
8. Colour and flavour as liked.

21. **CARAMEL WALNUTS**

Ingredients:

Marzipan
Walnuts

Dipping Syrup (No 22)

Method:

1. Form marzipan into balls.
2. Place halved, shelled walnuts on each side.
3. Allow to dry for 12 hours.
4. Dip in syrup, allow to set on an oiled plate and place in cases.

22. **DIPPING SYRUP**

Ingredients:

500 g Granulated Sugar
250 ml Water

Pinch Cream of Tartar

Method:

1. Dissolve sugar slowly in water. Stirring gently.
2. Add cream of tartar.
3. Boil to 148°C (crack), without stirring.

PRESERVING

HOME FREEZING

BOTTLING FRUIT

PICKLES AND CHUTNEY

JAMS AND JELLIES

HOME FREEZING

I. INTRODUCTION

Home freezing is a quick and efficient method of preserving a wide variety of foods. If treated correctly, frozen foods retain much of their original fresh condition, flavour, appearance and nutritive value.

Foods can be frozen in quantities to suit the family's requirements and at a time when a particular food is in peak condition and when in plentiful supply.

In home-freezing, a low temperature is used to inhibit the multiplying of spoilage organisms and enzymes which cause food to deteriorate. The success and safety of the food therefore depends on the maintenance of a low temperature.

Fahrenheit	Celsius	
35–40°	1–4°	Recommended temperature range for main cabinet of home refrigerator
32°	0°	Freezing point of water
21°	-6°	Temperature of frozen food in storage compartment of a one-star refrigerator*
10°	-12°	Temperature of frozen food in storage compartment of a two-star refrigerator**
0°	-18°	Temperature of frozen food in storage compartment of a three-star refrigerator*** **also** Storage temperature for food in a freezer
-5° -12°	-21° -24°	Freezing fresh food in a home freezer
-30°	-34°	Temperature at which foods are quick-frozen commercially

Successful freezing depends on reducing the temperature of food to -18°C (0°F) within 24 hours using the fast-freeze facility (see manufacturer's guide) and maintaining it at that temperature. This prevents the formation of large ice crystals which cause rupturing of the cell walls of the food, and on thawing, could result in a limp, flavourless product.

It is important to remember that the spoilage organisms will be activated when the food is thawing. Thawed food must therefore be used immediately and **NEVER** refrozen.

2. **FREEZERS**

I. Chest or top-opening freezer

This type is slightly more economical to run, as cold air is heavier than warm air when the lid is opened there is little loss of cold. Defrosting therefore should only be necessary every 6 months.

An organised system should be adopted to ensure that food is used in rotation. Baskets or other containers are a help in this system.

2. Upright or front-opening freezer

(a) One-door model:

This type is fitted with shelves and the contents are easily seen. However, cold is lost when the door is open and this could cause a rise in temperature in the cabinet. The running cost is higher and more frequent defrosting is necessary than with the chest type although most modern freezers are now automatically self-defrosting.

(b) Two-door model:

Top section is used for foods which are used frequently. Lower section is for long-term storage as the door will not require to be opened so often.

There are some two-compartment refrigerator or freezer cabinets available. These are useful when space is limited.

3. **PACKAGING**

Wrapping materials must be:

1. Vapour and moisture proof, e.g. heavy-gauge polythene bags.
2. Free from taste and smell.
3. Non-toxic.
4. Able to withstand low temperatures.
5. Economical on storage space.
6. Not too expensive, e.g. margarine tubs.

Sealing

When liquids are being frozen, e.g. fruit purée or soup, a head space of (1–2 cm) should be left to allow for expansion on freezing.

Other packages should be filled almost to the brim, **excluding as much air as possible**. These may be heat sealed or twisted and folded and tied with a plastic-covered wire or sealed with a special freezer tape.

Labelling

Always label food with quantity or number of servings and date of freezing etc. Use in rotation. Write labels with a spirit-based pen and use labels which will stick in a damp condition.

4. **RULES FOR FREEZING**

1. Freeze only top quality products.
2. Freeze food which is at its peak of freshness.
3. Handle quickly food designed for the freezer.
4. Observe the basic rules of hygiene.
5. Follow general and specific directions given by manufacturers.
6. Only use packaging materials which are guaranteed to be sufficiently moisture- and vapour-proof, and resistant to cross-contamination during storage at -18°C or 0°F.
7. Pack foods in usable quantities.
8. Extract as much air as possible from each package and then completely seal.
9. Label and date packages.
10. Cool food as quickly as possible to room temperature or below, before putting into freezer. Do not put hot food in the refrigerator to cool as this will increase the temperature and put the fridge's contents at risk.
11. Limit additions of food to the freezer to quantities advised by the manufacturer of your freezer – usually one tenth of the capacity (28-litre space can hold 12–14 kg of food).
12. Allow spaces between packages added to the freezer, for fast freezing.
13. Observe suggested time limits for storage (page 438).
14. Do not let freezer temperature rise above -18°C or 0°F.
15. **NEVER** refreeze defrosted frozen foods.
16. Reseal part-used packages carefully (e.g. peas) excluding as much air as possible.

5. **PREPARATION OF FOODS FOR THE FREEZER**

All fresh vegetables should be blanched to prevent the development of "off flavours" by enzyme action and to preserve the colour. The vegetables should be prepared and then blanched in approximately 3 litres of boiling water to each 500 g so that the water returns to the boil in 1 minute after the addition of vegetables. Blanching time varies according to different vegetables.

After blanching, plunge vegetables (except potatoes) into ice cold water (for same length of time as for blanching) to cool quickly and to prevent overcooking.

6. A GUIDE TO THE PREPARATION OF THE MORE COMMON VEGETABLES FOR FREEZING

Vegetable	Preparation	Blanching and Cooling Times (same for both)
Beans (French or Runner)	Cut off ends and string if necessary. Cut into lengths of 2 cm	2 mins
Broccoli	Choose close heads. Divide into florettes and trim stalks	3–4 mins
Brussels Sprouts	Use small brussels sprouts. Prepare as for cooking (page 184)	3 mins
Carrots	Use only young tender fresh carrots. Cut off tops. Blanch and rub skin off	5 mins
Cauliflower	Break into even-sized florettes	3 mins
Peas	Choose young tender peas; shell	I mins
Potatoes (Roast)	Peel small potatoes	Blanch for 3 minutes in oil (180°C) and leave to cool
Potatoes (Mashed)	Prepare, cook and mash in normal way	Cool quickly
Chips	Prepare chips	As for roast potatoes but for 2 minutes only

7. A GUIDE TO THE PREPARATION OF FRUIT FOR FREEZING

Selection of fruit

Select fruit in perfect condition, free of any bruises or blemishes, and prepare according to kind. Wash only if necessary.

Syrup strengths for freezing fruit:

Light .—225 g sugar dissolved in 1.2 litres of water

Medium.—500 g sugar dissolved in 1.2 litres of water

Heavy .—I kg sugar dissolved in 1.2 litres of water

Allow approximately 300 ml of syrup per 500 g of fruit. Pack the prepared fruit into rigid containers and pour over the cold syrup to cover completely. Allow 1–2 cm headspace.

436

Fruit	Preparation	Pack
Apples (cooking/ eating, fresh)	Peel, core and slice, and blanch for 2 minutes	Mix blanched fruit with 100 g of sugar to each 500 g fruit
Apples (cooked)	Peel, core and stew with the juice of a lemon and minimum of water, using 100 g of sugar to each 500 g of fruit	Pack when cool in rigid containers allowing 2 cm head space
Brambles	Prepare as for eating	Mix with 100 g of sugar to 500 g fruit, or pack in a medium syrup
Blackcurrants	Prepare as for jam, jelly or pies	For jam or jelly – freeze without sugar or pack in a light syrup For cooking – mix with sugar as brambles above
Gooseberries	Top and tail	Dry pack – without sugar or pack in a medium syrup
Peaches	Blanch whole fruits in boiling water for 30 seconds then plunge into iced water. Skin, cut in half and remove stone.	Pack in a heavy syrup with juice of half a lemon to prevent discolouration. Allow 2 cm headspace.
Pears	Wash, peel and core. Halve, quarter or slice depending on size	Poach in heavy syrup, with the juice of half a lemon, for one and a half minutes. Cool in poaching syrup then pack in rigid container leaving 2 cm headspace
Plums	Wash, cut in half and remove stone	Syrup – as for gooseberries or without sugar
Greengages	As for plums	As for gooseberries
Damsons	As for plums	As for gooseberries
Raspberries	Prepare as for eating	Dry pack without sugar or mix 100 g sugar to 500 g fruit or cover with a medium syrup
Strawberries	Freeze small whole berries, removing stalks. Quarter or slice large berries	Pack as for raspberries
Rhubarb	Use young tender rhubarb cut into lengths of 2 cm. Blanch for 1 minute	Dry pack without sugar or stew, cool and freeze as apples

8. GUIDE TO PREPARATION, STORAGE TIME AND THAWING OF FROZEN FOODS

If foods are packed correctly, quick frozen, and stored at a steady temperature of -18°C or below they will keep indefinitely but taste, texture and colour will ultimately deteriorate.
The table below is a general guide to the length of time foods may remain frozen in prime condition provided the product is correctly packed and the packaging remains intact.

Food	Preparation	Packaging	Storage Time	Thawing
Meat	Wipe. Trim fat if necessary. If possible, buy "blast frozen" meat from butcher	Wrap in double layer of foil, and seal in a freezer bag	6–8 months (Fatty meat keeps for a shorter time than lean meat)	Thaw slowly, preferably overnight in refrigerator
Mince	Must be very fresh	Place in a freezer bag, excluding as much air as possible	2 months	Thaw slowly, preferably overnight in refrigerator
Offal	Rinse in cold water to remove excess blood, then dry on paper towel	Wrap in freezer wrap (cling film which will withstand freezer temperatures	2 months	Thaw slowly, preferably overnight in refrigerator
Sausages and Hamburgers	Must be very fresh	Freezer bags in usable numbers	2 months	Can be cooked from frozen state but they need longer time. Ensure product is thoroughly cooked throughout
Bacon	Cut off excess fat	Freeze with layers of paper between, in usable amounts. Overwrap with freezer wrap	1 month	3–4 hours in refrigerator

	Preparation	Packaging	Storage time	Thawing
Poultry	Wipe out inside with a paper towel. Cover any bones to stop them protruding through bags	Freezer bags or wrap	6–9 months (The more fat the shorter time it will store)	Thaw thoroughly, ensuring no ice crystals remain in cavity of whole birds. 24 hours in refrigerator
White Fish	Wash (and skin if required)	Freeze with layers of greaseproof paper between in usable amounts in freezer bags	3 months	Small fish cooked from frozen state. Others thaw 2–3 hours
Oily Fish	Clean	Wrap each fish or fillet in freezer wrap	2 months	Thaw slowly. Time depending on size of fish
Shellfish	Cook	Freezer bags	1 month; if ready frozen follow manufacturer's instructions	Thaw overnight in refrigerator
Cooked Meat Dishes	Make as usual, cool quickly	Plastic or tin foil container well sealed	2 months	In refrigerator overnight
Cooked Fish Dishes	As cooked meat	As cooked meat	1 month	As cooked meat
Paté	Make paté, press, cool quickly and turn out	Wrap in tin foil and then seal in freezer bag	1 month	In refrigerator overnight
Pastries, Pies, etc, Cooked	Make as usual in foil dish or buy ready-made	Overwrap in freezer wrap then seal in freezer bag	3 months	In refrigerator overnight
Fruit Pies	Make without cooking	Wrap as pastries, pies	3 months	Cook from frozen
Pastry Cases	Freeze unfilled	Store in box and seal	3 months	Heat from frozen
Pizzas		Freeze, then wrap in foil or freezer wrap	2–3 months	Heat from frozen

Vegetables	See chart (page 436)			Cook from frozen
Roast Potatoes	"			"
Chips	"			"
Fruit	See chart (page 437)	Freezer bags	6 months	2–3 hours
Puddings (except custard)	Make as usual	Cover with foil, seal	3 months	Thaw in refrigerator 4–6 hours
Bread		Freezer bags	6 months	2–3 hours; (can toast from frozen)
Cakes (high-fat)	Make as usual	Freezer bag/wrap	6 months	1–2 hours
Cakes (low-fat)	Make as usual	Freezer bag/wrap	3 months	1–2 hours
Cakes (Iced)	Make as usual	Freeze and then wrap in freezer wrap	2 months	1–2 hours
Butter (unsalted)		Wrap with freezer wrap	6 months	Overnight in refrigerator
Butter (salted)		As unsalted	3 months	As unsalted
Frozen cream, 40% fat and over		In manufacturer's packaging, unopened	3 months	Overnight in refrigerator
Ice Cream		In lidded tub	2 months	
Egg Whites		In small containers. Remove from containers and seal in freezer bags	6 months	2 hours
Soup (Broths)	Make as usual, cool quickly, remove fat	Freeze in containers leaving 2 cm headspace	3 months	Thaw overnight in refrigerator
Stock	Make as usual, cool quickly, remove fat	Freeze in containers leaving 2 cm headspace	6 months	Thaw overnight in refrigerator
Herbs	Chop finely, put into ice tray with very little water to cover	Remove and store in freezer bag	6 months	Use from frozen in soups and sauces

BOTTLING FRUIT

9. INTRODUCTION

Preserving fruits and vegetables is simply keeping them in a condition fit for consumption longer than would normally be the case.

Spoilage is caused by the growth of moulds, yeasts and bacteria which are naturally present on fruits and vegetables and in the air. Enzymes which are chemical substances present in all living matter, also cause spoilage.

In preservation, the aim is to stop the growth of these substances and to prevent more micro-organisms having access to the fruits and vegetables during storage.

In the bottling of fruits, heat, which destroys moulds, yeasts, bacteria and enzymes, is applied and the bottles are sealed against the entrance of more organisms. Some fruits are more difficult to sterilise than others and so the temperature is varied accordingly.

With the exception of tomatoes **the bottling of vegetables is not recommended**, as they are difficult to sterilise and require special treatment.

10. THE CHOICE OF BOTTLING JARS

There are many varieties of jars obtainable but all depend on a lid which rests on a rubber ring, making an airtight joint, after a vacuum has been formed during processing. Manufacturer's instructions must be carefully followed.

Vacuum Bottles: Generally those used in home bottling of fruit are screw-band bottles.

Rubber Rings: These must fit well and be pliable and in good condition. Perished rings when stretched will not return to their original size. It is not advisable to use rings more than once.

Lids: These must be free from corrosion.

Note: All jars and rings must be scrupulously clean before use. Rubber rings should be soaked in warm water for 15 minutes, then dipped in boiling water.

11. CHOICE AND PREPARATION OF FRUIT

1. Fruit should be of good quality and perfectly sound, i.e. free of any bruising or blemishes.
2. Soft fruits should be firm and just ripe to give a good result.
3. Gooseberries should be bottled when under-ripe.
4. Stone fruits should be firm and ripe.
5. Fruit should be freshly gathered and of uniform size and ripeness.
6. Prepare the fruit according to kind and wash in cold water, if necessary. This can be done in a colander.

Fruit	Preparation
Apples	Wash, peel, core and cut into slices or rings. As they discolour quickly, place in cold water to which the juice of half a lemon has been added
Pears	Best results are obtained by using dessert pears: they should be fully ripe. Peel, halve and core the pears. Place in water with the juice of half a lemon to prevent discolouration. Cooking-pears require to be stewed before bottling. Dissolve 100–150 g sugar in 500 ml water. Stew the pears gently until barely tender
Apricots	Remove the stalks and wash in cold water. They may be bottled whole or the stones may be removed
Peaches	Skin fruit by dipping in boiling water for 1 minute and then place in cold water. May be bottled whole or halved
Plums	Remove stalks and wash in cold water. May be packed whole or in halves
Damsons, Greengages, Cherries	Remove stalks. Rinse in cold water
Raspberries, Brambles, Loganberries	Remove hulls and handle as little as possible. Fruit should be free from maggots. Rinse in cold water. Drain well on paper towels
Strawberries	These lose their colour when bottled and also shrink a good deal. Remove the calyx and rinse in cold water. Put strawberries in a bowl and cover with boiling syrup made from 200 g sugar to 500 ml water. Leave overnight. Use this syrup to cover fruit after packing into bottles
Redcurrants, Blackcurrants	Remove stalks and rinse in cold water
Rhubarb	Should be preserved when young and tender. Wipe the stalks and cut into lengths of 3 cm
Gooseberries	Top and tail, wash. Prick skins or cut off a small slice at either end of the berry when topping and tailing to prevent fruit shrivelling
Tomatoes	Dip in boiling water for 30 seconds, then dip in cold water and remove skin. They may be bottled whole or cut in halves or quarters to give a tight pack

12. FRUIT SYRUP

Ingredients:

125–250 g Sugar   500 ml Water
   (according to preference)

Method:

1. Place sugar and water in saucepan and dissolve slowly.

2. Bring to the boil and boil for 5 minutes.

3. Use as required.

Note: Fruit can also be bottled using natural fruit juice. This can be used to make fruit syrup.

13. BOTTLING METHODS

There are many methods of processing fruit. The chief methods suitable for home bottling of fruit are:

1. Water bath method

This is recommended for reliable results if suitable equipment is available.

A pan or fish kettle should be used which is deep enough to immerse the bottles in water when standing on a false bottom (cardboard, thick paper or wood).

Method:

1. Prepare fruit according to kind (page 441–42).
2. Pack firmly into jars without bruising and well fill the jars.
3. Fill jars to overflowing with hot syrup.
4. Adjust rubber ring and lid and fit screw band which must be loosened slightly after screwing up.
5. Ensure water in pan is warm (40°C) and put in the bottles so that they do not touch each other or the side of pan.
6. Heat the water to simmering point (90°C) in 25–30 minutes and hold at simmering point for necessary time, depending on fruit used (see Table, page 444).
7. Remove bottles from pan. Tighten any screw bands and leave till next day before testing seal.
8. To test, take off screw bands and lift bottles by the lids. If the lid comes off, the fruit must be used within two days or re-processed at once.
9. Store in a cool, dry, dark place.

2. Oven method

This is very satisfactory for gooseberries and plums but is not recommended for fruits which readily discolour, such as pears and apples.

1. Warm jars and allow oven to heat to 150°C, No. 2.
2. Prepare fruit according to kind (page 441–42).
3. Pack firmly into warm jars and fill to within 2 cm of the top with boiling syrup or water.
4. Place on rubber ring and metal disc. (Screw bands are put on after processing.)
5. Place filled jars 4 cm apart on a baking sheet lined with newspaper in the centre of the oven and leave for the time recommended see table (page 444).
6. After processing, screw bands on and tighten.
7. Test next day as step 8 in water bath method.

14. FRUIT PROCESSING CHART

Fruit	Method 1 – Water Bath	Method 2 – Oven	
	Time Retained	Time	
		½–2 kg Prepared weight	2½–4½ kg Prepared weight
Apple (slices)	2 mins	30–40 mins	45–60 mins
Apricots (whole)	10 mins	40–50 mins	55–70 mins
Brambles	2 mins	30–40 mins	45–60 mins
Cherries	10 mins	40–50 mins	55–70 mins
Blackcurrants/Redcurrants	10 mins	30–40 mins	45–60 mins
Damsons	10 mins	40–50 mins	55–70 mins
Gooseberries	10 mins	30–40 mins	45–60 mins
Greengages (whole)	10 mins	40–50 mins	55–70 mins
Loganberries	2 mins	30–40 mins	45–60 mins
Peaches (halves)	20 mins	50–60 mins	65–80 mins
Pears	40 mins	60–70 mins	75–90 mins
Plums	10 mins	40–50 mins	55–70 mins
Plums (halves)	20 mins	50–60 mins	65–80 mins
Raspberries	2 mins	30–40 mins	45–60 mins
Rhubarb	10 mins	30–40 mins	45–60 mins
Strawberries	2 mins	30–40 mins	45–60 mins
Tomatoes (whole)	40 mins	60–70 mins	75–90 mins
Tomatoes (solid pack)	50 mins	70–80 mins	85–100 mins

PICKLES AND CHUTNEY

15. INTRODUCTION

Vinegar is the chief means of preserving the ingredients in pickles and chutney by lowering the pH. A good quality vinegar should be used so that sufficient acetic acid is present to prevent the growth of yeasts, moulds and bacteria. Salt also acts as a preservative and should be used as per the recipe, e.g. in a brine solution.

Pickled vegetables:

1. The general method is to wash the vegetables thoroughly and soak them in brine (500 g salt to 4 litres water) for 48 hours.
2. Wash vegetables again and pack into jars.
3. Completely cover with spiced vinegar, below. Seal.

Sealing:

1. Many jars now have lids which have been treated to make them acid resistant. These are very suitable.
2. Metal caps may be used, but they must not come in contact with the chutney. Ceresin discs, obtainable for the purpose, or several thicknesses of waxed or greaseproof paper must be put inside the lid.
3. Plastic tops can be bought with directions for use.

Note: Cold vinegar is used for vegetables requiring a crisp finish, e.g. onions and cabbage. Hot vinegar is used for soft types, e.g. walnuts.

16. SPICED VINEGAR

Ingredients:

1 litre Vinegar (malt *or* white *or* a mixture)	1 teaspoonful whole Allspice or
Small piece Cinnamon Stick	Pickling Spice
5 Cloves	Small piece Mace

Method:

1. Add the spices (tied in muslin) to the vinegar.
2. Put all in a pan with a tight-fitting lid and bring to boiling point.
3. Remove from heat, leave covered and infuse for 2 hours.
4. Lift out the spice bag and use the vinegar as required.

17. PICKLED BEETROOT

Method:

1. Cut cold, cooked beetroot into thin slices.
2. Pack into bottles and cover with cold, spiced vinegar.
3. Seal and do not use for at least one week.

18. PICKLED ONIONS

Method:

1. Select small, white, round onions. Skin.
2. Put in brine (500 g salt to 4 litres water).
3. Leave for 12 hours. Drain.
4. Put in a fresh brine of the same strength for a further 24–36 hours.
5. Remove from brine, wash thoroughly in cold water and drain well.
6. Pack in jars, cover with cold spiced vinegar.
7. Seal and store for 3–4 months before using. To seal, see 15 above.

19. **PICKLED MUSHROOMS**

Method:

1. Wash mushrooms thoroughly.
2. Put in stewpan and sprinkle with a little salt and pepper. Add a blade of mace.
3. Cook slowly till liquor flows. Shake well and continue cooking till all liquor has evaporated.
4. Cover with vinegar. Bring to boil and put in jars.
5. Top up to cover with boiling vinegar, if necessary, and seal (page 445).

20. **PICKLED WALNUTS**

Method:

1. Gather the walnuts before the shell has formed. They should be tested by pricking with a needle.
2. Put in brine (500 g salt to 4 litres water) and let them soak for 6 days.
3. Change the brine and soak the nuts for a further week.
4. Drain, spread them on plates and expose to the air until they become black (about 1 day).
5. When quite black, pack the nuts in jars and cover well with spiced vinegar. Seal (page 445) and leave for a month or longer before use.

21. **PICKLED RED CABBAGE**

Method:

1. Choose cabbage that is firm and a good colour.
2. Remove any discoloured outer leaves and the hard core, and then shred the cabbage.
3. Put in a large bowl in layers with salt sprinkled between. Leave for 24 hours.
4. Drain thoroughly, rinsing off any surplus salt.
5. Pack loosely in jars or bottles and cover with cold spiced vinegar. Seal (page 445).
6. Use after a week. It loses its crispness after 2–3 months' storage.

22. **PICKLED CAULIFLOWER**

Method:

1. Choose firm fresh cauliflowers and break into sprigs.
2. Put in a large container and cover with brine (500 g salt to 4 litres water). Allow to stand for 24 hours.
3. Drain thoroughly, pack into bottles or jars and cover with cold spiced vinegar.
4. Seal jars (page 445).

23. **PICKLED DAMSONS OR PEACHES**

Ingredients:

2 kg Damsons *or* Peaches   500 ml spiced Vinegar
1 kg Sugar

Method:

1. Wash and stalk fruit. Prepare the fruit as required (page 442).
2. Dissolve the sugar in the spiced vinegar.
3. Simmer the fruit in the spiced vinegar till tender.
4. Drain off the liquid and pack the fruit into jars.
5. Boil the vinegar until slightly thick and use, while hot, to cover the fruit.
6. Seal securely (page 445).

24. **PICKLED SPICED APPLES**

Ingredients:

1 kg Crab Apples *or* other small   1 kg Sugar
   Apples   750 ml Spiced Vinegar

Method:

1. Dissolve sugar in spiced vinegar.
2. Prick the apples, or cut in halves, and simmer in the syrup until tender but not broken.
3. Pack the apples carefully into jars.
4. Reduce the syrup to 500 ml and pour, while boiling, over the fruit.
5. Seal jars (page 445).

25. **APPLE CHUTNEY**

Ingredients:

750 ml Vinegar   2 level teaspoonfuls Salt
150 g Onions   1–2 level teaspoonfuls ground Ginger
1 kg Cooking Apples   150 g Raisins *or* Sultanas
25 g Mustard Seeds, optional   ½ level teaspoonful Cayenne
350 g Sugar   *or* ½ level teaspoonful Chilli Pepper

Method:

1. Chop or mince apples and onions.
2. Lightly crush mustard seeds and soak in 250 ml of the vinegar (this should be left overnight).
3. Put all ingredients, except the remaining vinegar and the sugar, in a pan and cook gently, with pan lid on, till fruit and onions are soft.
4. Add remaining vinegar and sugar and continue cooking until fairly thick and no free vinegar remains. Stir occasionally to prevent burning.
5. Pour before cold into warm jars and seal (page 445).

26. APPLE AND GINGER CHUTNEY

Ingredients:

1 kg Cooking Apples	250 g Brown Sugar
1 litre Vinegar	1 clove Garlic
500 g Dates	4 Chillies
100–200 g Preserved Ginger	50 g Salt
in syrup, drained	1 Onion (chopped)

Method:

1. Peel and chop apples roughly and cook in vinegar, with onion until soft.
2. Tie garlic and chillies in muslin and add to vinegar.
3. Add chopped dates, ginger and salt. Boil till soft and pulpy. Remove spices.
4. Pour into warm jars and seal (page 445).

27. RHUBARB CHUTNEY

Ingredients:

1 kg Rhubarb	25 g ground Ginger
750g Sugar	1 level teaspoonful Pepper
500 g Sultanas	1 level teaspoonful Cloves
500 g Onions	750 ml Vinegar
25 g Salt	

Method:

1. Wipe and cut rhubarb into small pieces.
2. Skin and slice onions thinly.
3. Mix all in a large pan.
4. Boil slowly for 40 minutes or until thick.
5. Put into jars; seal (page 445).

28. TOMATO CHUTNEY

Ingredients:

2 kg Tomatoes	½ level teaspoonful Paprika
150 g Onions	Pinch Cayenne
250 ml Vinegar	15 g Salt
½ level teaspoonful Mixed Spice	250 g Sugar

Method:

1. Skin the tomatoes by dipping in boiling water for 30 seconds (page 202). Cut up tomatoes roughly.
2. Chop or mince the onions and cook with the tomatoes until thick and pulpy.
3. Add half the vinegar and spices and cook until thick.
4. Add sugar, remaining vinegar and cook until soft and pulpy.
5. Bottle while hot and seal (page 445).

29. GREEN TOMATO CHUTNEY

Ingredients:

2 kg Green Tomatoes	12 Chillies
500 g Apples	15 g Fresh Ginger Root
250 g Raisins	15 g Salt
500 g Brown Sugar	750 ml Vinegar
500 g Shallots	

Method:

1. Cut up tomatoes, peel and cut up apples and shallots, and chop raisins.
2. Bruise ginger and chillies and tie in muslin.
3. Put all in pan, bring to boil and simmer until soft and pulpy.
4. Remove muslin bag and bottle chutney while hot.
5. Seal (page 445).

30. VEGETABLE MARROW AND APPLE CHUTNEY

Ingredients:

2 kg Vegetable Marrow	1 kg Cooking Apples
500 g Onions	500 g soft Brown Sugar
250 g Sultanas	50 g Salt
1 litre spiced Vinegar	

Method:

1. Peel, core and seed marrow. Cut in small pieces and place in bowl layered with salt, leave overnight.
2. Peel, core and chop apples and onion.
3. Drain marrow, add the apples, onions, sultanas and 500 ml vinegar.
4. Simmer until soft, stirring frequently.
5. Add remainder of vinegar and sugar. Cook slowly until thick.
6. Pour into warm jars and seal (page 445).

JAMS AND JELLIES

31. INTRODUCTION

The characteristics of good jam and jelly are full fruit flavour, good colour, firm set and good keeping qualities. For successful jam making, the correct proportions of pectin, acid and sugar to fruit and liquid are essential.

Sugar is the preservative, but this must be present in the correct proportion so that, when combined with the pectin and acid of the fruit, a firm gel is produced. A good gel generally ensures good keeping qualities, but overboiling, especially after the addition of sugar, will spoil both colour and flavour.

Fruit	The fruit should be just ripe and in good condition, gathered when dry and preserved as soon as possible. Some fruits make better jam than others because they contain a high proportion of pectin and acid which are necessary for a good gel. These good gelling fruits are often mixed with fruit poor in pectin and acid, e.g. green apples with brambles
To Test for Pectin	The fruits which provide enough pectin to give a well-set jam are soon learned by experience, but the following tests may be made: 1. Take a teaspoonful of juice, free from seeds and skin, after simmering the fruit till soft 2. Put into a cup and allow to cool 3. Add one tablespoonful of methylated spirit and shake together gently and leave to stand for about a minute. A jelly-like lump will form if there is plenty of pectin. If the jelly is not very firm and in several smaller lumps, then there is moderate pectin content; lots of small jelly like clots indicate a poor pectin level. Commercial pectin is available with full instructions for fruits lacking in pectin. Preserving sugar with added pectin (check label) is also widely available 4. For a very good jelly clot add 1 ¼ kg sugar to 1 kg fruit or 1250 ml juice: For a moderate clot add 1 kg sugar to 1 kg fruit or 1250 ml juice; For poor pectin levels use 750 g sugar to 1 kg fruit or 1250 ml juice
Sugar	Either cane or beet sugar may be used. Preserving sugar dissolves more easily than granulated or castor sugar. Warming the sugar in a low oven helps it dissolve more quickly
Acid	Fruits vary in the amount of acid and pectin they contain. Acid is necessary for the setting quality of the jam, and maintaining good colour. The most common low-acid fruits used in jam making include eating apples, brambles, cherries and pears. The following acids can be added to 1.8 kg of low-acid fruit: 2 tablespoons of lemon juice *or* ½ teaspoonful of citric *or* tartaric acid The acid should be added to the fruit before cooking

The Pan	A preserving pan should be made of metal and heavy-bottomed to prevent burning and should be large enough to allow jam to boil up well. Stainless steel pans are recommended
Scalding	When straining jellies, the bag should be scalded first with boiling water. Place the clean bag into a large colander in the sink and pour over a kettleful of boiling water. Once drained, the jelly bag is now ready for use
Cooking	Fruit should be heated and well-pulped (with or without the addition of water) before sugar is added. This is important to free the pectin and acid. Slow, covered cooking is best at this stage to prevent evaporation. Sugar should be completely dissolved before jam boils; then jam should be boiled very rapidly till setting point is reached
Test for Setting	A teaspoonful of jam put on a cold plate (kept in the freezer for a short time) and allowed to cool should skin over. When pushed with the finger it should wrinkle
Temperature Test	Place a sugar thermometer into a jug of hot water, both before and after testing. For a good set, the jam should be boiled to 104.5°C (220°F) assuming the proportions of pectin and acid are correct
Skimming	If necessary, this should be done quickly with a spoon dipped in boiling water. A small piece of fresh butter may be added to the jam to prevent the scum rising. If the inside of the pan is rubbed with butter the jam is less liable to stick
Potting	Jars must be clean and warm. The washed jars should be placed upside down on an oven tray lined with a clean folded tea towel and then placed in a warm oven (100°C). Jelly should be potted at once, but jam should be cooled to 85°C and stirred before potting. Pots should be filled to the rim – the jam shrinks a little on cooling. A jam funnel is useful, but not essential, for this task
Covering	Immediately after potting, a well-fitting disc should be pressed carefully onto the surface of the jam. The jars may either be tied down at once, or protected from the air and tied down when quite cold. Alternatively, the jars should be filled to 1 cm from the top, the lid screwed on tightly immediately and then inverted. (Use rubber gloves and be careful!) This allows the hot jam to sterilise the headspace. Turn back over after 2 minutes
Labelling and Storing	Any spillages should be wiped from the surfaces. Once cold, jars should then be labelled with the type of jam and the date made. Jars should be stored in a dark airy cupboard, free from damp and excessive heat

32. APRICOT JAM (DRIED FRUIT)

Ingredients:

500 g dried Apricots   1.5 kg Sugar
2 litres Water   50 g Almonds (optional)
or Juice of 1 Lemon
1 level teaspoonful Citric or Tartaric Acid

Method:

1. Wash apricots and soak in measured cold water, covered, for at least 24 hours.
2. Put apricots and water in preserving pan and simmer 30 minutes.
3. Add lemon juice, sugar and almonds (finely shredded, if using).
4. Stir till sugar is dissolved then boil rapidly until setting point is reached.
5. Skim, pot and cover.

33. BLACKCURRANT JAM

Ingredients:

1 kg Blackcurrants   2 kg Sugar
1250 mls Water

Method:

1. Wash fruit and put in preserving pan with water and bring to boiling point.
2. Simmer until skins are soft (about 10 minutes).
3. Add sugar and stir until dissolved.
4. Boil quickly till it reaches setting point. Skim.
5. Allow to cool slightly and stir before potting.
6. Cover.

34. DAMSON JAM

Ingredients:

1 kg Damsons   1.5 kg Sugar
1 litre Water

Method:

1. Wash damsons and put in preserving pan with water.
2. Cook slowly until fruit is well broken down.
3. Add sugar and stir until it dissolves.
4. Bring to boil and remove as many stones as possible.
5. Boil rapidly until setting point is reached.
6. Skim, pot and cover (page 451).

35. GOOSEBERRY JAM

Ingredients:

1 kg green Gooseberries   2 kg Sugar
1 litre Water

Method:

1. Put gooseberries and water in preserving pan and cook gently for
   20 minutes.
2. Add sugar and allow to dissolve.
3. Bring to boil and boil rapidly until setting point is reached.
4. Skim, cool and stir before potting.
5. Cover (page 451).

36. PLUM, GREENGAGE OR APRICOT JAM

Ingredients:

1 kg Plums   1 ¼ kg Sugar
500 ml Water

Method:

1. Wash the fruit and put in preserving pan with water. Simmer until the fruit is
   well broken down.
2. Add sugar, stir till dissolved.
3. Boil quickly until setting point is reached.
4. Allow to cool, skim and stir before potting.
5. Cover (page 451).

37. RASPBERRY JAM (1)

Ingredients:

1 kg Raspberries   1 kg Sugar

Method:

1. Put fruit in pan and warm until juice flows. Simmer until fruit is soft and well
   broken down.
2. Add sugar and stir till dissolved.
3. Boil rapidly till setting point is reached. Skim.
4. Stir till slightly cool before potting.
5. Cover (page 451).

38. RASPBERRY JAM (2)

Ingredients:

1 kg Raspberries   1.5 kg Sugar

Method:

1. Warm fruit in preserving pan till juice flows. Mash fruit till well broken down.
2. Add sugar and dissolve slowly.
3. Boil rapidly for 5 minutes.
4. Skim, pot and cover (page 451).

39. FREEZER RASPBERRY JAM

Ingredients:

500 g Raspberries   I kg Castor Sugar
½ bottle Certo (a commercial pectin 2 tablespoonfuls Lemon Juice
often used in home jam making)

Method:

1. Mix raspberries and sugar together, stir well and leave to stand in warm place for I hour.
2. Add Certo and lemon juice, stir for 2 minutes.
3. Pour into small dry containers (not glass) and leave I cm headspace.
4. Cover with airtight lid.
5. Leave in warm place for 48 hours.
6. Put in freezer.

Note: Keeps well in freezer for 6 months.

40. RHUBARB JAM

Ingredients:

I kg Rhubarb   I kg Sugar
Juice I Lemon

Method:

1. Wipe the rhubarb and cut in 2 cm lengths.
2. Put in glass or stainless steel bowl with the sugar sprinkled on in layers. Add the lemon juice.
3. Cover and leave overnight.
4. Put in preserving pan and bring to boil.
5. Boil rapidly till thick.
6. Skim, pot and cover (page 451).

41. RHUBARB AND GINGER JAM

Ingredients:

I kg Rhubarb   *or*   100–150 g crystallised Ginger
I kg Sugar   I ½ level teaspoonfuls ground Ginger
½ Lemon

Method:

1. Wipe and cut up rhubarb.
2. Put in glass or stainless steel bowl with sugar in layers. Add lemon juice, cover and leave overnight.
3. Strain off juice into preserving pan. Add ginger and boil 15 minutes.
4. Add rhubarb and boil 15 minutes longer.
5. Skim, pot and cover (page 451).

42. **STRAWBERRY JAM (1)**

Ingredients:

1 kg hulled Strawberries   1 kg Sugar

Method:

1. Heat strawberries in preserving pan until juice flows (about 15 minutes).
2. Add sugar and boil quickly for 15 minutes. Skim.
3. Allow jam to cool. Stir before potting.
4. Cover (page 451).

Note: This jam has a fine flavour but must be made from dry fruit in good condition. It does not gel, but is syrupy.

43. **STRAWBERRY JAM (2)**

Ingredients:

1 kg hulled Strawberries   1 kg Sugar
250 ml Fruit Juice (Gooseberry *or* Redcurrant)
Juice ½ Lemon

Method:

1. Put strawberries in pan with fruit juice.
2. Simmer until fruit is soft.
3. Add sugar and allow to dissolve.
4. Bring to boiling point and boil quickly until setting point is reached.
5. Skim, allow to cool slightly, stir and pot.
6. Cover (page 451).

Note: Commercial pectin may be used instead of fruit juice – use according to direction.

44. **VEGETABLE MARROW JAM**

Ingredients:

1 kg Vegetable Marrow   1 Lemon
1 kg Sugar   10 g bruised Ginger

Method:

1. Peel the marrow and cut in cubes.
2. Sprinkle some of the sugar over and leave for 12 hours.
3. Put into preserving pan with remainder of the sugar and ginger tied loosely in muslin.
4. Dissolve sugar and bring to boil.
5. Boil quickly until marrow is clear (about 45 minutes), remove muslin.
6. Add grated rind and juice of lemon and skim and pot jam.
7. Cover (page 451).

45. MINCEMEAT

Ingredients:

100 g Raisins	100 g Brown Sugar
100 g Sultanas	1 level teaspoonful Cinnamon
200 g Currants	1 level teaspoonful mixed Spice
500 g Apples	1 level teaspoonful Nutmeg
100 g Shredded Suet	Pinch Salt
1 Lemon Rind finely grated and Juice	125 ml Brandy
50 g Mixed Peel (chopped)	*or* Sherry

Method:

1. Wash fruit.
2. Peel and core apples and put through mincer or roughly grate.
3. Mix fruit, apple, suet, peel, sugar, spices and salt.
4. Add grated lemon rind, juice and brandy or sherry.
5. Mix well until moist; pot and cover (page 451).
6. Store for one month before using.

46. BRAMBLE JELLY

Ingredients:

1.5 kg Brambles	Water
500 g Cooking Apples	Sugar

Method:

1. Wash fruit, cut up apples. Put in preserving pan with water to almost cover.
2. Simmer till tender, mash well. Strain through scalded jelly bag and allow to drip overnight.
3. Measure the juice and allow 1 kg sugar to each 1250 mls.
4. Heat juice and dissolve sugar in it.
5. Boil rapidly to setting point.
6. Skim, quickly pour into warm jars and cover (page 451).

47. DAMSON JELLY

Ingredients:

1 kg Damsons	Sugar (1 kg sugar for each 1250 mls juice)
500 g Cooking Apples	Water

Method:

1. Wash fruit, cut up apples. Put all in pan and cover well with water.
2. Simmer slowly till tender.
3. Mash well and strain overnight through a scalded jelly bag or muslin.
4. Measure juice and allow 1 kg sugar for each 1250 mls juice.
5. Dissolve sugar in juice, then boil rapidly until setting point is reached.
6. Skim, quickly pour into warm jars and cover (page 451).

Note: A second extraction may be made and mixed with first extraction before measuring (see redcurrant jelly, page 457).

48. **REDCURRANT JELLY**

Ingredients:

    1 kg Redcurrants   Sugar
    750 ml Water

Method:

1. Wash fruit without removing stalks.
2. Put in preserving pan with water and simmer till quite tender. Mash well.
3. Strain though scalded jelly bag and allow to drip overnight.
4. Measure the juice and allow 1 kg sugar to each 1250 mls.
5. Heat juice and dissolve sugar in it.
6. Boil rapidly to setting point.
7. Skim, quickly pour into warm jars, and cover (page 451).

Make as Redcurrant Jelly:

    Apple Jelly   **Blackcurrant Jelly**
    Gooseberry Jelly   **Raspberry Jelly**

Note: A greater yield of jelly can be got by returning the remaining pulp to jelly pan and adding enough water to make a soft mash. This is boiled and strained and added to the first extraction before measuring. However, the resulting jelly will not be as clear.

49. **REDCURRANT JELLY (UNCOOKED)**

Ingredients:

    To every 1.5 kg redcurrants, allow 500 g raspberries
    To every 1250 mls of resulting juice, allow 1¼–1.5 kg sugar

Method:

1. Squeeze the fruit through a cloth and to every 1250 mls of resulting juice allow 1¼–1.5 kg sugar for good result.
2. Stir till sugar is dissolved, fill at once into small jars, cover (page 451). Store in refrigerator.

50. **ROWAN AND APPLE JELLY**

Ingredients:

    1.5 kg Apples   Water
    500 g Rowans   Sugar

Method:

1. Wash rowans and remove stalks.
2. Cut up apples and put with rowans in preserving pan. Cover with water.
3. Simmer until tender. Mash well. Strain through scalded jelly bag.
4. Measure juice and allow 1 kg sugar to each 1250 mls of juice.
5. Heat juice and dissolve sugar in it.
6. Boil rapidly to setting point.
7. Skim, pot and cover (page 451).

51. **MINT JELLY**

Ingredients:

1.5 kg Bright Green Cooking Apples   Sugar
Bunch fresh Mint   Water
Juice 2 lemons

Method:

1. Wash and cut up fruit. Simmer with a few sprigs of mint, the lemon juice and enough water until soft and pulpy.
2. Strain and allow 500 g sugar to each 750 ml.
3. Heat the juice, add the sugar and stir till dissolved. Boil rapidly for 5 minutes.
4. Wash and bruise a bunch of fresh mint and hold this in the jelly for 5 minutes or add some finely chopped mint to strengthen the flavour and enhance the colour.
5. Continue boiling until setting point is reached.
6. Pot in small jars and cover (page 451).

52. **THICK MARMALADE**

Ingredients:

1 kg bitter Oranges (Seville)   3½ litres Water
1–2 Lemons   Sugar

Method:

1. Wash oranges and lemons and cut into halves.
2. Remove pips and put in a small bowl. Squeeze out the juice into a large bowl.
3. Cut the fruit into very thin slices, or mince, or liquidise with some of the measured water, and add to the juice.
4. Cover the pips with some of the measured water and add the remainder to the pulp. Leave overnight.
5. Put the pulp into a large preserving pan and add the juice strained from the pips.
6. Boil pulp until rind is quite tender.
7. Measure the pulp and add sugar, allowing 1 kg to each litre pulp.
8. Dissolve sugar and bring all to boiling point.
9. Boil till setting. Skim and cool.
10. Stir before potting. Cover (page 451).

53. **GRAPEFRUIT MARMALADE**

Ingredients:

500 g Fruit (2 parts grapefruit, 1 part lemon)

Method:

Make as you would thick marmalade, above.

54. THREE-FRUIT MARMALADE

Ingredients:

2 Grapefruits ⎫   4 litres Water
2 Lemons   ⎬ 1.5 kg Fruit   Sugar
2 sweet Oranges ⎭

Method:

Follow method for thick marmalade (page 458).

55. FOUR-FRUIT MARMALADE

Ingredients:

1 large Jaffa Orange   1 Lemon
1 large Grapefruit   2 kg Sugar
1 Cooking Apple   2½ litres Water

Method:

1. Peel, core and chop apple.
2. Continue as for quick marmalade, below.

56. SWEET ORANGE MARMALADE

Ingredients:

500 g Oranges   2 litres Water
2 Lemons   Sugar

Method:

Follow method for thick marmalade, but use 1 kg sugar to 1½ litres pulp.

57. QUICK MARMALADE

Ingredients:

1 kg Bitter (Seville) Oranges   2 Lemons
4 litres Water   4 kg Sugar

Method:

1. Halve fruit, remove pips, squeeze out juice.
2. Mince or liquidise fruit.
3. Put juice, fruit and water on to cook.
4. Tie pips in muslin and cook along with fruit.
5. Simmer until tender, approx. 1 hour 30 minutes; remove bag of pips.
6. Add sugar, dissolve and boil until set; skim, stir, pot and cover (page 451).
Note: Yields 14–16 pots.

58. JELLY MARMALADE

Ingredients:

1 kg Bitter (Seville) Oranges   2 litres cold Water
1 Lemon   Sugar

Method:

1. Wash fruit, remove rind thinly from half the oranges and cut into shreds. Lay aside.
2. Remove white pith from these oranges and discard pith.
3. Cut up these skins together with remaining oranges and lemon.
4. Put fruit in jelly pan and cover with water.
5. Simmer for 1 hour. Boil shreds separately in enough water to cover till tender, 20 minutes approximately.
6. Pour pulp through jelly bag or muslin. Allow to drip.
7. Add shreds to juice; measure.
8. Allow 1 kg sugar to each 1250 mls juice. Put in jelly pan and dissolve sugar.
9. Boil till setting (about 10 minutes).
10. Skim, cool, stir, pot and cover (page 451).

WINES AND DRINKS

WINES

DRINKS

WINES

I. WINE MAKING

Essential ingredients:

    1. Fruits or Root Vegetables, Herbs, Flowers or Cereals.

    2. Sugar.

    3. Water.

    4. Wine Yeast – or if this is unobtainable – Brewers' Yeast or Dried Yeast.

Fruits contain natural yeast, which will ferment but sometimes give off flavours, therefore it is advisable to use specially prepared yeasts.

Insecticides are widely used on fruit trees and bushes. Fruit should, therefore, be washed before use.

Essential utensils:

    1. Suitable large containers, e.g. large plastic bucket, glass (4 litre) storage jars.

    2. Jelly bag or close-textured butter muslin.

    3. Filter, measures, syphoning tubing.

    4. Fermentation traps.

    5. Clean glass bottles, corks.

    Note: Polythene utensils may be used, but metal utensils should not be used.

Miscellaneous points:

    1. Do not leave the wine at any time in direct sunlight, particularly red wine as it loses its colour.

    2. An even temperature of 12°C is essential during fermentation periods otherwise fermentation will not be satisfactory.

    3. Almost any fruit, flower, vegetable, herb or cereal may be used in the making of wine. A few recipes only are given, but many reliable books on homemade wines have been published in recent years.

    4. When wine is bottled, all bottles to be kept must be well filled.

General processes:

    1. Preparation of the fruit, vegetables, etc, according to kind (the recipe will indicate this).

    2. Addition of the measured amount of water.

    3. The mixture of fruit, etc and water should be put into a wide-mouthed container like a plastic bucket, and allowed to stand for some days (the recipe will give the number) at a constant temperature of about 12°C. It must be stirred frequently and kept covered to prevent wine-flies and dust from getting into it.

    4. The mixture is then strained through a jelly bag or double muslin; and returned to the bucket.

    5. The yeast should now be added to the strained mixture. Usually this is done

by making a starter bottle of the wine yeast. When fermenting, add to wine. This ensures a more even distribution of the yeast throughout the mixture as it sinks slowly to the bottom of the container. Cover the container as before.

6. Allow the fermenting mixture to stand at a constant temperature of 12°C till all signs of vigorous fermentation have ceased. Fermentation is indicated by a hissing sound, and bubbles rising to the surface.

7. The fermented mixture, or must, should now be strained into glass jars, if the amount of wine is small, the mixture can be strained into clean bottles. Cork the container well and put in a fermentation lock. Allow the wine to stand till all the signs of fermentation have ceased. This may take a month or more. All containers must be full.

8. Sediment will fall to the bottom of the containers and the wine should gradually become clear. Sometimes isinglass or gelatine are added to a wine which will not clear. (Other methods of getting rid of a cloudy effect will be found in books on wine-making.) Once the wine is clear, it should be "racked off" or poured off into clean bottles, care being taken not to disturb the "less", or sediment, at the bottom of the container.

9. Cork the bottles tightly.

10. Storage is important. Bottles are usually placed on their sides in a cool, dry place away from light. The wine is usually ready to use after 1 year's storage, but the longer it is kept, the better the flavour.

Note: Generally the proportions given in the recipes will give a medium strength sweet or dry wine. If a more full-bodied wine is desired, slightly reduce the amount of water added. If a stronger wine is desired, increase the amount of sugar and yeast. Sweet wines can be made by slightly increasing the amount of sugar added and using fully ripened fruit. Dry wines can be made by slightly reducing the amount of sugar added. It is necessary to experiment before arriving at the desired strength and degree of sweetness or dryness.

2. BRAMBLE WINE

Ingredients:

1.5 kg ripe Brambles	10 g Dried Yeast
1–1.5 kg Sugar	4 litres boiling Water

Method:

1. Put washed berries in a plastic bucket, pour boiling water over them.
2. Cover the bucket with muslin and keep it in a warm place, 12°C, for 10 days, mashing and stirring the mixture well every day.
3. Strain off the juice and discard the pulp. Add the sugar, stir till it dissolves.
4. Add yeast and pour into glass jar, fit fermentation lock, allow to stand in a warm place.
5. When fermentation ceases, syphon into clean bottles.
6. Cork tightly. Store for 1 year before using. This wine improves greatly with keeping.

Note: Raspberry wine can be made in a similar way.

3. **DANDELION WINE**

Ingredients:

4 litres Dandelion Flowers	1 Lemon
1.5 kg Sugar	Thinly pared rind 1 Orange
4 litres boiling Water	Small piece Root Ginger

Method:

1. Put yellow flower petals into a plastic bucket. Pour boiling water over them.
2. Cover the bucket with muslin and keep in a warm place, 12°C, for 3 days, stirring the mixture well and frequently.
3. Strain into preserving pan, add rinds of lemon and orange, sugar and ginger.
4. Remove pith from lemon and slice lemon thinly.
5. Add to liquid, boil gently 30 minutes.
6. Cool, add yeast, pour into jar and fit fermentation lock.
7. When fermentation ceases, syphon into bottles.
8. Cork tightly. Store for 6 months at least.

4. **DAMSON WINE**

Ingredients:

2 kg Damsons (ripe)	10 g Dried Yeast
1.5 kg Sugar	Rind 1 Lemon
4 litres boiling Water	

Method:

1. Put washed damsons in plastic bucket. Pour boiling water over them, and mash fruit. Add lemon rind.
2. Cover the bucket with muslin and allow to stand 5 days, stirring each day.
3. Strain and squeeze fruit through muslin; add sugar, stir to dissolve.
4. Add yeast, pour into jar, fit on fermentation lock. Allow to stand in a warm place.
5. When fermentation ceases, syphon, into clean bottle.
6. Cork tightly. Store for 1 year before using.

5. **ELDERBERRY WINE**

Ingredients:

2 kg Elderberries (ripe)	10 g Dried Yeast
1.5 kg Sugar	4 litres Water

Method:

1. Boil berries for 30 minutes in measured water.
2. Strain juice through bag or double muslin.
3. Add sugar while still hot, stir to dissolve, and allow to cool.
4. Add yeast, and pour into jar, fit fermentation lock, allow to stand in a warm place.
5. When fermentation ceases syphon, into clean bottles.
6. Cork tightly. Store for 1 year or more before using.

6. FRUIT WINE

Ingredients:

6 Lemons (sliced)	1.5 kg Sugar
6 Oranges	4 litres Water
1 kg Raisins	10 g Dried Yeast

Method:

1. Put all ingredients except yeast into a plastic bucket.
2. Mix well, leave 24 hours at 12°C.
3. Add yeast.
4. Stir mixture well, once a day for 10 days.
5. Strain juice through jelly bag into a clean jar.
6. Fit fermentation lock and leave till fermentation ceases.
7. Syphon into clean bottles.
8. Cork tightly. Store for 6 months to 1 year.

7. GOOSEBERRY WINE

Ingredients:

2 kg Gooseberries	1 kg Sugar to each 2 litres of Juice
4 litres Water	10 g Dried Yeast

Method:

1. Wash, top and tail the gooseberries which should be picked before they change colour.
2. Bruise them well and place in a plastic bucket. Add water, mix and mash well. Cover with a cloth and leave for two days.
3. Strain and measure the liquid. Put this with sugar into the bucket, stirring well.
4. Add yeast, pour into fermentation jar, fit fermentation lock, leave in a warm place until fermentation ceases.
5. Syphon into clean bottles and cork tightly.

8. RHUBARB WINE

Ingredients:

2½ kg juicy Rhubarb	1.5 kg Sugar
1 Lemon	4 litres Water
10 g Dried Yeast	

Method:

1. Wipe the rhubarb, cut into small lengths without removing skin.
2. Put into plastic bucket, crush to extract juice.
3. Pour on measured water, cover, leave in warm place 10 days. Stir well each day.
4. Strain juice, add sugar, lemon juice and thinly-pared rind. Stir until sugar is dissolved.
5. Add yeast, pour into jar, fit fermentation lock, allow to stand in a warm place.

6. When fermentation ceases, syphon into clean bottles.
7. Cork tightly. Store for one year before using.

9. PARSNIP WINE

Ingredients:

2 kg Parsnips	4 litres boiling Water
10 g Dried Hops	10 g Dried Yeast
1 kg Demerara Sugar	

Method:

1. Scrub parsnips, pare, cut up roughly and boil gently in measured water, 15 minutes.
2. Add hops and boil 10 minutes. Strain.
3. Add sugar while still hot and stir till dissolved.
4. Add yeast, pour into jar, fit fermentation lock. Allow to stand in a warm place.
5. When fermentation ceases, syphon into clean bottles.
6. Cork tightly. Store for a few months before using.

10. ROSE HIP WINE

Ingredients:

4 litres Rose Hips	2 kg Sugar
4 litres cold Water	12.5 g Dried Yeast

Method:

1. Gather hips when they are red. Top and tail them and wash well.
2. Cut them into pieces and put into a plastic bucket. Add the water and mash the rose hips by hand or with a wooden spoon.
3. Cover and leave for 1 week, stirring the mixture well every day.
4. Strain the mixture through muslin and discard pulp. Add the sugar and stir till dissolved.
5. Add yeast, pour into jar and fit fermentation lock. Allow to stand in a warm place.
6. When fermentation ceases, syphon into clean bottles.
7. Cork tightly. Store for at least 6 months before using.

11. SHERRY

Ingredients:

1.5 kg Blue Raisins	1.5 kg Brown Sugar
250 g Grapes	12.5 g Dried Yeast
250 g Barley	4 litres boiling Water
2 Potatoes	

Method:

1. Wash and slice potatoes with skins on and put in bucket with boiling water.
2. Add raisins, grapes, barley and sugar.

467

3. When cool add yeast. Stand in a warm place.
4. Cover the bucket and leave mixture one week, stirring well each day.
5. Strain through jelly bag; if necessary filter.
6. Put into jar to allow fermentation to finish and any sediment to be precipitated.
7. Bottle, cork tightly. Can be used almost at once, but improves with keeping.

12. ELDERFLOWER CHAMPAGNE

Ingredients:

2–3 Heads of Elderflowers	1 Lemon
¾–1 kg Sugar	4 litres Water
2 tablespoonfuls White Wine Vinegar	

Method:

1. Put all ingredients into a plastic bucket or other suitable container. Leave for 24 hours.
2. Strain and bottle the champagne in screw-top bottles.
3. Store the bottles on their sides. After two weeks the wine should be ready for use.

13. SLOE GIN

Ingredients:

Sloes – sound and ripe	Demerara Sugar
Gin	

Method:

1. Prick the sloes well with a sharp fork and put them into clean glass jars, two-thirds full.
2. Add demerara sugar packed tightly to within 2 cm of the top of the jars.
3. Pour in enough gin to fill the jars.
4. Screw on lids or stoppers tightly and turn the jars upside down several times to help to dissolve the sugar.
5. Repeat this twice every day for a week or so. Loosen the stoppers a little after inverting.
6. Store the gin for 4–6 months, then drain off into clean bottles through double muslin
7. The gin is then ready for use.

Note: Don't soak the fruits for longer than necessary as the flavour of the gin can be impaired. Taste after 4 months. This method also works for making damson gin, though white sugar is recommended. The gin-soaked fruits from sloe or damson gin can then be soaked in sherry for a further 6 months, to make damson or sloe sherry.

DRINKS

Use lemonade bottles with screw-tops or bottling jars. Sterilise before using. On opening the bottles the contents should be used within a few days.

14. BLACKCURRANT DRINK (1)

Ingredients:

I dessertspoonful Blackcurrant Jam   250 ml boiling Water
Sugar and Lemon Juice to taste

Method:

1. Put all ingredients into a jug and stir well.
2. Cover, and allow to stand in a warm place 20 minutes.
3. Strain through muslin.

15. BLACKCURRANT DRINK (2)

Ingredients:

Blackcurrants   Water

Proportions:

300 g Sugar and 250 ml Water to every 500 ml of the resulting Blackcurrant Juice

Method:

1. Put blackcurrants into a pan with enough water to keep them from sticking. Bring to the boil stirring all the time. Boil 1 minute.
2. Strain through jelly bag, squeeze to extract all juice. Measure.
3. Dissolve sugar in hot water and add blackcurrant juice.
4. Pour into sterilised bottles, place on tops or lids and half screw down.
5. Place bottles in a deep pan of cold water. Bring to simmering point and keep at that temperature for 20 minutes.
6. Remove from heat and screw down tops tightly.
7. Dilute as required.

16. REDCURRANT DRINK

Make as blackcurrant drink (2), above.

17. DAMSON DRINK

Make as blackcurrant drink (2), above.

18. **RASPBERRY DRINK**

Ingredients:

Raspberries   Water

Proportions:

300 g Sugar and 250 ml Water to every 500 ml of the resulting Raspberry Juice

Method:

1. Put raspberries in a pan with a little water. Bring to the boil stirring all the time. Boil for 1 minute.
2. Crush berries with a wooden spoon.
3. Proceed as for blackcurrant drink (page 469).

19. **LEMONADE (CONCENTRATED)**

Ingredients:

3 Lemons   750 g–1 kg Sugar
500 ml boiling Water   50 g Citric Acid

Method:

1. Peel lemon rind thinly, cover with some of the measured water.
2. Pour the remaining water onto sugar and citric acid. When cold add the lemon juice and the strained liquid from the rind.
3. Bottle.
4. Dilute as required.

20. **LEMONADE**

Ingredients:

2 Lemons   500 ml boiling water
100 g Sugar (*or* more according to taste)

Method:

1. Wash the lemons and remove thin strips of lemon rind without pith and squeeze out the juice.
2. Put rind and sugar into a jug and pour the boiling water over.
3. Cover and leave till cold, add lemon juice, strain and use.

Note: Imperial Drink may be made by adding one rounded teaspoonful of cream of tartar to the lemonade before serving.

This amount would provide a sufficient amount to give several drinks in one day.

Orange and grapefruit drinks can be made similarly.

21. **ORANGEADE (CONCENTRATED)**

Make as for lemonade, above, using ¾ kg sugar.

22. BOSTON CREAM

Ingredients:

750 g Sugar

40 g Tartaric Acid

2 litres Water

2 teaspoonfuls Lemon Essence

I Egg White

Method:

1. Dissolve the sugar in 500 ml of measured water, bring to boil.
2. Add remaining water and tartaric acid. Stir till dissolved.
3. Add lemon essence and beaten white of egg.
4. Pour into bottles. Dilute as required.

Note: A pinch of bicarbonate of soda can be added to a glass to make a fizzy drink. Because raw white is an ingredient, it is probably best not to serve the drink to children, the elderly, the infirm or pregnant women.

23. CIDER CUP

Ingredients:

500 ml Fresh Orange Juice

500 ml can Cider

Few slices Orange, Apple, Cucumber

250 ml Soda Water

Ice Cubes

Method:

1. Mix orange juice, cider and soda water. Chill.
2. Add orange, apple and cucumber.
4. Add ice cubes, serve very cold.

24. BARLEY WATER

Ingredients:

75 g Pearl Barley

25 g Sugar

I litre cold Water

Strips Lemon Rind

Method:

1. Scald the barley, put in a pan with the measured water.
2. Add lemon rind, bring to boiling point, simmer 1–2 hours.
3. Strain, add sugar and a little lemon juice.

Note: The barley may be used once or twice again. Patent barley may be used. Grapefruit may be used instead of lemon.

25. **MILK SHAKES**

Ingredients:

250 ml Milk

Fruit Syrup *or* Fruit Purée to taste, e.g. Banana, Apricot, Blackcurrant.

Note: The fruit chosen should have a distinctive flavour.

Alternative additions: Chocolate Powder

Ice-cream

Method:

Beat milk and flavouring well together, sweeten to taste.

If desired, add ice-cream before serving.

MISCELLANEOUS

1. **COATING BATTER (1)**

Ingredients:

100 g sieved Plain Flour   125 ml tepid Milk *or* Water
1 level teaspoonful Salt   ½ level teaspoonful Baking Powder

Method:

1. Mix the flour and salt.
2. Gradually add enough tepid water or milk to give a coating consistency.
3. Beat well. Just before using, add baking powder.

2. **COATING BATTER (2)**

Ingredients:

4 level tablespoonfuls Breadcrumbs   ½ level teaspoonful Salt
75 g Plain Flour (sieved)   1 Egg
About 125 ml Milk

Method:

1. Mix the dry ingredients.
2. Beat the egg well and gradually add the milk to it.
3. Add to the dry ingredients, beating very thoroughly.
4. Let it stand at least half an hour, in a cool place before using. Use as a coating for fish, fruit and vegetables.

3. **COATING BATTER (3)**

Ingredients:

100 g Plain Flour (sieved)   125 ml tepid Water
Pinch Salt   2 Egg Whites (stiffly-beaten)
1 tablespoonful Vegetable Oil (scant)

Method:

1. Mix flour and salt.
2. Make a hole in the centre of flour, add the oil and, by degrees, the tepid water.
3. Beat well and set aside for 1 hour.
4. Just before using, fold in the stiffly-beaten egg whites.

4. **YEAST COATING BATTER**

Ingredients:

100 g Plain Flour (sieved)   ½ level teaspoonful Sugar
5 g Dried Yeast   125 ml tepid Milk

Method:

1. Dissolve sugar in milk and sprinkle on yeast and leave to froth.
2. Sieve the flour into a warm bowl.
3. Mix milk mixture into the warmed flour. Beat well.
4. Leave to rise and use as required.

5. **YORKSHIRE PUDDING (1)**

Ingredients:

100 g Plain Flour (sieved)	250 ml Milk
1 Egg	Pinch Salt

Servings: 8
Time: 30 minutes in one tin; 20 minutes in patty tins
Oven Temperature: 200°C, Gas No. 6
Position in Oven: One-third from top

Method:

1. Mix sieved flour and salt. Drop the egg into centre of flour.
2. Add one-third milk; mix and beat well.
3. Gradually add remainder of milk, cover, set aside in a cool place for 30 minutes. Stir before using.
4. Heat cooking fat until hot in a small roasting tin or in patty tins.
5. Pour in prepared batter and bake for 30 minutes if large, and 20 minutes if individual.
6. Serve, cut into large pieces.

6. **YORKSHIRE PUDDING (2)**

Ingredients:

75 g Plain Flour (sieved)	250 ml Milk
Salt	1 Egg

Servings: 8
Time: 30 minutes in single tin; 20 minutes in patty tins
Oven Temperature: 200°C, Gas No. 6
Position in Oven: One-third from top

Method:

1. Blend flour with egg and half the milk.
2. Boil remainder of milk, add to blended flour. Use batter at once. Cook as in Yorkshire pudding (1), steps 4 to 6.

7. **BOILED RICE**

Ingredients:

100 g Rice (long grain)	1 level teaspoonful Salt
Water	Lemon Juice

Method:

1. Wash rice in cold water.
2. Boil water in a fairly large pan; add salt and a few drops of lemon juice.
3. Add the rice and boil 10–12 minutes without the lid.
4. Test a grain of rice between finger and thumb. When soft, drain and pour boiling water through.
5. Return to pan and shake gently over heat to dry.

Note: As there are many easy-cook rices available, read instructions on packet.

8. **MARINADE**

Ingredients:

½ tablespoonful Vegetable Oil
1 teaspoonful mixed Vinegars
½ teaspoonful chopped Parsley
½ teaspoonful chopped Shallot
Cayenne Pepper and Salt

Method:

Mix together and use to marinade fish or meat.

9. **GLAZE (QUICKLY MADE)**

Ingredients:

1 teaspoonful Meat Extract   2 level teaspoonfuls powdered Gelatine
125 ml Stock

Method:

1. Melt the extract and gelatine in the hot stock.
2. Allow to cool until of correct consistency.

10. **ROLLS OF BACON**

Method:

1. Cut thinly-sliced streaky bacon into pieces about 5 cm long.
2. Roll up keeping the rolls hollow.
3. Push the rolls onto a skewer.
4. Grill or bake in a moderate oven about 10 minutes.

11. **SALTED ALMONDS, WALNUTS, OR CASHEW NUTS**

Ingredients:

50 g Nuts   Salt
25 g clarified Butter *or* Olive Oil

Method:

1. Blanch (see Glossary of Cooking Terms) and skin the nuts. Dry.
2. Heat oil.
3. Fry nuts, stirring well, until lightly browned and crisp.
4. Drain, to remove surplus fat, sprinkle with salt.

12. **BROWNED CRUMBS**

Ingredients:

50 g Breadcrumbs   25 g Butter

Method:

1. Heat the butter without discolouring.

2. Add the crumbs and stir over a moderate heat until of the desired colour, being careful to have them all of a uniform shade. Season and use.

Note: Can be made on a tray in the oven. Dot with butter and stir occasionally.

13. DRIED BREADCRUMBS FOR COATING

Method:

1. Place the scraps and crusts of bread on a tin, and put into the oven until dry and lightly browned.
2. Place on a board and crush with rolling pin, or reduce to crumbs in a food processor.
3. Rub through a wire sieve and they are ready for use.

14. RENDERED FAT

Ingredients:

Beef *or* Mutton Fat

Method:

1. Cut fat into small pieces, place in strong pan and heat gently till it becomes liquid and any solid remaining part becomes clear.
2. Stir frequently. Strain. This may be done in a tin in the oven.

15. TO CLARIFY BUTTER

Method:

1. Melt butter slowly in a saucepan without discolouring.
2. Skim off any froth.
3. Pour off the clear butter leaving any sediment behind.

16. THICKENED GRAVY (AFTER A ROAST)

Ingredients:

Sediment from roasting pan   250 ml Stock (appropriate to the dish)
2 level teasponfuls Cornflour

1. Pour fat from roasting tin, leaving the sediment.
2. Add 250 ml stock and boil up. Thicken with blended cornflour, allowing 2 level teaspoonfuls to 250 ml.

INDEX

	No	No.	Cakes
...nolina Soufflé	117	1	Swiss Roll
...man Apple Tart	120	2	Madeira Cak...
...ed Chocolate	123	3	Jam Sandw...
...ple Amber	128	6	Welsh Cheesca...
...rnflour Mould	134	7	Cocoanut Bu...
...tewed Prunes	135	8	Gingerbread
...ple Charlotte	140	15	Shortbread
...wiss Cream	154	39	Brown Bread
...nnoise Pudding	160	43	German Biscu...
...p Fruit "	168	53	Fruit Cake
...nilla Cream	169	65	Genoese Pastr...
...Trifle	170	79	Windsor Cake
...tana Pudding	171	80	German Poun...
...nge Chartreuse	181	85	Cream Buns
...ffee Soufflé	188	90	Tea Cakes
...rlotte Russe	191	95	French Brea...
...	193	100	...